# Fostering Communication and Learning With Underutilized Technologies in Higher Education

Mohammed Banu Ali
*Institute of Management, University of Bolton, UK*

Trevor Wood-Harper
*University of Manchester, UK*

A volume in the Advances in Educational Technologies and Instructional Design (AETID) Book Series

IGI Global
PUBLISHER of TIMELY KNOWLEDGE

Published in the United States of America by
IGI Global
Information Science Reference (an imprint of IGI Global)
701 E. Chocolate Avenue
Hershey PA, USA 17033
Tel: 717-533-8845
Fax: 717-533-8661
E-mail: cust@igi-global.com
Web site: http://www.igi-global.com



Library of Congress Cataloging-in-Publication Data

Names: Ali, Mohammed Banu, editor. | Wood-Harper, A. T., editor.
Title: Fostering communication and learning with underutilized technologies in higher education / Mohammed Banu Ali and Trevor Wood-Harper, editors.

Description: Hershey, PA : Information Science Reference, 2021. | Includes bibliographical references and index. | Summary: "This book explores underutilized technologies in higher education that foster communication and learning"-- Provided by publisher.
Identifiers: LCCN 2020013993 (print) | LCCN 2020013994 (ebook) | ISBN 9781799848462 (hardcover) | ISBN 9781799857273 (paperback) | ISBN 9781799848479 (ebook)
Subjects: LCSH: Education, Higher--Effect of technological innovationss on. | Artificial intelligence--Educational applications.
Classification: LCC LB2395.7 .F679 2021 (print) | LCC LB2395.7 (ebook) | DDC 378.1/7344678--dc23
LC record available at https://lccn.loc.gov/2020013993
LC ebook record available at https://lccn.loc.gov/2020013994

This book is published in the IGI Global book series Advances in Educational Technologies and Instructional Design (AE-TID) (ISSN: 2326-8905; eISSN: 2326-8913)

British Cataloguing in Publication Data
A Cataloguing in Publication record for this book is available from the British Library.



For electronic access to this publication, please contact: eresources@igi-global.com.

# Advances in Educational Technologies and Instructional Design (AETID) Book Series

Lawrence A. Tomei
Robert Morris University, USA

ISSN:2326-8905
EISSN:2326-8913

## Mission

Education has undergone, and continues to undergo, immense changes in the way it is enacted and distributed to both child and adult learners. In modern education, the traditional classroom learning experience has evolved to include technological resources and to provide online classroom opportunities to students of all ages regardless of their geographical locations. From distance education, Massive-Open-Online-Courses (MOOCs), and electronic tablets in the classroom, technology is now an integral part of learning and is also affecting the way educators communicate information to students.

The **Advances in Educational Technologies & Instructional Design (AETID) Book Series** explores new research and theories for facilitating learning and improving educational performance utilizing technological processes and resources. The series examines technologies that can be integrated into K-12 classrooms to improve skills and learning abilities in all subjects including STEM education and language learning. Additionally, it studies the emergence of fully online classrooms for young and adult learners alike, and the communication and accountability challenges that can arise. Trending topics that are covered include adaptive learning, game-based learning, virtual school environments, and social media effects. School administrators, educators, academicians, researchers, and students will find this series to be an excellent resource for the effective design and implementation of learning technologies in their classes.

## Coverage

- Higher Education Technologies
- Virtual School Environments
- Adaptive Learning
- Hybrid Learning
- Digital Divide in Education
- Instructional Design
- Curriculum Development
- Collaboration Tools
- E-Learning
- Classroom Response Systems

IGI Global is currently accepting manuscripts for publication within this series. To submit a proposal for a volume in this series, please contact our Acquisition Editors at Acquisitions@igi-global.com or visit: http://www.igi-global.com/publish/.

The Advances in Educational Technologies and Instructional Design (AETID) Book Series (ISSN 2326-8905) is published by IGI Global, 701 E. Chocolate Avenue, Hershey, PA 17033-1240, USA, www.igi-global.com. This series is composed of titles available for purchase individually; each title is edited to be contextually exclusive from any other title within the series. For pricing and ordering information please visit http://www.igi-global.com/book-series/advances-educational-technologies-instructional-design/73678. Postmaster: Send all address changes to above address. 

## Titles in this Series

*For a list of additional titles in this series, please visit:*
*https://www.igi-global.com/book-series/advances-educational-technologies-instructional-design/73678*

***Simulation and Game-Based Learning in Emergency and Disaster Management***
Nicole K. Drumhiller (American Public University System, USA)
Information Science Reference • © 2021 • 300pp • H/C (ISBN: 9781799840879) • US $195.00

***Impact of AI Technologies on Teaching, Learning, and Research in Higher Education***
Shivani Verma (Km. Mayawati Government Girls P.G. College, India) and Pradeep Tomar (Gautam Buddha University, India)
Information Science Reference • © 2021 • 295pp • H/C (ISBN: 9781799847632) • US $195.00

***Practical Perspectives on Educational Theory and Game Development***
Fabio Perez Marzullo (Federal University of Rio de Janeiro, Brazil)
Information Science Reference • © 2021 • 300pp • H/C (ISBN: 9781799850212) • US $185.00

***Ethical Research Approaches to Indigenous Knowledge Education***
Ntokozo Mthembu (University of South Africa, South Africa)
Information Science Reference • © 2021 • 262pp • H/C (ISBN: 9781799812494) • US $185.00

***Digital Learning Architectures of Participation***
Nigel Ecclesfield (FRSA, UK) and Fred Garnett (FRSA, UK)
Information Science Reference • © 2021 • 289pp • H/C (ISBN: 9781799843337) • US $165.00

***Participatory Pedagogy Emerging Research and Opportunities***
Martha Ann Davis McGaw (Davis McGaw Family Foundation, USA) and Simone McGaw Evans (Emory University, Atlanta, USA & University of Georgia, Clarkston, USA)
Information Science Reference • © 2021 • 150pp • H/C (ISBN: 9781522589648) • US $155.00

***Visual Approaches to Instructional Design, Development, and Deployment***
Shalin Hai-Jew (Kansas State University, USA)
Information Science Reference • © 2021 • 228pp • H/C (ISBN: 9781799839460) • US $185.00

***Teaching Language and Literature On and Off-Canon***
José Manuel Correoso-Rodenas (Universidad Complutense de Madrid, Spain)
Information Science Reference • © 2020 • 370pp • H/C (ISBN: 9781799833796) • US $195.00

IGI Global
PUBLISHER of TIMELY KNOWLEDGE

701 East Chocolate Avenue, Hershey, PA 17033, USA
Tel: 717-533-8845 x100 • Fax: 717-533-8661
E-Mail: cust@igi-global.com • www.igi-global.com

# Table of Contents

# Detailed Table of Contents

The scale, magnitude, and diversity of higher education teaching/learning and higher education institutions (HEIs) have resulted in corresponding diverse datafication representations. Contrary to conventional datafication, where the objective is profitability (e.g., adopting facial recognition for improved policing), the datafication of HEIs should be analysed, understood, and interpreted for its unique diversity, practice, and consequences. The result of the COVID-19 pandemic has forced a paradigm shift from conventional/traditional classroom-based teaching to online teaching, which has resulted in enhanced data collection. Taking a post-digital perspective on modern practices in higher education literature, this chapter argues for an organic view, in which the datafication must consider the aspects of teaching, learning, and educational context that are absent in digital data. The findings from the discussion lead to the conclusion that datafication can complement expert judgement in HEIs when informed by the unification of pedagogy and technology.



The role of information technology (IT) transforming higher education (HE) institutions is flourishing. Students, lecturers, and faculty staff adopt overarching platforms and applications that are driven by ubiquitous technology such as big data and cloud computing to support their teaching and learning activities. In this chapter, the authors analysed cases of EdTechs (apps) used in the higher education institutions (HEIs) and their impact on teaching and learning processes. They draw the benefits, challenges, and appropriate cases pertaining to the apps used in HEIs in supporting such processes. They find that EdTechs have a high potential to provide better education for students, easier teaching process for lecturers, and clearer managerial process for administrators and faculty members. The chapter concludes that while EdTechs used during the pandemic can provide an alternative learning experience, it still lacks in providing optimal learning engagement.



Higher education institutions (HEIs) are currently developing a significant research interest in transferring from traditional to novel practices in teaching and learning through the use of modern technological tools and platforms. The integration of digital technologies in higher education has tended to focus on improving academic professionals in developing countries like Saudi Arabia. This chapter was driven by a desire to understand ICT implementation in higher education institutions (HEIs) by professionals using digital transformation in Saudi Arabia. This chapter discusses the implementation of digital transformation in teaching and learning at HEIs in Saudi Arabia. This aim is achieved throughout several objectives, beginning by reviewing the related literature and presenting theoretical frameworks. The literature review will provide the possibility of identifying the focal trends related to the topic.

# Foreword

Information and Communication Technology (ICT) is integral to the development of higher education institutions (HEIs) since it has revolutionised how they conduct their academic practices and procedures. Such reforms has led to communication and learning playing a huge role in facilitating academic operations, which calls for a consensus on a brand of ICT that caters to the personal development needs of HEI multi-stakeholders. This book refers to ICTs as underutilised technologies that have the ability to change the status quo, as well as rethinking about ICT strategies in the higher education context in a way that leads to a better understanding of stakeholders' needs and gives more consideration towards resulting implications. The book draws on the social and technical implications of technologies (sociotechnical systems), which can be observed in underutilised technologies, including organisational and personal issues that lead to making adoptive decisions concerning emerging ICTs. The limited coverage on the application of underutilised technologies for HEIs indicates the need to inform about the potentials of underutilised technologies to enhance and foster institutional practices such as communication and learning. Knowledge is a high priority to HEIs and thus will make the extra effort to improve their ICT infrastructure to address some the key issues the industry faces both internally and externally. Ultimately, the book is inspired to develop theory to support HEIs awareness of underutilised technologies and support institutional practices, thereby helping to shed some light on the potential suitability of such technologies.

Editors present a series of chapters developed by determined and knowledgeable authors concerning the different underutilised technologies and their role in developing pedagogy, as well as learning/teaching/communication practices. It unearths some very new and previously untreated issues, such as employing cloud computing, internet of things (IoT), artificial intelligence and big data among others to provide intelligent shared computing provision to enhance simplicity, scalability and efficiency. This includes meeting stakeholder expectations and preferences from the sharing of quality information resources to facilitating collaboration between multi-stakeholders operating in higher education.

Fostering communication and learning with underutilised technologies in higher education provides a unique outlook on the current and future position of technological developments in pedagogy and its role in shaping learning for future generations. These concepts heralds the emergence of new learning technology frameworks that combines conventional learning methods and modern technological innovations. The book also brings to the attention of both academics and practitioners the notion of developing learning, teaching and communication in the higher education domain through technological paradigms such as cloud computing, Internet of Things, Gamification, Artificial Intelligence and Smart Learning Spaces among others. The book is also inspired by a number of engaging and insightful frameworks and models such as aspectual analysis, systematic literature analyses, sociotechnical theory and case study analysis among others. The book even deliberates on recent world issues such as the COVID-19 pandemic and its impact on underutilised ICTs, such as video-conferencing through the Zoom application which has recently boomed in wake of the pandemic. The driving notion of this book is the application of these technological paradigms in higher learning settings and how they foster communication and learning in different ways. For that reason, there is a critical need for a principled way of managing knowledge through underutilised technologies in order to provide a more positive pedagogical outcome. This book is both conceptually elegant and operationally useful and is a much-needed contribution.

Editors weaves the phenomena in this book like a determined artist who is fixated on providing a beautiful and intricate work of art that people can appreciate. This can be symbolic of the editor's determination and goal of sharing knowledge in their domain, while anticipating future issues like a skilled researcher who needs to better allocate knowledge as a public good. The book brings together the conceptual richness of a new way of diagnosing existing pedagogical gaps through the application of underutilised technologies, while providing a practical perspective of linking this to the development of learning, teaching and communication in higher education settings and for the requisite institutional change for long-term competitive advantage. The book identifies archetypes of emerging technology trends that help diagnose and uncover pedagogical problems, while directly linking that with technological interventions.

Finally, the book does something that will, in my opinion, becoming increasingly important in the coming years: It sets the stage for better management of pedagogy through current and future underutilised technologies. As the technological landscape continues to develop rapidly, technical techniques for pedagogy will increasingly influence institutional performance for higher education. Editors book is showing us the way of the future of fostering communication and learning with underutilised technologies in higher education. I am honoured and proud to write the foreword to this immensely useful and innovative book.

*Brij B. Gupta*
*National Institute of Technology, Kurukshetra, India*

# Preface

## OVERVIEW

Information and Communication Technology (ICT) plays a huge role in the development of modern society, particularly for higher education institutions (HEIs) where ICT has fundamentally changed the way in which they carry out their academic practices and procedures (Dintoe, 2018). The radical reforms in ICTs has a fundamental impact on how Universities carry out their everyday operations, where communication and learning play a huge role in facilitating these operations. This calls for a consensus on a brand of ICT that caters to not only the University's needs, but also stakeholders' personal communication and learning needs. ICTs in the context of this book refer to underutilised technologies that have the ability to change the status quo, as well as rethinking about ICT strategies in the higher education context in a way that leads to a better understanding of stakeholders' needs and gives more consideration towards resulting implications. Mumford (2006) explores the social and technical implications of technologies (sociotechnical systems), which can also be observed in Underutilised technologies. This includes the organisational and personal issues that lead to making adoptive decisions concerning emerging ICTs.

Existing ICTs often fail to meet University requirements owing to a slow rate of adoption of novel underutilised technologies in University settings. In spite of the considerable ICT investments to enhance education across various countries, there is a lack of evidence to support the widespread adoption of underutilised technologies in the education sector. However, the education sector is investing heavily in underutilised technologies, but adoption compared to the private sector has lagged behind. Barriers of underutilised technologies in higher education settings have identified a number of emerging patterns, such as the significant resistance towards novel underutilised technologies among stakeholders and a lack of collaborative support in existing educational ICTs have contributed to the lack of ICT adoption in the higher education domain. A lack of technical support and training, limited information sharing capabilities, and lack of tools to benefit from educational underutilised technologies off-campus are among other impediments of ICT adoption in the higher education domain. The most prevalent barrier to educational underutilised technologies is the security of data and the privacy and protection of University repositories, including performance social and financial risks. Data security upholds the idea of data confidentiality, integrity and availability, and ultimately protect institutional data.

Institutions are employing a wide range an emerging underutilised technologies such as cloud computing, internet of things (IoT), artificial intelligence and big data among others to complement existing systems such as virtual learning environments (VLE) and monitoring and progression systems. For example, Willcocks et al. (2014) states that cloud computing (CC) is a service-based innovation that offers shared computing provision to enhance simplicity, scalability and efficiency. In the context of underutilised technologies, CC could potentially meet stakeholder expectations and preferences by promoting the sharing of quality information resources to facilitate collaboration or communication between multi-stakeholders operating in higher education, offer better service delivery, usability and flexibility, and overcoming user-resistance towards new/emerging technologies.

Underutilised technologies could help Universities to improve not only their higher education practices (e.g. teaching and research capabilities), but also compete on the world stage of education and ultimately enhance their reputation. Additionally, there appears to be a need for emerging and underutilised technologies for HEIs owing to stakeholders' needs related to their use of ICT and addressing the pragmatic difficulties like facilitating access to information resources for research purposes. There is also missed opportunities for discussing how underutilised technologies for higher education can encourage quick and reliable communication between stakeholders. There is a need to explore underutilised technologies for HEIs to foster communication and teaching/learning between stakeholders involved in University settings.

## CONTEXTUAL FIT

The contextual fit of this book refers to the underutilised technologies that could give HEIs insight into the complex nature of the benefits and challenges associated with these innovations. Higher education plays a significant role in our daily lives as it enables us to gain knowledge about a wide variety of topics, improves academic skills and provides the opportunity to pursue better careers (Darling-Hammond et al., 2020). Today, there are many key issues, both internal and external, facing HEIs, particularly with regards to managing a number of institutional practices and adopting underutilised technologies, while catering to the needs of its stakeholders. This has a direct impact on stakeholders and the institution itself in terms of the delivery of quality teaching/learning and research. Within the past few decades, research-quality plays a significant role in higher education in terms of how it is conceptualised, theorised and practiced to enhance student learning and knowledge development. University level education, in particular, is an area that has been understudied with respect to how institutional practices, such as communication and learning. The rationale for considering higher education stems from personal experiences of working in higher education, as well as becoming aware of the existing problems and frustrations with existing ICTs adopted within the University. Assessing the suitability of underutilised technologies for HEIs is vital towards the enhancement of everyday practices, as well as keeping stakeholders satisfied (M. Ali, 2019; M. B. Ali, 2019).

This book covers a range of underutilised technologies and provides cases in the higher education context, such as cloud computing, artificial intelligence, gamification, virtual learning environments, blockchain, Internet of Things and big data among others. Although these technologies have been around for quite some time, they have been overlooked in higher education to foster communication and learning development and how they can impact pedagogical outcomes in this arena. So there is a need to study the higher education context to determine the extent of how prevalent these technologies are in creating value contributions toward the development of contemporary pedagogical practice.

There is limited coverage on the application of underutilised technologies for HEIs. This book aims to inform about the potentials of underutilised technologies to enhance and foster institutional practices such as communication and learning. It is important that HEIs obtain vital knowledge on the ways in which they can enhance their existing ICTs in order to address some the key issues the industry faces as a whole from the perspective of their stakeholders. Ultimately, this book intends to develop theory to support HEIs awareness of underutilised technologies to support institutional practices, thereby helping to shed some light on the potential suitability of such technologies.

## TARGET AUDIENCE

The target audiences of this book are mainly scholars and teachers who are interested in areas, such as information systems, IT Management, Business Studies and emerging technologies. The book covers a range interests ranging from cloud computing and ubiquitous technologies to alternative online technologies such as artificial intelligence, virtual learning spaces and gamified systems. The book will also spark the interest of practitioners e.g. IS managers who are responsible for systems planning the development within their organisation/institution, as well as other stakeholders of higher education e.g. administrators, facility leaders and course leaders of business and computing schools. Table 1 provides a reading guide for interested practitioners in the field:

*Table 1. Reading guide for practitioners*

| Reader Interests | Chapter(s) | Section(s) |
|---|---|---|
| Background of technologies and rationale | All | Introductions |
| Key Concepts | All | Discussions |
| Key ubiquitous and smart technologies | 1, 2, 3, 4, 5, 6, 15 | Main bodies |
| Communication, teaching and learning systems | 1, 3, 4, 6, 7, 8, 9, 15 | Main bodies |
| HE cases | All | Cases and main bodies |
| Conclusions | All | Conclusion |

## ORGANISATION OF THE BOOK

The book is organised into fifteen chapters with a brief description of each as follows:

Chapter 1 reviews the barriers and opportunities of the IoT to determine a potential communication and information sharing culture in HEIs. The authors indicate that stakeholders wish for a better collaborative learning environment, improved information sharing and productive efficiency, yet IoT has a number of privacy, data security and interoperability concerns that hinder stakeholders' acceptance of IoT. The authors also reveal that IoT as an ICT strategy could potentially fulfil HEIs system expectations, though stakeholders remain undecided about accepting IoTs.

Chapter 2 analyses gamification as a novel technology that encourages student learning. This chapter reviews the implementation of a gamified application to support students' learning in terms of learning important facts concerning their study program. It concludes that tailored feedback was less effective than generic feedback. Session limits were found to not circumvent binging without a reduction in sessions.

Chapter 3 examines AI applications in higher education using a systematic review approach. The author reveals several areas of AI education applications in academic support services and institutional and administrative services, including profiling and prediction, assessment and evaluation, adaptive systems and personalisation, and intelligent tutoring systems.

Chapter 4 evaluates and assesses the impact of big data and cloud computing in higher education. The authors adopt a systematic literature research approach that employs qualitative content analysis to establish their position with regards to the impact, benefits, challenges, and opportunities of integrating big data and cloud computing to facilitate teaching and learning. The authors found that the key opportunities of cloud computing big data interventions for higher education range from efficiency to the provision of frequent formative feedback, while the key challenges ranged from ethical issues regarding tracking students to user resistance from traditional system users.

Chapter 5 examines artificial intelligence technology, its benefits, and integration to Higher Education with particular emphasis on learning and teaching. The authors show that the consequences of AI development cannot be predicted today, but it appears to be very probable that AI applications will turn out to be a critical enabler for educational adoption of technology for the foreseeable future. The authors conclude that AI-based systems have a high potential to provide extensive support to students, lecturers, and faculty members throughout the student lifecycle.

Chapter 6 argues for an organic view, in which the datafication must consider the aspects of teaching, learning, and educational context that are absent in digital data. The authors revealed that datafication can complement expert judgement in HEIs when informed by the unification of pedagogy and technology.

Chapter 7 explores existing literature relating educational technologies (EdTech) used in the Higher Education Institutions (HEIs) and their impact on teaching and learning processes. The authors draw on the benefits, challenges and appropriate cases pertaining to the apps (EdTechs) used in HEIs in supporting such processes. The authors found that technology-based systems have a high potential to provide better education for students, easier teaching process for lecturers, and clearer managerial process for administrators and faculty members. The authors conclude that while online tools used during the pandemic can provide an alternative learning experience, it still lacks in providing optimal learning engagement.

Chapter 8 analyses the implementation of digital transformation in teaching and learning at HEIs in Saudi Arabia. Using aspectual analysis, the authors reveal a gap in literature in ICT and digital transformation studies in Saudi Arabia in terms of examining the perceptions and practices of students and professionals when using ICT in HEIs in Saudi universities.

Chapter 9 examines the main elements of virtual learning environments (VLE), together with an evaluation of the VLE blackboard system design and discuss how blackboard facilitates teaching, learning and communication in HEIs. The authors revealed that the weaknesses of blackboard could be compensated by the opportunities, whilst threats should be considered by the policy makers to enrich the teaching and learning experience.

Chapter 10 discusses measures to enhance student engagement in online learning settings within HEIs during post-Covid 19. The authors present measures to enhance student engagement and an enhanced framework in Online Learning in HEIs. The authors propose the EFSEOL framework to examine the opportunities for teaching and learning in higher education. It was found that the EFSEOL framework could encourage pedagogical development to retain the integrity of core values for higher education.

Chapter 11 examines the use of technology in moments of extreme internationalised interference. Using the COVID-19 pandemic as a ground for change, students enrolled in presential courses in Spain, Malta and the United Kingdom were interviewed in order to understand how they are coping with having contact with their academic life exclusively online. The student's impressions, LMS software and results (assignments and exams) were also discussed and the solutions provided by lecturers and students were analysed. The authors revealed that the unprecedented pandemic generated by the COVID-19 has led to several global consequences, disrupting the international community not only on a health perspective but also forbidding transit and shutting down countries. The authors conclude that higher education institutions were in turn faced with an unexpected new challenge: change from a face-to-face learning environment to an online learning tool which would in turn ensure the continuity of the semester.

Chapter 12 examines Knowledge Management (KM) in HEIs and the role of communication and organisational learning when working in partnerships. The authors reveal that essential for improving performance of HE Partnerships is the adoption of communication and learning technologies. The authors reveal three emerging KM factors from the former that HEIs should measure, including Social Capital; Monitoring and Review Meetings and; Continuing Professional Development of Staff Communication. The authors conclude that KM is essential for HEIs to identify and adopt or adapt communication and learning technologies through structured evaluation of the partnership performance.

Chapter 13 examined what faculty members have experienced after taking part in a University intervention known as the TeachTech Program. The authors employed an online interview method to solicit past and present TeachTech Program participants to share their experiences. Using the key phrase extraction functions from QDA Miner and WordStat, authors found the following phrases related to their experiences: "incorporate technology," "collaborate sessions," hybrid version," "desire to learn," and "solve problems."

Chapter 14 analyses the 'REALab' consultancy programme, piloted and funded by the University of Manchester, which allowed a group of multidisciplinary researchers to address representation and inclusion of underrepresented groups at the Museum of Science and Industry in Manchester (MSI). The authors presented a case study into the collaboration process between academic and heritage institutions. The authors revealed that the advantages of MSI as a professional and educational non-profit and their collaboration with the authors as researchers instead of consultants, is the connection offered to the public. The authors also revealed a personal approach to the problem, acknowledging the difficulties in changing how the museum operates.

Chapter 15 analyses prospective applications for teaching and learning in a scaled environment or university campus. The authors evaluated the potential of IoT and blockchain for the development of new smart campuses and smart university applications with primary implementations as well as their communications technologies. The authors revealed that blockchain integration does hold some potential future challenges, such as scalability and service flexibility problems, long-distance low-power communications, requirement of novel communication technologies, integration issues, lack of smart campus standards and public initiatives and issues with seamless integration of outdoor and indoor smart campus applications. In spite of these challenges, blockchain has the potential to be integrated into the smart campus via applications for teaching and learning, promote activities in research and innovation and provide applications for community-based knowledge transfer.

## CONCLUSION

The book contributes to the ICT/IS field, with its exploration of the suitability of underutilised technologies to foster communication and learning in higher education. The theoretical implication of this book is the identification of an uncommon messy situation through exploring the impact of collaboration/ communication and information culture on the adoption of underutilised technologies in higher education. This complimented through the methodological implications, such as presenting comprehensive case studies of Universities adopting underutilised technologies. Cases revealed some interesting trends pertaining to the current state of technology use and propositions of underutilised technologies to foster communication and learning in University settings, even under toughest of periods, such as the Covid-19 pandemic. While, face-to-face online video-conferencing software, for example, provide an alternative learning experience outside the classroom amidst a pandemic, they still lack the optimal learning engagement since the quality of the technology used to power such tools determines how effective they are in fostering communication and learning.

This book also recognises the benefits and challenges of underutilised technologies in higher education for teaching and learning support. One such area of concern that was a common theme throughout the book is the lack of collaboration among stakeholders, which is down to the poor existing state of ICTs deployed in HEIs. Despite this, Universities are starting to embrace underutilised technologies to revolution collaborative learning and teaching and to keep up with the latest education technology trends. This was also linked to the stakeholders' resistance towards embracing a novel system that they are unaccustomed to as they felt that they could not trust such systems owing to the problems with the existing ones. Finally, practical contributions to the book included the presentation of models such as EFSEOL to foster communication and learning through the use of underutilised technologies.

The themes of communication and learning has a great impact on this book owing to the exploration of new ICTs as a means to enhance these capabilities, as well as facilitate stakeholder roles and higher education practices, such as teaching, research and management. Assessing the suitability of underutilised technologies is reflected by the stakeholder needs and expectations. The case studies provided in the chapters give a clear indication that Universities still have a long way to go in providing the optimal technologies to foster communication and learning. This is not because Universities are incapable of using these technologies, rather the limitations of the technologies themselves hindering the development of communication and learning.

*Mohammed Banu Ali*
*Institute of Management, University of Bolton, UK*

*Trevor Wood-Harper*
*University of Manchester, UK*

## REFERENCES

Ali, M. (2019). Cloud Computing at a Cross Road: Quality and Risks in Higher Education. *Advances in Internet of Things*, *9*(3), 33–49. doi:10.4236/ait.2019.93003

Ali, M. B. (2019). Multiple Perspective of Cloud Computing Adoption Determinants in Higher Education a Systematic Review. *International Journal of Cloud Applications and Computing*, *9*(3), 89–109. doi:10.4018/IJCAC.2019070106

Darling-Hammond, L., Flook, L., Cook-Harvey, C., Barron, B., & Osher, D. (2020). Implications for educational practice of the science of learning and development. *Applied Developmental Science*, *24*(2), 97–140. doi:10.1080/10888691.2018.1537791

Dintoe, S. (2018). Information and communication technology use in higher education: Perspectives from faculty. *International Journal of Education and Development Using ICT, 14*(2).

Mumford, E. (2006). The story of socio-technical design: Reflections on its successes, failures and potential. *Information Systems Journal, 16*(4), 317–342. doi:10.1111/j.1365-2575.2006.00221.x

Willcocks, L., Venters, W., & Whitley, E. (2014). *Moving to the Cloud Corporation*. Palgrave Macmillan. doi:10.1057/9781137347473

# Acknowledgment

I would like to extend my appreciation to all academic individuals who have supported and contributed to this book, through either providing feedback and/or comments, in addition to contributing to the reviewing process. I would also like to thank my colleagues and family for being supportive and patient during the process of writing this valuable book.

*Mohammed Banu Ali*

I would like to give my sincerest gratitude to Mohammed Ali for his valuable contributions and considerable support as a co-editor of this book. I would also like to give a big thank you to all of the contributing authors of this book, without whom would have not been possible to produce. Lastly, I am grateful to IGI Global for providing a platform to publish this book and to share our research interests and specialist subject areas.

*Trevor Wood-Harper*

# Chapter 1
# Internet of Things (IoT) to Foster Communication and Information Sharing:
## A Case of UK Higher Education

**Mohammed Banu Ali**
https://orcid.org/0000-0001-5854-8245
*Institute of Management, University of Bolton, UK*

## ABSTRACT

*IoT is a rapidly emerging technology in education that attracts researchers, students, and administrators. This chapter reviews the opportunities and challenges of the IoT to determine whether there are potential communication and information sharing cultures in higher education institutions (HEIs). Despite the findings revealing stakeholders' demand for a better collaborative learning environment and better information sharing capabilities, IoT has various security and interoperability concerns that present an unattractive prospect for HE stakeholders to embrace IoT. IoT has the potential to meet HEIs system expectations, though stakeholders remain distant toward embracing IoTs. This indicates that stakeholders are not ready to embrace IoTs, thus prompting the need to study why stakeholders are resistant towards the IoT.*

## INTRODUCTION

Modern Information and Communication Technology (ICT) solutions and strategies have recently transformed the traditional educational process resulting in better quality education systems at various levels of learning (Maksimović, 2018). There are currently seven known categories of technologies, tools, and strategies have been a potential game changer in the education sector: visualization technologies, social media technologies, learning technologies, Internet technologies, enabling technologies, digital strategies and consumer technologies (Rushby & Surry, 2016). The Internet of Things (IoT), for example,

DOI: 10.4018/978-1-7998-4846-2.ch001

is an internet technology that has enabled small devices to become connected to the Internet, which in turn provides an opportunity to make remarkable developments in many facets of life (Majeed & Ali, 2018). IoT in the education domain has successfully bridged the gap between the requirements needed for both traditional education systems and contemporary education systems through the transformation of an interconnected sharing and collaborative environment. This has been brought together by internet based information and communication tools and strategies that form this sharing culture.

Kevin Ashton first coined the term "Internet of Things" in 1999, which describes a unique set of interoperable objects connected via radio-frequency identification (RFID) technology (Gawali & Deshmukh, 2019). Similarly, Oberländer et al. (2018, p. 488) states that IoT facilitates the connectivity of physical objects that include sensors and actuators in the form of data communication technologies that are powered by the internet. These definitions suggest that the significant growth and ubiquitous penetration of the IoT can be attributed to the rapid increase in smart device usage within the past decade.

The advanced development and ubiquitous nature of internet technology has led to a world where devices are able to be interconnected to the internet, thus providing anytime anywhere access to information. The IoT are a technological innovation of pervasive computing that is developing a worldwide network of the information society, which facilitates novel and complex services (Patel & Cassou, 2015). For example, Universities are currently using the IoT, such as campus-wide Wi-Fi that allow students and staff to use their mobile devices to access information regarding the campus according to their location e.g. guiding lost students using interactive map data or even check the availability of study rooms. By 2023, the size of the IoT in Education market is expected to grow to $11.3B due to the increased use of connected devices in educational institutions (Petrov, 2019).

Various supporting technologies are responsible for the IoT growth, such as developments in smart devices, broadband availability, reduced cost of connected devices and energy efficient systems (Talari et al., 2017). Similarly, a 2015 report about the IoT found that the rise of other technologies, such as cloud computing (M. Ali, 2019; Ali, 2020; M. B. Ali, 2019; Mohammed Banu et al., 2018) and big data has influenced the technological ecosystem that has facilitated the emergence of the IoT (Rose, Eldridge, & Chapin, 2015). With the proliferation of smart technologies, the IoT is a new wave of ubiquitous connectivity. Moreover, Gómez et al. (2013) asserted that developments in nanotechnology (small technologies used mainly in the scientific field) have facilitated the manufacturing of miniature devices that can be inserted into various systems with additional functionality of efficiently connecting to the Internet.

Although the IoT is an emerging technology that brings together both virtual and physical devices based on existing ICTs, there are several limitations such as a lack of security, privacy and trust in the IoT, which may dissuade stakeholders from embracing the technology (Hsu & Lin, 2018). For those reasons, this research explores the opportunities and challenges pertaining to the IoT as an ICT strategy to facilitate communication and information sharing among stakeholders associated with Higher Education Institutions (HEIs).

## THEORETICAL BACKGROUND

The IoT today are fostering new technological innovations that are changing the face of industry. This growing trend has been fostered because of the convergence pertaining to wireless technologies and the developments in the internet. This makes any object a smart device that is able to communicate unobtrusively. Although the IoT provides opportunities to enhancing information and communication driven decision-making (ICD) (Krotov, 2017; Pauget & Dammak, 2018; Wei & Zhou, 2018), there are a number of key issues that could potentially affect the integration of the IoT into Higher Education (HE) regarding information sharing and collaboration.

Zhu, Yu, and Riezebos (2016) found that the ubiquitous nature of improved access to information facilitates the development of connected communities where educational stakeholders, particularly students can share ideas with their peers and other stakeholders such as their tutors/teachers. For example, the IoT devices can facilitate live streaming of other classrooms situated in schools in different parts of the world. In the same vein, the IoT-enabled learning spaces uniquely facilitate the ubiquitous access to information, as well as contexts that connect people, processes, data and things on demand via smart devices (Middleton et al., 2014; Whitmore et al., 2015).

The application of digital technology as a strategy or tool to share and distribute information have become favourable targets in data mining (Njeru, Omar, Yi, Paracha, & Wannous, 2017). Njeru et al. (2017) found that the benefits retained from using visualization tools is improved collaboration/information sharing. Despite information sharing not being a new paradigm, the indelible nature of the digital footprint resulting from the information that is shared online is a concern, particularly regarding the sharing of individuals' information without their consent (Whitmore et al., 2015).

Research by Hansen and Reich (2015) found that the different access levels to information resources and technologies influence stakeholder success, particularly among students (stakeholder success in the student context would be improved learning outcomes, better access to information for research purposes and improved collaboration with other stakeholders such as teachers). The authors argue that there is concern about the equal access to online information since stakeholders do not have the same level of access to technological resources. Similarly, poorer students are more likely to have limited access to ubiquitous learning platforms, thereby restricting their success. In the same vein, Fraga-Lamas et al. (2016) argued there is limited access to information resources and secure communications for defence and public safety, which indicates the need to integrate the IoT in sectors such as public safety and education. This will help to improve the rate of access to important online information.

Du et al. (2018) discovered that although information disclosure is a privacy related issue, which could be argued as a technical challenge related to The IoT technology, it has a direct impact on users' personal information and not only the system itself. The authors go on to mention that the information exchanged among users and The IoT vendors could be disclosed by these human actors and not the result of a system exploit or attack. Therefore, this creates not only a technical issue, but also a personal issue in the potential disclosure of information that is exchanged between human actors on a personal level.

Dery et al. (2014) found that mobile communication technology practices have considerably evolved within a relatively short period in both work and non-work contexts. With respect to IoT, this type of mobile communication technology has also rapidly evolved through a seamless platform communication that not only facilitates knowledge management and knowledge availability, but it also provides stakeholders with a sense of engagement via unique value-added learning experiences across varying distances using The IoT enabled tools or strategies (Zhu et al., 2016). The ubiquitous nature of communication facilitated by The IoT renders itself as a platform that supports collaborative research in which students and faculty can work together and share ideas anytime anywhere in one centralised space. Likewise, Demirer, Aydın, and Çelik (2017) state that owing to the pervasive nature of smart devices, The IoT technologies are a potential game changer in the provision of seamless learning in both informal and formal communication spaces in education settings.

Concerning a lack of support, the IoT have become a standard in various industries, where data ownership is questioned by organisations, particularly when comping to regulatory policies related to sharing data with third parties. This issue is pertinent given the limited support surrounding the ownership of the IoT data (Janeček, 2018). For HE, data ownership is even more pertinent owing to the large quantities data produced by the IoT in Universities is accessed by third party vendors offering services to them. Berman and Cerf (2017) questioned about the social and ethical behaviour of the IoT. The authors argued while technological innovation should not be limited, developing effective models for governing the IoT is needed to guide social behaviour and ethical use of the IoT technologies that promote efficiency.

According to Harwood & Gerry (2017), a lack of knowledge and/or understanding of or familiarity with the IoT can result in user resistance among human actors or system users. Confidence in the IoT therefore becomes critical, as organisations have to build users' trust in using the IoT. Despite this important issue, the nature of trust in a system can vary based on the agency of human actors and machine objects that operate within a network. Therefore, it is vital for actors and objects to work collectively or collaboratively owing to the complex adaptive socio-technical nature of the IoT, which comprise of various benefits that come from interdependencies situated in networked systems.

The interoperability of the IoT presents series of security challenges, such as cyber-attacks and authorised access to data. Noura, Atiquzzaman, and Gaedke (2018) found that despite industry proposals to overcome the IoT interoperability problem, there is still very little ground that can address these issues. The authors found that the lack of standards and limited cutting-edge technologies hinders the development of the IoT.

Hsu and Lin (2018) found that when sharing information using the IoT, there is a growing threat regarding the perceived privacy risk related to the application of these smart technologies. Given the likely increase in the IoT driven data sharing for the education system, data security becomes a matter of security and risk. The vendors who provide support for the processes within the IoT ecosystem further influence such vulnerability (Fraile, Tagawa, Poler, & Ortiz, 2018). To further support the claim of vulnerability in the IoT, a report compiled by Arxan, IBM and the Ponrmon Institute found that 80% of the IoT devices were not tested for any vulnerabilities owing to the quick deployment of these applications in order to meet user demands (Forrest, 2017). This confirms the security concerns associated with the IoT platforms, which in turn can compromise its sharing and communicative potentials. Strategies or tools that could avert potential security threats that originate from the IoT devices because of their varying privacy and security requirements are limited (Islam, Kwak, Kabir, Hossain, & Kwak, 2015). The lack of standards and legal restrictions on data sharing could in turn thwart the application of the IoT in other contexts, particularly in higher education, where security would be a high priority given the security standards required to protect stakeholders' personal information.

Although the IoT is a potential game-changer to different sectors, the technology itself can be a potential threat towards not only individuals' roles, but also to the entire information sharing and communication ethos. This is because individuals can communicate and share information with each other on a social level, but the introduction of the IoT could instil fear in potential users and be a threat to not only their job position, but also their social interactions with others. This may result in potential users to reject the technology or fear it as it could be a personal threat to their social life and career. From the related work, several key issues have been identified: information issues, communication issues and technology issues in the IoT. Information refers to the data issues in the IoT devices used in HEIs, communication refers to the collaborative and communicative issues between HEI stakeholders, which are generated from the IoT devices, and technology refers to the hardware/software side of the IoT devices or the technical issues

*Table 1. Different Perspectives of IoT Integration Issues*

| Category | Key Issues | Reference |
|---|---|---|
| *Information* | Better access to information<br>Limited access to information resources<br>Promote information sharing<br>Information Disclosure | Du et al. (2018)<br>Fraga-Lamas et al. (2016)<br>Hansen and Reich (2015)<br>Njeru et al. (2017)<br>Whitmore et al. (2015)<br>Zhu et al. (2016) |
| *Communication* | Enhance collaboration<br>Lack of support<br>Limited Understanding of the IoT<br>Encouraging Learner Engagement<br>Lack of Trust | Berman and Cerf (2017)<br>Demirer et al. (2017)<br>Harwood & Gerry (2017)<br>Janeček (2018)<br>Zhu et al. (2016) |
| *Technological* | Interoperability issues<br>Security issues<br>Privacy issues<br>Technophobia | Forrest (2017)<br>Fraile et al. (2018)<br>Hsu and Lin (2018)<br>Islam et al. (2015)<br>Noura et al. (2018)<br>Mani & Chouk (2018) |

that can arise from using the IoT devices in HEIs. In short, the key issues derived from the literature have been summarised in Table 1. This facilitates the development of the proposed model.

## THEORETICAL FRAMEWORK

Actor-network theory (ANT) refers to an analytical method that is used to analyse various sociotechnical contexts from a conceptual perspective (Lee & Chen, 2011). ANT describes and explores socio-technical processes in a heterogeneous network with focus on the interactions among various human and nonhuman actors. In particular, Latour (1987) and Callon (1991) in Lee & Chen (2011) explains that ANT describes how relationships are developed between human and nonhuman actors and their mutual benefits via the network. In our paper, human actors refer to HE stakeholders or potential the IoT users, such as teachers, students, and administrators, whereas non-human actors refer to the technological artefact, namely the IoT to support the human actors (Sarker, Sarker, & Sidorova, 2006). Since ANT has been widely applied to IS studies in fields such as business (Guilloux et al., 2013), healthcare (Cho et al., 2008), e-government (Heeks & Stanforth, 2007) and information security (Tsohou et al., 2015) to explore the role of actors in a given technological scenario, such as implementation, makes ANT an ideal for the paper.

ANT concepts related to our paper include: **Punctualisation**, which refers to looking at a technology as a whole. For example, looking at the IoT tools and strategies from a holistic point of view. **Inscription**, which refers to aligning actors with actants. For example, aligning users or stakeholders, such as students, teachers and admins with IT artefacts to facilitate institutional practices, namely the IoT. **Storytelling**, which refers to the successful experience of integrating and using technological artefacts. For example, can the integration the IoT as an IT tool/strategy for HE facilitate institutional practices, such as teaching and research, as well as promoting information sharing and collaboration among HE stakeholders. **Translation**, which is linked to effectiveness and efficiency of an innovation based on four sub-concepts, including Problematisation, Interessement, Enrolment and Mobilization. For example, can the aforementioned sub-concepts improve the efficiency and effectiveness of the IoT to enhance institutional practices, as well as promote information sharing and collaboration. And **Black boxing**, which refers to aligning the interests of many actors. For example, can the IoT cater to the needs held by HE stakeholders?

Despite the plethora of research on the IoT in organisational contexts, there is still an underlying problem concerning the wider aspects that affect the application of the IoT in higher education (Qin, Li, Zhang, Gao, & He, 2014). This prompts the need to explore this problem to address communication and sharing information issues in the HE domain. Figure 1 illustrates the proposed framework:

*Figure 1. Research Framework of IoT and ANT Concepts through ICT Lens*

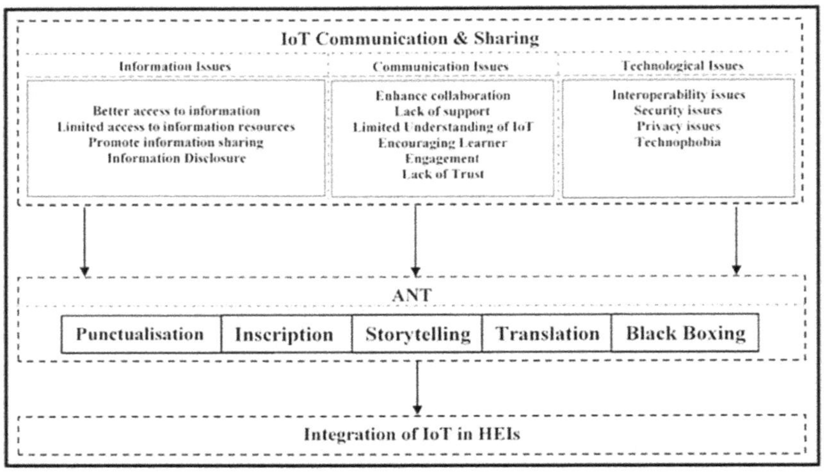


## METHOD

A qualitative research method was used to address the following "how" question:

*How IoT technology meets the informational, communication and system needs of University stakeholders?*

The unit of analysis or research population are University stakeholders comprising of students, teachers and administrators. A case study was carried out on two high-ranking University situated in North-West England. For the sample size and categories of participants, 40 participants made up of undergraduate/postgraduate students and lecturers and admins across the two Universities were interviewed (see Table 2). These particular participant groups were chosen because these are potential users of the IoT in HE and their perception of the opportunities and challenges of this innovation could influence their decision to use the IoT to support their institutional practices. To protect participants' personal identities, pseudonyms replaced their real names.

For data collection, individual interviews and focus groups with supporting documentation were conducted. Interview and focus group questions were designed as means to contextually frame participants' responses within the ANT framework. In particular, a semi-structured interview protocol was

*Table 2. Summary of Participants*

| No. | Participant | Code | No. | Participant | Code |
|---|---|---|---|---|---|
| University A | | | University B | | |
| **UA1** | Student | S1A | **UB1** | Student | S1B |
| **UA2** | Student | S2A | **UB2** | Student | S2B |
| **UA3** | Student | S3A | **UB3** | Student | S3B |
| **UA4** | Student | S4A | **UB4** | Student | S4B |
| **UA5** | Student | S5A | **UB5** | Student | S5B |
| **UA6** | Student | S6A | **UB6** | Student | S6B |
| **UA7** | Student | S7A | **UB7** | Student | S7B |
| **UA8** | Student | S8A | **UB8** | Student | S8B |
| **UA9** | Admin | A1A | **UB9** | Admin | A1B |
| **UA10** | Admin | A2A | **UB10** | Admin | A2B |
| **UA11** | Admin | A3A | **UB11** | Admin | A3B |
| **UA12** | Admin | A4A | **UB12** | Admin | A4B |
| **UA13** | Admin | A5A | **UB13** | Admin | A5B |
| **UA14** | Teacher | T1A | **UB14** | Teacher | T1B |
| **UA15** | Teacher | T2A | **UB15** | Teacher | T2B |
| **UA16** | Teacher | T3A | **UB16** | Teacher | T3B |
| **UA17** | Teacher | T4A | **UB17** | Teacher | T4B |
| **UA18** | Teacher | T5A | **UB18** | Teacher | T5B |
| **UA19** | Teacher | T6A | **UB19** | Teacher | T6B |
| **UA20** | Teacher | T7A | **UB20** | Teacher | T7B |

developed comprising of various questions and sub-questions aligned to the research questions. Semi structured interviews were used as a set of specific pre-defined questions needed to be asked about the topic in order to collect the most accurate and relevant data. Semi-structured interviews also created the opportunity to improvise during the interview process (Myers & Newman, 2007) in order to collect supplementary data that was not collected from the main narrative of the interview sessions, but would be equally as relevant and interesting as the main narrative data.

The structure of the interview protocol comprised of open-ended questions that captured the participants' responses that aligned with the research questions, which in turn enabled the participants to elaborate on their responses. For the focus groups, similar questions were asked in an open-ended discussion among a selected sample of the participants. Two focus groups were held. The first comprised of eight students, five admins and seven teachers from University A's population and a further two from each respected participant group was selected for University B. The interviews and focus groups took place over a three-month period between September and December 2018.

Finally, the interview and focus group transcripts were transcribed and were imported to a qualitative analysis tool known as Nvivo. The main themes and sub-themes were coded by applying nodes to each of them. This helped to unearth new concepts from the data and categorise them based on ANT theory.

*Figure 2. Coded Themes*

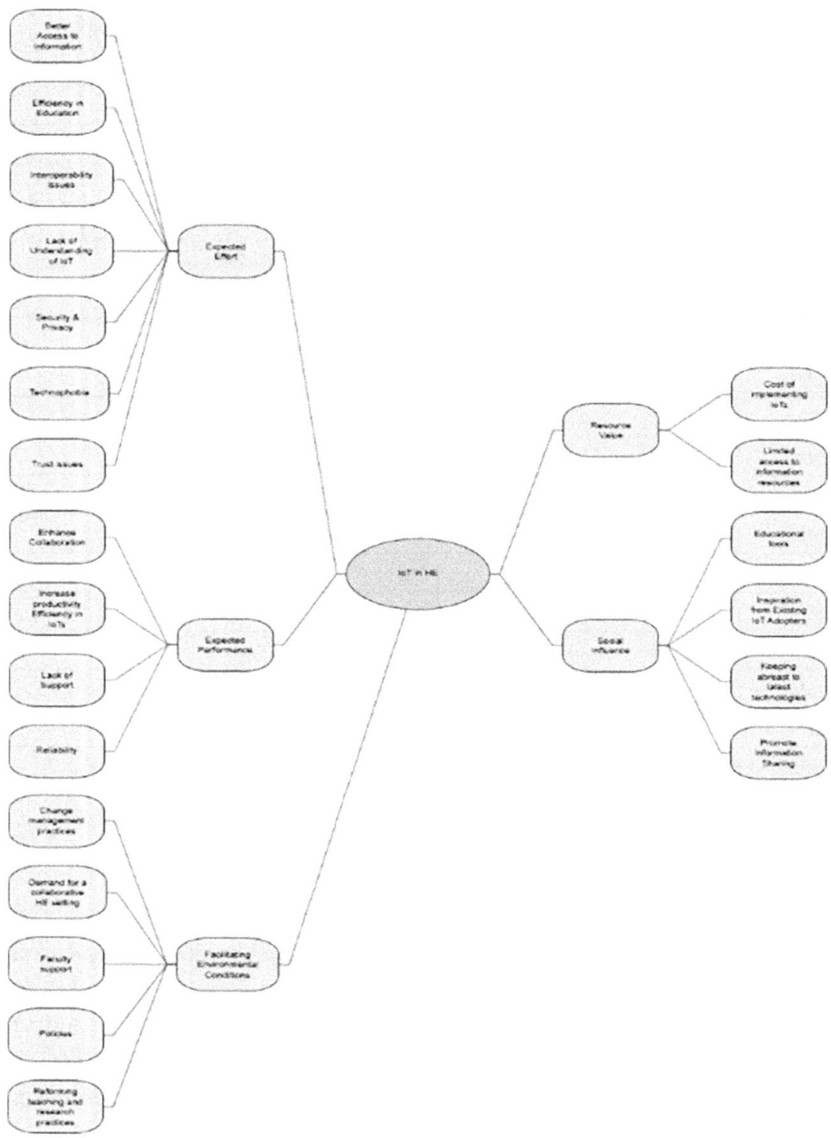

This contributed towards the validity of the research findings. Theme diagrams were created to highlight the main themes. Figure 2 illustrates the coded themes from the data analysis process using Nvivo.

## FINDINGS

The key components of the ANT framework helped to determine the potential integration of strategic innovation in the form of a novel technology (IoT). The following ANT predictors or concepts in the context of this research are defined below:

- **Punctualisation**: Looking at the IoT tools and strategies from a holistic point of view.
- **Inscription**: Aligning users or stakeholders, such as students, teachers and admins with IT artefacts to facilitate institutional practices, namely the IoT.
- **Storytelling**: the integration the IoT as an IT tool/strategy for HE to potentially facilitate institutional practices, such as teaching and research, as well as promoting information sharing and collaboration among HE stakeholders.
- **Translation**: the effectiveness and efficiency of the IoT based on four sub-concepts, including Problematisation, Interessement, Enrolment and Mobilization to enhance institutional practices, as well as promote information sharing and collaboration.
- **Black boxing**: the IoT to potentially cater to the similar benefits held by HE stakeholders.

The participants' beliefs and perceptions towards a potential the IoT technology converged around five central themes that reflected the proposition of the ANT framework as shown in Figure 3. These include Expected Performance, Expected Effort, Social Influence, Facilitating Environmental Conditions and Resource value, in addition the ANT concepts mentioned above. Moreover, the key themes were mapped to the appropriate ANT theme. These themes were born out of the concepts sharing similar characteristics, which were then categorised accordingly.

"Performance expectancy" emerged strongly amongst the admin side. They noted that the ability to integrate the IoT technology as a strategy to enhance productivity and efficiency were most prominent in influencing their potential use of the technology. The admins noted that the IoT could potentially help untether researchers from the field using sensor technology as they collect, as well as autonomously transmit, share and communicate data from remote locations (A1A, A2B and A4B). This capability makes this technology ideal for enhancing institutional practices, such as information sharing and communication.

Students emphasised a need for a reliable integrated system or platform like the IoT to enable cross-departmental access to information (S1A and S8B). The inefficiency and unreliability of using paper-based methods register for some courses was also highlighted (S2A and S4B). The IoT was perceived as an efficient and reliable integrated system that can bring all university departments within a shared working environment.

The performance expectancy also emerged as a substantial enabler that influences the potential integration of the IoT technology amongst the admins. The reliability of the IoT technology is an essential issue in determining its integration to enhance communication/collaboration and information sharing. The admins mentioned about the lack of support from vendors hindering the potential acceptance of the IoT owing to trust issues between the University and the vendors (A3A, A4A and A5B).

"Expected effort" emerged thematically across the participant responses. Most of the teachers expressed excitement about the potential use of the IoT technology owing to potential opportunities that this technology is likely to play in the teaching and learning process. They explained that the IoT is expected to make their job processes more manageable, enhance their collaboration with students, and provide better access to course materials.

The IoT would also be used in the teaching and learning process if there are guaranteed efficiencies such as better engagement with their students and promote more efficient education practices (T1A, T2B and T7B). Similarly, there is likely to be an increased desire to apply the IoT as an educational tool/strategy if it can intuitively be used to accomplish specific tasks. For example, the lectures stated that if the IoT were compatible with pedagogy ethos of the University, it would influence their acceptance of the technology (T3B and T5B). It was argued by the admins that technophobia, interoperability issues

*Figure 3. IoT Themes & Concepts in HE through ICT & ANT Lens*

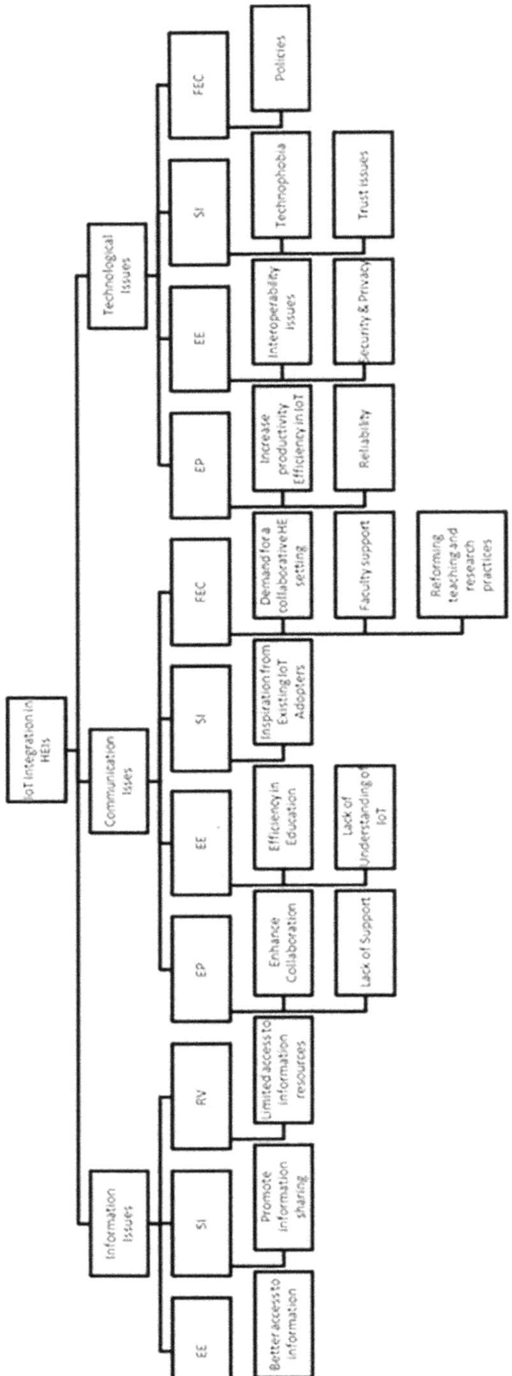

a lack of understanding of the IoT and security and privacy influence the acceptance of the technology (A4A, A1B and A3B). A lack of trust in the IoT, as well as having a lack of knowledge of the IoT would more than likely lead to a rejection of the technology (A2A, A5A and A5B).

Similarly, a potential dilemma could occur from the integration of the IoT if there is an ongoing level of interruption in the classroom when a student is struggling with the technology, as well as other students being distracted when attempting to help them (T6A and T4B). The efficiency that the IoT are set out to create, thus presents greater disruption.

The participants also mentioned that having an understanding of the IoT-enabled education is a key determinant to potential the IoT integration. If the IoT were to be embraced in HE, both teachers and students have to perceive the technology as being useful in order to promote collaboration and information sharing between them. The challenge with the IoT is the technology's ability to maintain the effective management of information, which in turn hinders collaboration and information sharing capabilities (S3A and S6B).

The response from the teacher and student participants showed that they have a high preference for digital content. They emphasised that they are more likely to use The IoT in the event of reducing the amount of effort in their ability to conduct institutional activities such as enhancing ubiquitous access to information and untethering them from physical learning spaces.

"Social influence" was found to be a high predictor of the potential integration of the IoT technology amongst the participants. Admins noted that the desire to keep abreast of trending technology could influence their choice to use The IoT. Participant A5B noted that they moved towards working with the IoT devices owing to the influence from collaborative projects they had worked on with their technically minded colleagues.

A community of members including admins, students and teachers have established research camps that aim to promote information sharing and collaboration via the IoT. Technically driven research spaces influenced their decision to use the IoT devices (S4A and S5B).

The student participants emphasised that it is essential to keep well informed of emergent technologies such as the IoT. An understanding of the IoT affords them with the skills applicable in today's digital economy (S7A and S2B). Further, the student participants explained that they have opted to adopt the IoT technology because they perceive themselves as being technologically advanced. They also believe this has allowed them to conduct trending research projects that are likely to positively influence the kind of job opportunity they seek after college (S5B and S6A).

In terms of "facilitating environmental conditions", the administrators noted that despite the effort by HEIs to attract and accommodate student's technological needs, having their smart gadgets connected to campus Wi-Fi must be carefully weighed against implementation challenges and security threats that are likely to evolve (A4B and A5A).

Education policies are paramount when it comes to adopting new technologies (T2B and T7B). The participant further reiterated that policies that encourage and explicitly support the integration of the IoT into collaborative teaching and learning. Teachers noted that it is essential to have strategies that foster change management practices to reduce barriers to the IoT integration (T3A and T7A). Teachers also mentioned the need for professional development programs that should incorporate the IoT tools/strategies to encourage early adoption of these technologies (T4A and T2B). They noted that this would help educators develop innovative methodologies and appropriate pedagogies that reshape classroom experiences (T1B, T2A and T3B). One student argued that embracing a particular educational tool requires faculty to support the IoT enabled learning environment (S7A and S8B).

It was also noted that it is crucial to set up policies that facilitate collaboration in the IoT ecosystem between institutions of higher education and private industry to promote its successful implementation within higher education (A3A and A2B). The students pointed out that the role of faculty is paramount in influencing students to adopt the IoT (S7B and S8B). They elucidated that faculty members have the flexibility to select their pedagogical tools and given their power of choice, this is paramount in controlling the decision of tools that meet their pedagogical needs at the lowest cost for students (S7A and S8B).

In terms of "resource value", while the cost of adopting the IoT was not an outstanding factor in influencing the use of the technology amongst faculty, both students and administrators mentioned that despite the positive reputation the IoT has received from other sectors, the costs and inadequate institutional resources to support effective technology integration had influenced its use (S1B, A4B and T1B).

Administrators mentioned that despite the primary objective of institutions of higher education being to educate students; however, there are other competing interests for the limited resources which may affects the institution-wide adoption of the IoT in their University (A2B and A4A). Despite the proliferation of educational technology, Universities fully adopt the IoT as an educational tool (T4B). The integration of the IoT into the education system is a gradual process due to the cost and challenges of implementation (A3B and T2A).

## Significance of ANT

Information issues relate to the themes EE, SI and RV, and the ANT concepts of storytelling, translation, black boxing and punctualisation. Translation in the sense that mobilisation of the IoT allows for better information sharing capabilities. Black boxing because the concept of better information access is a shared benefit among students, teachers and admins. Punctualisation in the sense that the wider issues of the IoT in HEIs limited information resources present a wider impediment of the IoT non-adoption in HEIs. Inscription in the sense that students, admins and teachers can use the same the IoT to support institutional practices such as the concept of promoting information sharing.

Communication issues relate to the themes EP, EE, SI and FEC, and the ANT concepts of black boxing, storytelling, punctualisation and inscription. Black boxing in the sense that the concept of enhanced communication is a shared benefit among students, teachers and admins. Storytelling in the sense that the IoT integration can facilitate the concept of enhanced collaboration and increased productivity efficiency in the IoT, as well as provide support for faculty and a means to reform teaching and research practices. Similarly, translation in the sense that mobilisation of the IoT facilities collaboration among HEI stakeholders. In terms of punctualisation, the wider issues of the IoT in HEIs such as concepts like, inspiration from existing the IoT adopters that present a wider opportunity of the IoT adoption in HEIs, as well as the wider barriers to the IoT adoption such as a lack of understanding of the IoT.

Technological issues relate to the themes EP, EE, SI and FEC, and the ANT concepts of storytelling, punctualisation and inscription. In terms of punctualisation, the wider technical issues of the IoT in HEIs such as concepts like reliability issues interoperability issues, security and privacy issues, trust issues and technophobia that present a wider impediment of the IoT non-adoption in HEIs. Storytelling in the sense that the IoT integration can help HEIs to introduce new policies to include the IoT as part of HEIs' ICT strategy to facilitate collaboration and information sharing capabilities.

In summary, the themes and concepts deduced from the above analysis in relation to ANT theory are summarised in Table 3. This was achieved by first categorising the concepts taken from the empirical findings into the key themes. This facilitated the categorisation of the themes into the three main perspectives covered in this paper, namely the informational, communicative and technological perspectives. Categorising the themes according to the relevant perspective then facilitated the categorisation of which ANT theme each perspective belonged to in order to highlight a relationship between the perspectives and the ANT themes. The adapted framework in Figure 4 highlights this process based on Table 3.

*Table 3. Summary of Empirical Study Findings*

<table>
<tr><th colspan="2">Themes</th><th>Concepts</th><th>ANT Concepts</th><th>Stakeholder(s)</th></tr>
<tr><td rowspan="3">Information Issues</td><td>Expected Effort (EE)</td><td>Better access to information</td><td rowspan="3">Black boxing<br>Punctualisation<br>Storytelling<br>Translation</td><td rowspan="3">A1B, A2A, A2B, A3B, A4A, A4B, A5A, A5B, S1B, S2B, S3A, S4A, S5B, S6A, S6B, S7A, T1A, T1B, T2A, T2B, T3B, T4B, T5B, T6A, T7B</td></tr>
<tr><td>Social Influence (SI)</td><td>Promote information sharing</td></tr>
<tr><td>Resource value (RV)</td><td>Limited access to information resources<br>Information Disclosure</td></tr>
<tr><td rowspan="4">Communication Issues</td><td>Expected Performance (EP)</td><td>Enhanced Collaboration<br>Lack of Support<br>Increase productivity Efficiency</td><td rowspan="4">Black boxing<br>Inscription<br>Punctualisation<br>Storytelling</td><td rowspan="4">A1A, A1B, A2A, A2B, A3A, A3B, A4A, A4B, A5A, A5B, S1A, S2A, S2B, S3A, S4A, S5B, S6A, S7A, S7B, S8A, S8B, T1A, T1B, T2A, T2B, T3A, T4A, T3B, T3B, T4B, T7A, T7B</td></tr>
<tr><td>Expected Effort (EE)</td><td>Efficiency in Education<br>Lack of Understanding of the IoT</td></tr>
<tr><td>Social Influence (SI)</td><td>Inspiration from Existing the IoT Adopters<br>Limited Understanding of the IoT<br>Encouraging Learner Engagement</td></tr>
<tr><td>Facilitating Environmental Conductions (FEC)</td><td>Demand for a collaborative HE setting<br>Faculty support<br>Reforming teaching and research practices</td></tr>
<tr><td rowspan="4">Technological Issues</td><td>Expected Performance (EP)</td><td>Reliability issues</td><td rowspan="4">Punctualisation<br>Storytelling</td><td rowspan="4">A1A, A1B, A2A, A2B, A3A, A3B, A4A, A4B, A5A, A5B, S1A, S2A, S2B, S3A, S4A, S5B, S6A, S7A, S7B, S8A, S8B, T1A, T1B, T2A, T2B, T3A, T4A, T3B, T3B, T4B, T7A, T7B</td></tr>
<tr><td>Expected Effort (EE)</td><td>Interoperability issues<br>Security issues<br>Privacy issues</td></tr>
<tr><td>Social Influence (SI)</td><td>Technophobia<br>Trust issues</td></tr>
<tr><td>Facilitating Environmental Conductions (FEC)</td><td>Policies</td></tr>
</table>

## DISCUSSION

This descriptive case study design allowed participants to share their perceptions of the IoT technology. The discussion aligns to the research questions of the study. The findings provided insight into how insight into how a potential the IoT strategy can facilitate communication and information sharing within HE.

As the IoT becomes a new normal in HEIs, stakeholders are looking for new strategies to enhance performance, engagement, and behaviour. Integrating the IoT into HE provides the opportunity to store, analyse, and share data. Data could potentially be used to personalise instructions tailored to match the

*Figure 4. Adapted Framework Drawn upon the IoT and ANT Concepts from an ICT Perspective*

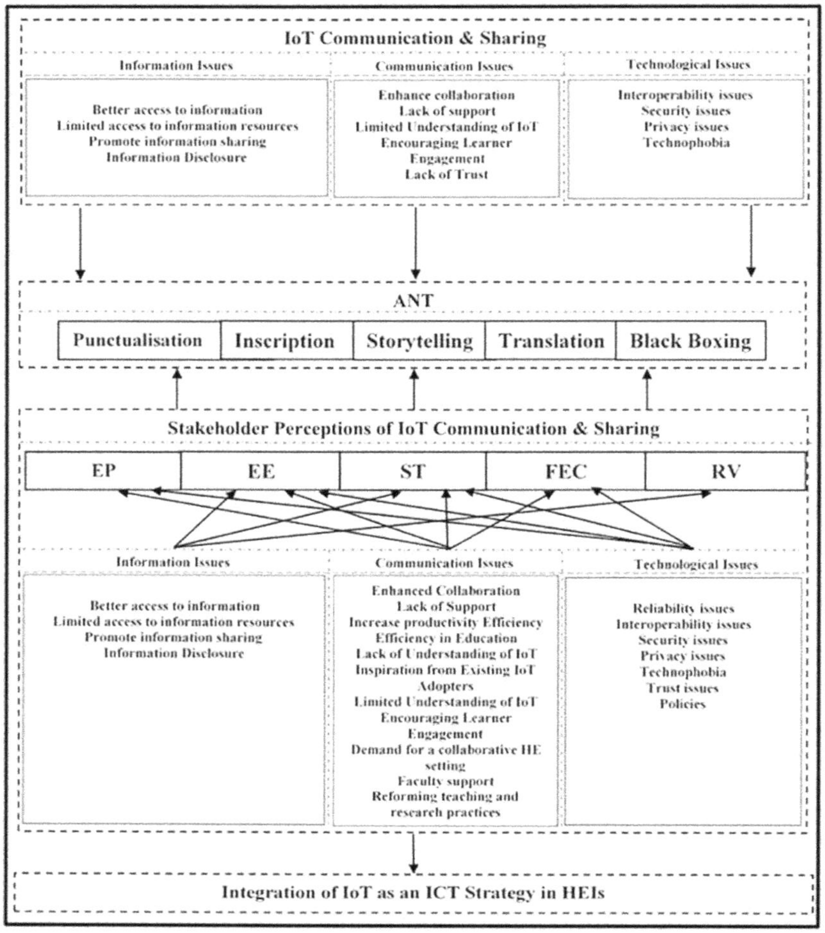


needs and expectations of HEI stakeholders, such as admins, teachers and students. This data can then be leveraged to create new strategies that enhance collaboration and information sharing in HE settings.

The beliefs and perceptions reported to influence the IoT integration in HEIs include expected performance, expected effort, social influence, facilitating environmental conductions and resource value. The key themes were guided by the propositions of the Actor Network Theory (ANT) and the ICT topology adopted throughout this paper.

PE had a significant impact on the potential integration of the IoT technology among the HEI stakeholders. It became more apparent that the IoT as an IT strategy to could potentially create a shared working space that promotes collaboration and work productivity. Relatedly, teachers could embrace the IoT as an IT strategy to improve efficiency in their teaching research practices, such as grading and preparing course materials. Stakeholders highlighted that they would only accept the IoT for teaching and learning if it aligned with their individual needs and efficiencies. Despite this, there is a need for professional development in order to raise awareness about the IoT and how this aligns with existing curricula. Therefore, ongoing training about the IoT and its integration into the teaching and learning process is vital to raise such awareness.

Other themes that were deduced from the findings were EE, SI and FEC, which were perceived as benefits to the IoT integration to promote collaboration and information sharing (Njeru et al., 2017). For example, teachers appear to be convinced by the idea that the IoT can only be realised through training and support to increase the uptake of the IoT in HEIs. To improve the buy-in into integrating the IoT, administrators are required to increase teachers' awareness about why the IoT cannot only improve their efficiency but can also act as an IT strategy that can facilitate and promote collaboration and information sharing to increase efficiency and provide a better teaching and learning experience.

Despite the significant costs of integrating technologies like the IoT, this had very little impact on teachers' behaviour towards integrating the IoT in that teachers and students would utilise the technology availed to them by administrators. Cost can be perceived as key barrier to administrators while efficiency was more of a concern for teachers. Nevertheless, to promote efficiency among teachers with the availed technology, administrators are expected to draft policies as part of its IT strategy that support professional development to raise awareness of the IoT and how this can promote collaboration and information sharing to enhance HEI practices.

Information issues were found to relate to the ANT concepts of storytelling, translation, black boxing and punctualisation. This included the mobilisation of the IoT for better information sharing capabilities, better information access as a shared benefit among students, teachers and admins and limited information resources as a wider impediment of the IoT non-adoption. These findings represent a link between the sociotechnical aspect of ANT and the information component the ICT topology in a sense that the integration of the IoT as a potential information-sharing tool can help to meet or hinder stakeholders' informational needs.

Communication issues were found to relate to the ANT concepts of storytelling, punctualisation and inscription. This included enhanced communication as a shared benefit among students, teachers and admins, enhanced collaboration, increased productivity efficiency, provision of support for faculty, reforming teaching and research practices, mobilisation of the IoT, facilitating collaboration among HEI stakeholders, inspiration from existing the IoT adopters and a lack of understanding of the IoT. These findings represent a link between the sociotechnical aspect of ANT and the communication component the ICT topology in a sense that the integration of the IoT as a potential collaboration tool can help to meet or hinder stakeholders' informational needs.

Technological issues were found to relate to the ANT concepts of storytelling, punctualisation and inscription. This included the wider technical issues of the IoT in HEIs such as reliability issues, interoperability issues, security and privacy issues, trust issues and technophobia that present a wider impediment of the IoT non-adoption in HEIs. This also includes the introduction of new policies to include the IoT as part of HEIs' ICT strategy to facilitate collaboration and information sharing capabilities. These findings represent a link between the sociotechnical aspect of ANT and the technological component the ICT topology in a sense that the integration of the IoT as a potential innovative technology can help to meet or hinder stakeholders' system needs.

In short, HEIs are potential incubators of the IoT if integrated into the education system. HEIs are expected to facilitate its use as collaborative and sharing tools on a management platform across various educational institutions. If the IoT are to gain traction across HE, it is crucial to understand where different stakeholders are positioned in the spectrum of technological awareness.

## CONCLUSION

With the current education system transitioning from a traditional to a data-driven education process, the uptake of the IoT within HEIs is slowly gaining traction. The integration of the IoT in HEIs can offer potential affordances to institutional practices. Opportunities include better collaborative learning, improved information sharing and productive efficiency that is driven by ubiquitous tools that can used as a potential ICT strategy to facilitate these practices for HEI stakeholders. With the increased integration of the IoT to the teaching and learning process, the HE sector is very likely to transition to competency based learning driven by IT tools. Despite the IoT highlighting several potential opportunities in the teaching and learning process, it is equally important to regard the barriers to the IoT integration in HEIs. This paper found that the IoT as a potential IT strategy could come with potential risks such as privacy concerns, data security and interoperability issues.

Information, communication and technological issues were found to relate to the ANT concepts and findings highlighted a link between the sociotechnical aspect of ANT and the information, communication and technological components of the ICT topology. Despite the opportunities the IoT can bring to HEIs, stakeholders have contrasting perceptions of the IoT as a potential information sharing and communication strategy to meet their system expectations, and therefore are undecided about their willingness to embrace the IoT.

The research findings drawn on recommendations for future research. Considerations for future research are required to determine the best practices or strategies to integrate the IoT in HEIs. The low level of awareness of IoT technology amongst the HEI stakeholders' prompts further additional research to explore the reasons why HEI stakeholders are reluctant to embrace the IoT. This also includes how pedagogical strategies can be developed to implement the IoT as a potential IT strategy that can facilitate institutional practices, as well as promote information sharing and collaboration amongst HEI stakeholders. Further research could also draw on developing best practices from a faculty perspective who are likely to be early adopters of the IoT in HEIs, and thus could be a persuading factor for faculty to adopt the IoT into their pedagogy. This could help to develop a network of faculty members to promote the potentials of the IoT to persuade other potential adopters. For security and privacy, future research could draw on how HEIs could address cyber-attacks in the event of integrating the IoT into their curricula.

### Future Recommendation

- Although this paper provided insight and rigour contributions to IoT theory and practice a future researcher should consider adopting a mixed method to generalise the outcome of the empirical findings.
- Future researcher and practitioners could benefit from adopting an innovation theory such as DoI and TAM.

## REFERENCES

Ali, M. (2019). Cloud Computing at a Cross Road: Quality and Risks in Higher Education. *Advances in Internet of Things*, *9*(3), 33–49. doi:10.4236/ait.2019.93003

Ali, M. (2020). Multi-Perspectives of Cloud Computing Service Adoption Quality and Risks in Higher Education. In D. B. A. Mehdi Khosrow-Pour (Ed.), Handbook of Research on Modern Educational Technologies, Applications, and Management (2nd ed.). IGI Global.

Ali, M. B. (2019). Multiple Perspective of Cloud Computing Adoption Determinants in Higher Education a Systematic Review. *International Journal of Cloud Applications and Computing*, *9*(3), 89–109. doi:10.4018/IJCAC.2019070106

Demirer, V., Aydın, B., & Çelik, Ş. B. (2017). *Exploring the educational potential of Internet of Things (IoT) in seamless learning The Internet of Things: Breakthroughs in Research and Practice*. IGI Global.

Dery, K., Kolb, D., & MacCormick, J. (2014). Working with connective flow: How smartphone use is evolving in practice. *European Journal of Information Systems*, *23*(5), 558–570. doi:10.1057/ejis.2014.13

Du, J., Jiang, C., Gelenbe, E., Xu, L., Li, J., & Ren, Y. (2018). Distributed Data Privacy Preservation in IoT Applications. *IEEE Wireless Communications*, *25*(6), 68–76. doi:10.1109/MWC.2017.1800094

Forrest, C. (2017). *80% of IoT apps not tested for vulnerabilities, report says*. Retrieved 24th Feb 2019 from https://www.techrepublic.com/article/80-of-IoT-apps-not-tested-for-vulnerabilities-report-says/

Fraga-Lamas, P., Fernández-Caramés, T. M., Suárez-Albela, M., Castedo, L., & González-López, M. (2016). A Review on Internet of Things for Defense and Public Safety. *Sensors (Basel)*, *16*(10), 1644. doi:10.339016101644 PMID:27782052

Fraile, F., Tagawa, T., Poler, R., & Ortiz, A. (2018). Trustworthy industrial IoT gateways for interoperability platforms and ecosystems. *IEEE Internet of Things Journal*, *5*(6), 4506–4514. doi:10.1109/JIOT.2018.2832041

Gawali, S. K., & Deshmukh, M. K. (2019). Energy Autonomy in IoT Technologies. *Energy Procedia*, *156*, 222–226. doi:10.1016/j.egypro.2018.11.132

Gómez, J., Huete, J. F., Hoyos, O., Perez, L., & Grigori, D. (2013). Interaction system based on internet of things as support for education. *Procedia Computer Science*, *21*, 132–139. doi:10.1016/j.procs.2013.09.019

Guilloux, V., Locke, J., & Lowe, A. (2013). Digital business reporting standards: Mapping the battle in France. *European Journal of Information Systems*, *22*(3), 257–277. doi:10.1057/ejis.2012.5

Hansen, J. D., & Reich, J. (2015). Democratizing education? Examining access and usage patterns in massive open online courses. *Science*, *350*(6265), 1245–1248. doi:10.1126cience.aab3782 PMID:26785488

Harwood, T., & Garry, T. (2017). Internet of Things: Understanding trust in techno-service systems. *Journal of Service Management*, *28*(3), 442–475. doi:10.1108/JOSM-11-2016-0299

Heeks, R., & Stanforth, C. (2007). Understanding e-Government project trajectories from an actor-network perspective. *European Journal of Information Systems*, *16*(2), 165–177. doi:10.1057/palgrave.ejis.3000676

Hsu, C.-L., & Lin, J. C.-C. (2018). Exploring factors affecting the adoption of Internet of Things services. *Journal of Computer Information Systems*, *58*(1), 49–57. doi:10.1080/08874417.2016.1186524

Islam, S. M. R., Kwak, D., Kabir, M. H., Hossain, M., & Kwak, K. (2015). The Internet of Things for Health Care: A Comprehensive Survey. *IEEE Access: Practical Innovations, Open Solutions*, *3*, 678–708. doi:10.1109/ACCESS.2015.2437951

Janeček, V. (2018). Ownership of personal data in the Internet of Things. *Computer Law & Security Review*, *34*(5), 1039–1052. doi:10.1016/j.clsr.2018.04.007

Krieger, D. J., & Belliger, A. (2014). *Interpreting Networks: Hermeneutics, Actor-Network Theory & New Media*. Transcript.

Krotov, V. (2017). The Internet of Things and new business opportunities. *Business Horizons*, *60*(6), 831–841. doi:10.1016/j.bushor.2017.07.009

Lee, S. M., & Chen, L. (2011). An integrative research framework for the online social network service. *Service Business*, *5*(3), 259–276. doi:10.100711628-011-0113-y

Majeed, A., & Ali, M. (2018). *How Internet-of-Things (IoT) making the university campuses smart? QA higher education (QAHE) perspective*. Paper presented at the Computing and Communication Workshop and Conference (CCWC), 2018 IEEE 8th Annual.

Maksimović, M. (2018). IoT concept application in educational sector using collaboration. *Facta Universitatis, Series: Teaching. Learning and Teacher Education*, *1*(2), 137–150.

Mani, Z., & Chouk, I. (2018). Consumer Resistance to Innovation in Services: Challenges and Barriers in the Internet of Things Era. *Journal of Product Innovation Management*, *35*(5), 780–807. doi:10.1111/jpim.12463

Manwaring, K., & Clarke, R. (2015). Surfing the third wave of computing: A framework for research into eObjects. *Computer Law & Security Review*, *31*(5), 586–603. doi:10.1016/j.clsr.2015.07.001

Middleton, C., Scheepers, R., & Kristiina, V. T. (2014). When mobile is the norm: Researching mobile information systems and mobility as post-adoption phenomena. *European Journal of Information Systems*, *23*(5), 503–512. doi:10.1057/ejis.2014.21

Mohammed Banu, A., Trevor, W.-H., & Mostafa, M. (2018). Benefits and Challenges of Cloud Computing Adoption and Usage in Higher Education: A Systematic Literature Review. *International Journal of Enterprise Information Systems*, *14*(4), 64–77. doi:10.4018/IJEIS.2018100105

Myers, M. D., & Newman, M. (2007). The qualitative interview in IS research: Examining the craft. *Information and Organization*, *17*(1), 2–26. doi:10.1016/j.infoandorg.2006.11.001

Nimmo, R. (2011). Actor-network theory and methodology: Social research in a more-than-human world. *Methodological Innovations Online*, *6*(3), 108–119. doi:10.4256/mio.2011.010

Njeru, A. M., Omar, M. S., Yi, S., Paracha, S., & Wannous, M. (2017). *Using IoT technology to improve online education through data mining*. Paper presented at the 2017 International Conference on Applied System Innovation (ICASI). 10.1109/ICASI.2017.7988469

Noura, M., Atiquzzaman, M., & Gaedke, M. (2018). Interoperability in Internet of Things: Taxonomies and Open Challenges. *Mobile Networks and Applications*.

Oberländer, A. M., Röglinger, M., Rosemann, M., Kees, A., Ågerfalk, P., & Tuunainen, V. (2018). Conceptualizing business-to-thing interactions – A sociomaterial perspective on the Internet of Things. *European Journal of Information Systems*, *27*(4), 486–502. doi:10.1080/0960085X.2017.1387714

Patel, P., & Cassou, D. (2015). Enabling high-level application development for the Internet of Things. *Journal of Systems and Software*, *103*, 62–84. doi:10.1016/j.jss.2015.01.027

Pauget, B., & Dammak, A. (2019). The implementation of the Internet of Things: What impact on organizations? *Technological Forecasting and Social Change*, *140*, 140–146. doi:10.1016/j.techfore.2018.03.012

Petrov, C. (2019). *Internet Of Things Statistics 2020*. Available: https://techjury.net/stats-about/internet-of-things-statistics/

Qin, W., Li, B., Zhang, J., Gao, S., & He, Y. (2014). *Design and Implementation of IoT Security System Towards Campus Safety*. Paper presented at the Advanced Technologies in Ad Hoc and Sensor Networks, Berlin, Germany. 10.1007/978-3-642-54174-2_27

Rose, K., Eldridge, S., & Chapin, L. (2015). *The internet of things: An overview*. The Internet Society.

Rushby, N., & Surry, D. (2016). *The Wiley Handbook of Learning Technology*. Wiley.

Sarker, S., Sarker, S., & Sidorova, A. (2006). Understanding Business Process Change Failure: An Actor-Network Perspective. *Journal of Management Information Systems*, *23*(1), 51–86. doi:10.2753/MIS0742-1222230102

Talari, S., Shafie-Khah, M., Siano, P., Loia, V., Tommasetti, A., & Catalão, J. (2017). A review of smart cities based on the internet of things concept. *Energies*, *10*(4), 421. doi:10.3390/en10040421

Tsohou, A., Karyda, M., Kokolakis, S., & Kiountouzis, E. (2015). Managing the introduction of information security awareness programmes in organisations. *European Journal of Information Systems*, *24*(1), 38–58. doi:10.1057/ejis.2013.27

Wei, P., & Zhou, Z. (2018). Research on security of information sharing in Internet of Things based on key algorithm. *Future Generation Computer Systems*, *88*, 599–605. doi:10.1016/j.future.2018.04.035

Whitmore, A., Agarwal, A., & Da Xu, L. (2015). The Internet of Things—A survey of topics and trends. *Information Systems Frontiers*, *17*(2), 261–274. doi:10.100710796-014-9489-2

Xia, F., Yang, L. T., Wang, L., & Vinel, A. (2012). Internet of Things. *International Journal of Communication Systems*, *25*(9), 1101–1102. doi:10.1002/dac.2417

Zhu, Z.-T., Yu, M.-H., & Riezebos, P. (2016). A research framework of smart education. *Smart Learning Environments*, *3*(1), 4. doi:10.118640561-016-0026-2

## ADDITIONAL READING

Fernández-Caramés, T. M., & Fraga-Lamas, P. (2019). Towards Next Generation Teaching, Learning, and Context-Aware Applications for Higher Education: A Review on Blockchain, IoT, Fog and Edge Computing Enabled Smart Campuses and Universities. *Applied Sciences (Basel, Switzerland)*, *9*(21), 4479. doi:10.3390/app9214479

Immordino, K. M., Gigliotti, R. A., Ruben, B. D., & Tromp, S. (2016). Evaluating the Impact of Strategic Planning in Higher Education. *Educational Planning*, 35-48.

## KEY TERMS AND DEFINITIONS

**Actor-Network Theory:** An approach that promotes social and natural worlds that exist in a continuously shifting network of relationships.

**Collaborative Technology:** Technologies or tools that promote the collaboration or cooperation between organisations and people.

**Higher Education:** Tertiary education where academic courses are taught.

**Information Sharing:** The practice of exchanging and disclosing information to another party using online tools.

**Internet of Things:** Online computing devices that are embedded in everyday objects, which allows for the sending and receiving of data.

**Ubiquitous Tools:** Applications that enable users to access them from any device at any given period.

# Chapter 2
# Gamification Tools to Facilitate Student Learning Engagement in Higher Education:
## A Burden or Blessing?

**Mark Schofield**
*UK Academic Consultations, UK*

## ABSTRACT

*Gamification is a novel technology that can potentially motivate student learning. This chapter reflects on the implementation of a gamified application to support students' learning in terms of learning important facts concerning their study program. The scope of the chapter refers to two design features in which tests were conducted on the different configurations in a field experiment among UK university students. The initial feature identified was feedback, where it was anticipated that engagement would increase, with tailored feedback having a greater impact than generic feedback. The next feature identified was circumventing users from binge gaming through session limits, as this may potentially prevent deep learning. The findings suggest that tailored feedback was less effective than generic feedback, contradicting the initial anticipation. Session limits were found to not circumvent binging without a reduction in sessions. The findings suggest that gaming properties of gamified applications could impact sustaining and encouraging play.*

## INTRODUCTION

Novel technologies have paved the way for learners to have a more engaging and immersive learning experience, offering exciting opportunities to collaborate with their instructors and colleagues in new ways. Gamification is a novel technology that has the potential to motivate student learning. Deterding et al. (2011) define gamification as "the use of game-design elements in non-game contexts" (p.9). Though within the past decade, gamification has attracted much attention within various sectors, which has seen

DOI: 10.4018/978-1-7998-4846-2.ch002

successful outcomes such as rapid growth with a number of cases reporting that businesses, educators and web designers have applied gamification as a means to motive and engage learners (Mollick & Rothbard, 2014; Subhash & Cudney, 2018). Despite the achievements of gamification, investigations into when and how gamification can be applied to achieve the most engaging learning experience in higher education settings have been overlooked.

The wider interest in gamification has prompted various studies across various topical areas aimed at certain audiences and disciplines. In 2012, an early literature review (around the time gamification started to take off) by Connolly and Boyle (Connolly et al., 2012) found over 100 empirical studies investigating the impact of gamification in various contexts. By contrast, Nah et al. (2014) conducted a more recent review which investigated gamification in the education context and only found 15 studies that discussed gamification in education settings. In addition, the latter review indicates that gamification has the potential to increase student engagement for improving their learning outcomes which are influenced by a number of situational factors such as the utilisation of tailored feedback (Burgers et al., 2015; Hatala et al., 2014; Lustria et al., 2013). For that reason, the scope of this chapter is to examine whether tailored feedback can reveal whether gamified learning tools can foster student engagement for higher education and whether this is a burden or a blessing for achieving learning outcomes.

In some contexts, players often binge games for prolonged periods of time as opposed to periodically spacing out play over a number of sessions. Several authors argue against the prolonged exposure to gamified tools, suggesting that distributed practice can enhance learning through learning a new skill or developing knowledge by effectively spreading learning across a number of short time intervals (Dunlosky et al., 2013; Heidt et al., 2016; Rohrer, 2015). However, gamification for learning engagement can only succeed when students game for prolonged periods of time in order to process a sufficient amount of new information to achieve their learning outcomes (Welbers et al., 2019). The dilemma here is that prolonged periods of gaming can potentially take away the learning element and becomes a mere leisure activity or a source of entertainment. So main objective of this chapter is to determine whether gamified learning tools for higher education learning is a burden or a blessing.

This chapter hypothesises whether learning engagement from persistent play would a) encourage enforce distributed learning or b) limit enforce distributed learning. Testing this hypothesis calls for the creation of experimental conditions where persistent play would either positively or negatively impact learning participation and engagement.

## THEORETICAL BACKGROUND

### Gamification

In spite of its inception, which dates back to 2008 and its current popularity, gamification is still in its infancy. Brett Terill (2008) is often the first to be credited for the inception of the term and discussed gamification in a blog to define the act of taking game mechanics and applying them to other web properties to increase engagement. Currently, gamification is not limited to the web, but it can also engage people, motivate action, promote learning, and solve problems through incorporating game design elements in contexts such as non-game environments (Aparicio et al., 2019; Deterding et al., 2011; Mollick & Rothbard, 2014). The scope of our paper was investigating the properties of gamification to stimulate learning in higher education contexts; however, gamification is related, but is not the same as game-based learning.

Gamification refers to game design elements in a non-game context, though game-based learning refers to using actual games to obtain skills or knowledge. Cheong et al. (2013) argue that gamification is a continuum that incorporates games, as well as activities to which game elements have been added. Gamified multiple choice quiz app is a middle ground between the former two areas mentioned by Cheong et al. In addition to these elements, tested gamification mechanics are incorporated in the app, such as avatars, experience points, and badges (Barata et al., 2015). Thus, the application can be classified as a gamified multiple choice quiz, which is akin to Cheong's application.

Academic interest in effectively using game design elements dates back at least 30 years to Malone (Malone, 1982) who studied the appealing features of computer games for the purpose of using these features to make user interfaces more interesting and enjoyable. Sweetser and Wyeth (2005) contributed greatly to our understanding of the features that make games enjoyable by developing a scale to measure game enjoyment, although they did not elaborate on the use of these features in a non-game context. Fu et al. (2009) developed a scale to measure the enjoyment of people playing educational games. Cózar-Gutiérrez and Sáez-López (2016) recently reported that teachers' interest in and perceived innovativeness of using games in the classroom is strong, showing a desire to understand the best practices in incorporating games and gamified education in the classroom.

Despite academic interest in understanding and using the appealing features of games, academia has been slow to react to the surge of gamification projects in businesses and on the Internet (Chitra, 2020). Initial support for the efficacy of gamification mainly came from businesses, where the idea that tasks can be made more efficient and engaging by wrapping them in game design elements rapidly gained popularity. Yu-Kai Chou, an influential gamification expert, collected and published a list of 95 documented gamification cases, based on the criterion that the documentation reports return on investment indicators (Chou, 2013). These cases show that gamification can indeed have a strong, positive impact on engagement and performance in various activities.

Although it is not reported how these cases were selected, and there could very well be a bias toward successful cases, this adds weight to the claim that gamification can work, given the right context and implementation. A recent literature study of academic gamification research found that most studies on the subject verified that gamification can work, even though effects differ across contexts. By context, the authors refer to the type of activity being gamified, such as exercise, sustainable consumption, monitoring, or education. Features such as feedback options and the way in which the level of difficulty adapts to a player's skills can be critical to a game's success and need to be investigated in more detail.

## Impact of Feedback on Efficacy of Gamifying Learning

Hammer and Lee (2011) argue that feedback is central to the potential of gamification. First, to make a person feel that they are successfully improving and heading toward a goal, games can provide explicit feedback to show this progress. Studies indicate that even simple, virtual reward systems such as experience points and badges can increase the engagement of players (Denny, 2013; Fitz-Walter et al., 2011). For instance, Hatala et al. (2014) conducted a meta-analysis to investigate if feedback positively impacted learning of procedural skills in medical education. Their results demonstrate that providing feedback moderately enhances learning. In addition, they found that terminal feedback (i.e. feedback given at the end of the learning activity) was more effective than concurrent feedback (i.e. feedback given during the learning activity). These analyses point toward the effectiveness of using feedback as a mechanism to enhance learning.

However, not all feedback is equally effective in achieving its goal (Burgers et al., 2015; Kluger & DeNisi, 1996). For instance, one study shows that the effectiveness of negative feedback (i.e. feedback emphasising the elements that could be improved upon) and positive feedback (i.e. feedback emphasising the elements that went well during an activity) depends on the task at hand (Burgers et al., 2015). Negative feedback was more effective than positive feedback when the problem could immediately be repaired (e.g. in the case of a game which enables a new session to be started immediately). By contrast, positive feedback was more effective than negative feedback when repair was delayed (e.g. in the case of a game which only enables one session per specified time period). Thus, when using feedback, it is important to match the specific type of feedback to the specific task at hand.

One type of feedback which has been associated with enhancing effectiveness is the use of tailored feedback over generic feedback (De Vries et al., 2008; Krebs et al., 2010). In tailored feedback, the specific content is personalised ("tailored") to the individual, through mechanisms like personalisation (i.e. addressing the receiver by name) or by adapting the feedback to their individual performance (e.g. by including descriptive statistics that refer to the receiver's personal performance). By contrast, generic feedback is similar for all addressees receiving the feedback. Tailored messaging may take the form of, for example, frequent prompt or reminder emails (Neff & Fry, 2009), often edited (or tailored) to include information specific to particular participants (Schneider et al., 2013). While simple interventions such as emails can increase participants' logging into online systems, tailored information can further increase desired behaviours in specific cases (Krebs et al., 2010; Neff & Fry, 2009). Thus, for the current study, we expect a similar pattern leading to students receiving feedback play more sessions of the gamified app compared to students receiving no feedback.

Nevertheless, other studies show different results (Kroeze et al., 2006; Noble et al., 2015). For instance, a systematic review by Kroeze et al. (2006) demonstrates that the effectiveness of tailoring depends on the specific kind of behaviour targeted. For instance, for 11 out of 14 interventions targeting fat reduction, the authors found positive effects of tailoring over a generic intervention. By contrast, for only 3 out of 11 interventions targeting physical education, did the authors find such positive effects of tailoring. Thus, the question whether or not tailoring improves effectiveness may also be dependent on contextual factors like the targeted behaviour. In the current study, we aim to motivate students to continue using a gamified app to increase learning. For this specific context, we do not yet have information on whether tailoring is an effective strategy or not. Yet, given that, across behaviours, tailoring typically boosts performance compared to generic information (Krebs et al., 2010) we expect that students receiving tailored feedback play more sessions of the gamified app compared to students receiving generic feedback.

## Educational Distributed Practice

In pilot studies of the application used in this study, it was observed that some players tended to binge play. Within a matter of days, they would play so many sessions that they quickly learned the answers to most questions. Although this can be considered as a success in terms of engagement, it can actually be harmful for long term recall. One of the challenges for gamification in a learning task and more so for games for learning is thus not to create as much engagement as possible, but to create the right type and amount of engagement to best achieve the learning goal.

One of the goals of any education intervention is to stimulate deep learning, which means that students retain the most important information, even when the education intervention has been completed. In that light, many studies highlight the positive aspects of distributed practice. This means that students spread ("distribute") their learning and practice activities over a number of relatively short time intervals, as compared to cramming all learning in one long session. For instance, a recent study by Heidt et al. (2016) contrasted two versions of a training program meant to teach students how to conduct a specific type of police interview. One of the versions contained a single session of two hours containing all information, while the other version spaced the program into two one hour sessions (i.e. distributed learning). Results demonstrated that, on average, participants in the distributed learning condition performed better in that they asked more open questions and were able to elicit more detailed information through these open questions. This suggests that distributed learning could positively enhance training outcomes.

This study by Heidt et al. (2016) is not the only one that shows these advantages of distributed learning. A review by Dunlosky et al. (2013) argues that distributed practice is one of the best researched topics in the field of education studies. Typically, distributed practice focuses on two elements, referring to the spacing of activities (i.e. the number of learning activities planned to cover all materials) and the time lag between activities. Dunlosky's review demonstrated that distributed practice enhances learning across a variety of learning contexts (Barata et al., 2015; Cózar-Gutiérrez & Sáez-López, 2016; Welbers et al., 2019). Thus, the literature suggests that it is better to spread out learning over several sessions instead of concentrating it in one large binge.

Many studies on distributed practice focus on specific training programs with set dates for education activities (such as the interview training sessions described by Heidt et al. (2016). Gamification interventions offer the technological possibilities of also stimulating distributed learning on an individual basis through computer design. One way to do this is by imposing a daily limit on players. Such a daily limit prevents users from gorging on all content in one large binge and may instead stimulate players to return to the content on later dates, thus encouraging distributed practice. However, an important condition for this feature is that it should not reduce the overall amount of sessions played. We test whether this effect can be achieved through gamification, whether students with a daily limit play an equal amount of sessions on more different days compared to students without a daily limit in playing the gamified app.

## Increased Complexity

To motivate a person to achieve their best performance, games can be designed to interactively increase the difficulty of an activity to match the player's growth in skill (Barata et al., 2015; Garris et al., 2002; Malone, 1982). Ensuring the right level of challenge can, however, be difficult depending on the goal of an educational or serious game. In the current study, the goal of the app is knowledge acquisition, letting students learn a list of facts. For this type of learning task, it is not always possible to implement progressive difficulty levels. In our case, the facts are mostly orthogonal, in the sense that there is no overarching skill that can be learned, as would for instance be the case for math or language acquisition tasks. Players thus either know the answer to a question or they do not, and when posed a novel question, players have no previous skill to rely on. This complicates the goal of keeping players perform at their best (Barata et al., 2015; Chitra, 2020; Cózar-Gutiérrez & Sáez-López, 2016; Deterding et al., 2011; Nah et al., 2014; Wolfenden, 2019).

Still, it is possible to influence how well players perform based on what questions are asked. If players perform very well, to the point where they might experience the activity to be too easy, one might next present more difficult questions such as those that the player has not yet answered before in previous rounds. Conversely, if a player is performing poorly, one might present easy questions, for example, questions that the player had already answered correctly in previous rounds. This interactive selection of questions is a distinct advantage compared to textbook learning. Furthermore, this is where an important potential lies for client-server infrastructures. Many contemporary applications connect to servers, making it possible for the host of a game to monitor and aggregate playing results. This global-level information can be used to optimise the question selection algorithm, for instance by determining how difficult questions are based on average performance.

At present, there does not appear to be any empirical support that player performance on a quiz affects prolonged play. In the current study, we test this assumption by analysing to what extent prolonged play can be predicted by a player's recent performance. Based on the theory that the level of challenge should be neither too low nor too high in view of an individual's mastery of the task (Garris et al., 2002; Giora et al., 2004), we expect that players get demotivated if the task is too easy or too difficult. This implies that the effect of recent performance on prolonged play with most playing at the level of "optimal innovation" (Giora et al., 2004) when the task is neither too easy nor too difficult. Thus, we hypothesise that students' prolonged play impacts their performance very poorly or very well.

# METHOD

## Participants

This research was conducted within a UK University between November 2019 and January 2020. Students were informed about an application we used to support our research known as Knowingo (https://knowingo.com/) through distributing emails. To confirm their participation, students were asked to fill out a short survey that could be completed on their smartphones. The survey link was distributed via email with a QR code. After the students had completed the survey, they were granted a request to access the app once they had received an invite code within the next 24hrs. The app was free to download from the Google Play and Apple Store, for which students were guided in the campaign material and in the concluding statements of the introductory survey.

In total, 654 students responded to the survey and willingness to participate in the research for which 436 were contacted for completing the survey and fulfilling the conditions of the research. Table 1 summarises the descriptive statistics of the participants.

*Table 1. Participants Summary*

| Variable | Levels | N | % |
|---|---|---|---|
| *Gender* | Male | 235 | 54% |
| | Female | 201 | 46% |
| *Age* | 18-21 | 178 | 41% |
| | 22-25 | 146 | 33% |
| | 26-31 | 80 | 18% |
| | >31 | 32 | 8% |
| *University Year* | First year | 223 | 51% |
| | Second year | 127 | 29% |
| | Third year | 86 | 20% |

Overall, a greater number of male participants (54%) took part in the research, most of whom were in their early to mid-twenties (33%). The majority of interested participants were first year students, which is unsurprising given the high population of young students. This is because the information in the app was more appealing to the younger population and felt that the app and the information (e.g. exam regulation details and policies) it provides was more relevant to them given its modern appeal.

Based on the literature review developed in the previous section, this research proposes several hypotheses:

**H1**: Student feedback significantly increases playtime sessions compared to students who do not receive feedback

**H2**: Tailored feedback encourages students to engage in more play more sessions compared to students receiving generic feedback

**H3**: Students with restricted play engage in the same number of sessions on more different days compared to students with no restrictions playing the gamified app

**H4**: Students' prolonged play impacts their performance very poorly or very well.

## Design

The experiment had a 2 (daily limit: present vs. absent) 3 (no feedback, generic feedback, personalised feedback) between subjects experimental design. Participants in the condition with a daily limit were limited in their play to four sessions per day. Participants in the condition without a daily limit could play as many sessions per day as they wanted. Participants were randomly assigned to the six conditions.

Participants in the feedback conditions received a weekly email on Monday for three consecutive weeks that encouraged them to play (if they did not play that week) or to play more. The difference between the generic and personalised feedback conditions was limited to the information provided in the email. Participants in the generic feedback condition were not addressed by name, and the email only reported whether or not they played in the previous week. Participants in the personalised feedback condition were addressed by their first name, and the email reported the exact number of sessions they played in the previous week. The encouragement message also changed depending on how many sessions were played. The personalised feedback condition deliberately did not include additional support, such as offering tips or replying to specific questions that the participant answered incorrectly. The condition thereby focuses purely on whether the participant was addressed as a generic and anonymous user versus as an individual that is personally monitored. The effect investigated in this study is thus only a communication effect and not an effect of offering a different learning experience.

The number of participants per condition is reported in Table 2. The distribution of participants is not perfectly balanced, because not all students who completed the survey (upon which they were assigned to a condition) actually participated.

## Application

The application used for this study, Knowingo (https://knowingo.com/), was developed by a partner company. It is normally licensed to businesses that use it as a tool to disseminate factual knowledge throughout their organisations. Traditionally, learning this type of knowledge would require employees

*Table 2. Participants per Condition*

| | Condition | | | |
|---|---|---|---|---|
| | **None** | **Generic** | **Tailored** | **Total** |
| *No limit* | 14 | 13 | 19 | 46 |
| *Limit* | 17 | 20 | 18 | 55 |
| *Total* | 31 | 33 | 37 | 101 |

to study non-interactive documents. The purpose of Knowingo is to make this type of knowledge acquisition more engaging and efficient by presenting the learning task as a multiple choice quiz.

By itself, a simple multiple-choice quiz still lacks many important game elements. To make the application more engaging, Knowingo therefore incorporates various tested gamification features. The first time players log in, they need to choose an avatar that is visible to themselves and other players whom they can challenge. By playing, and by giving the right answers, players receive experience points to grow in levels and unlock virtual rewards. Each day players also receive new quests, such as playing for streaks of correct answers that give additional experience and rewards.

Furthermore, the game algorithm has been designed to make users play short consecutive sessions. Sessions consist of seven questions, and each question has a time limit. To prevent users from getting bored or frustrated, the selection of questions takes the session history of users into account. If players are performing poorly, they can be given more easy questions or questions that they already answered before to boost their score, and if players have perfect scores, they are more likely to receive new and difficult questions. One of the development goals of the application is to optimise this question selection algorithm by using the client-server infrastructure to collect information from all users, in order to learn the difficulty of different questions and use this to provide an adaptive learning experience. The version used in this study does not yet implement this adaptive learning experience.

For the current study, the Knowingo app was used to help students learn relevant information about their university, ranging from exam regulations to social events. We developed 200 unique multiple choice questions, each with four possible answers, to ensure that there would be enough content to prevent users from getting the same questions too often. For example, some of the questions were: "what does ECTS stand for?" "what must you always bring to an exam?," "who can help you with course registration issues?," and "when is the pub quiz in the [campus cafe]?"

## FINDINGS

### Predictors of Player Participation

To test the hypotheses about the effects of feedback on player participation, we analysed the variance in the number of sessions played by each participant. Note that this is a heavily over-dispersed count variable: most participants only played one or a few sessions, but there are also several players that continued for more than 200 sessions. Contrary to our hypothesis, we did not find a significant effect of feedback messages in general on the number of sessions played. Therefore, we reject H1.

Our second hypothesis was that the tailored feedback messages have a stronger effect on the number of sessions played than the generic feedback messages—or, given that we did not find a general effect of feedback, that there would be an effect for tailored feedback. However, our results showed that tailored feedback messages did not have an effect, but rather the other way around. The number of sessions played is significantly higher for participants in the generic feedback condition.

Additionally, male participants tend to play more sessions compared to female, and older participants tend to play less sessions.

## Effect of Daily Limit on Prolonged Play

Our third hypothesis concerns the impact of a daily limit, where we hypothesised that students with a daily limit play a similar amount of sessions on more different days compared to students without a daily limit. We tested the unique number of days played as the dependent variable. For this analysis, we only included participants that at least once played four or more sessions on one day (n ¼ 35), since the other participants would not have experienced an effect of the daily limit. To account for the small sample size, we only included two independent variables: the daily limit condition (dichotomous) controlled for the number of sessions played. The results show that participants in the daily limit condition indeed played on more unique days. Based on these results, we can accept H3.

Playing on more different days, however, would not be beneficial to learning if the overall number of sessions played suffers from the daily limit condition. Our results showed that participants in the daily limit condition—who could only play four sessions each day—did not play less sessions overall compared to participants without a daily limit. The nonparametric Mann–Whitney–Wilcoxon test shows that the difference is not significant. This supports H3. This indicates that participants in the daily limit condition were not less motivated than those without a daily limit, but rather spread out their sessions over more different days, which is the intended effect of this feature.

## Effect of Performance on Prolonged Play

To investigate whether a player's experience of difficulty affects their motivation to play (H4), we analysed whether their performance in each individual session affects the probability to continue playing. For this analysis, we analysed the individual sessions that are nested in participants. The dependent variable, prolonged play, indicated whether participants played a new session within 15 minutes after finishing the current session. Our independent variable of interest is session performance, which indicates how many of the seven questions in the current session were answered correctly. We control for the participants' streak, which is the number of times participants already continued playing (with 15 minute intervals). We also control for the daily limit condition and its interaction with one's streak, since participants in this condition cannot continue playing after four sessions.

Results show a negative effect of performance on prolonged play. This indicates that participants might indeed lose motivation or become bored the more they perform above their average. This is in line with H4 that there is an inverted u-curve relation between performance and prolonged play. However, we did not find any indications that participants also lose motivation if they are performing below their average. This is likely related to a ceiling effect in performance: on average, 5.6 out of 7 questions were answered correctly. This suggests that for many students, the questions in the current application might not have been challenging enough. Based on these results, we conclude that H4 is partly supported.

## DISCUSSION

This study investigated the use of a quiz app designed to support university students to acquire essential information about how their university functions and analysed how manipulating game features and feedback can enhance engagement and learning. The first part of our study examined the effect of feedback on player participation. No differences were found between the feedback conditions and the no feedback condition. However, a closer inspection of the generic versus personalised ("tailored") feedback conditions revealed that generic feedback does have a positive effect on player participation, whereas this could not be established for the personalised feedback. Personalised feedback, which included personally identifiable information (e.g. the number of sessions one had played thus far), might possibly induce a boomerang effect (Wattal et al., 2012). This is an important topic for future studies, which could focus on whether the amount and type of personalisation makes a difference. In particular, a potential explanation that requires inquiry is that it could matter whether personalisation has a clear benefit to the user. In our study, the personalised feedback condition deliberately did not receive additional help or benefits. More personalisation might not induce a boomerang effect if it is clear to benefit the user, such as feedback on specific answers or links with more information.

While not a prominent focus of this study, it is interesting to note that player participation was also affected by player demographics. Male and older students tended to play more sessions compared to female and younger students, respectively. Understanding the effects of player demographics is important for effective use of gamification, because it can inform the development of applications with specific audiences in mind. However, we recommend caution in generalising our results in this regard. Prior research shows mixed findings, for instance, in gender effects for both engagement and learning outcomes (Khan et al., 2017; Su & Cheng, 2015). Current research into gamification is rather diverse, with different types of applications built for different learning goals, which makes it difficult to draw conclusions on effects of social and cultural factors. A meta-analysis of demographic factors in gamification would be a welcome contribution to the field.

The second part of the study investigated whether introducing a daily limit on the number of sessions a participant can play per day can promote distributed learning. A daily limit feature can prevent people from binge playing a game, but a concern is that users will simply play less sessions, rather than maintain their interest over a longer period of time. Findings of this study show that participants in the daily limit condition indeed played on more different days compared to participants that could "binge" as many sessions as they wanted, while playing a similar amount of sessions. So, it seems the daily limit did not demotivate them and spread out the learning experience over more sessions. This suggests that including a daily limit in the gamified app in an education setting can be a useful tool to prevent binge playing and enhance distributed learning.

Finally, we investigated whether a participant's performance in the game affects prolonged play. Results show that if participants perform very well (in the current study often having a perfect score), they become less likely to continue playing, which confirms the importance of ensuring that participants are sufficiently challenged. For a multiple choice quiz about mostly independent facts, it can be difficult to manipulate the difficulty of the learning task. However, it is possible to estimate the likelihood that a participant answers a question correctly and to use this to manipulate performance. By using a client-server architecture, where all user data is collected, information from all users can be used to improve this estimate. More large-scale research with this type of application can help us better understand how performance affects prolonged play.

## CONCLUSION

In conclusion, while our findings are preliminary, we are cautiously optimistic about continuing this line of research in the future. Our findings suggest that careful manipulation of game mechanisms can have an impact on sustaining and encouraging play via a gamified application. Despite the limitations of our study, we are encouraged by these findings and hope to continue this line of work in gamifying educational settings.

This study has several limitations that need to be taken into account. The number of unique participants in our sample was small due to a relatively small sample population. In addition, we found that three factors made it difficult to get students to play. First, voluntary participation might be perceived by students as additional and unnecessary work. Since we are interested in the extent to which the app alone manages to engage students, we did not offer any form of compensation for participating. Second, the app is mainly directed at students that know little about the university, such as starting year students, so our pool of all students in the School of Social Sciences is (purposefully) too broad in the first period of our data collection. Third, the current project, which served as a pilot, was launched in the spring, which is close to the end of the academic year. To compensate for the low participation rate, we included a second wave of data collection only pertaining to first year students and starting the data collection earlier that is in the autumn. The relative response rates in the second period are higher compared to the first period, but the number of interested students remains to be a small minority.

Aside from limiting our sample, this also tells us something important about the challenges of gamification projects in natural occurrences of an educational field setting, where it would be inappropriate to compensate students for participation. This calls for more field research that investigates whether and how we can get students to actually participate. The results of this study do show hope: once students started playing, a non-trivial number of students did become engaged, with some students playing for many hours. More than improving the game itself, the challenge could be to have students take that first step. In addition, experimental research into the efficacy of educational games may complement the valuable insights from field studies. Further research could also incorporate gamified applications that are driven ubiquitous technologies such as cloud computing (Ali, 2018; Ali, 2020; Ali et al., 2020; Mohammed Banu et al., 2018) that could provide better use of educational resources and attract new users to gamified services.

## REFERENCES

Ali, M. (2018). The Barriers and Enablers of the Educational Cloud: A Doctoral Student Perspective. *Open Journal of Business and Management*, *7*(1), 1–24. doi:10.4236/ojbm.2019.71001

Ali, M. (2020). Multi-Perspectives of Cloud Computing Service Adoption Quality and Risks in Higher Education. In D. B. A. Mehdi Khosrow-Pour (Ed.), Handbook of Research on Modern Educational Technologies, Applications, and Management (2nd ed.). IGI Global.

Ali, M. B., Wood-Harper, T., & Ramlogan, R. (2020). A Framework Strategy to Overcome Trust Issues on Cloud Computing Adoption in Higher Education. In Modern Principles, Practices, and Algorithms for Cloud Security (pp. 162-183). IGI Global. doi:10.4018/978-1-7998-1082-7.ch008

Aparicio, M., Oliveira, T., Bacao, F., & Painho, M. (2019). Gamification: A key determinant of massive open online course (MOOC) success. *Information & Management*, *56*(1), 39–54. doi:10.1016/j.im.2018.06.003

Barata, G., Gama, S., Jorge, J., & Gonçalves, D. (2015). Gamification for smarter learning: Tales from the trenches. *Smart Learning Environments*, *2*(1), 10. doi:10.118640561-015-0017-8

Burgers, C., Eden, A., van Engelenburg, M. D., & Buningh, S. (2015). How feedback boosts motivation and play in a brain-training game. *Computers in Human Behavior*, *48*, 94–103. doi:10.1016/j.chb.2015.01.038

Cheong, C., Cheong, F., & Filippou, J. (2013). Quick Quiz: A Gamified Approach for Enhancing Learning. PACIS, Chitra, K. (2020). Adoption of Gamification tool in Higher Education: An empirical study. *Studies in Indian Place Names*, *40*(3), 3132–3146.

Chou, Y. (2013). *Comprehensive List of 90+ Gamification case studies with ROI Stats*. Retrieved 8th Mar from https://gamificationplus.uk/comprehensive-list-90-gamification-cases-roi-stats/

Connolly, T. M., Boyle, E. A., MacArthur, E., Hainey, T., & Boyle, J. M. (2012). A systematic literature review of empirical evidence on computer games and serious games. *Computers & Education*, *59*(2), 661–686. doi:10.1016/j.compedu.2012.03.004

Cózar-Gutiérrez, R., & Sáez-López, J. M. (2016). Game-based learning and gamification in initial teacher training in the social sciences: An experiment with MinecraftEdu. *International Journal of Educational Technology in Higher Education*, *13*(1), 2. doi:10.118641239-016-0003-4

De Vries, H., Kremers, S., Smeets, T., Brug, J., & Eijmael, K. (2008). The effectiveness of tailored feedback and action plans in an intervention addressing multiple health behaviors. *American Journal of Health Promotion*, *22*(6), 417–424. doi:10.4278/ajhp.22.6.417 PMID:18677882

Denny, P. (2013). The effect of virtual achievements on student engagement. *Proceedings of the SIGCHI Conference on Human Factors in Computing Systems.*

Deterding, S., Dixon, D., Khaled, R., & Nacke, L. (2011). From game design elements to gamefulness: defining gamification. *Proceedings of the 15th International Academic MindTrek Conference: Envisioning Future Media Environments.*

Dunlosky, J., Rawson, K. A., Marsh, E. J., Nathan, M. J., & Willingham, D. T. (2013). Improving students' learning with effective learning techniques: Promising directions from cognitive and educational psychology. *Psychological Science in the Public Interest*, *14*(1), 4–58. PubMed

Fitz-Walter, Z., Tjondronegoro, D., & Wyeth, P. (2011). Orientation passport: using gamification to engage university students. *Proceedings of the 23rd Australian Computer-Human Interaction Conference.*

Fu, F.-L., Su, R.-C., & Yu, S.-C. (2009). EGameFlow: A scale to measure learners' enjoyment of e-learning games. *Computers & Education*, *52*(1), 101–112.

Garris, R., Ahlers, R., & Driskell, J. E. (2002). Games, motivation, and learning: A research and practice model. *Simulation & Gaming*, *33*(4), 441–467. doi:10.1177/1046878102238607

Giora, R., Fein, O., Kronrod, A., Elnatan, I., Shuval, N., & Zur, A. (2004). Weapons of mass distraction: Optimal innovation and pleasure ratings. *Metaphor and Symbol*, *19*(2), 115–141. doi:10.120715327868ms1902_2

Hammer, J., & Lee, J. (2011). Gamification in Education: What, How, Why Bother. *Academic Exchange Quarterly*, *15*(2).

Hatala, R., Cook, D. A., Zendejas, B., Hamstra, S. J., & Brydges, R. (2014). Feedback for simulation-based procedural skills training: A meta-analysis and critical narrative synthesis. *Advances in Health Sciences Education: Theory and Practice*, *19*(2), 251–272. doi:10.100710459-013-9462-8 PMID:23712700

Heidt, C. T., Arbuthnott, K. D., & Price, H. L. (2016). The effects of distributed learning on enhanced cognitive interview training. *Psychiatry, Psychology and Law*, *23*(1), 47–61. doi:10.1080/13218719.2015.1032950

Khan, A., Ahmad, F. H., & Malik, M. M. (2017). Use of digital game based learning and gamification in secondary school science: The effect on student engagement, learning and gender difference. *Education and Information Technologies*, *22*(6), 2767–2804. doi:10.100710639-017-9622-1

Kluger, A. N., & DeNisi, A. (1996). The effects of feedback interventions on performance: A historical review, a meta-analysis, and a preliminary feedback intervention theory. *Psychological Bulletin*, *119*(2), 254–284. doi:10.1037/0033-2909.119.2.254

Krebs, P., Prochaska, J. O., & Rossi, J. S. (2010). A meta-analysis of computer-tailored interventions for health behavior change. *Preventive Medicine*, *51*(3-4), 214–221. doi:10.1016/j.ypmed.2010.06.004 PMID:20558196

Kroeze, W., Werkman, A., & Brug, J. (2006). A systematic review of randomized trials on the effectiveness of computer-tailored education on physical activity and dietary behaviors. *Annals of Behavioral Medicine*, *31*(3), 205–223. doi:10.120715324796abm3103_2 PMID:16700634

Lustria, M. L. A., Noar, S. M., Cortese, J., Van Stee, S. K., Glueckauf, R. L., & Lee, J. (2013). A meta-analysis of web-delivered tailored health behavior change interventions. *Journal of Health Communication*, *18*(9), 1039–1069. doi:10.1080/10810730.2013.768727 PMID:23750972

Malone, T. W. (1982). Heuristics for designing enjoyable user interfaces: Lessons from computer games. *Proceedings of the 1982 Conference on Human Factors in Computing Systems*.

Mohammed Banu, A., Trevor, W.-H., & Mostafa, M. (2018). Benefits and Challenges of Cloud Computing Adoption and Usage in Higher Education: A Systematic Literature Review. *International Journal of Enterprise Information Systems*, *14*(4), 64–77. doi:10.4018/IJEIS.2018100105

Mollick, E. R., & Rothbard, N. (2014). *Mandatory fun: Consent, gamification and the impact of games at work*. The Wharton School research paper series.

Nah, F. F.-H., Zeng, Q., Telaprolu, V. R., Ayyappa, A. P., & Eschenbrenner, B. (2014). Gamification of education: a review of literature. *International Conference on HCI in Business*.

Neff, R., & Fry, J. (2009). Periodic prompts and reminders in health promotion and health behavior interventions: Systematic review. *Journal of Medical Internet Research*, *11*(2), e16.

Noble, N., Paul, C., Carey, M., Blunden, S., & Turner, N. (2015). A randomised trial assessing the acceptability and effectiveness of providing generic versus tailored feedback about health risks for a high need primary care sample. *BMC Family Practice*, *16*(1), 95. doi:10.118612875-015-0309-7 PMID:26243144

Rohrer, D. (2015). Student instruction should be distributed over long time periods. *Educational Psychology Review*, *27*(4), 635–643. doi:10.100710648-015-9332-4

Schneider, F., de Vries, H., Candel, M., van de Kar, A., & van Osch, L. (2013). Periodic email prompts to re-use an internet-delivered computer-tailored lifestyle program: Influence of prompt content and timing. *Journal of Medical Internet Research*, *15*(1), e23. doi:10.2196/jmir.2151 PMID:23363466

Su, C. H., & Cheng, C. H. (2015). A mobile gamification learning system for improving the learning motivation and achievements. *Journal of Computer Assisted Learning*, *31*(3), 268–286. doi:10.1111/jcal.12088

Subhash, S., & Cudney, E. A. (2018). Gamified learning in higher education: A systematic review of the literature. *Computers in Human Behavior*, *87*, 192–206. doi:10.1016/j.chb.2018.05.028

Sweetser, P., & Wyeth, P. (2005). GameFlow: A model for evaluating player enjoyment in games. *Computers in Entertainment*, *3*(3), 3–3. doi:10.1145/1077246.1077253

Terill, B. (2008). *My Coverage of Lobby of the Social Gaming Summit*. Retrieved 7th Mar from http://www.bretterrill.com/2008/06/my-coverage-of-lobby-of-social-gaming.html

Wattal, S., Telang, R., Mukhopadhyay, T., & Boatwright, P. (2012). What's in a "name"? Impact of use of customer information in e-mail advertisements. *Information Systems Research, 23*(3-part-1), 679-697.

Welbers, K., Konijn, E. A., Burgers, C., de Vaate, A. B., Eden, A., & Brugman, B. C. (2019). Gamification as a tool for engaging student learning: A field experiment with a gamified app. *E-Learning and Digital Media*, *16*(2), 92–109. doi:10.1177/2042753018818342

Wolfenden, B. (2019). Gamification as a winning cyber security strategy. *Computer Fraud & Security*, *2019*(5), 9–12. doi:10.1016/S1361-3723(19)30052-1

## ADDITIONAL READING

Barata, G., Gama, S., Jorge, J., & Gonçalves, D. (2015). Gamification for smarter learning: Tales from the trenches. *Smart Learning Environments*, *2*(1), 10. doi:10.118640561-015-0017-8

Chitra, K. (2020). Adoption of Gamification tool in Higher Education: An empirical study. *Studies in Indian Place Names*, *40*(3), 3132–3146.

Chou, Y. (2013). *Comprehensive List of 90+ Gamification case studies with ROI Stats*. Retrieved 8th Mar from https://gamificationplus.uk/comprehensive-list-90-gamification-cases-roi-stats/

Cózar-Gutiérrez, R., & Sáez-López, J. M. (2016). Game-based learning and gamification in initial teacher training in the social sciences: An experiment with MinecraftEdu. *International Journal of Educational Technology in Higher Education*, *13*(1), 2. doi:10.118641239-016-0003-4

Hammer, J., & Lee, J. (2011). Gamification in Education: What, How, Why Bother. *Academic Exchange Quarterly*, *15*(2).

Khan, A., Ahmad, F. H., & Malik, M. M. (2017). Use of digital game based learning and gamification in secondary school science: The effect on student engagement, learning and gender difference. *Education and Information Technologies*, *22*(6), 2767–2804. doi:10.100710639-017-9622-1

Mollick, E. R., & Rothbard, N. (2014). Mandatory fun: Consent, gamification and the impact of games at work. *The Wharton School research paper series*.

Wolfenden, B. (2019). Gamification as a winning cyber security strategy. *Computer Fraud & Security*, *2019*(5), 9–12. doi:10.1016/S1361-3723(19)30052-1

## KEY TERMS AND DEFINITIONS

**Adaptive Learning:** An educational method supported by computer algorithms to develop interactions with the learner and the delivery of customised resources and learning activities to fulfil learners' unique needs.

**Binge Gaming:** The process of playing games too long to the point where the player passes out.

**Deep Learning:** A sub-set of machine learning in artificial intelligence (AI) with network capabilities supporting learning unsupervised from unstructured data.

**Feedback:** The act of providing constructive criticism on another individuals' work or actions.

**Gamification:** The process of deploying everyday game play elements such as points scoring or completion to other areas of activity, which is used as an online marketing method to encourage engagement with a given product/service.

**Higher Education:** Tertiary sector education in which undergraduate, post-graduate and doctoral courses are taught in university settings.

**Learning Engagement:** The extent of a learner's participation in their courses and educational experience.

# Chapter 3
# Bibliographical Analysis of Artificial Intelligence Learning in Higher Education:
## Is the Role of the Human Educator and Educated a Thing of the Past?

**Mohammed Ali**
https://orcid.org/0000-0001-5854-8245
*Centre for Islamic Finance, UK*

**Mohammed Kayed Abdel-Haq**
*Centre for Islamic Finance, UK*

## ABSTRACT

*This chapter provides an overview of research on AI applications in higher education using a systematic review approach. There were 146 articles included for further analysis, based on explicit inclusion and exclusion criteria. The findings show that Computer Science and STEM make up the majority of disciplines involved in AI education literature and that quantitative methods were the most frequently used in empirical studies. Four areas of AI education applications in academic support services and institutional and administrative services were revealed, including profiling and prediction, assessment and evaluation, adaptive systems and personalisation, and intelligent tutoring systems. This chapter reflects on the challenges and risks of AI education, the lack of association between theoretical pedagogical perspectives, and the need for additional exploration of pedagogical, ethical, social, cultural, and economic dimensions of AI education.*

DOI: 10.4018/978-1-7998-4846-2.ch003

## INTRODUCTION

Software applications in the field of Artificial Intelligence (AI) in higher education (HE) have been increasing over the last few years and are starting to gain a great deal of traction. AI in education has been the subject of research for some 30 years. AI and adaptive learning technologies have made some important developments in educational technology, with adoption times between 2-3 years (Becker et al., 2019; Johnson et al., 2016). Experts predict that AI in education is set to grow by 43% by 2022, although a 2019 report predicts that in HE, AI applications that aim to enhance the teaching and learning experience are expected to grow even more significantly (Becker et al., 2019). With significant investments by private organisations like Google, which obtained the European start up Deep Mind for $400m, as well as non-profit public-private partnerships like the German Research Center for Artificial Intelligence (DFKI), there is a huge possibility that the current wave of Internet will have a greater impact on HE institutions (HEIs) (Popenici & Kerr, 2017).

Using AI in education has been the subject of huge debates for the past 30 years (Cioffi et al., 2020; Jackman et al., 2010; Jiang et al., 2017; Liu et al., 2018; O'Donovan et al., 2019; Smart & Burrell, 2015). Broadly speaking, educators have only now began to explore the potential pedagogical opportunities that AI applications can provide for supporting learners throughout the student life cycle. Although there are significant opportunities that AI can provide for higher teaching and learning, new ethical implications and risks are attached to the development of AI applications in HE. For instance, budget cuts could tempt administrators to replace the human teachers with profitable automated AI solutions. This may instil fear into faculty members, teaching assistants, student counsellors, and administrative staff that AI solutions will take their jobs. In spite of the human implications of AI (Kearney et al., 2019), AI has the potential to advance the capabilities of learning analytics, though such systems require huge amounts of data, including confidential information about students and faculty, which raises serious issues of privacy and data protection. For that reason, it would be interesting to explore the fresh ethical implications and risks in the field of AI enhanced education. Russell and Norvig (2016) emphasise that AI researchers should consider the ethical implications of their work, and thus we are interested to explore the ethical implications and risks in AI enhanced education. The purpose of this chapter is to determine whether AI learning systems will impact the human educator and educated in HE in terms of replacing their teaching and learning skills with those of a machine or application in HE, as well as the ethical implications of such applications. Owing to the growing interest of educators in the AI field, this warrants the need to review the AI literature in HE. This paper specifically addresses the following research question by means of systematic literature review (Booth et al., 2016; Liberati et al., 2009; David Moher et al., 2009):

**RQ1:** *How is AI-enhanced education conceptualised and what are the ethical implications, challenges and risks in HE?*
**RQ2:** *How does AI enhance educational practices in HE?*

Although the AI field originates from engineering and computer science, it is greatly influenced by other disciplines ranging from philosophy and economics to cognitive and neurosciences. Owing to the interdisciplinary nature of this area of study, there is a lack of consensus among AI researchers on a common definition of AI (Tegmark, 2017). In terms of introducing AI-based tools and services in HE, several authors claim that AI has already been introduced to HE, though many teachers do not understand its scope and in particular, what it comprises. For our analysis of AI in HE, it is ideal to clarify the appropriate terminology. We posit that authors of the current literature refer to learning as a social exercise in which interaction and collaboration are central to the learning process (Jonassen et al., 1995).

## BACKGROUND

This section provides a background of AI in education, including definitions, characteristics and methods that AI applications may comprise of, prior to reviewing the existing AI education literature. The inception of AI dates back to the 1950s in which John McCarthy first used the term in a short workshop he had organised in 1956 (Russell & Norvig, 2016, p.17). Studying AI is based on the conjecture that the features of intelligence or aspects of learning can theoretically be described as a machine that is able to simulate such features. An attempt to determine how to make machines use language is made, including form abstractions, concepts, problem solving and human development and improvement. According to Baker and Anissa (2019), AI can be defined as "Computers which perform cognitive tasks, usually associated with human minds, particularly learning and problem-solving" (p.10). The authors explain that AI does not refer to a single technology, but rather a range of technologies and methods, like machine learning, natural language processing, data mining, neural networks or algorithms.

In the AI literature, there is often an equal mentioning of AI and machine learning. Machine learning refers to a method of AI for supervised and unsupervised classification and profiling, e.g. estimating the outcome of student dropouts from a course or the number of course admissions or to identify topics chosen by students for their assignments. According to Popenici and Kerr (2017), machine learning refers to "a subfield of artificial intelligence that includes software able to recognise patterns, make predictions, and apply newly discovered patterns to situations that were not included or covered by their initial design" (p.2). The idea behind rational agents is vital to AI as Russel & Norvig (2010) point out: "An agent is anything that can be viewed as perceiving its environment through sensors and acting upon that environment through actuators" (p.34). For example, the vacuum cleaner robot is a type of intelligent agent, but this becomes a highly complex subject when thinking about other agents like an automated taxi.

AI experts in the field can tell the difference between strong and weak AI (Russel & Norvig, 2010, p.1020) and general or narrow AI (Baker & Smith, 2019, p.10). This raises the question of whether machines have the ability to actually think freely or even develop consciousness in the future, as opposed to merely simulating thinking and demonstrating rational behaviour. Despite the speculation that AI will develop to a point where its human creators will control or lose control are equally good as it is detrimental to the development of HE, the likelihood of a strong or general AI in the near future is low. Consequently, this is a case of GOFAI or "good old fashioned AI", which the philosopher John Haugeland refers to as a sense of agents and information systems that believe they are intelligent (Haugeland, 1989). Owing to this understanding of AI, it question the potential areas of AI applications in the HE arena. Luckin et al. (2016) refer to three categories associated with the currently available AI software applications in education, namely personal tutors, intelligent support for collaborative learning and intelligent virtual reality.

Other uses of AI in HE include intelligent tutoring systems (ITS) which can simulate one-to-one personal tutoring. According to learner models, algorithms and neural networks, ITS have the capability of making decisions related to students' learning path and help students to engage in dialogue via cognitive scaffolding. This shows the vast potential of ITS, particularly in large-scale distance teaching institutions, where many modules are run with thousands of students and where it is impossible to conduct human one-to-one tutoring. Nevertheless, facilitating and moderating online collaboration has is required (Salmon, 2000). AI education has the potential to contribute to collaborative learning through facilitating adaptive group formation according to learner models, as well as through supporting online group interactions that a human tutor can use to guide students towards a given course's aims and objectives. Drawing on ITS, intelligent virtual reality (IVR) can also be used to engage and guide students in actual virtual reality and game-based learning environments. For example, teachers, facilitators or students' peers are the virtual agents in virtual or remote labs (Perez et al., 2017).

Given the recent developments in AI education and the wider access and availability of big data (student data) and learning analytics, Luckin et al. (2016) referred to the term "renaissance in assessment" (p.35). AI has the ability to offer just-in-time feedback and assessment. As well as stop-and-test, AI education can be integrated into learning activities in order to continuously monitor student achievement via algorithms that can help to accurately predict whether a student is failing an assignment or dropping out of a course (Bahadir, 2016).

Recently, Baker and Smith (2019) conducted a report in which emphasises an approach to educational AI tools from several perspectives, namely learner-facing, teacher-facing and system-facing AI education. Learner-facing AI tools refer to learning software for students e.g. ITS or personalised learning management systems. Teachers use teacher-facing systems to reduce his or her workload through automating administrative activities, such as assessment, feedback and plagiarism detection. AI education tools also help to understand students' learning progression to allow teachers to proactively provide support and guidance where needed. Administrators and managers use system-facing tools for information acquisition within institutions, e.g. monitoring attrition patterns across Universities. Ultimately, using AI-powered systems can significantly enhance the efficiency of many educational institutions, reduce operating costs, provide greater visibility and improve the overall responsiveness of educational institutions. However, ensuring that AI serves learners and educators and to address the ethical concerns and mitigate them, there is a need to explore AI learning systems and their impact on HE stakeholders, in addition to the issues related to AI-enhanced applications to foster pedagogical development.

In the HE context, student lifecycle concept (Reid, 1995) is used in this research as a framework to describe a number of AI based services on the broader institutional level, in addition to supporting the narrow academic teaching and learning process.

## METHOD

A systematic review was carried out to answer specific questions based on an explicit, systematic and replicable search strategy, including an inclusion and exclusion criteria that helps to identify studies that are included and omitted (Gough et al., 2017). Later, the findings are synthesised from the studies that met the inclusion criteria to provide clarity in the application in practice, as well as identifying research gaps and inconsistencies. This research maps 146 articles regarding AI in HE.

### Search Strategy

The initial search keywords and criteria can be seen in tables 1 and 2, respectively for the SLR included peer reviewed English written articles, reporting on AI at any education level, indexed in three international databases; Elton B. Stephens Company (EBSCO) Education Source, Web of Science and Scopus (covering titles, abstracts, and keywords). Since there are concerns pertaining to the peer review processes within the scientific community, articles used in this review were restricted to peer reviewed publications, namely articles from reputable journals given their general trustworthiness in academia and the rigorous and critical review methods undertaken (Nicholas et al., 2015). The search was undertaken in December 2019, with an initial 2654 records identified.

After the removal of duplicate articles, the articles were then limited to those published during or after 2010, as this was around the time when iPhone's Siri was introduced; an algorithm-based personal assistant, started as an AI project and later acquired by Apple Inc. from the US Defence Advanced Research Projects Agency (DARPA). Another decision was made based on limited the corpus to articles discussing applications of AI in HE only.

## Screening and Interrater Reliability

The 1549 titles and abstracts from the searched papers were screened. At the first screening stage, there was a requirement of sensitivity as opposed to specificity, that is, the papers included instead of excluded. Reaching a consensus called for reasons for inclusion and exclusion of the first 80 articles.

After initial screening, 332 potential articles remained for screening on full text (see Fig.1). However, 41 articles could not be retrieved, either through the library order scheme or by contacting authors. Therefore, 291 articles were retrieved, screened and coded, and following the exclusion of 149 papers, 146 articles remained for synthesis.

*Table 1.Initial Search String*

| Topic | Search Terms |
|---|---|
| **AI** | "artificial intelligence" OR "machine intelligence" OR "intelligent support" OR "intelligent virtual reality" OR "chat bot*" OR "machine learning" OR "automated tutor" OR "personal tutor*" OR "intelligent agent*" OR "expert system" OR "neural network" OR "natural language processing" |
| ***AND*** | |
| **Education level** | "HE" OR college* OR undergrad* OR graduate OR postgrad* OR "K-12" OR kindergarten* OR "corporate training*" OR "professional training*" OR "primary school*" OR "middle school*" OR "high school*" OR "elementary school*" OR "vocational education" OR "adult education" |
| ***AND*** | |
| **Learning setting** | learn* OR student* |

*Table 2. Final Inclusion and Exclusion Criteria*

| Inclusion Criteria | Exclusion Criteria |
|---|---|
| Published 2010 - Dec 2019 | Published before 2010 |
| English written papers | Non-English written papers |
| Empirical primary research | Not empirical primary research |
| HE context | Not in HE context |
| Indexed in Web of Science, Scopus or EBSCO Educational Source | Not indexed in Web of Science, Scopus or EBSCO Educational Source (not a journal or has no relevance to AI) |
| AI use in education or HE | No learning setting |

*Figure 1. PRISMA Diagram (Adapted from the PRISMA Group 2009)*

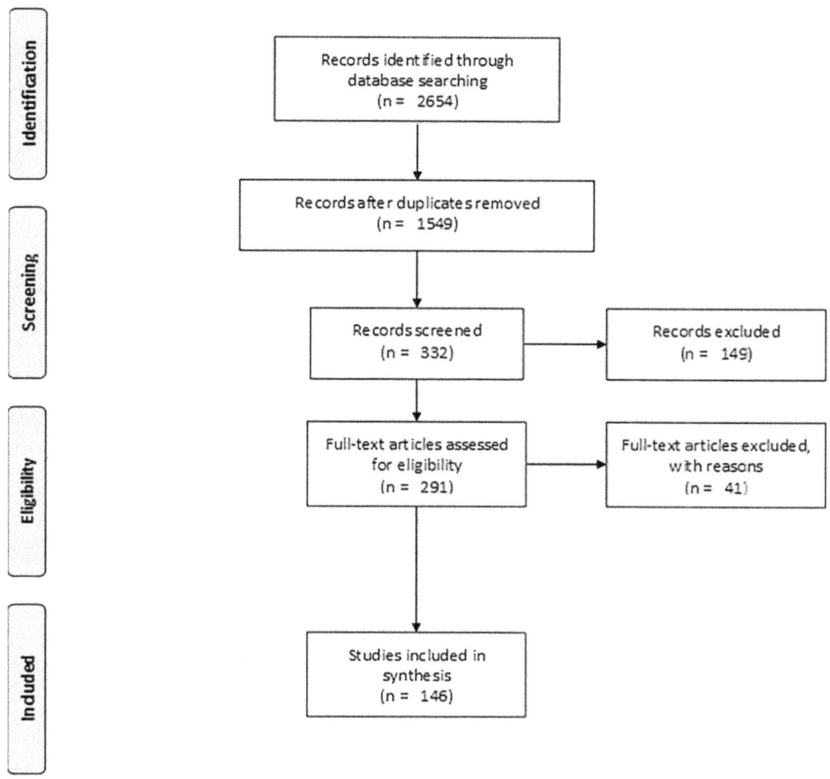


## Coding, Data Extraction and Analysis

For data extraction, the articles were uploaded into an SLR software known as EPPI Reviewer and a coding system was developed. Codes included article information (year of publication, journal name, countries of authorship, discipline of first author), study design and execution (empirical or descriptive, educational setting) and how AI was used (applications in the student life cycle, specific applications and methods). Articles were also coded on whether challenges and benefits of AI were present, and whether AI was defined.

Although this SLR was undertaken as rigorously as possible, each review is limited by its search strategy. Despite the large and international in scope of the databases used, by applying the criteria of peer-reviewed articles published only in English, research published on AI in other languages were not included in this review. This also applies to research in conference proceedings, book chapters or grey literature, or those articles not published in journals that are indexed in the three databases searched. Future research could consider using a larger number of databases, publication types and publication languages, in order to widen the scope of the review. However, serious consideration would then need to be given to project resources and the manageability of the review.

## FINDINGS

There was a noticeable increase in the papers published from 2007 onwards given their dissemination across 104 different journals as of 2020. The greatest number of articles were published in the International Journal of Artificial Intelligence in Education (n = 11), followed by Computers & Education (n = 8), and the International Journal of Emerging Technologies in Learning (n = 5). Nineteen journals were published at least two articles on AI in HE from 2007 to 2019. For the geographical distribution analysis of articles, the country of origin of the first author was taken into consideration (n = 38 countries). Nineteen countries contributed at least two papers, and it reveals that 50% of all articles come from only four countries: USA, China, Taiwan, and Turkey.

Again, the affiliation of the first author was taken into consideration. Researchers working in departments of Computer Science contributed by far the greatest number of papers (n = 61) followed by Science, Technology, Engineering and Mathematics (STEM) departments (n = 29). Only nine first authors came from an Education department, some reported dual affiliation with Education and Computer Science (n = 2), Education and Psychology (n = 1), or Education and STEM (n = 1). Thus, 13 papers (8.9%) were written by first authors with an Education background. It is noticeable that several were published in the same journal, i.e. the International Journal of Artificial Intelligence in Education (Goralski & Tan, 2020; Zawacki-Richter et al., 2019).

### Analytical Method

Thirty studies (20.5%) were coded as being theoretical or descriptive in nature. The vast majority of studies (73.3%) applied quantitative methods, whilst only one (0.7%) was qualitative in nature and eight (5.5%) followed a mixed methods approach. The purpose of the qualitative study, involving interviews with ESL students, was to explore the nature of written feedback coming from an automated essay scoring system compared to a human teacher (Dikli, 2011 in Bailey, 2019). In many cases, authors employed quasi experimental methods, being an intentional sample divided into the experimental group, where an AI application (e.g. an intelligent tutoring system) was applied, and the control group without the intervention, followed by pre and post-tests (Adamson et al., 2014).

### General AI Applications

There are many different types and levels of AI mentioned in the articles; however only five out of 146 included articles (3.6%) provide an explicit definition of the term "Artificial Intelligence". The main characteristics of AI, described in all five studies, are the parallels between the human brain and artificial intelligence. The authors conceptualise AI as intelligent computer systems or intelligent agents with human features, such as the ability to memorise knowledge, to perceive and manipulate their environment in a similar way as humans, and to understand human natural language (Huang, 2018; Lodhi et al., 2018; Welham, 2008),

Dodigovic (2007) defines AI in her article as follows (p. 100): "Artificial intelligence (AI) is a term referring to machines which emulate the behaviour of intelligent beings. AI is an interdisciplinary area of knowledge and research, whose aim is to understand how the human mind works and how to apply the same principles in technology design. In language learning and teaching tasks, AI can be used to emulate the behaviour of a teacher or a learner" (p.100). Dodigovic is the only author who gives a definition of

AI, and comes from an Arts, Humanities and Social Science department, taking into account aspects of AI and intelligent tutors in second language learning.

A stunningly low number of authors, only two out of 146 articles (1.5%), critically reflect upon ethical implications, challenges and risks of applying AI in education. Li (2007) deals with privacy concerns in his article about intelligent agent supported online learning: Privacy is also an important concern in applying agent-based personalised education. As discussed above, agents can autonomously learn many of students' personal information, like learning style and learning capability. In fact, personal information is private. Many students do not want others to know their private information, such as learning styles and/or capabilities. Students might show concern over possible discrimination from instructors in reference to learning performance due to special learning needs. Therefore, the privacy issue must be resolved before applying agent-based personalised teaching and learning technologies (Li, 2007, p.327).

Another challenge of applying AI is mentioned by Welham (2008) concerning the costs and time involved in developing and introducing AI-based methods that many public educational institutions cannot afford (p.295).

## AI Applications in HE

As mentioned before, we used the concept of the student life-cycle as a framework to describe the various AI based services at the institutional and administrative level (e.g. admission, counselling, library services), as well as at the academic support level for teaching and learning (e.g. assessment, feedback, tutoring). Ninety-two studies (roughly 63.0%) were coded as relating to academic support services and forty-eight (roughly 32.8%) as administrative and institutional services, six studies (roughly 4.1%) covered both levels. The majority of studies addressed undergraduate students (n = 91, roughly 62.1%) compared to eleven (roughly 7.5%) focussing on postgraduate students, and another forty-four (roughly 30.1%) that did not specify the study level.

The iterative coding process led to the following four areas of AI applications with 17 sub-categories, covered in the publications: a) adaptive systems and personalisation, b) assessment and evaluation, c) profiling and prediction, and d) intelligent tutoring systems. Some studies addressed AI applications in more than one area. The nature and scope of the various AI applications in HE are described along the lines of these four application categories in the following synthesis.

## Profiling and Prediction

The basis for many AI applications are learner models or profiles that allow prediction, for example of the likelihood of a student dropping out of a course or being admitted to a programme, in order to offer timely support or to provide feedback and guidance in content related matters throughout the learning process. Classification, modelling and prediction are an essential part of educational data mining (Krishna et al., 2018).

Most of the articles (roughly 55.4%, n = 32) address issues related to the institutional and administrative level, many (roughly 36.2%, n = 21) are related to academic teaching and learning at the course level, and five (roughly 8.6%) are concerned with both levels. Articles dealing with profiling and prediction were classified into three sub-categories; admission decisions and course scheduling (n = 7), dropout and retention (n = 23), and student models and academic achievement (n = 27). One study that does not fall into any of these categories is the study by Ge and Xie (2015), which is concerned with forecasting the costs of a Chinese university to support management decisions based on an artificial neural network.

All of the 58 studies in this area applied machine-learning methods, to recognise and classify patterns, and to model student profiles to make predictions. Thus, they are all quantitative in nature. Many studies applied several machine-learning algorithms (e.g. ANN, SVM, RF, NB) and compared their overall prediction accuracy with conventional logistic regression. Machine learning methods were found to have outperformed logistic regression in all studies in terms of their classification accuracy in percent.

## Intelligent Tutoring Systems

All of the studies investigating intelligent tutoring systems (ITS) (n = 29) are only concerned with the teaching and learning level, except for one that is contextualised at the institutional and administrative level. The latter presents StuA, an interactive and intelligent student assistant that helps newcomers in a college by answering queries related to faculty members, examinations, extra curriculum activities, library services, etc. (Lodhi et al., 2018).

The most common terms for referring to ITS described in the studies are intelligent (online) tutors or intelligent tutoring systems (Miwa et al., 2014), although they are also identified often as intelligent (software) agents (Schiaffino et al., 2008), or intelligent assistants (Casamayor et al., 2009). According to Welham (2008), the first ITS reported was the SCHOLAR system, launched in 1970, which allowed the reciprocal exchange of questions between teacher and student, but not holding a continuous conversation.

## Assessment and Evaluation

Assessment and evaluation studies also largely focused on the level of teaching and learning (86%, n = 31), although five studies described applications at the institutional level. In order to gain an overview of student opinion about online and distance learning at their institution, Ozturk et al. (2017) used sentiment analysis to analyse mentions by students on Twitter, using Twitter API Twython and terms relating to the system. This analysis of publicly accessible data, allowed researchers insight into student opinion, which otherwise may not have been accessible through their institutional LMS, and which can inform improvements to the system. Two studies used AI to evaluate student Prior Learning and Recognition (PLAR). Kalz et al. (2008) used Latent Semantic Analysis and ePortfolios to inform personalised learning pathways for students, and Biletska et al. (2010) used semantic web technologies to convert student credentials from different institutions. This could provide information from course descriptions and topics, to allow for easier granting of credit. The final article at the institutional level, Sánchez et al. (2016) used an algorithm to match students to professional competencies and capabilities required by companies, in order to ensure alignment between courses and industry needs.

Overall, the studies show that AI applications can perform assessment and evaluation tasks at very high accuracy and efficiency levels. However, due to the need to calibrate and train the systems (supervised machine learning), they are more applicable to courses or programs with large student numbers. Articles focusing on assessment and evaluation applications of AI at the teaching and learning level, were classified into four sub-categories; automated grading (n = 13), feedback (n = 8), evaluation of student understanding, engagement and academic integrity (n = 5), and evaluation of teaching (n = 5).

## Adaptive Systems and Personalisation

Most of the studies on adaptive systems (roughly 85%, n = 23) are situated at the teaching and learning level, with four cases considering the institutional and administrative level. Two studies explored undergraduate students' academic advising (Alfarsi et al., 2017), and Nguyen et al. (2018) focused on AI to support university career services. Ng et al. (2011) reported on the development of an agent-based distance LMS, designed to manage resources, support decision making and institutional policy, and assist with managing undergraduate student study flow (e.g. intake, exam and course management), by giving users access to data across disciplines, rather than just individual faculty areas.

There does not seem to be agreement within the studies on a common term for adaptive systems, and that is probably due to the diverse functions they carry out, which also supports the classification of studies. Some of those terms coincide in part with the ones used for ITS, e.g. intelligent agents (Li, 2007; Ng et al., 2011). The most general terms used are intelligent e-learning system (Kose & Arslan, 2016), adaptive web-based learning system (Lo et al., 2012), or intelligent teaching system (Ji & Liu, 2016). As in ITS, most of the studies either describe the system or include a pilot study but no longer-term results are reported. Results from these pilot studies are usually reported as positive, except in Vlugter et al. (2009), where the experimental group that used the dialogue-based computer assisted language-system scored lower than the control group in the delayed post-tests.

The twenty-three studies focused on teaching and learning can be classified into five sub-categories; teaching course content (n = 7), recommending/providing personalised content (n = 5), supporting teachers in learning and teaching design (n = 3), using academic data to monitor and guide students (n = 2), and supporting representation of knowledge using concept maps (n = 2). However, some studies were difficult to classify, due to their specific and unique functions, helping to organise online learning groups with similar interests, supporting business decisions through simulation, or supporting changes in attitude and behaviour for patients with Anorexia Nervosa, through embodied conversational agents. Aparicio et al. (2018) present a study where no adaptive system application was analysed, rather students' perceptions of the use of information systems in education in general and biomedical education in particular were analysed, including intelligent information access systems.

## CONCLUSION

In this paper, we have explored the field of AI education research in terms of authorship and publication patterns. It is evident that American, Chinese, Taiwanese and Turkish researchers (approximately 50% of the publications as first authors) from Computer Science and STEM departments (roughly 62%) dominate the field. The leading journals are the International Journal of Artificial Intelligence in Education, Computers & Education, and the International Journal of Emerging Technologies in Learning. More importantly, this study has provided an overview of the vast array of potential AI applications in HE to support students, faculty members, and administrators. They were described in four broad areas (profiling and prediction, intelligent tutoring systems, assessment and evaluation, and adaptive systems and personalisation) with seventeen sub-categories. This structure, which was derived from the systematic review, contributes to the understanding and conceptualisation of AI education practice and research.

Conversely, there is a lack of longitudinal studies and the substantial presence of descriptive and pilot studies from the technological perspective. This includes the prevalence of quantitative methods, especially quasi experimental methods in empirical studies, which show that there is still substantial room for educators to aim at innovative meaningful research and practice with AI education that could have learning impacts within HE, e.g. adopting design-based approaches. A recent systematic literature review on personalisation in educational technology coincided with the predominance of experiences in technological developments, which also often used quantitative methods. Misiejuk and Wasson (2017) noted in their systematic review on Learning Analytics: “there are very few implementation studies and impact studies” (p.61), which is also similar to the findings in the present article.

The full consequences of AI development cannot yet be foreseen today, but it seems likely that AI applications will be a top educational technology issue for the future generation. AI-based tools and services have a high potential to support students, faculty members and administrators throughout the student lifecycle. The applications that are described in this article provide enormous pedagogical opportunities for the design of intelligent student support systems, and for scaffolding student learning in adaptive and personalised learning environments. This applies in particular to large HE institutions (such as open and distance teaching universities), where AI education might help to overcome the dilemma of providing access to HE for very large numbers of students (mass HE). On the other hand, it might also help them to offer flexible, but also interactive and personalised learning opportunities, for example by relieving teachers from burdens, such as grading hundreds or even thousands of assignments, so that they can focus on their real task: empathic human teaching.

We should not strive for what is technically possible, but always ask ourselves what makes pedagogical sense. In China, systems are already being used to monitor student participation and expressions via face recognition in classrooms (so called Intelligent Classroom Behaviour Management System, Smart Campus) and display them to the teacher on a dashboard. This is an example of educational surveillance, and it is highly questionable whether such systems provide real added value for a good teacher who should be able to capture the dynamics in a learning group (online and in an on campus setting) and respond empathically and in a pedagogically meaningful way. In this sense, it is crucial to adopt an ethics of care (Prinsloo, 2017) to start thinking on how we are exploring the potential of algorithmic decision-making systems that are embedded in AI education applications. Furthermore, we should also always remember that AI systems “first and foremost, require control by humans. Even the smartest AI systems can make very stupid mistakes. AI Systems are only as smart as the date used to train them” (Kaplan & Haenlein, 2019, p.25). Some critical voices in educational technology remind us that we should go beyond the tools, and talk again about learning and pedagogy, as well as acknowledging the human aspects of digital technology use in education (Castañeda & Selwyn, 2018). The new UNESCO report on challenges and opportunities of AI education for sustainable development deals with various areas, all of which have an important pedagogical, social and ethical dimension. For example, ensuring inclusion and equity in AI education, preparing teachers for AI-powered education, developing quality and inclusive data systems, or ethics and transparency in data collection, use and dissemination (Pedró et al., 2019).

We also found that the lack of theory might be a syndrome within the field of educational technology in general. In a recent study, Hew et al. (2019) found that more than 40% of articles in three top educational technology journals were wholly atheoretical. The systematic review by Bartolomé et al. (2018) also revealed this lack of explicit pedagogical perspectives in the studies analysed. The majority of research included in this systematic review is merely focused on analysing and finding patterns in data to develop models, and to make predictions that inform student and teacher facing applications, or to support administrative decisions using mathematical theories and machine learning methods that were developed decades ago (Russel & Norvig, 2010). This kind of research is now possible through the growth of computing power and the vast availability of big digital student data. However, at this stage, there is very little evidence for the advancement of pedagogical and psychological learning theories related to AI driven educational technology.

Finally, it is crucial to emphasise that educational technology should not only highlight technology, but also highlight pedagogical, ethical, social, cultural and economic dimensions of AI education. Selwyn (2016) writes: "The danger, of course, lies in seeing data and coding as an absolute rather than relative source of guidance and support. Education is far too complex to be reduced solely to data analysis and algorithms. As with digital technologies in general, digital data do not offer a neat technical fix to education dilemmas, no matter how compelling the output might be" (p.106). Hence, we urge further research should be developed within this area.

## FUTURE RESEARCH AND RECOMMENDATIONS

Based on our conclusions, we propose several recommendations:

- Our research was mainly restricted to secondary data analysis of technical papers, so future research could empirically explore the technical aspects of AI education through a wider perspective lens; this is based on Selwyn's view, which dictates that education is too complex to be reduced to data analysis and algorithms and that AI as a digital technology cannot offer technical solutions to education dilemmas;
- Our findings also showed a lack of AI education studies in the European regions with the majority coming from the Americas and China, Taiwanese and Turkish and thus more studies coming from European regions may help to provide a broader perspective of the culture of AI education from different regions around the world;
- A lack of critical reflection of the pedagogical and ethical implications as well as risks of implementing AI applications in HE were noted in our findings. In particular, the ethical implications point to privacy issues, which were rarely addressed in the reviewed papers. This calls for more research on the integration of AI applications throughout the student lifecycle, to harness the enormous opportunities that they afford for creating intelligent learning and teaching systems.
- It is an important implication of this systematic review, that researchers are encouraged to be explicit about the theories that underpin empirical studies about the development and implementation of AI education projects (perhaps through cloud computing technology) (M. Ali, 2019; M. B. Ali, 2019; Ali et al., 2020). This will help to expand research to a broader level, helping us to understand the reasons and mechanisms behind this dynamic development that will have an enormous impact on HE institutions in the various areas we have covered in this review.

## REFERENCES

Adamson, D., Dyke, G., Jang, H., & Rosé, C. P. (2014). Towards an agile approach to adapting dynamic collaboration support to student needs. *International Journal of Artificial Intelligence in Education, 24*(1), 92–124. doi:10.100740593-013-0012-6

Alfarsi, G. M. S., Omar, K. A. M., & Alsinani, M. J. (2017). A rule-based system for advising undergraduate students. *Journal of Theoretical & Applied Information Technology, 95*(11).

Ali, M. (2019). Cloud Computing at a Cross Road: Quality and Risks in Higher Education. *Advances in Internet of Things, 9*(3), 33–49. doi:10.4236/ait.2019.93003

Ali, M. B. (2019). Multiple Perspective of Cloud Computing Adoption Determinants in Higher Education a Systematic Review. *International Journal of Cloud Applications and Computing, 9*(3), 89–109. doi:10.4018/IJCAC.2019070106

Ali, M. B., Wood-Harper, T., & Ramlogan, R. (2020). A Framework Strategy to Overcome Trust Issues on Cloud Computing Adoption in Higher Education. In Modern Principles, Practices, and Algorithms for Cloud Security (pp. 162-183). IGI Global. doi:10.4018/978-1-7998-1082-7.ch008

Aparicio, F., Morales-Botello, M. L., Rubio, M., Hernando, A., Muñoz, R., López-Fernández, H., Glez-Peña, D., Fdez-Riverola, F., de la Villa, M., Maña, M., Gachet, D., & Buenaga, M. (2018). Perceptions of the use of intelligent information access systems in university level active learning activities among teachers of biomedical subjects. *International Journal of Medical Informatics, 112*, 21–33. doi:10.1016/j.ijmedinf.2017.12.016 PMID:29500018

Bahadir, E. (2016). Using Neural Network and Logistic Regression Analysis to Predict Prospective Mathematics Teachers' Academic Success upon Entering Graduate Education. *Educational Sciences: Theory and Practice, 16*(3), 943–964.

Bailey, L. W. (2019). *Educational Technology and the New World of Persistent Learning*. IGI Global. https://books.google.co.uk/books?id=3_CBDwAAQBAJ

Baker, T., & Anissa, N. (2019). *Educ-AI-tion rebooted? Exploring the future of artificial intelligence in schools and colleges.* Retrieved 4th Apr from https://media.nesta.org.uk/documents/Future_of_AI_and_education_v5_WEB.pdf

Becker, S. A., Brown, M., Dahlstrom, E., Davis, A., DePaul, K., Diaz, V., & Pomerantz, J. (2019). *NMC horizon report: 2018 higher education edition*. EDUCAUSE. https://library.educause.edu/-/media/files/library/2019/4/2019horizonreport.pdf

Booth, A., Sutton, A., & Papaioannou, D. (2016). *Systematic Approaches to a Successful Literature Review*. SAGE Publications. https://books.google.co.uk/books?id=DKj0CwAAQBAJ

Casamayor, A., Amandi, A., & Campo, M. (2009). Intelligent assistance for teachers in collaborative e-learning environments. *Computers & Education, 53*(4), 1147–1154. doi:10.1016/j.compedu.2009.05.025

Cioffi, R., Travaglioni, M., Piscitelli, G., Petrillo, A., & De Felice, F. (2020). Artificial Intelligence and Machine Learning Applications in Smart Production: Progress, Trends, and Directions. *Sustainability*, *12*(2), 492. doi:10.3390u12020492

Dodigovic, M. (2007). Artificial intelligence and second language learning: An efficient approach to error remediation. *Language Awareness*, *16*(2), 99–113. doi:10.2167/la416.0

Ge, C., & Xie, J. (2015). Application of Grey Forecasting Model Based on Improved Residual Correction in the Cost Estimation of University Education. *International Journal of Emerging Technologies in Learning*, *10*(8), 30. doi:10.3991/ijet.v10i8.5215

Goralski, M. A., & Tan, T. K. (2020). Artificial intelligence and sustainable development. *International Journal of Management Education*, *18*(1), 100330. doi:10.1016/j.ijme.2019.100330

Gough, D., Oliver, S., & Thomas, J. (2017). An introduction to systematic reviews. *Sage (Atlanta, Ga.)*.

Haugeland, J. (1989). *Artificial Intelligence: The Very Idea*. MIT Press. https://books.google.co.uk/books?id=zLFSPdIuqKsC

Huang, S.-P. (2018). Effects of using artificial intelligence teaching system for environmental education on environmental knowledge and attitude. *Eurasia Journal of Mathematics, Science and Technology Education*, *14*(7), 3277–3284. doi:10.29333/ejmste/91248

Jackman, S. R., Witard, O. C., Jeukendrup, A. E., & Tipton, K. D. (2010). Branched-Chain Amino Acid Ingestion Can Ameliorate Soreness from Eccentric Exercise. *Medicine and Science in Sports and Exercise*, *42*(5), 962–970. doi:10.1249/MSS.0b013e3181c1b798 PMID:19997002

Ji, Y., & Liu, Y. (2016). Development of Intelligent Teaching System Based on 3D Technology in the Course of Digital Animation Production. *International Journal of Emerging Technologies in Learning*, *11*(09), 81–86. doi:10.3991/ijet.v11i09.6116

Jiang, F., Jiang, Y., Zhi, H., Dong, Y., Li, H., Ma, S., Wang, Y., Dong, Q., Shen, H., & Wang, Y. (2017). Artificial intelligence in healthcare: Past, present and future. *Stroke and Vascular Neurology*, *2*(4), svn-2017–svn-000101. doi:10.1136vn-2017-000101 PMID:29507784

Johnson, L., Becker, S. A., Cummins, M., Estrada, V., Freeman, A., & Hall, C. (2016). *NMC horizon report: 2016 higher education edition*. The New Media Consortium.

Jonassen, D., Davidson, M., Collins, M., Campbell, J., & Haag, B. B. (1995). Constructivism and computer-mediated communication in distance education. *american. Journal of Distance Education*, *9*(2), 7–26. doi:10.1080/08923649509526885

Kearney, E., Shemla, M., van Knippenberg, D., & Scholz, F. A. (2019). A paradox perspective on the interactive effects of visionary and empowering leadership. *Organizational Behavior and Human Decision Processes*.

Kose, U., & Arslan, A. (2016). Intelligent e-learning system for improving students' academic achievements in computer programming courses. *International Journal of Engineering Education*, *32*(1), 185–198.

Krishna, K. P., Kumar, M. M., & Sri, P. A. (2018). Student information system and performance retrieval through dashboard. *International Journal of Engineering & Technology, 7*(2.7), 682-685.

Li, X. (2007). Intelligent agent–supported online education. *Decision Sciences Journal of Innovative Education*, *5*(2), 311–331. doi:10.1111/j.1540-4609.2007.00143.x

Liberati, A., Altman, D. G., Tetzlaff, J., Mulrow, C., Gøtzsche, P. C., Ioannidis, J. P., Clarke, M., Devereaux, P. J., Kleijnen, J., & Moher, D. (2009). The PRISMA statement for reporting systematic reviews and meta-analyses of studies that evaluate health care interventions: Explanation and elaboration. *PLoS Medicine*, *6*(7), e1000100. doi:10.1371/journal.pmed.1000100 PMID:19621070

Liu, L. F., Li, Y., Xiong, Y., Cao, J., & Yuan, P. (2018). An EEG study of the relationship between design problem statements and cognitive behaviours during conceptual design. *Artificial Intelligence for Engineering Design, Analysis and Manufacturing*, *32*(3), 351–362. doi:10.1017/S0890060417000683

Lo, J.-J., Chan, Y.-C., & Yeh, S.-W. (2012). Designing an adaptive web-based learning system based on students' cognitive styles identified online. *Computers & Education*, *58*(1), 209–222. doi:10.1016/j.compedu.2011.08.018

Lodhi, P., Mishra, O., Jain, S., & Bajaj, V. (2018). StuA: An intelligent student assistant. *IJIMAI*, *5*(2), 17–25. doi:10.9781/ijimai.2018.02.008

Luckin, R., Holmes, W., Griffiths, M., & Corcier, L. B. (2016). *Intelligence Unleashed: An Argument for AI in Education*. Pearson. https://books.google.co.uk/books?id=3OZduwEACAAJ

Misiejuk, K., & Wasson, B. (2017). *State of the field report on learning analytics*. Academic Press.

Miwa, K., Terai, H., Kanzaki, N., & Nakaike, R. (2014). An intelligent tutoring system with variable levels of instructional support for instructing natural deduction. *Information and Media Technologies*, *9*(1), 132–140. doi:10.1527/tjsai.29.148

Moher, D., Liberati, A., Tetzlaff, J., & Altman, D. (2009). PRISMA Group: Methods of systematic reviews and meta-analysis: preferred reporting items for systematic reviews and meta-analyses: the PRISMA statement. *Journal of Clinical Epidemiology*, *62*(10), 1006–1012. doi:10.1016/j.jclinepi.2009.06.005 PMID:19631508

Moher, D., Liberati, A., Tetzlaff, J., & Altman, D. G. (2009). Preferred reporting items for systematic reviews and meta-analyses: The PRISMA statement. *Annals of Internal Medicine*, *151*(4), 264–269. doi:10.7326/0003-4819-151-4-200908180-00135 PMID:19622511

Nguyen, J., Sánchez-Hernández, G., Armisen, A., Agell, N., Rovira, X., & Angulo, C. (2018). A linguistic multi-criteria decision-aiding system to support university career services. *Applied Soft Computing*, *67*, 933–940. doi:10.1016/j.asoc.2017.06.052

Nicholas, D., Watkinson, A., Jamali, H. R., Herman, E., Tenopir, C., Volentine, R., Allard, S., & Levine, K. (2015). Peer review: Still king in the digital age. *Learned Publishing*, *28*(1), 15–21. doi:10.1087/20150104

O'Donovan, P., Gallagher, C., Leahy, K., & O'Sullivan, D. T. J. (2019). A comparison of fog and cloud computing cyber-physical interfaces for Industry 4.0 real-time embedded machine learning engineering applications. *Computers in Industry*, *110*, 12–35. doi:10.1016/j.compind.2019.04.016

Ozturk, Z. K., Cicek, Z., & Ergul, Z. (2017). Sentiment Analysis: An Application to Anadolu University. *Acta Physica Polonica A, 132*(3), 753–755. doi:10.12693/APhysPolA.132.753

Perez, S., Massey-Allard, J., Butler, D., Ives, J., Bonn, D., Yee, N., & Roll, I. (2017). Identifying productive inquiry in virtual labs using sequence mining. *International Conference on Artificial Intelligence in Education.*

Popenici, S. A., & Kerr, S. (2017). Exploring the impact of artificial intelligence on teaching and learning in higher education. *Research and Practice in Technology Enhanced Learning, 12*(1), 22. doi:10.1007/978-3-319-61425-0_24

Prinsloo, P. (2017). Fleeing from Frankenstein's monster and meeting Kafka on the way: Algorithmic decision-making in higher education. *E-Learning and Digital Media, 14*(3), 138–163. doi:10.1177/2042753017731355

Russell, S., & Norvig, P. (2016). *Artificial Intelligence: A Modern Approach.* CreateSpace Independent Publishing Platform. https://books.google.co.uk/books?id=PQI7vgAACAAJ

Sánchez, L. E., Santos-Olmo, A., Álvarez, E., Huerta, M., Camacho, S., & Fernández-Medina, E. (2016). Development of an Expert System for the Evaluation of Students' Curricula on the Basis of Competencies. *Future Internet, 8*(2), 22. doi:10.3390/fi8020022

Schiaffino, S., Garcia, P., & Amandi, A. (2008). eTeacher: Providing personalized assistance to e-learning students. *Computers & Education, 51*(4), 1744–1754. doi:10.1016/j.compedu.2008.05.008

Selwyn, N. (2016). *Is Technology Good for Education?* Wiley. https://books.google.co.uk/books?id=XLtQDAAAQBAJ

Smart, O., & Burrell, L. (2015). Genetic programming and frequent itemset mining to identify feature selection patterns of iEEG and fMRI epilepsy data. *Engineering Applications of Artificial Intelligence, 39*, 198–214. doi:10.1016/j.engappai.2014.12.008 PMID:25580059

Tegmark, M. (2017). *Life 3.0: Being Human in the Age of Artificial Intelligence.* Penguin Books Limited. https://books.google.co.uk/books?id=3_otDwAAQBAJ

Vlugter, P., Knott, A., McDonald, J., & Hall, C. (2009). Dialogue-based CALL: A case study on teaching pronouns. *Computer Assisted Language Learning, 22*(2), 115–131. doi:10.1080/09588220902778260

Welham, D. (2008). AI in training (1980–2000): Foundation for the future or misplaced optimism? *British Journal of Educational Technology, 39*(2), 287–296. doi:10.1111/j.1467-8535.2008.00818.x

Zawacki-Richter, O., Marín, V. I., Bond, M., & Gouverneur, F. (2019). Systematic review of research on artificial intelligence applications in higher education–where are the educators? *International Journal of Educational Technology in Higher Education, 16*(1), 39. doi:10.118641239-019-0171-0

## ADDITIONAL READING

Hinojo-Lucena, F.-J., Aznar-Díaz, I., Cáceres-Reche, M.-P., & Romero-Rodríguez, J.-M. (2019). Artificial intelligence in HE: A bibliometric study on its impact in the scientific literature. *Education in Science*, *9*(1), 51. doi:10.3390/educsci9010051

Popenici, S. A., & Kerr, S. (2017). Exploring the impact of artificial intelligence on teaching and learning in HE. *Research and Practice in Technology Enhanced Learning*, *12*(1), 22. doi:10.118641039-017-0062-8 PMID:30595727

Zawacki-Richter, O., Marín, V. I., Bond, M., & Gouverneur, F. (2019). Systematic review of research on artificial intelligence applications in HE–where are the educators? *International Journal of Educational Technology in HE*, *16*(1), 39.

## KEY TERMS AND DEFINITIONS

**Adaptive Systems:** A system that possesses interacting or interdependent entities that can respond to change within a given setting.

**Artificial Intelligence:** Systems performing tasks through human simulated actions, such as decision making and translation.

**E-Learning:** Teaching and learning systems driven by online and computing technologies.

**HE:** Tertiary education in which University courses are taught.

**Intelligent Tutoring Systems:** A computer that can provide instruction or feedback to learners without human instructor intervention.

**Machine Learning:** An application of AI that can develop computer programs with the capacity of accessing data and use it for learning.

**Pedagogical Systems:** Systems that can create organised, purposeful, and pedagogical or instructive influence for learners.

# Chapter 4
# Cloud Computing Big Data Adoption Impacts on Teaching and Learning in Higher Education:
## A Systematic Review

**Fahad Nasser Alhazmi**
*King Abdulaziz University, Saudi Arabia*

## ABSTRACT

*There is a rapid evolution in the purpose and value of higher education brought about by technological advancement and data ubiquity. Data mining and advanced predictive analytics are increasingly being used in higher education institutions around the world to perform tasks, ranging from student recruitment, enrolment, predicting student behaviour, and developing personalised learning schemes. This chapter evaluates and assesses the impact of big data and cloud computing in higher education. The authors adopt systematic literature research approach that employs qualitative content analysis to establish their position with regards to the impact, benefits, challenges, and opportunities of integrating big data and cloud computing to facilitate teaching and learning.*

## INTRODUCTION

The advancement in technology has impacted every facet of human endeavour and the higher education sector is consequently not left out. The impact of technology has infused the heart of higher education teaching and learning and contributes to providing and enhancing student experience and positive engagement. In today's world, technology has been cleverly infused in higher education teaching and learning to augment various elements, components, and processes like teaching, learning, curriculum design, and assessment. When associated with apt learning objectives and standards, the impact is overwhelming.

DOI: 10.4018/978-1-7998-4846-2.ch004

For instance, some universities have already partnered with IBM to provide cloud-based access to the emergent big data analytics platform – IBM's supercomputer Watson. Even though the service provided is only basic, it still provides an illustration of the impact of big data and cloud computing on teaching and learning in higher education. The paradigm of higher education is constantly evolving, therefore emphasizing the need for rapid and dynamic adaptation by higher education institutions. There are strict requirements from accrediting and regulatory agencies, government and parastatals, as well as other stake holders to explore new methods and techniques for enhancing and monitoring student success and experience.

Within the higher education, technology trends comprising data mining and predictive analytical techniques are progressively being adopted in higher education for the purpose of classifying students to categories based on performance, learning history, and future prospect. Higher education institutions that have seldom collaborated with commercial partners, have commenced the adoption of these methods to recommend courses, monitor student progress, customise learning curriculum, and even develop collaborative networks amongst students. Big data analytics is a critical component of business intelligence and industrial analytics and is fast becoming part of a revolutionary and disruptive technology for higher education in which the ability to forecast individual consequences completely transforms management and allows institutions to better understand their students (and their needs) by exploiting the vast amounts of data that higher education institutions generate in their day-to-day actions (Collins et al., 2018; Poonia et al., 2018; Wang et al., 2018).

On the other hand, the last two decades has witnessed the evolution of distributed computing, a disruptive technology that has altered the application of scientific and commercial applications. This progress has birthed several more recent and relevant applications. The most recent member of this family and consequence of the development of distributed computing is Cloud computing. Using Cloud environment, all the applications can be delivered as a web service (Ali, 2019; Ali et al., 2019, Ali et al., 2020). Cloud facilitates the delivery of applications, software development languages and server/hardware as a service. The concept of cloud computing relates to the delivery of IT services that typically run in a web browser as a service. These services range from modifications or enhancements of common applications, such as email, admin/secretarial and personal finance to innovative solutions such as virtual and physical social networks. A very critical and essential service provided by cloud computing is the storage of digital data. Therefore, cloud computing can be defined as a computing platform that is resident in a network provider's data centre and is able to randomly and rapidly give its numerous servers the capabilities to deliver a wide range of services to its clients (Dillon et al., 2010). The notion of 'cloud' is a metaphor that represents the internet. In other words, the cloud refers to a computing paradigm, one where tasks are allocated to a permutation of services, software and connections read over a network. This holistic network comprising the servers, client base, and connections is collectively referred to as the cloud. Performing computing on a large scale on the cloud creates opportunities for users to access computing resources at a clustered level. Rather than purchase, develop, maintain and administer their personal data centres, firms prefer to purchase this computing power and storage capacity as a service from a provider, typically on a 'pay-as-you-use' model, just as with regular bills of electricity or water. This model has also been described as "utility computing," in which the availability of computing resources is addressed as any other metered utility service (Jain and Bhardwaj, 2010).

Cloud computing serves many functions and can provide solutions to a myriad of challenges posed, even in the higher education institutions. Typical uses of cloud computing in the higher education sector include cloud computing as Personal Learning Environments (PLEs), which can substitute for organisation-wise Virtual Learning Environments (VLEs)/LMS, like blackboard, with various personalised functions to meet their personal needs and preferences. Second, it can enable ubiquitous computing and learning. For students, with the availability of cloud computing, there is the introduction of the element of flexibility, meaning that the students are no longer tied to their lecture classrooms or halls. Cloud computing offers live chat sessions, video conferencing facilities, collaboration for online assessments and virtual labs, which have actually expanded the borders of the classroom, and all but eradicated the limitation of geographical distance and time.

Consequently, this chapter aims to evaluate and assess the impact of big data and cloud computing in higher education. We adopt systematic literature research approach to establish our position with regards to the impact, benefits, challenges, and opportunities of integrating big data and cloud computing to facilitate teaching and learning. Adopting a systematic literature review process, this chapter aims to identify and discuss the impact of big data and cloud computing on higher education teaching and learning, as well as touch on the disadvantages and challenges of completely adopting these technologies in higher education.

## LITERATURE REVIEW

This section presents a review of existing literature on big data analytics and cloud computing adoption by Higher Educational Institutions (HEIs). The aim is the identification of frameworks, models and architectures that have so far been proposed for establishing cloud computing services inside HEIs, as well as how these are integrated for big data analytics. The section commences with a basic description of concepts in the field of cloud computing and big data analytics. It then proceeds to review existing frameworks and academic articles.

## BASIC DESCRIPTIONS OF CLOUD COMPUTING AND BIG DATA ANALYTICS

### Cloud Computing

The concept of cloud computing as a term was first mentioned by John McCarthy in 1960s where he referred to it as the ability of providing computing facilities to the public as a service – like a utility. Although the business model of providing computing as a service is not novel and has been in used in the provision of essential amenities such as in the water, electric and telephone sectors, it is still in its beginning in computing. In the early 1990s, the term "cloud" was used in numerous perspectives and appeared in many articles' diagrams to signify large networks. However, the term 'Cloud Computing' really gained popularity after its use by then Google's CEO Eric Schmidt in 2006, where he used it to denote the business model for delivering services over the internet (Campbell-Kelly et al., 2008; Erl et al., 2013; Hwang et al., 2011; Jain and Bhardwaj, 2010).

There is no consensus standard definition for cloud computing and this ambiguity obviously creates misunderstanding about a clear, succinct and precise definition of this technology (Rittinghouse and Ransome, 2016). The authors in Vaquero et al. (2008) performed a critical and comparative analysis of many definitions from a variety of academic publications in order to formulate a standardised definition of cloud computing. Armbrust et al. (2010) presents an alternative approach, which differentiated between the definitions of the two terms – cloud and utility computing. In the paper, the authors defined the data centre components (i.e. hardware and software) as the "cloud" while the service being rendered as the "utility computing". In summary, the authors defined "cloud computing" as the accumulation of the implemented software services and utility computing (Ali et al., 2018).

However, the National Institute of Standards and Technology (NIST) presents a definition of cloud computing that is rapidly becoming the globally-accepted definition, both in literature and industry (Lee et al., 2014; Sokol and Hogan, 2013; Yang and Huang, 2013) . The description of cloud computing, according to NIST is "a model for enabling convenient, on-demand network access to a shared pool of configurable computing resources (e.g., networks, servers, storage, applications and services) that can be rapidly provisioned and released with minimal management effort or service provider interaction" (Lee et al., 2014). Furthermore, the International Organization for Standardization (ISO) and the International Electrotechnical Commission (IEC) have defined cloud computing in their respective standard documentation as "a paradigm for enabling network access to a scalable and elastic pool of shareable physical or virtual resources with self-service provisioning and administration on-demand" (Antonopoulos and Gillam, 2010).

## Big Data Analytics

In conventional data analytics, extract, transform, and load (ETL) processes (Kelly, 2014) that are used to store structured data into data warehouses from enterprise software such as CRM, ERP, and financial database systems. Consequently, consistent reports run on the stored data are used to create dashboards and data visualizations that are often used as analytic and decision-making components. The advent of social networking sites (SNS) and media, smart phones, the internet, interconnected devices, and sensors have contributed to the evolving nature of big data. This precipitated the need for new methods, models, and techniques to manipulate big data, resulting in a field of research analytics known as big data analytics (BDA).

Big data refers to gigantic datasets with sizes ranging from thousands of gigabytes, terabytes to petabytes, exabytes, and beyond, coming from a variety of sources, therefore is heterogeneous (semi-structured or unstructured) and is generated at increasing velocity. It is important to note that big data should not be mistaken for a dataset that has expanded to the point that it can no longer be analysed on a spread sheet, nor is it a database that happens to be extremely large. Some characteristics differentiate big data from traditional data are tabulated in Table 1. As can be seen, the table distinguishes big data from conventional or traditional data on the basis of the listed characteristics. It is important to comprehend the nature of big data in order to decide on the methods, tools, and technologies to control and manage it effectively.

Big data is typically characterised by Vs, which appear to be increasing year-on-year. However, in (Katal et al., 2013), big data is characterised by three dimensions – Volume, Variety, and Velocity. Additional Vs including Veracity, Value, and Variability further refine the description and characterisation of the term big data. As Table 1 shows, big data is typically semi-structured and unstructured in nature and is mainly obtained from a range of sources, such as, sensor, computerised, device-generated data, social media and web data, etc. With big data, the data are generated at constantly increasing rates. Veracity relates to the inherent issues of ambiguity and authenticity of data, for instance being of low quality or lacking trust to enable it being used in decision-making. The dimension value explores big data using analytical techniques in order to provide essential insight from the data to allow businesses make more

*Table 1. Comparative Analysis of Big and Conventional Data*

| Characteristic | Big Data | Conventional Data |
|---|---|---|
| Volume | Thousands of gigabytes, terabytes, petabytes, exabytes, and beyond | Megabytes to few hundred Gigabytes |
| Nature and Location | Typically, semi-structured or highly unstructured (text, likes, tweets, images, motion pictures, sound recordings, etc.) | Typically consists of highly structured and comprises a single discipline sub-discipline. The data is often in ordered and even records, such as an ordered spreadsheet or time series dataset |
| Reproducibility | Replication of big data is rarely feasible | Conventional data projects can easily be repeated |
| Analysis | Big data is typically analysed orderly in small incremental steps. In big data, the data can be extracted, examined, transformed, normalized, visualized, interpreted, and re-analysed with different analytical methods | Conventional data projects typically need to be analysed alongside the data |
| Frameworks and tools | HDFS, NoSQL, Hadoop, Storm, Spark | Relative DBMS, ETL tools and SQL |
| Data Preparation | Big data typically comes from diverse data sources and is organised by many people | In this data type, the data user formulates her own data for her use |

accurate and timely decisions for future prospects. The term variability, (Katal et al., 2013) refers to data flow variations for heavy loads. For instance, an instance where numerous concurrent events on a social media platform cause a steep spike in the demand for/of the data.

### Big Data Analytics and Cloud Computing Adoption in HEIs

In this section, qualitative content analysis methodology (Mayring, 2004) on the adoption of big data analytics and cloud computing services by HEIs is performed and a systematic review process is applied on this collection of academic articles. This process adopted to perform a Systematic Literature Review (SLR) followed the steps outlined below.

## METHODOLOGY

The first step in this process involved a definition of the search terms in a manner that all the concerned research areas – adopting big data analytics and cloud computing in HEIs – were covered. Consequently, the proposed keywords include big data analytics, cloud computing, cloud computing services, information and communication technology services for higher education and big data and cloud computing for higher education. Next, each of these keywords were searched on popular online electronic databases – Google Scholar, Elsevier Science direct, IEEE Xplore and Web of Science. The search was constrained to articles published in English language. Furthermore, the search was constrained to only include articles from the last 10 years (i.e. 2010 to 2020). The contextual analysis was performed using the article title, abstract, and manuscript text. The outcome of the systematic literature review methodology described above resulted in 147 papers, which focused on adopting big data analytics and cloud computing technology in HEIs.

Aggregating the papers in terms of chosen methodology, of the 147 identified papers, 36 percent performed exploratory analyses that investigated the implementation and use of big data and cloud computing services respectively, while 19 percent applied quantitative survey methodology to obtain the analysed data about the adoption of this technology. Another 13 percent adopted literature survey methodology. 11 papers adopted case study methodology, which accounted to 8 percent of the papers as shown in Table 2.

*Table 2. Summary of Methodologies used in the papers*

| Methodology | Percentage | Value |
|---|---|---|
| Exploratory analysis | 36% | 53 |
| Quantitative Survey | 19% | 28 |
| Systematic Literature Review | 13% | 19 |
| Hypothesis | 12% | 17 |
| Case Study | 11% | 16 |
| Observation | 9% | 14 |

The review process mainly focused on identifying frameworks, models and architectures that were used for adopting big data analytics and cloud computing in HEIs. The empirical analysis of the resultant dataset showed that only three papers of the identified papers proposed computing frameworks, while four papers described big data analytics and cloud computing models. Finally, five papers proposed cloud computing architectures.

## Frameworks for Cloud Computing Adoption in HEIs

Yang (2011) presents an enhanced framework for e-education that adopted open standards for cloud services. The framework is delineated into two parts – service and management phases. The service subsystem is further logically split into execution cloud, managing the virtual machines through service scheduler, core middleware, service monitor, hype visor and storage cloud merged, which are in the management subsystem and are provided according to the user's requests. The management subsystem accepts the user`s requests through user-front-end and parses the same to the service subsystem stage after determining whether the service is satisfied locally, or it needs to be transmitted to alternative cloud locations. In Saidhbi (2012), a hybrid cloud computing framework for Ethiopian Universities Hybrid Cloud (EUHC) is presented. The framework comprises of four layers, including the user interface layer – which has three parts (user portal, service catalogue, and service repository) for accessing different services provided in the three other layers. The other three layers provide varying levels of cloud services (SaaS, PaaS, and IaaS).

Subramanian and Seshasaayee (2014) present three frameworks representing a roadmap for developing a best practice for the adoption of big data and cloud computing in Indian universities. The first framework proposes the hybrid cloud as a solution for security and capacity compromises. The second framework represents the workflow approach, which can be deliberated as a principled decision-making process concerning service provisioning on the basis of the scalable and 'pay as you use' model. The third framework provides an explanation of how the hybrid cloud works through all the universities and schools. The article presented in (Liu and Li, 2011) presents a cloud-based platform for digitalising a university campus, which adopts a Service Oriented Architecture (SOA) and virtualization technologies. The framework comprises three layers: (i) The infrastructure layer, (ii) the application layer, which provides the operational environment built around three requirements that define the required services, managing them and providing uniform access to various services as well as the convenience that comes with using them at a cloud platform. These requirements are met through the SOA architecture. The Third layer comprises the service offering layer which supports instant IT services provided through the network to satisfy the users' requests in various forms – IaaS, PaaS or SaaS.

Conghuan (2011) proposes a service computing model for communication between local campus clouds to manage the activities of universities and proposing the efficient sharing of resources. The model proposes multiple local campus clouds. Each campus cloud is programmed to provide given services by virtualising a set of resources. This set of virtualised resource is recorded in the service pool. Consequently, the service pool delivers the requisite incorporation of a learning platform and teaching environment for distributed resources under certain conditions, which provides the requested services.

## The Adoption of Big Data Analytics in HEIs

As previously stipulated, big data provides higher education institutions an opportunity to strategically use their IT resources to improve the quality of educational services, guide students to provide student experience, deliver higher completion rates, and improve student persistence. Many business organisations around the world adopt big data analytics in business intelligence and areas including market and financial forecasting. Over the past decade, Big Data has attracted the interest of academia. Consequently, academic institutions are migrating to cloud architectures and, with the increased adoption of digital devices by users in these ecosystems, is resulting in a situation where more data is being generated in these institutions than ever before, therefore creating significant opportunities for using Big Data analytics techniques to find patterns in the data that can enhance decision-making.

Big Data presents a suitable framework for efficiently exploiting the enormous array of data in shaping the future of higher education (Görnerup et al., 2013). The adoption of Big Data application in higher education institutions (HEIs) is attributed to technological innovation and development, which have accelerated the growth of big data analytics in higher education institutions. According to Williamson (2017), Data Warehouses and Cloud Computing combined with greater proprietorship of digital devices by end users in the educational network make it possible to obtain, manage and sustain enormous amounts of data. These Information Technologies present critical resources that – when exploited by policy makers – are beneficial in compelling institutional strategy and policy making for the future. IT makes accessible sophisticated platforms that deliver computing power that is essential for analysing massive datasets and transforming these into important information. Data mining technologies, when applied, apply descriptive statistics to develop patterns from the massive amounts of collected data for actionable information (Eynon, 2013). Big Data Analytics is important in tackling a momentous amount of pressing issues for education systems. Such issues include (i) increasing effectiveness of HEIs, (ii) exploiting intuitions from learning experiences, (iii) delivering high-quality education for all, which may be tailored to individual learners' needs; and (iv) furnishing students with appropriate skills for their future.

## CASES OF BIG DATA ANALYTICS AND CLOUD COMPUTING ADOPTION IN HEIS

For this section, let the assumption remain that big data analytics for higher education refers to the science of analysing institutional data from various sources using complex statistical, mathematical and machine learning-based quantitative models, and predictive models to enhance data-driven decision making. Big data analytics has been employed in higher education to provide academic, management and administrators the liberty to observe and obtain more insight about their respective institutions and learners and transform that knowledge into insight for informed decision-making. This section presents a practical application of big data analytics in higher education.

### Case 1: Learning Analytics for Academic Student Tracking

The rapid advancement in the volume and veracity of data obtained by HEIs has resulted in a spike in the flow of data. Through learning analytics, HEIs can improve understanding of their learners' challenges and apply the resultant insight to emphatically enhance the improvement (Slade and Prinsloo, 2013). The ability to understand the learning needs of individual students should comprise the motivating factor for the adoption of learning analytics in HEIs. A successful case of implementing learning analytics in a HEI is the Rio Salado University in Arizona, which developed a learning analytics software for tracking student progress in courses, and the resultant analytics of the collected data in order to drive decision-making. The university enrols over 41,000 students in both online and in-campus courses. The application was developed to centre on personalisation, which involves providing assistance to non-traditional students to achieve academic goals through personalised intermediations (Crush, 2019).

### Case 2: Cloud Computing in Higher Education

As stated in the preceding sections, cloud computing has the potential to increase flexibility and expose HEI users to a broad range of educational resources. This includes providing them with access to infrastructure, software, hardware, and platform at any time in any place provided there is internet access. Within HEIs, the users of cloud computing (i.e. students, lecturers, admin staff, developers, programmers and researchers) all adopt the overarching platform for delivery of the given service. Amongst the existent cloud service models (see Section 2.2.2), the software-as-a-service (SaaS) model is the most commonly applied service model in HEIs. The authors in Akande and Van Belle (2014) explored the adoption of SaaS cloud computing in South African HEIs, having the main motive of determining the viability of the adoption of SaaS in HEIs. The paper also articulated the benefits and limitations of SaaS in HEIs.

This findings from the study revealed that most South African HEIs were sensitive to the existence of SaaS and are typically employing public and hybrid cloud services, with none using community cloud services. Furthermore, in South African HEIs, SaaS is mainly applied towards student management (i.e. student recruitment, enrolment, financial disbursement, graduation, and alumni. SaaS is also employed for admin systems including human resource management (HR), customer relationship management (CRM), supply chain management, finance and payroll and asset management. In summary, the study supported the claim that cloud computing was beneficial to HEIs. To confirm this calls for an analysis of the benefits and challenges of cloud computing in HEIs.

## BENEFITS OF BIG DATA AND CLOUD COMPUTING IN HEIS

As previously stated, Big Data typically integrates the research field of learning analytics (Siemens and Long, 2011), which is rapidly-growing area of research. However, rather than focus on the – rather peripheral – application of Big Data analytics in student tracking analytics, Big Data can provide opportunities and challenges for HEIs. Siemens and Long (2011) showed that Big Data presents an intriguing framework for efficiently exploiting the broad range of data and eventually moulding the future of higher education.

Analytics can be used to improve the quality of teaching in HEIs. Just as in businesses, the value of performance or monitoring dashboards applied towards improving teaching or course provision is also highlighted by the literature. For instance, in the University of Wollongong, Australia, analytics of social network data showed interaction patterns that surface in sections that are local. On the other hand, the learners themselves, particularly when in their early years of higher education, often have little or no idea of their performance in comparison with their peers, thereby having gaps in essential knowledge, lacking key study skills. Consequently, providing students with better information relating to their progression and what is required in order to meet their educational goals represents an important use of learning analytics for improving teaching and learning quality. This action has the potential to transform their learning and understanding of how they learn by providing frequent formative feedback as the students advance through their studies. It also enables them to compare themselves to their contemporaries, adding a competitive component and adding a check that enables them to keep up with the group or the progress of successful students in previous groups. Meanwhile, other universities use analytics systems to assist students choose future modules, building up on historical data about career picks, aptitudes and grades of previous modules to provide optimal pathways through their studies.

## CHALLENGES OF BIG DATA AND CLOUD COMPUTING IN HEIS

The research field of Big Data Analytics is receiving increased interest in many HEIs with many scholars supporting its relevance for enhancing the success of higher education. To improve the quality of learning outcomes, it is critical that the massive amounts of data generated by educational systems should be effectively analysed to expedite suitable responses to emergent challenges. However, the challenges to the adoption of Big Data in Education typically include ethical aspects of tracking student data, failure to correlate vital business problems with big data solutions. Furthermore, users or executives are typically rooted in old technologies constitutes another challenge. Third, the cost of computational resource and manpower can also result in a challenge for the adoption of big data analytics and cloud computing.

More so, there is also the shortage of data warehouses and analytical methods and algorithms as well as issues with data quality, which basically leaves most data uncollected resulting in no analyses. It is observed in the literature that prevalent analytics use is limited mainly to the functional aspects of student enrolment administration, progress, and resource optimisation. This peripheral space of application of analytics is mainly due to the barriers of cost, data availability and quality, culture, know-how, and communication. In reality, attaining a well-structured and handy big data ecosystem with distinct encouragements for all parties poses challenges in many aspects. These are segments such as regulation, policy making, public administration and management. This calls for progress of practical models for big data. Big Data analytics in HEIs also faces the strict test of discovering the means to mine knowledge from the widespread datasets generated daily and the distillation of the extracted data into usable information for administrators, students, instructors, and the public. Tracking big data is costly, and therefore organisational managers must be persuaded that analysing such data will yield tangible results prior to investing in the technology.

Big Data also presents many analytical issues that require recurrent updating of instruments and expertise, meaning that HEIs need to have sufficient finances to accommodate these concerns. Furthermore, there also exist genuine concerns about privacy, especially given that the data is obtained from online sources. This, in combination with the 'digital divide' in many countries presents hindrances to fully exploiting the power of Big Data analytics and cloud computing for the benefit of the users of the educational systems (Dede et al., 2016). In summary, the challenges associated with the manipulation and analysis of Big Data using cloud computing are broadly due to its defining properties – volume, velocity, veracity, variety and value. The challenge is in the integration of heterogeneous data sources in this era. For instance, in HEIs, there is the need for the integration, synchronisation, and aggregation of data from sensors, cameras, social media, and legacy systems, all of which are in different formats, size, structure, etc. Table 3 provides a summary of the key opportunities and challenges of cloud computing stated above:

*Table 3. Summary of Key Opportunities and Challenges of Cloud Computing*

| Opportunities | Challenges |
|---|---|
| Efficiency | Ethical issues regarding tracking student data |
| Improve the quality of teaching and course provision | User resistance from traditional system users |
| Improve the quality of teaching and course provision | High cost of computational resource and manpower |
| Provision of frequent formative feedback | Shortage of data warehouses and analytical methods |
| Supports future career development | Issues with data quality |
| | Lack of cloud competency |
| | Difficulties maintaining a well-structured and handy big data ecosystem |
| | Complex big data analytics in HEIs |
| | Privacy issues |

## CONCLUSION

A popular saying "knowledge is power" implies that the more one knows, the more control he/she has. In HEIs, when tutors are provided with insight into the individual progression of their students, they are able to take action if things are going in the wrong direction. Consequently, technology-based learning provides data that, when analysed can provide this intuition, illuminating what works and what does not work so that learning outcomes can be enhanced using informed mediation. Within HEIs, there is increasing data growth, although most of it is distributed across desktops in departments, faculties, or schools, and typically come in different formats, increasing the difficulty of retrieving nor consolidating it. On the other hand, notwithstanding the many critics and deterrents of the widespread adoption of cloud computing, it appears obvious that Cloud Computing is not going away anytime soon. Cloud computing guarantees a revolutionary migration in the provision of computing resources within an organisation. Currently, it is penetrating into many domains and areas of endeavour, from computer science to engineering, student recruitment to learning analytics; from research laboratories to enterprise IT infrastructures. Educational institutes are at the genesis of a changeover period during which they will encounter many challenges relating to cloud adoption. Despite the many benefits of adopting cloud computing and big data analytics in higher education, there will always be demerits that will impede adoption of the technology.

Limitations of the research is the lack of empirical support since a systematic approach was adopted. Cases were presented, but only for a select few HEIs. Other cases conducted through empirical enquiry may yield different findings since each University is different and thus cloud computing may not be the ideal fit for meeting their institutional goals. Empirical enquiry could help to rectify this issue. So this leads to conducting potential future studies. Future studies could the topic of cloud computing adoption in HEIs further to analyse the benefits and challenges from a wider lens. For example, a PESTLE analysis could be conducted to determine the political, economic, social, technological, legal and environmental determinants and barriers to cloud computing big data. This may provide a greater insight why HEIs may choose to adopt or not adopt ubiquitous technologies. Another study could also look at the benefits and challenges through a sociotechnical lens where interactions between HEI stakeholders and potential cloud technology may help to unravel further reasons for adoption and non-adoption of cloud computing. A comparison of cloud computing and other ubiquitous technologies such as Internet of Things could also help to reveal some interesting trends of ubiquitous technology adoption in HEIs to foster teaching and learning.

## REFERENCES

Akande, A. O., & Van Belle, J.-P. (2014). Cloud computing in higher education: A snapshot of software as a service. In *2014 IEEE 6th International Conference on Adaptive Science & Technology (ICAST)*. IEEE. 10.1109/ICASTECH.2014.7068111

Ali, M. (2019). Cloud Computing at a Cross Road: Quality and Risks in Higher Education. *Advances in Internet of Things*, *9*(3), 33–49. doi:10.4236/ait.2019.93003

Ali, M. B. (2019). Multiple Perspective of Cloud Computing Adoption Determinants in Higher Education a Systematic Review. *International Journal of Cloud Applications and Computing*, *9*(3), 89–109. doi:10.4018/IJCAC.2019070106

Ali, M. B., Wood-Harper, T., & Mohamad, M. (2018). Benefits and challenges of cloud computing adoption and usage in higher education: A systematic literature review. *International Journal of Enterprise Information Systems*, *14*(4), 64–77. doi:10.4018/IJEIS.2018100105

Ali, M. B., Wood-Harper, T., & Ramlogan, R. (2020). A Framework Strategy to Overcome Trust Issues on Cloud Computing Adoption in Higher Education. In Modern Principles, Practices, and Algorithms for Cloud Security (pp. 162-183). IGI Global. doi:10.4018/978-1-7998-1082-7.ch008

Antonopoulos, N., & Gillam, L. (2010). *Cloud computing*. Springer. doi:10.1007/978-1-84996-241-4

Armbrust, M., Fox, A., Griffith, R., Joseph, A. D., Katz, R., Konwinski, A., Lee, G., Patterson, D., Rabkin, A., Stoica, I., & Zaharia, M. (2010). A view of cloud computing. *Communications of the ACM, 53*(4), 50–58. doi:10.1145/1721654.1721672

Campbell-Kelly, M., Garcia-Swartz, D. D., Aspray, W., & Ceruzzi, P. E. (2008). The rise, fall, and resurrection of software as a service: historical perspectives on the computer utility and software for lease on a network. In *The Internet and American Business* (pp. 201–230). MIT Press Cambridge.

Collins, C., Andrienko, N., Schreck, T., Yang, J., Choo, J., Engelke, U., Jena, A., & Dwyer, T. (2018). Guidance in the human–machine analytics process. *Visual Informatics*, *2*(3), 166–180. doi:10.1016/j.visinf.2018.09.003

Conghuan, Y. (2011). A service computing model based on interaction among local Campus Clouds. In *2011 6th International Conference on Computer Science & Education (ICCSE)*. IEEE. 10.1109/ICCSE.2011.6028668

Crush, M. (2019). Monitoring the PACE of student Learning: Analytics at Rio Salado Community University. *Campus Technology*.

Dede, C. J., Ho, A. D., & Mitros, P. (2016). Big data analysis in higher education: Promises and pitfalls. *EDUCAUSE Review*.

Dillon, T., Wu, C., & Chang, E. (2010). Cloud computing: issues and challenges. In *2010 24th IEEE International Conference on Advanced Information Networking and Applications*. IEEE. 10.1109/AINA.2010.187

Erl, T., Puttini, R., & Mahmood, Z. (2013). *Cloud computing: concepts, technology & architecture*. Pearson Education.

Eynon, R. (2013). *The rise of Big Data: what does it mean for education, technology, and media research?* Academic Press.

Görnerup, O., Gillblad, D., Holst, A., & Bjurling, B. (2013). *Big data analytics-a research and innovation agenda for Sweden*. The Swedish Big Data Analytics Network.

Hwang, K., Dongarra, J. J., & Fox, G. C. (2011). *Distributed and cloud computing: clusters, grids, clouds, and the future internet*. Morgan Kaufmann.

Jain, L., & Bhardwaj, S. (2010). Enterprise cloud computing: Key considerations for adoption. *International Journal of Engineering and Information Technology*, *2*, 113–117.

Katal, A., Wazid, M., & Goudar, R. H. (2013). Big data: issues, challenges, tools and good practices. In *2013 Sixth International Conference on Contemporary Computing (IC3)*. IEEE. 10.1109/IC3.2013.6612229

Kelly, J. (2014, Feb 5). *Big data: Hadoop, business analytics and beyond* [Blog post]. Wikibon.

Lee, K., Lee, S., & Yang, H.-D. (2014). Towards on cloud computing standardization. *International Journal of Multimedia & Ubiquitous Engineering*, *9*(2), 169–176. doi:10.14257/ijmue.2014.9.2.17

Liu, N., & Li, G. (2011). Research on digital campus based on cloud computing. In *International Conference on Computer Education, Simulation and Modeling*. Springer. 10.1007/978-3-642-21802-6_34

Mayring, P. (2004). Qualitative content analysis. *A companion to Qualitative Research, 1*, 159–176.

Poonia, P., Jain, V. K., & Kumar, A. (2018). Short Term Traffic Flow Prediction Methodologies: A Review. *Mody University International Journal of Computing and Engineering Research, 2*, 37–39.

Rittinghouse, J. W., & Ransome, J. F. (2016). *Cloud computing: implementation, management, and security*. CRC Press.

Saidhbi, S. (2012). A cloud computing framework for Ethiopian Higher Education Institutions. *IOSR Journal of Computer Engineering, 6*, 1–9.

Siemens, G., & Long, P. (2011). Penetrating the fog: Analytics in learning and education. *EDUCAUSE Review*, *46*, 30.

Slade, S., & Prinsloo, P. (2013). Learning analytics: Ethical issues and dilemmas. *The American Behavioral Scientist*, *57*(10), 1510–1529. doi:10.1177/0002764213479366

Sokol, A.W., & Hogan, M.D. (2013). *NIST Cloud Computing Standards Roadmap*. NIST.

Subramanian, S., & Seshasaayee, A. (2014). Review & Proposal for a Cloud based Framework for Indian Higher Education. *International Journal of Engineering and Computer Science*, *3*, 3689–3694.

Vaquero, L.M., Rodero-Merino, L., Caceres, J., & Lindner, M. (2008). *A break in the clouds: towards a cloud definition*. Academic Press.

Wang, J., Ma, Y., Zhang, L., Gao, R. X., & Wu, D. (2018). Deep learning for smart manufacturing: Methods and applications. *Journal of Manufacturing Systems*, *48*, 144–156. doi:10.1016/j.jmsy.2018.01.003

Williamson, B. (2017). Big data in education: The digital future of learning, policy and practice. *Sage (Atlanta, Ga.)*.

Yang, C., & Huang, Q. (2013). *Spatial cloud computing: a practical approach*. CRC Press. doi:10.1201/b16106

Yang, Z. (2011). Study on an Interoperable Cloud framework for e-Education. In *2011 International Conference on E-Business and E-Government (ICEE)*. IEEE. 10.1109/ICEBEG.2011.5887174

## ADDITIONAL READING

Askari, S. H., Ahmad, F., Umair, S., & Khan, S. A. (2018). Cloud Computing Education Strategies: A Review. In Exploring the Convergence of Big Data and the Internet of Things (pp. 43-54). IGI Global. doi:10.4018/978-1-5225-2947-7.ch004

Feng, J., Yang, L. T., Gati, N. J., Xie, X., & Gavuna, B. S. (2019). Privacy-preserving computation in cyber-physical-social systems: A survey of the state-of-the-art and perspectives. *Information Sciences*.

Stergiou, C., Psannis, K. E., Gupta, B. B., & Ishibashi, Y. (2018). Security, privacy & efficiency of sustainable Cloud Computing for Big Data & IoT. *Sustainable Computing: Informatics and Systems, 19*, 174-184.

Tawalbeh, L. A., & Saldamli, G. (2019). Reconsidering big data security and privacy in cloud and mobile cloud systems. *Journal of King Saud University - Computer and Information Sciences*.

Wazid, M., Das, A. K., Hussain, R., Succi, G., & Rodrigues, J. J. P. C. (2019). Authentication in cloud-driven IoT-based big data environment: Survey and outlook. *Journal of Systems Architecture*, *97*, 185–196. doi:10.1016/j.sysarc.2018.12.005

## KEY TERMS AND DEFINITIONS

**Adoption:** The acceptance of technologies in an organisational setting.

**Big Data:** A large volume of structured and unstructured data that inundates an organisation.

**Cloud Computing:** The use of applications, storage, and processing facilities to deliver on-demand computing services over the internet on a pay-per-use basis.

**Data Analytics:** The process of probing datasets to determine what information they contain.

**E-Learning:** Learning via online applications and systems.

**Higher Education:** University taught education.

**Pedagogy:** The practice of teaching in a learning environment.

# Chapter 5
# Opportunities and Challenges of Adopting Artificial Intelligence for Learning and Teaching in Higher Education

**Aniekan Essien**
*Department of Management, University of Sussex Business School, Falmer, UK*

**Godwin Chukwukelu**
*University of Manchester, UK*

**Victor Essien**
*Teeside University, UK*

## ABSTRACT

*This chapter provides a sense of what artificial intelligence is, its benefits, and integration to higher education. Seeing through the lens of the literature, this chapter will also explore the emergence of artificial intelligence and its attendant use for learning and teaching in higher education institutions. It begins with an overview of artificial intelligence and proceeds to discuss practical applications of emerging technologies and artificial intelligence on the manner in which students learn as well as how higher education institutions teach and develop. The chapter concludes with a discussion on the challenges of artificial intelligence on higher education.*

## INTRODUCTION

Over the past two decades the term *artificial intelligence* (AI) has received an increased interest in academia and practice. Although the foundations for AI from assembly and procedural language, object-oriented computer programming, data mining, and machine learning have been laid several decades ago, some uncertainty regarding consequences of the full adoption of AI to the society and economy remains.

DOI: 10.4018/978-1-7998-4846-2.ch005

Recent breakthroughs towards natural language processing (NLP), computer vision, image recognition, text-to-speech and speech-to-text have further accentuated the capabilities of AI.

AI adoption can result in significant social and economic benefits since computers can quickly analyse and learn from vast amounts of data at higher accuracy and speed. Furthermore, AI can improve efficiency in nearly all sectors of human endeavour, ranging from transportation, healthcare, industrial manufacturing, and financial sectors. In each of these sectors, research into the integration of AI to processes is on the increase to infuse methods for efficient and cost effective data-driven decision-making (Collins et al., 2018; Poonia et al., 2018; Wang et al., 2018). According to a report by Gov.UK, AI adoption could add an additional £630bn to the UK economy by 2035 (Hall and Pesenti, 2019). To this end, there is a shortage of AI experts in the UK, therefore teaching of AI in HEIs via industry-funded master's degrees and research in AI at leading UK universities should be increased (Hall and Pesenti, 2019).

AI is currently progressing an already has positive impacts on services within higher education. For instance, many universities already partner with IBM to provide cloud-based access to the emergent AI platform – IBM's supercomputer Watson – to automate simple, repetitive, and typically administrative tasks, such as attendance reminder, classifying feedback, and student support. Even though only the basic service is provided, it provides an illustration of the impact of AI on teaching and learning in higher education. From the foregoing, it is imminent to increase the adoption of AI for educational purposes, in order to equip students or learners with relevant skills that can fill skill gaps in domains. Furthermore, answers to the following questions can make clearer the hurdles that need to be overcome to adopt AI for higher education teaching and learning.

i. How can AI be integrated to the teaching curriculum?
ii. Can AI be used to assess and provide feedback to students automatically?
iii. What impact will AI have to classroom size?
iv. What are the ethical implications of integrating AI for HEI teaching / learning?

Addressing these questions will lead to better understanding and provide a discussion that can benefit higher education regulatory bodies that can improve the visibility of AI in the society and economy.

## ARTIFICIAL INTELLIGENCE

The term artificial intelligence was popularized in the 1950s, when Alan Turing postulated an answer to the question of assigning the term 'intelligent' to a system designed by a human. In his solution, Turing presented a game known as 'the imitation game', a quiz that tests the ability of a human listener to distinguish if a conversation made is with a machine or another human. If this distinction is undetected, it can be concluded that we have an intelligent system, referred to as artificial intelligence (AI). According to Russell and Norvig (2016), artificial intelligence strives to build and understand intelligent entities. AI is typically described as a computer system that possesses the ability to accomplish tasks linked with intelligent beings. In lay terms, an AI is a machine that thinks, understands, learns, solves problems, plays chess, etc. As this definition arguably suffices for the term 'intelligence' and is tautological, AI can also be defined as a *scientific discipline*. AI has produced many significant outcomes in recent times, even at its infancy and although it is impossible to predict the future in detail, it is now apparent that computers intelligent systems can have a tremendous impact on everyday living.

Since the emergence of the concept of AI in 1956, there have been efforts to unravel numerous theoretical underpinnings of AI, which are affected by chemistry, biology, linguistics, mathematics, and other advancements in the field of AI. In this chapter, we insinuate a simplistic literature-informed characterisation to enable an analysis of the impact of AI on teaching and learning in higher education institutions. Accordingly, we define AI to refer to computing systems that can perform human-like tasks for instance, learning, adaptation, self-correction, and processing data for complex tasks.

## THE EMERGENCE OF ARTIFICIAL INTELLIGENCE IN HIGHER EDUCATION

The advent and adoption of new technologies in learning and teaching has rapidly progressed over the past decades. Looking through the present-day lens, the arguments that have ensued in institutions over students being allowed to use what are now seen as elementary technologies. For instance, in a longitudinal study conducted between 1993 and 2005, the authors relate to the previously existent fierce and contentious debate that surrounded the use of calculators and spell check programs for students with learning disabilities (Lazarus et al., 2009). Today, assistive technologies — such as text-to-speech, speech-to-text, text completion, spell checkers, and search engines — are some typical instances of technologies that were originally designed to assist people with disabilities. These technological solutions have been expanded and can now be found as generic features in all personal computers, mobile devices, or wearable devices. These technologies now supplement the learning relations of all students' worldwide, augmenting teaching and design of educational encounter. Furthermore, the adoption of artificial intelligence (AI) enhances tools and instruments in Universities around the world, which are ranging from internet search engines, smartphone features and apps, to public transport and household appliances. A popular application of artificial intelligence iPhone's Siri that represents a classic example of AI solutions (Luckin, 2017). Google adopts AI to drive its search engines and maps, and all new automobiles use AI for a variety of tasks ranging from engine diagnostics to preventive maintenance and navigation. Furthermore, self-driving technology is already at an advanced stage, and some companies have made this a top priority, for instance, Tesla, Volvo, Mercedes, and Google (Mueck and Karls, 2018). This represents a major step towards altering the complex effort of integrating education and AI.

## AI APPLICATIONS IN HIGHER EDUCATION

A recent study of Zawacki-Richter et al. (2019) used student life-cycle to describe the numerous AI-based services at the management or organisational and administrative level (e.g. admission provision, counselling, and library services), in addition to the academic support level for teaching and learning (e.g. assessment, feedback, tutoring). From the findings, the authors reveal that 92 studies (63.0%) were related to academic support services and 48 (32.8%) as administrative and institutional services while six studies (4.1%) covered both levels. Furthermore, majority of the studies focused on undergraduate students (n = 91, 62.3%) in comparison to 11 (7.5%) that focused on postgraduate students, and an additional 44 (30.1%) that did not specify the level of study. Accordingly, two groups of applications of AI in education are identified, which will be discussed below.

### Admission Profiling and Prediction

Machine learning is a subfield of artificial intelligence that aims to develop systems that 'learn' from data. Consequently, many AI applications are machine learning models or systems that are used for prediction, for example of the probability of a student abandoning a course or being admitted to a programme, which can be used to provide timely support or provide formative or summative feedback to students throughout their learning process. According to the authors in Zawacki-Richter et al. (2019), articles dealing with profiling and prediction were categorised into three sub-categories - (i) admission decisions and course scheduling (n = 7), (ii) drop-out and retention (n = 23), and (iii) student models and academic achievement (n = 27). In terms of prediction, machine learning models are mainly applied to predict and classify tasks based on extracted patterns from training data to model student profiles to make predictions. Many studies have applied several machine learning and deep learning algorithms (e.g. CNN, LSTM, ANN, SVM, Random Forest, Naïve Bayes, etc.) Findings from the studies showed that machine learning methods outperformed classic regression-based models in all studies in terms of classification accuracy.

### Admission Decisions and Course Scheduling

In the educational context, AI is currently being applied in admission decisions and course scheduling. In a study by Chen and Do (2014), the authors mention that "an accurate prediction of students' academic performance is of importance for making decisions around admission as well as providing better educational services in the wider scheme of things" (p. 18). Within the literature, Zawacki-Richter et al. (2019) identified four articles that aimed to predict the probability of a prospective student being admitted to university. These studies have been implemented in Turkey, for instance, in Acikkar and Akay (2009), where few candidates were selected for a school for Physical Education and Sports in Turkey based on their physical abilities, respective scores in the National Selection and Placement Examination, and their prior graduation grade point average (GPA). The study adopted a support vector machine (SVM) algorithm for classifying the student admission decision and the model was able to predict admission decisions to an accuracy of 97.17% in 2006 and 90.51% in 2007. Another study, Andris, Cowen, and Wittenbach (2013) also applied the SVM to identify spatial patterns that may benefit prospective college students originating from specific geographic regions in the USA. Moreso, Kardan, Sadeghi, Ghidary, and Sani (2013) also presented a study that empirically analysed data to find the factors that influence student course selection, which include course and instructor characteristics, workload, mode of delivery and examination time, to develop a predictive model for course selection prediction. The model comprised an Artificial Neural Network (ANN) and was tested on two Computer Engineering and Information Technology Masters programs. In another study, the authors in Feng, Zhou, and Liu (2011) analysed enrolment data from 25 Chinese provinces as training data to predict the registration rates in other provinces using an ANN.

## AI AND TEACHING/LEARNING IN HIGHER EDUCATION

The adoption of new technologies for learning and teaching has rapidly evolved over the past decades. Consequently, the adoption of speech-to-text, text-to-speech, predictive text, assistive typing, spell checking, and search engines constitute examples of technologies that impacted teaching and learning. Today, these technologies constitute daily living and are generic features in many devices, such as, personal computers, mobile phones, and wearable devices. Similarly, AI is enhancing the devices and tools used in educational campuses worldwide. Ranging from the basic Siri in the iPhone or Alexa in Google devices, this low complexity AI solution comprises a set of intelligent algorithms that can be used as a virtual assistant. Google maps, used by almost everyone, incorporates AI into its map searching, and is now being integrated to smart vehicles. Consequently, the students are now in the forefront of a plethora of opportunities and possibilities for learning and teaching, incorporating AI.

The growing interest in the use and application of AI is gaining traction in the higher education sector (universities). The most likely reason for the accelerated adoption of AI in higher education will be due to financial pressure related to the increasing number of higher education students. The shift towards Massive Open Online Courses (MOOCs) has also presented universities with potential means of cutting teaching staff. In the UK, some universities have adopted the trend, for instance, University of Warwick, which created a new department completely from casual teaching staff, which functions in a way like outsourced staff.

Current students quickly embrace the novelties in learning. Currently, human-AI interaction could be facilitated by transferring the existing knowledge from tools helping people with disabilities. These solutions can stimulate teachers to employ them in education to augment learners and teachers for a more engaging process. The notion of cyborgs, which refer to "a crossbreed of a human and a machine" (Mitcham, 2005), are no longer as far away as we may envisage, as the potential to combine human capacities with new technologies are already being implemented at an accelerated pace. At the rate of technological advancement, most disability will be gone in 50 years" (de Lange, 2015). Hugh Herr, director of the Biomechatronics group at the MIT Media Lab and works Harvard–MIT Division of Health Sciences and Technology, reports about the progress the company is making in producing technologically-advanced prosthetics and exoskeletons, as well as pioneering bionic technology for people living with a disability. Complex systems exploiting machine learning algorithms can engage in in complex processing tasks between humans and machines that can be employed in education and learning. This opens to a new age for higher education institutions.

This type of human-like machine interaction and system presents the instantaneous potential to change the way one learns, accesses, and creates information. However, it remains to be seen how long it will take to implement this kind of application to augment human memory and reasoning. Whichever way, if the current wave of AI and technological advancement cause a shift in the focus of 'cyborgs' from the perspective of science-fiction to reality by augmenting the capacities of for teachers and students, it is promising to apply cyborgs in teaching and research in universities. It is only a matter of time before the recent wave of enthusiasm and investments in artificial intelligence impacts on universities. The most probable factor will relate to financial pressures that come with the multitude of students undertaking higher education, mainly enforced by the universalisation of higher education. Consequently, the international student market will pose itself as a convincing motivation to adopt AI solutions. The current 'outsourcing' of academic staff, evident in the low number of academics and tenured positions, is now a discussion that is open to an overthrow by intelligent machines (Grove, 2015). In the UK, there have been various proposals to adopt a similar approach, for instance in the University of Warwick, where a new department has been created to employ only casual teaching staff and outsource teaching (Gallagher, 2017). The notion of humanity and the possibilities of humans stand to be redefined by technology at an accelerated pace. In summary, technology is rapidly growing the potential to use AI functions to augment human skills and abilities. However, it is useful to mention the quote by Andreas Schleicher, "Innovation in education is not just a matter of putting more technology into more classrooms; it is about changing approaches to teaching so that students acquire the skills they need to thrive in competitive global economies"(Schleicher, 2015).

## THE IMPACT OF AI IN HIGHER EDUCATION

Within the literature, that AI opens a new discussion on teaching and learning in higher education (Ciolacu et al., 2018; Vohra and Das, 2011; Xing and Marwala, 2017). Existing studies mention that AI is not ready to replace lecturers yet, however, it can augment or supplement them. The existing evidence of AI-based algorithms facilitate daily human routines, for instance credit scores checking, loan applications to employment shortlisting, which could be re-implemented for similar tasks in higher education domain. This vital crossroad demands a cautious investigation from an academic standpoint, as this can enable the identification of technological advancement as a potential replacement of the facets of pedagogical work. When properly applied, the potential of integrating AI within higher education extends possibilities for teaching, learning, and research. This section discusses about the evolving field of artificial intelligence in higher education.

Over the world, AI is advancing at an accelerated pace, and now impacts almost all facet of human endeavour including teaching and learning. A typical example of this can be found when universities use an emergent form of AI, IBM Watson. The IBM Watson is currently being deployed and used to provide student advice for Deakin University in Australia and therefore allows 24/7 advice 365 days of the year (Eassom, 2015). Although being used to perform simple repetitive and comparatively predictable tasks that can be performed by existing and complex algorithms, the application of Watson represents a prime illustration of the potential impact of AI on the organisational staff profile in higher education institutions. This represents a paradigm change in terms of the quality of service, high turnaround for time within the university, and improve the organisation of its workforce.

The main objective of AI in higher education teaching and learning is to enhance human intellectual capability to enhance the educational development, rather than to constrain it to be represented as a set of procedures for content delivery, regulation, and assessment. With the emergence of AI, it is particularly pertinent for educational institutions to remain ready if the 'power of control' over the antecedent algorithms that run them is not dominated by technical powers. In the work of Frank Pasquale (2015), 'The Black Box Society', he states that decisions that were previously based on 'human reflection' are now made automatically. In typical software engineering and development, the software "encodes thousands of rules and commands that are computed within a fraction of a second" (Pasquale 2015). Consequently, humans do not only have a 'quasi-concentrated and powerful domination' over this software, but also face an unintended lack of transparency about algorithms and how they are used. The programmers who control algorithms that run AI systems now have unparalleled and proxy influence over people and every sector of a contemporary society. The internal machinations of mega-corporations such as the GAFA – Google, Amazon, Facebook and Apple – do not follow an egalitarian model, but those of generous autocrats who know the 'best practice' and enforce or implement these – with no consultation – on their internal or external subjects. Higher education learning is contemptuous when the freedom of thinking and analysis is stifled in any way or form, as manipulations and the limitation of the knowledge about the AI systems misrepresents and cancels in-depth comprehension and the consequent advancement of knowledge. If the further advancement of AI gets to a point where the agenda of universities is set by a handful of technological 'big guns', as well as the monopoly of their information and the ethos of universities, then higher education is likely going to be heading to a very different age. These set of potential threats is too critical to be ignored and unexplored with mettle and caution.

## BENEFITS OF AI IN HIGHER EDUCATION

Many opportunities exist for adopting AI in higher education. For instance, the continuous increase in student numbers, cost of staffing, and external financial pressures suggest universities to adopt new technologies as a measure to survive. This is evident with massive open online courses (MOOCs), which imply no physical space for teaching, more students for a single lecturer and online means of interaction. This enables universities to increase their market share worldwide. Soon became apparent that the key challenge is to extend the human ability of tutors to actively interact with a large numbers of students studying from different time zones, at different progress rates and background knowledge. The unresolved challenge is how to assist students to progress efficiently through the learning encounter to achieve their set of goals. In an article by Sian Bayne, she states that the current standpoint of automated methods in teaching "are driven by a productivity-oriented solutionism," not by a pedagogical perceptive, so it is necessary to re-explore a humanistic perception for mass education to switch the "cold technocratic imperative" (Bayne, 2015). The author makes this claim on the grounds of her experience obtained by the creation and delivery of a MOOC by the University of Edinburgh. The course had about 90,000 students from over 200 countries. It is evident that MOOCs continue to be perceived as a different type of online course, interesting and beneficial, but not aimed at or capable of changing the structure and function of universities. Research about this theme reflects the inability of MOOCs to deliver on the potential promises of its many proponents.

## CHALLENGES OF AI IN HIGHER EDUCATION

Within the literature, there are various levels of AI mentioned, though only a limited number of articles provide an unequivocal description of the term "Artificial Intelligence". The authors theorise AI as intelligent computer systems with human-like features, such as the ability to memorise knowledge, to perceive and manipulate their environment in a similar way as humans, and to understand human natural language. The broad challenges of AI centre around privacy, the use of AI in human-centric activities, cost of development and the absence of teacher-like presence. These are discussed below.

### Privacy

In today's world, the availability of interconnectivity leads to data ubiquity. However, there is growing concern about the issue of privacy and confidentiality in data sharing and globality. Findings from studies have shown that the wider public will express loud concerns about privacy of their personal information, but be less than cautious about protecting it (Dwyer et al., 2007; Kaur et al., 2019). Although majority of the information available to artificial intelligent systems are optional, it still raises concerns, thereby making students gradually more uncomfortable with revealing a great deal of personal information online. Therefore, a critical concern for students in this context is privacy. Typical questions that arise from these concerns are 'how is my private data handled?' 'Who (else) has access to the information?' In terms of AI for educational purposes, 'whose role is it – student, educator or technology applicator – to ensure the student or educator understands his/her right to privacy and applies it accordingly?' Consequently, privacy is a key obstacle that has plagued the widespread adoption of AI in higher education. Furthermore, privacy raises a vital point of concern in the application of agent-based systems in higher education. As presented above, AI-based intelligent systems can unconventionally learn and memorise many students' personal information, for instance, learning style, efficiency and capability. Moreover, personal information is meant to be confidential and not to be learned by a third party. Many students may not be willing for others to know their confidential information, such as learning styles, deficiencies and/or capabilities. The consequence of this is that students may raise concerns over possible discrimination from tutors or educators relating to learning academic performance due to special learning needs. Therefore, the issue of privacy must be solved before adopting agent-based artificial intelligent systems for teaching and learning technologies.

## AI in Human-Centric Activities

Although advancement in the fields of machine learning and artificial intelligence opens up novel opportunities (and challenges) for higher education, it is pertinent to mention at this point that education is exceedingly a human-centric venture, rather than a technology-centric one. Consequently, notwithstanding the rapid progression in AI, the notion of solely relying on the technology is a precarious conduit. Furthermore, it is critical to focus attention on the fact that humans can and should identify difficulties, critique, detect risks, and query pertinent aspects that range from issues such as explain-ability, justification, rationale, confidentiality, and control to the requirement of nurturing ingenuity and opens the door to luck or chance and unanticipated paths in teaching and learning. The excitement of the emergence and universality of AI can lead to an undisputed remedy that can leave many potential higher education learners susceptible to the wheels of reality, for instance, that tragic event of the driverless car – a system that was considered to be a perfect software – accident.

## Absence of Classroom Feel and Cost

A typical adoption of intelligent technology in education is evident in distance learning schemes. Although it has many benefits, distance education opens new challenges to teaching and learning. First, online students lack reciprocal face-to-face contact with their educators, meaning that it is more problematic for them to know each other and build interactive, collaborative interactions like in the conventional classroom. Therefore, in online learning or education, they may find it difficult to choose appropriate classmates for group projects. For instance, some group members may not turn up and/or contribute less to the group coursework because many online or adult students have busy work and family schedules. This typically triggers disagreements among group members. In fact, many online instructors acknowledge that many of their conventional teaching pedagogies are ineffective in the virtual classroom. Occasionally, a single online course system does not include all the fundamental functions for online teaching, and instructors – therefore – must adopt other auxiliary tools. For example, Blackboard currently does not have a screen-sharing ability, therefore instructors must use the screen-sharing function of other platforms (i.e. Skype, etc.) to exhibit how to use a given computer software. Another challenge of applying

*Table 1. A summary of the benefits and challenges that helped to form our conclusions*

| Benefits | Challenges |
|---|---|
| Promotes automated teaching methods | Privacy issues, namely users feeling uncomfortable about using their personal information on the internet |
| Promotes collaboration between students and teachers through ubiquitous technologies | AI in Human-Centric Activities |
| Encourages student enrolment | Absence of Classroom Feel and Cost |
| Efficient and timely feedback | |

AI in higher education is mentioned in (Welham, 2008), which relates to the costs and time involved in developing and sustaining AI-based methods. This cost refers to amounts in terms of financial and manpower resources that many public educational institutions cannot afford.

## CONCLUSION

The prospect of the application of AI has made it impossible to ignore constant discussions about the potential impacts of the adoption of AI in the higher education teaching and learning, as well as how universities will adapt to this trend. The threat of technological innovation and the attendant job 'transposition' and replacement implies that there is need for equipping students with requisite skillsets to thrive and remain relevant. Consequently, this calls for a reconsideration of teaching curricula and pedagogical underpinnings. The use of technological solutions to detect plagiarism, provide feedback, etc. already contribute to questioning who is responsible for the teaching and learning agenda. In summary, the time is now right for universities to reconsider their core teaching and pedagogical models with relation to AI solutions and their proprietors. Additionally, higher education institutions should explore the plethora of opportunities (and challenges) opened by the prospect to embrace AI in teaching and learning. These elucidations can present new opportunities for teaching and learning in education, while encouraging long-term learning in a reinforced pedagogical model that can retain the integrity of core values and strengthen the cause for higher education.

The absolute consequences of AI development cannot be predicted today, but it appears to be very probable that AI applications will turn out to be a critical enabler for educational adoption of technology for the foreseeable future. Consequently, AI-based systems have a high potential to provide extensive support to students, lecturers, and faculty members throughout the student lifecycle. Two basic applications of AI in education have been presented in this chapter and provide immense pedagogical prospects for integrating intelligent systems to education, as well as tools capable of supporting student learning in advanced, conducive, and personalised learning environments. This potential is applicable in large higher education institutions (HEIs), where artificial intelligence and education might assist in overcoming the predicament of delivering access to higher education for large number of students. This could also be supplemented with other ubiquitous technologies such as cloud computing which can further enhance the teaching and learning experience through the provision of interactive content via a range of mobile devices on the go and outside of the traditional classroom.

## REFERENCES

Acikkar, M., & Akay, M. F. (2009). Support vector machines for predicting the admission decision of a candidate to the School of Physical Education and Sports at Cukurova University. *Expert Systems with Applications*, *36*(3), 7228–7233. doi:10.1016/j.eswa.2008.09.007

Andris, C., Cowen, D., & Wittenbach, J. (2013). Support vector machine for spatial variation. *Transactions in GIS*, *17*(1), 41–61. doi:10.1111/j.1467-9671.2012.01354.x

Bayne, S. (2015). Teacherbot: Interventions in automated teaching. *Teaching in Higher Education*, *20*(4), 455–467. doi:10.1080/13562517.2015.1020783

Chen, J.-F., & Do, Q. H. (2014). Training neural networks to predict student academic performance: A comparison of cuckoo search and gravitational search algorithms. *International Journal of Computational Intelligence and Applications*, *13*(01), 1450005. doi:10.1142/S1469026814500059

Ciolacu, M., Tehrani, A. F., Binder, L., & Svasta, P. M. (2018). Education 4.0-Artificial Intelligence Assisted Higher Education: Early recognition System with Machine Learning to support Students' Success. In *2018 IEEE 24th International Symposium for Design and Technology in Electronic Packaging (SIITME)*. IEEE.

Collins, C., Andrienko, N., Schreck, T., Yang, J., Choo, J., Engelke, U., Jena, A., & Dwyer, T. (2018). Guidance in the human–machine analytics process. *Visual Informatics*, *2*(3), 166–180. doi:10.1016/j.visinf.2018.09.003

De Lange, C. (2015). Welcome to the bionic dawn. *New Scientist*, *227*(3032), 24–25. doi:10.1016/S0262-4079(15)30881-2

Dwyer, C., Hiltz, S., & Passerini, K. (2007). Trust and privacy concern within social networking sites: A comparison of Facebook and MySpace. *AMCIS 2007 Proceedings*, 339.

Eassom, S. (2015). IBM Watson for education. *IBM Insights on Business, 1.*

Feng, S., Zhou, S., & Liu, Y. (2011). Research on data mining in university admissions decision-making. *International Journal of Advancements in Computing Technology*, *3*(6), 176–186. doi:10.4156/ijact.vol3.issue6.21

Gallagher, P. (2017, Sept. 24). The University of Warwick launches new department to employ all temporary or fixed-term teaching staff. *The Independent*.

Grove, J. (2015). Teach Higher 'disbanded' ahead of campus protest. *Times Higher Education, 2.*

Hall, W., & Pesenti, J. (2019). *Growing the Artificial Intelligence Industry in the UK*. Academic Press.

Kardan, A. A., Sadeghi, H., Ghidary, S. S., & Sani, M. R. F. (2013). Prediction of student course selection in online higher education institutes using neural network. *Computers & Education*, *65*, 1–11. doi:10.1016/j.compedu.2013.01.015

Kaur, R., Sharma, M., & Taruna, S. (2019). Privacy Preserving Data Mining Model for the Social Networking. In *2019 6th International Conference on Computing for Sustainable Global Development (INDIACom)*. IEEE.

Lazarus, S. S., Thurlow, M. L., Lail, K. E., & Christensen, L. (2009). A longitudinal analysis of state accommodations policies: Twelve years of change, 1993—2005. *The Journal of Special Education*, *43*(2), 67–80. doi:10.1177/0022466907313524

Luckin, R. (2017). The implications of artificial intelligence for teachers and schooling. *Future Frontiers: Education for an AI World*, 109–126.

Mitcham, C. (2005). *Encyclopaedia of science, technology, and ethics*. Academic Press.

Mueck, M., & Karls, I. (2018). *Networking Vehicles to Everything: Evolving Automotive Solutions*. Walter de Gruyter GmbH & Co KG.

Pasquale, F. (2015). *The black box society*. Harvard University Press. doi:10.4159/harvard.9780674736061

Poonia, P., Jain, V. K., & Kumar, A. (2018). Short Term Traffic Flow Prediction Methodologies: A Review. *Mody University International Journal of Computing and Engineering Research*, *2*, 37–39.

Russell, S., & Norvig, P. (2016). *Artificial intelligence: a modern approach*. Academic Press.

Schleicher, A. (2015). *Schools for 21st-Century Learners: Strong Leaders, Confident Teachers, Innovative Approaches*. International Summit on the Teaching Profession. ERIC. doi:10.1787/9789264231191-en

Vohra, R., & Das, N. N. (2011). Intelligent decision support systems for admission management in higher education institutes. *International Journal of Artificial Intelligence & Applications*, *2*(4), 63–70. doi:10.5121/ijaia.2011.2406

Wang, J., Ma, Y., Zhang, L., Gao, R. X., & Wu, D. (2018). Deep learning for smart manufacturing: Methods and applications. *Journal of Manufacturing Systems*, *48*, 144–156. doi:10.1016/j.jmsy.2018.01.003

Welham, D. (2008). AI in training (1980–2000): Foundation for the future or misplaced optimism? *British Journal of Educational Technology*, *39*(2), 287–296. doi:10.1111/j.1467-8535.2008.00818.x

Xing, B., & Marwala, T. (2017). Implications of the fourth industrial age for higher education. *The Thinker, 73*.

Zawacki-Richter, O., Marín, V. I., Bond, M., & Gouverneur, F. (2019). Systematic review of research on artificial intelligence applications in higher education–where are the educators? *International Journal of Educational Technology in Higher Education*, *16*(1), 39. doi:10.118641239-019-0171-0

## ADDITIONAL READING

Adamson, D., Dyke, G., Jang, H., & Rosé, C. P. (2014). Towards an agile approach to adapting dynamic collaboration support to student needs. *International Journal of Artificial Intelligence in Education*, *24*(1), 92–124. doi:10.100740593-013-0012-6

André, E., Baker, R., Hu, X., Rodrigo, M. M. T., & du Boulay, B. (2017). *Artificial Intelligence in Education: 18th International Conference, AIED 2017, Wuhan, China, June 28 – July 1, 2017, Proceedings*. Springer International Publishing. https://books.google.co.uk/books?id=SWgpDwAAQBAJ

Baker, T., & Anissa, N. (2019). *Educ-AI-tion rebooted? Exploring the future of artificial intelligence in schools and colleges.* Retrieved 4th Apr from https://media.nesta.org.uk/documents/Future_of_AI_and_education_v5_WEB.pdf

Goralski, M. A., & Tan, T. K. (2020). Artificial intelligence and sustainable development. *International Journal of Management Education*, *18*(1), 100330. doi:10.1016/j.ijme.2019.100330

Hinojo-Lucena, F.-J., Aznar-Díaz, I., Cáceres-Reche, M.-P., & Romero-Rodríguez, J.-M. (2019). Artificial intelligence in higher education: A bibliometric study on its impact in the scientific literature. *Education in Science*, *9*(1), 51. doi:10.3390/educsci9010051

Huang, S.-P. (2018). Effects of using artificial intelligence teaching system for environmental education on environmental knowledge and attitude. *Eurasia Journal of Mathematics, Science and Technology Education*, *14*(7), 3277–3284. doi:10.29333/ejmste/91248

Zawacki-Richter, O., Marín, V. I., Bond, M., & Gouverneur, F. (2019). Systematic review of research on artificial intelligence applications in higher education–where are the educators? *International Journal of Educational Technology in Higher Education*, *16*(1), 39. doi:10.118641239-019-0171-0

## KEY TERMS AND DEFINITIONS

**Artificial Intelligence:** A computer or robot's ability to perform human tasks, while developing knowledge.

**E-Learning:** Learning via online platforms or technologies.

**Higher Education:** University-focused education in which undergraduate, postgraduate, and doctoral courses are taught.

**ICT Adoption:** The acceptance of information communication technologies in organisations.

**Machine Learning:** Making computers learn without being programmed.

**Teaching Systems:** Systems that aim to facilitate teaching and learning practices.

# Chapter 6
# Exploring Datafication for Teaching and Learning Development:
## A Higher Education Perspective

**Mark Schofield**
*UK Academic Consultations, UK*

## ABSTRACT

*The scale, magnitude, and diversity of higher education teaching/learning and higher education institutions (HEIs) have resulted in corresponding diverse datafication representations. Contrary to conventional datafication, where the objective is profitability (e.g., adopting facial recognition for improved policing), the datafication of HEIs should be analysed, understood, and interpreted for its unique diversity, practice, and consequences. The result of the COVID-19 pandemic has forced a paradigm shift from conventional/traditional classroom-based teaching to online teaching, which has resulted in enhanced data collection. Taking a post-digital perspective on modern practices in higher education literature, this chapter argues for an organic view, in which the datafication must consider the aspects of teaching, learning, and educational context that are absent in digital data. The findings from the discussion lead to the conclusion that datafication can complement expert judgement in HEIs when informed by the unification of pedagogy and technology.*

## INTRODUCTION

The notion of datafication refers to rendering the social and natural world in machine-readable format. It involves the continuous transformation of the social, material elements and activities in our world to digital data. Furthermore, this transformation is succeeded by the transformation/analysis of the resulting data as comparable to its original source. Datafication is a prevalent phenomenon throughout society and humanity, in general (Beer, 2016). Besides influencing our comprehension and perception of healthcare, the military, commerce, tourism, etc., datafication has quickly permeated the teaching and learning in

DOI: 10.4018/978-1-7998-4846-2.ch006

education, as well as the higher education teaching and learning. The main objective of education is the impartation of quality teaching and knowledge in the mind of the learner that can be reproduced whenever called upon. However, a measure of teaching quality is not easy to come by and perhaps might be elusive due to its simplicity. According to Beer (2016), a prerequisite to the datafication of any element, component, or activity is the construction of a unit of measurement. Furthermore, while there exist many forms of measuring teaching quality, for instance, by measuring student engagement. Within literature, there is not a consensus about the definition of student engagement. There exists diverse interpretations of what student engagement can be referred. Conventionally, student engagement typically denotes the accumulation of students in higher educational institutional groups or boards, and their respective active/on-going involvement in the activities that occur in the institutions (Kuh & Hu, 2001). A recursive definition of student engagement can be found in Trowler, (2010) where the author described student engagement as the field of research "…concerned with the interaction between time, effort and other resources invested by both students and their HEIs intended to enhance the student experience …". This definition implies that student engagement is the product of a partnership/collaboration between the tutors and learners in their HEIs.

In recent times, there is a gradual, yet consistent, datafication of higher education teaching and learning. For instance, activities, learning outcomes and formative/summative feedback relating to teaching and learning are continually being 'datafied' and the resulting digital signatures are analysed and collected in the form of marks, student satisfaction scores, surveys, attendance monitoring, sickness absence reporting, administration, teaching enhanced learning, technology-led student feedback, marking turnaround times, learning analytics, and more. The consequences of this datafication extend way beyond education and pedagogy, into issues of politics, economics and social fairness, as can be perceived through a thorough investigation of two measurement paradigms – outcomes and student satisfaction. The outcomes of pedagogy (for instance, grades, work and salary) and student satisfaction surveys both deliver valuable information as a subset of a universal picture that can be used to develop a true picture of the quality of education or educational quality delivered. However, these measures are arguably unsuitable when considered as segregated substitutions for quality. First, the outcome measures focus on the result without interrogating if the efforts applied towards achieving these are concentrated in a desirable path (Biesta, 2009). In other words, the outcome measures neglect the value of exploration and critical thinking, and arguably the process of pedagogy, including teaching and learning and how this integrates with the specific needs of the students, or the societal current/prevalent needs (Naidoo & Williams, 2015). Furthermore, these metrics tend to be positioned towards measuring short-term goals rather than long-term solidity. The tutors consequently experience these pressures in the form of a persistent drive to "improve teaching standards" and whilst these test scores or outcome scores were generated to measure the output, they are in turn used as a performance yardstick to compare teachers against themselves, create league tables for schools and, gradually, ranking nation against nation (Steiner-Khamsi, 2003). A vital component that influences these advances is the transformation of complex educational procedures into digital (data) signatures, which can be used to sort, order, benchmark, compare and rank.

From the foregoing, the focus of this chapter is to discuss the role of datafication in pedagogy, as well as critically articulate the approaches to understanding tutelage and the apparent resistance triggered by the resultant 'theoretical' polarity within critical traditions. In using frame theory, this chapter argues that it is possible to seam together competing perspectives, and thereby develop a theoretical diversity necessary for understanding contemporary developments in teaching and learning in higher education institutions.

## EDUCATION-ORIENTATED DATAFICATION

The growing popularity of the notion 'datafication', especially the ubiquity of data and resultant algorithms presents novel methods of measuring, collecting, describing and representing social life with digits. The higher education sector is one of the most conspicuous spheres influenced by datafication, due to the fact that datafication transforms not only the ways in which the activities of teaching and learning are structured, but also the manner in which the future compeers currently do and will create reality with (and through) data. As previously mentioned, the datafication of higher education comprises the collection of data across all levels of the educational systems, including the individual, classroom, school, region, state, international, etc., about all the processes involved in the teaching, learning and management of the entire pedagogical endeavour. This proliferation of data disrupt conventional decision-making and opinion-forming procedures for educational stakeholders, such as the development of educational policies, school management, authorities, teachers, students and parents. For example, the collected data are used to enhance the development in the school, hold schools and teachers answerable, control access to schooling or to compare student achievements across countries. A use case of such raises anticipations with respect to amplified transparency, culpability, service orientation and civic contribution, but also attendant worries with respect to surveillance and control, confidentiality issues, power relations, and (novel) inequalities (Anagnostopoulos et al., 2013; Eynon, 2013; Livingstone & Sefton-Green, 2016; Lupton & Williamson, 2017).

Focusing on the educational sector, there is the availability of diverse and magnanimous amounts of data being generated intentionally for observing, surveying or assessment purposes. However, there is also some automatically generated data that is obtained via routine processes from a plethora of digital devices and systems that produce 'digital traces' (Hepp et al., 2018). In HEIs, for example, their structures are gradually being converted into 'data platforms' wherein 'a wide range of data tracking, sensing and analytics technologies are being mobilised' (Williamson, 2015). These digital data are dissimilar to 'non-digital' forms of data, as they may have the propensity to be exhaustive in scope, greatly detailed, and can be combined with a great flexibility and at different levels of aggregation. Such opportunities have previously always occurred on small or medium scales, but new data substructures and the plethora of predictive algorithms, resulting in advanced analytical capabilities allow for analytics of an unparalleled intricacy and scale. However, the causal algorithms and the manners in which the data are produced by the various HEIs or data providers, mathematicians as well as the role of software companies and educational technology providers are hardly understood.

From the foregoing, with the growing bid to expand the metric power from higher education institutions (HEIs) scaling across the social, cultural, economic and political practices, there is a resultant and dramatic increase in the applicability and execution of datafication within the educational sector. The increasing and persistent demands of quantifiable accountability (from sponsors, stakeholders, shareholders, parents, regulatory bodies, etc.), global large-scale assessments (resulting from the globalisation and multi-ethnicity of higher education), relative performance benchmarking, and the propagation of evaluation criteria or indicators in higher education together comprise a long lineage of what is referred to as accountability in governance or 'governance by numbers' (Piattoeva & Boden, 2020). Amongst the broader social, fiscal and partisan eagerness for 'big data', machine learning (ML) and artificial intelligence (AI), novel and emerging technologies, such as learning analytics, adaptive 'personalised learning' platforms, and robotic teaching assistants have all now been developed, presented, and in the early stages of being fully adopted to be implemented by education institutions. Recently, there has been a rapid and widespread integration of datafication in higher education, evident in the permeation of AI/ML, for instance, systems such as facial recognition (Andrejevic & Selwyn, 2019), student recruitment (Dennis, 2018) and 'emotion AI', which adopts new technology based on wearable biosensors, body gesture and facial expression analysis (McStay, 2018).

Specifically considering the higher education sector and higher education institutions (HEIs) in particular over the past two decades, there has been a rapid, widespread and dramatic increase in the scope of the collection and application of university data. This can be seen as a consequence of momentous struggles by the ruling and opposition political parties and businesses, focus groups, consultancies and sector agencies (Williamson, 2017). For this reason, research metrics are applied towards the audition, comparison, and assessment of the quality of research outputs, which is applied for the determination of the research quality and impact (Wilsdon, 2016). Besides, the rating of the specific university teaching quality and the 'value' of academic labour has rapidly amplified 'quantified control' and overabundance of the application of measurement metrics in the universities (Burrows, 2012). The proliferation of university rankings and league tables brings with it produce new types of responsive performances, as these institutions and individuals constantly seek for ways of maximising performance in terms of the measurement metrics, which they are scored on. Furthermore, the emergence of digital technologies and increasing research and global interests in 'big data' have now engorged the space of metric measurement across education systems, resulting in the increased fidelity of data analyses, enhancing the endorsement and application of data for various forms of audits, inspections, evaluations and decision-making (Dede et al., 2016). On the other hand, a political swing towards the gathering of student data is accelerating the development of significant technological developments and organisational activity. In other words, there is an increasing focus within the sector to increasingly more closely measuring and comparing students' benefits from learning, as well as student engagement, which quantifies student engagement. Conventionally, student engagement typically denoted the accumulation of students in higher educational institutional groups or boards, and their respective active/on-going involvement in the activities that occur in the institutions (Kuh and Hu 2001). In other words, student engagement should not be only described by something that can be measured using the subjective descriptives that are assessed only based on the form of learning outcomes.

Over the past two decades, however, there has been a constantly increasing research interest towards the definition of a more inclusive understanding of student engagement. Recently, the advancement of technologies, such as predictive learning analytics, technology-enhanced learning (TEL) and AI-led applications, originally produced from the recompense of in university research centres and labs, have now extended across the sector to execute these functions (Shum & Luckin, 2019). Consequently, student performance measures, mawkishness, engagement, and satisfaction are also treated as substitute measures of the performance of university staff, course modules, respective schools, and the institutions as a whole, leading to new claims that HE quality can be adduced from the analysis of large-scale student data (Williamson 2019).

## DATAFICATION OF TEACHING AND LEARNING IN HE

### The Role of Datafication in Higher Education (HE)

The ubiquity of 'data' collected via digital information systems through a process of datafication has emerged as a globally increasing topic and problem in recent times. For corporations, the increasing access to digital data is potentially a source of 'business intelligence' used to enhance decision-making, make efficient savings and gather profit. All over the world, governments are analysing data to obtain insight into its citizens' behaviours and understand wider social trends that can be applied to inform policymaking. Besides, there are drawbacks resulting from the use of data, for instance, when these data are used for more controversial purposes. Newly, Facebook user data was wrongly used by the data analytics consultancy, Cambridge Analytica, to 'micro-target' political advertising to voters in the 2016 EU referendum and US elections, while data breaches have become a common event. As political, commercial and public consciousness has increased around data controversies, there has been a corresponding increased understanding by researchers about the consequences and moral/ethical facet of data, analytics, algorithms and artificial intelligence (Sheikh, 2020).

Specifically focusing on the field of higher education teaching and learning or pedagogy, however, data has remained comparatively under-researched. It must however be mentioned that significant theoretical and technical developments in learning analytics, adaptive learning software, and artificial intelligence has arisen from academia, industry, groups, and government sources alike (Williamson 2017). Consequently, data obtained from HEIs can be used to provide insight into the processes of learning, the effects of pedagogies, curriculum design, and learning gain over time, especially as researchers in 'education data science' develop increasingly fine-tuned technologies and methods. Furthermore, the adoption of artificial intelligence (AI) now enhances tools and instruments used daily in metropolises and campuses around the world. Ranging from internet search engines, smartphone features and apps, to public transport and household appliances. A popular application of artificial intelligence in today's world is the complex set of algorithms that drives the iPhone's Siri and represents a classic example of AI solutions that have now permeated everyday life (Luckin, 2017). Google adopts AI to drive its search engines and maps, and all new automobiles use AI for a variety of tasks ranging from engine diagnostics to preventive maintenance and navigation. Furthermore, self-driving technology is already at an advanced stage, and some companies have made this a top priority, for instance, Tesla, Volvo, Mercedes, and Google (Mueck & Karls, 2018). This represents a major step towards altering the complex effort of integrating education and AI. Moreover, the data collected from HEIs may be used to predict the outcomes of student learning, detect risks, and 'personalise' the education system around individuals' needs (Ciolacu et al., 2018). A profitable industry in data-driven and analytical educational technologies has flourished on claims that data indicate a shift from uniform tests to adaptive, 'real-time' assessment technologies, and from school census data to personalised tracking and profiling (Boninger & Molnar, 2016). Such data-driven procedures are upsetting the primary education institutions, secondary, and higher education alike, often with accidental and perverse consequences (Bradbury & Roberts-Holmes, 2018; Manolev et al., 2019).

## Data Literacies and Inequalities

In today's world, there is a plethora of personal devices and crowd-led or social media platforms, such as Google, Facebook, Twitter and Amazon, which have collectively resulted in an unprecedented rate of data generation, collection, analysis, and reabsorption. On the one hand, several digital technology users consciously and conscientiously agree to providing masses of their personal and collective data on a daily basis. On the other hand, the data are collected without the individual's knowledge (Edwards & Taborda, 2016). This is evidently the case with individual/personal data, which is generated in droves by individuals on daily basis and often have little or no understanding of where, how or why the data are being collected. Thus, with the proliferation of data ubiquity, in everyday life, the intricacy of non-specialists to understand or decipher these underlying concepts is also becoming increasingly evident. According to Brunton and Nissenbaum (2015), this increasing gulf in knowledge is referred to as 'information asymmetry'. This is a situation where the data about individuals or a an individual is/are collected in situations that are not understood by the data generators, for purposes they definitely do not understand, and are used in ways we are not understand by them, to achieve an end objective that may not be beneficial to them. From the foregoing, resulting from this growing tension, there is an increased recognition of the need that individuals adopt more knowledgeable and critical positions towards how and why their data are being used. To be more specific, this subsection presents and argument in support of the notion of 'Personal Data Literacies'. Personal data refers to any piece of information that can identify an individual. Recently, specific interest has been drawn towards digital forms of personal data, which are drawn from a broad range of software and hardware sources, and take a variety of modes, including numbers, texts, symbols, images, electromagnetic waves, sensor information and sound.

Several devices or systems consciously or unconsciously collect data. For instance, these include data that users give to devices and systems. This might include location information, social media data (including videos, pictures, texts and tweets), emails and videos. The propagation of social media platforms such as Facebook, Instagram and Twitter has accelerated the rate at which these personal data that individuals consciously give to devices and systems are collected. The practices ratified through these platforms are habitually dramatic and controversial, resulting in what are typically perceived as rich and detailed sources of personal information. In another instance, personal data is collected automatically from the user device. These personal data practices are unintentional and include 'surveillance, and harvesting of personal device use, online searches and transactions by policing and security agencies, the Internet/data mining industry, and the development of tools and software that generate, analyse, interpret, and store big data sets' (Lupton & Williamson, 2017). The individual whose actions activate the creation of such personal data often has the least control as companies, governments, researchers and scientists seek to continually analyse and manipulate and reuse any collected information.

From the foregoing, the amplified pervasiveness of these types of personal data across manifold spheres has given rise to a variety of perspectives about the services and capabilities that prerequisite one being 'data literate'. For instance, there are many academic arguments within the computational sciences that mainly focus on highlighting the need for technical skills (Carlson et al., 2011), but information science typically focuses on the aptitude to trace and manage data (Prado & Marzal, 2013). The media and communication organisations perchance provides a more nuanced method to data literacies, where the emphasis is on creating and generating critical comprehensions of the verbal, spectators and representations of the resultant data. These explicit skills and methods can be applied to precise features of digital platforms in a variety of ways.

## Pedagogical Impacts

The bound of advancement in digital technology has surpassed that of pedagogy for the past two decades now. Although many benefits abound, it is well recognised by now that most regular countries only understand on the periphery how digital services and platforms work. Aggravating this challenge, most smart city and home technologies are fixed and in-built, problematic to perceive or analyse. As machine learning and artificial intelligence systems evolve and become more nuanced, automated decision-making becomes even more integrated with everyday life. Pedagogy, in combination with a strong qualitative disposition, can challenge quantification, datafication, and computational logics. In order to fully appreciate the impact of datafication on pedagogy, it is pertinent to involve the tutors or teachers. In a recent study (Roberts-Holmes & Bradbury, 2016), to understand the impact of datafication on pedagogy, a qualitative study was conducted, and the findings revealed that the teachers are sometimes overwhelmed by the datafication process. For instance, rather than challenge or undermine the prevalent regulations, some teachers are forced to intensify their workload to demonstrate constant and uninterrupted progress and development for all children at all times. In the datafication process, every child must be 'tracked' to ensure it is progressing continually. This represents the corrective power of indecision, where there is a great deal of discontent, brought about by a constant self-reforming, self-improving and showing progress. The constant need to demonstrate progress involves the creation of ever more complicated lattices, charts, graphs and tables having acronyms related to colour-codes in relation to their age, recorded as 'developing' and/or 'secure'.

In strict terms, datafication refers to the process of converting various developments, assets, activities and occurrences into forms that are machine-readable by digital technologies (Manolev et al., 2019). Datafication permits entities, relationships, occurrences, and progressions to be analysed for patterns and intuitions, typically today adopting computationally technical processes such as data/predictive analytics, machine learning and artificial intelligence. These data analysis systems rely on complicated algorithms to combine, analyse and make sense of a mammoth amount of individual data points, typically in millions or billions (i.e. big data). As a technical concept, big data has gained popularity in recent years. The technical and informational qualities of datafication in education are momentous due to the fact that they govern how students, tutors, institutions, universities, and systems can be measured, inspected, evaluated, judged and much more. The procedures for an international, large-scale computer assessment, for example, comprises software loaded on computer hardware in schools. Furthermore, network connections permit the student responses to flow to a central storehouse, as well as using spreadsheets for tabularising the results. Besides, servers and storage facilities are employed for storing the data, while security and encryption systems function to keep it safe. Finally, analytic software are used for processing the results prior to visualization programs, which can be used for communicating the analysed results.

In the higher education within the UK, there are streamed efforts being made to link the data captured from institutions' learning management systems, electronic reading lists (for example, from blackboard), and performing learning analytics platforms to other governmental datasets, predominantly through novel infrastructural provisions to permit the interoperability of the data and seamless integration across various platforms (Williamson, 2017). Linking individual-level learning data to other existing parallel data sources results in novel analytical and explanatory possibilities that can foster the development of courses and institutions that contribute to boosting students' learning ability to latter graduate outcomes, careers, and salaries. The potential here is the empowerment of the HEIs higher education institutions and students with intuitions about the courses and tutors/course developers that outperform in terms of quantifiable learning progress and student preparation for high-income graduate roles.

To summarise, datafication introduces the risk of pedagogic miniaturisation, especially when considering that only learning that can be 'datafied' is considered appreciated. In a very recent study, (Brown, 2020) describes the manner in which technologies, such as learning analytics dashboards, impose specific restrictions on how educators perceive their students. In other words, this dashboard introduces limits on the visibility that educators have over their students in their classrooms. It is worthy to mention here that it is in no way implied that the dashboards reduce visibility. After all, in large online courses/ programmes, tutors previously have very partial views of the student engagement, and these dashboards can thus direct the educator's attention to particular features of student activity and learning. As such, it can be pointed out to the tutor warnings like 'engagement' and 'risk of drop-out', which can be easily enumerated and envisaged through the activities of students on digital platforms. However, there is an imminent risk that pedagogy may be reformed to ensure it that it fits with the digital platforms that are required to generate the requisite data required to assess the students' learning. Furthermore, with datafication, as students become converted to quantitative categories, this may lead to a change in the perception of the tutors, as well as how the students see themselves as learners.

## DATAFICATION IN PRACTICE

In recent history, predictive analytics, machine learning and artificial intelligence processes have greatly permeated higher education. Consequently, there is a rapid transformation of existing functions, practices and tasks in higher education to 'machine-readable' ones, achieved by computational, data and digital technologies. This is in addition to the datafication of teaching, learning and administration. In other terms, datafication can be viewed as an advancement in automation and technology, as the processing of digital information by progressively proficient or 'advanced' technologies contribute towards automating a plethora of tasks. The COVID-19 pandemic significantly disrupted all facets of human endeavour, and putting a complete halt to all activities in nearly all sectors of the economy. One of the most affected sectors was the higher education. In the UK and across Europe in general, most teaching and learning in education was forced to be either online or dysfunctional. This meant that there was a shift towards online forms of pedagogical dissemination. From the foregoing, as higher education institutions (HEIs) have now commenced the consideration of a future that is a result of a disruption by Covid-19, it appears greatly probable that there will be a shift towards distant forms of learning, including online, blended, or distance learning. This is characterised by distance learning, datafication and automation.

In this subsection, there is the case for summarising some examples of datafication already in use, and those that are forced due to the COVID-19 pandemic (Table 1). In particular, two key forms of technologies influence datafication and automation, as they have become highlighted and emphasised in their use during the pandemic. These technologies are learning management systems (LMS) and online course modules/programs. Prior to the pandemic, there was a proliferation of the adoption of LMS in higher education, and this has consistently seen a dramatic rise ever since the pandemic. Currently, LMS constitute the fundamental components of the higher education courses globally, and as a result, the proprietary companies that provide these services have been forced to upgrade their services since they have probably gathered datasets from global locations about students. In the UK, the popular LMS include Blackboard, Moodle, and Canvas. A key advantage of LMS is their ability to integrate learning

*Table 1. Summary of Datafied Systems with Examples*

| Datafication Example | Examples | Definition |
|---|---|---|
| Learning Management System (LMS) | Blackboard<br>Moodle | A software application for the administration, documentation, tracking, reporting, automation and delivery of educational courses, training programs, or learning and development programs |
| Learning Experience Platforms (LXP) | AULA LXP | A learning environment that draws on targeted content, social media support, and intelligent recommendation |
| Online Program Management Infrastructures | Coursera<br>FutureLearn<br>Noodle partners<br>2U | A system that provides online services, such as market research, student recruitment and enrolment, course design and technology platforms, student retention, and placement of students in employment or training opportunities |

analytics, using an in-built module or third party collaborations. In recent times, the services provided by these LMS have extended to be used for automated recommender services. In other words, the result from the analytics process is applied towards student recruitment, advanced monitoring, as well as teacher notifications. This has opened up a multi-billion pound business sector that has seen the introduction of a number of new entrants.

In Learning experience platforms (LXP), the system is designed to automate the intelligent discovery and recommendation to the student relevant learning resources. In the UK, the AULA LXP, is adopted by multiple higher education institutions across the UK, and can be seen as a 'digital campus' platform that creates a partnership between academics, helping them design high-quality learning materials to deliver first-class student experiences. The company's 'LMS Data Importer' automates the integration of all content and information from legacy (i.e. older or existing) systems, and the platform also includes an Engagement API for performing in real-time the monitoring of student engagement, which offers personalised, targeted recommendations to educators for the improvement of the student experience.

Another example of datafication of higher education can be seen in online program management infrastructures. These refer to services that enable universities to deliver online/distance education courses. These infrastructures are prevalent in the US and UK, and can be extended to provide comprehensive data analytics within these platforms, thereby offering to the institutions the convenience of automating student tracking/monitoring using learning analytical methods. Popular online program management vendors include Coursera, FutureLearn, Noodle partners, 2U, etc. The company, 2U, provides a personalised operating system known as the 2U operating system (2UOS), which comprises an online teaching/learning platform, data analytics for information generation (about students, technical support, etc.) and incorporates machine learning/artificial intelligence. The 2UOS has prudently offered itself as a critical technology for universities that were able to transition from traditional/conventional classroom-based learning to online teaching during the COVID-19 pandemic.

## Model of Datafied Learning and Teaching in HE

The framework comprises of two datafication cycles: Design and Use. Design refers to the cycle comprising of various activities (e.g. learning and teaching practices) to reach a data practice, while use refers to the cycle that represents the generation, analysis and usage of data used to facilitate learning and teaching practices. Consequently, the use perspective can be seen as a lens for recognising data practices, while the design perspective serves as a methodology.

*Figure 1. Datafication Framework for Learning & Teaching Development in HE*

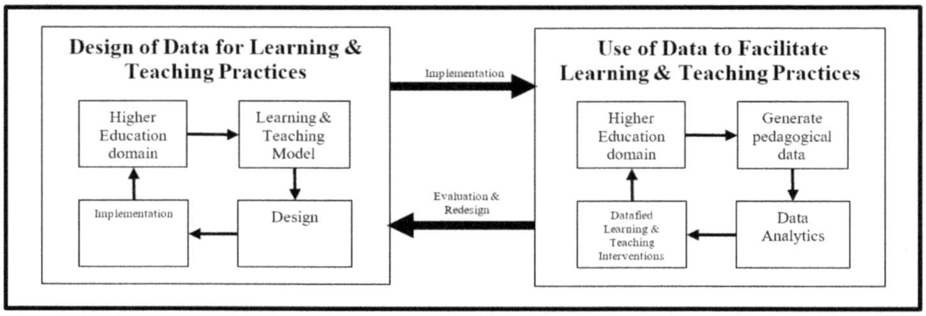


Many HEIs follow a similar datafication model as the one presented in Fig.1. UK universities in particular have engaged in extensive datafied smart campus developments. For example, the University of Northampton has recently established a smart campus complex that has the ability to track a student's location on campus and real-time online tracking of their learning progress, while the Manchester Metropolitan University has recently introduced engagement monitoring, digital wayfinding, lecture capture and cloud access a part of their innovative learning and teaching interventions (UCU, 2020). It can be concluded that despite datafied and automated systems often privileging the view that digital data-processing technologies provide accurate and precise representations of HE, social research on data and metrics argues that data are never entirely accurate since it is generated based on subjective social, institutional and political processes. In a learning and teaching scenario, this refers to the way in which data is generated and for what purpose influences how potential learners will learn from that data. We draw several conclusions as to why this is the case and provide recommendations for improvement going forward.

## CONCLUSION

This chapter has presented a series of literature-driven discussions of datafication in relation to higher education institutions. In addition, the chapter has also discussed the impact, challenges, potentials, and prospects of the proliferation of datafication regarding education, pedagogy, and curriculum design. the purpose of this chapter was to open up for debate, using an academic and literature-driven educational standpoint to elucidate, educate, and provoke constructing discourses with further scrutiny, shining light on the fact that the application of data in education are expected to intensify and escalate over the coming years. However, it is important to mention at this point that this chapter has in no way discounted the prospect of beneficial uses of data to inform pedagogy and curriculum. However, it has shone light on the role of datafication in higher education. Different from conventional datafication, where the main aim is profitability, the datafication of HEIs should be analysed, understood, and interpreted for its unique diversity, practice and consequences. Technologies such as learning analytics and education data science are continuing to mature and polish their methods, including close attention to a broad variety of ethical issues that are existent in literature. The critical perspectives outlined in this chapter, however, point to the enduring need for data literacy to students, subjects, and teachers alike, which will contribute to the antiquity, technicalities, epistemology, social costs, cultural exigence, and politics of datafication in education. Taking a techno-centric perspective on contemporary practices in higher education literature, this chapter presents an argument in support of an all-encompassing perspective, in which the datafication must consider the aspects of teaching, learning, and educational context that are absent in digital data. The findings from the discussion lead to the conclusion that datafication can complement expert judgement in HEIs when informed by the unification of pedagogy and technology. This has led to several key recommendations as follows:

HEIs and policy makers should engage with campus trade unions to promote the increased usage of datafication and automation in higher education. This should involve the establishment of a joint task group, including these trade unions on the use of automation in university settings. The task group includes datafication and automation experts in addition to educational experts to recognise the opportunities and challenges of datafication and automation in HEIs. Another recommendation is the University management should engage in meaningful dialogue with trade union representatives concerning the use of datafication and automation for learning and teaching development. Furthermore, University management should prepare for the expected increase of automation and its impact on pedagogy and academic roles. Formal consultation with appropriate trade unions through locally agreed arrangements should be carried out to inform Universities about the concerns of automation and datafied pedagogy. These recommendations inform future potential research on the role of campus trade unions on the development of datafied and automated pedagogical development in HEIs.

## REFERENCES

Anagnostopoulos, D., Rutledge, S. A., & Jacobsen, R. (2013). Mapping the information infrastructure of accountability. *The Infrastructure of Accountability: Data Use and the Transformation of American Education*, 1–20.

Andrejevic, M., & Selwyn, N. (2019). Facial recognition technology in schools: Critical questions and concerns. *Learning, Media and Technology*, 1–14. doi:10.1080/17439884.2020.1686014

Beer, D. (2016). *Metric power*. Springer. doi:10.1057/978-1-137-55649-3

Biesta, G. (2009). Good education in an age of measurement: On the need to reconnect with the question of purpose in education. *Educational Assessment, Evaluation and Accountability, 21*(1), 33–46.

Boninger, F., & Molnar, A. (2016). *Learning to be watched: Surveillance culture at school*. The Eighteenth Annual Report on Schoolhouse Commercialism Trends. National Center for Education Policy at the University of Colorado at Boulder. Http://Nepc. Colorado. Edu/Files/Publications/RB% 20Boninger-Molnar% 20Trends. Pdf

Bradbury, A., & Roberts-Holmes, G. (2018). How data impacts on early years educators. *Early Years Educator, 19*(10), 38–44. doi:10.12968/eyed.2018.19.10.38

Brown, M. (2020). Seeing students at scale: How faculty in large lecture courses act upon learning analytics dashboard data. *Teaching in Higher Education, 25*(4), 384–400. doi:10.1080/13562517.2019.1698540

Brunton, F., & Nissenbaum, H. (2015). *Obfuscation: A user's guide for privacy and protest*. Mit Press. doi:10.7551/mitpress/9780262029735.001.0001

Burrows, R. (2012). Living with the h-index? Metric assemblages in the contemporary academy. *The Sociological Review*, *60*(2), 355–372. doi:10.1111/j.1467-954X.2012.02077.x

Carlson, J. R., Fosmire, M., Miller, C., & Sapp Nelson, M. (2011). *Determining data information literacy needs: a study of students and research faculty libraries faculty and staff scholarship and research.* Academic Press.

Ciolacu, M., Tehrani, A. F., Binder, L., & Svasta, P. M. (2018). Education 4.0-Artificial Intelligence Assisted Higher Education: Early recognition System with Machine Learning to support Students' Success. *2018 IEEE 24th International Symposium for Design and Technology in Electronic Packaging(SIITME)*, 23–30.

Dede, C. J., Ho, A. D., & Mitros, P. (2016). Big data analysis in higher education: Promises and pitfalls. *EDUCAUSE Review*.

Dennis, M. J. (2018). Artificial intelligence and recruitment, admission, progression, and retention. *Enrollment Management Report*, *22*(9), 1–3. doi:10.1002/emt.30479

Edwards, J. S., & Taborda, E. R. (2016). Using knowledge management to give context to analytics and big data and reduce strategic risk. *Procedia Computer Science*, *99*, 36–49. doi:10.1016/j.procs.2016.09.099

Eynon, R. (2013). *The rise of Big Data: what does it mean for education, technology, and media research?* Taylor & Francis.

Hepp, A., Breiter, A., & Friemel, T. N. (2018). Digital Traces in Context| Digital Traces in Context—An Introduction. *International Journal of Communication*, *12*, 11.

Kuh, G. D., & Hu, S. (2001). The effects of student-faculty interaction in the 1990s. *The Review of Higher Education*, *24*(3), 309–332. doi:10.1353/rhe.2001.0005

Livingstone, S., & Sefton-Green, J. (2016). *The class: Living and learning in the digital age* (Vol. 1). NYU Press. doi:10.18574/nyu/9781479884575.001.0001

Luckin, R. (2017). The implications of artificial intelligence for teachers and schooling. *Future Frontiers: Education for an AI World*, 109–126.

Lupton, D., & Williamson, B. (2017). The datafied child: The dataveillance of children and implications for their rights. *New Media & Society*, *19*(5), 780–794. doi:10.1177/1461444816686328

Manolev, J., Sullivan, A., & Slee, R. (2019). The datafication of discipline: ClassDojo, surveillance and a performative classroom culture. *Learning, Media and Technology*, *44*(1), 36–51. doi:10.1080/17439884.2018.1558237

McStay, A. (2018). Emotional AI: The rise of empathic media. *Sage (Atlanta, Ga.)*.

Mueck, M., & Karls, I. (2018). *Networking Vehicles to Everything: Evolving Automotive Solutions*. Walter de Gruyter GmbH & Co KG.

Naidoo, R., & Williams, J. (2015). The neoliberal regime in English higher education: Charters, consumers and the erosion of the public good. *Critical Studies in Education*, *56*(2), 208–223. doi:10.1080/17508487.2014.939098

Piattoeva, N., & Boden, R. (2020). *Escaping numbers? The ambiguities of the governance of education through data*. Taylor & Francis. doi:10.1080/09620214.2020.1725590

Prado, J. C., & Marzal, M. Á. (2013). Incorporating data literacy into information literacy programs: Core competencies and contents. *Libri*, *63*(2), 123–134.

Roberts-Holmes, G., & Bradbury, A. (2016). The datafication of early years education and its impact upon pedagogy. *Improving Schools*, *19*(2), 119–128. doi:10.1177/1365480216651519

Sheikh, S. (2020). *Understanding the Role of Artificial Intelligence and Its Future Social Impact*. IGI Global.

Shum, S. J. B., & Luckin, R. (2019). Learning analytics and AI: Politics, pedagogy and practices. *British Journal of Educational Technology*, *50*(6), 2785–2793. doi:10.1111/bjet.12880

Steiner-Khamsi, G. (2003). The politics of league tables. *Journal of Social Science Education*.

Trowler, V. (2010). Student engagement literature review. *The Higher Education Academy*, *11*(1), 1–15.

University and College Union. (2020). The automatic university - a review of datafication and automation in higher education. *UCU*, 1-55.

Williamson, B. (2015). Algorithmic skin: Health-tracking technologies, personal analytics and the biopedagogies of digitized health and physical education. *Sport Education and Society*, *20*(1), 133–151. doi:10.1080/13573322.2014.962494

Williamson, B. (2017). Big data in education: The digital future of learning, policy and practice. *Sage (Atlanta, Ga.)*. Advance online publication. doi:10.4135/9781529714920

Wilsdon, J. (2016). The metric tide: Independent review of the role of metrics in research assessment and management. *Sage (Atlanta, Ga.)*.

## ADDITIONAL READING

Komenda, T., Reisinger, G., & Wilfried Sihn, A. (2019). A Practical Approach of Teaching Digitalization and Safety Strategies in Cyber-Physical Production Systems. *Procedia Manufacturing, 31*, 296-301.

Sanders, N. R. (2014). *Big Data Driven Supply Chain Management: A Framework for Implementing Analytics and Turning Information Into Intelligence*. Pearson Education. https://books.google.co.uk/books?id=-b2LAwAAQBAJ

Sundorph, E., & Mosseri-Marlio, W. (2016). Smart campuses: how big data will transform higher education. Accenture, 1-8.

Yan, H., & Hu, H. (2016, ). A Study on Association Algorithm of Smart Campus Mining Platform Based on Big Data. *2016 International Conference on Intelligent Transportation, Big Data & Smart City (ICITBS)*. 10.1109/ICITBS.2016.11

## KEY TERMS AND DEFINITIONS

**COVID-19:** A virus that led to a worldwide pandemic in 2020.

**Datafication:** Online tools and technologies designed to transform organisations into data-driven enterprises.

**Digital Technologies:** Electronic tools, systems, devices, and resources that generate, store, or process data.

**Higher Education:** Tertiary level education in which academic courses are taught.

**Learning Analytics:** Measuring and analysing learners and their contexts for the purpose of optimising learning within a desired learning setting.

**Pedagogy:** The practice of teaching in a learning setting.

# Chapter 7
# Emerging EdTechs Amidst the COVID-19 Pandemic:
## Cases in Higher Education Institutions

**Trevor Wood-Harper**
https://orcid.org/0000-0002-2246-3191
*Alliance Manchester Business School, UK*

## ABSTRACT

*The role of information technology (IT) transforming higher education (HE) institutions is flourishing. Students, lecturers, and faculty staff adopt overarching platforms and applications that are driven by ubiquitous technology such as big data and cloud computing to support their teaching and learning activities. In this chapter, the authors analysed cases of EdTechs (apps) used in the higher education institutions (HEIs) and their impact on teaching and learning processes. They draw the benefits, challenges, and appropriate cases pertaining to the apps used in HEIs in supporting such processes. They find that EdTechs have a high potential to provide better education for students, easier teaching process for lecturers, and clearer managerial process for administrators and faculty members. The chapter concludes that while EdTechs used during the pandemic can provide an alternative learning experience, it still lacks in providing optimal learning engagement.*

## INTRODUCTION

From early 2010s the research on how Information Technology (IT) transforms higher education (HE) institutions is flourishing. A rapid increase in online education across secondary and tertiary institutions all over the world is explained by the advent of the World Wide Web (www) (Allen and Seaman, 2017) and its penetration into conservative Higher Education Institutions (HEIs) (Stone, 2017; de Wit, 2018). In terms of adding apps into HEI learning processes, there are number of new technologies that could play a positive role. For instance, over the last years, Big Data has attracted the interest of academia. This technology provides higher education institutions to make more adjusted decision making on allocation

DOI: 10.4018/978-1-7998-4846-2.ch007

of IT resources that is expected "*to improve the quality of educational services, guide students to provide student experience, deliver higher completion rates, and improve student persistence*". HEIs are adopting cloud architectures and, new digital devices, entering digital platforms (Coursera), create ecosystems between students and lecturers. This often results in more data generation and new opportunities for Big Data-driven analytics to find patterns in the data, predictive maintenance, and prescriptive maintenance to play out several scenarios of future performance of the HEI (Ali, 2019a; Ali, 2019b; Ali, 2020).

Big data has provided new opportunities for more insight about student expectations, their intentions, and their challenges. This all contributes to better online learning process. Through new analytics, HEIs can improve "*understanding of their learners' challenges and apply the resultant insight to emphatically enhance the improvement*" (Slade and Prinsloo, 2013). Rio Salado University, which enrols over 41,000 students in both online and in-campus courses provides a good case of developing a new analytics software for tracking student performance, which could be used for more efficient decision-making. Such apps enable student-oriented learning environments, which helps non-traditional students to achieve high academic goals "*through personalised intermediations* "(Crush, 2019). In such settings, tutors get new insight into the individual progression of their students, and they are well informed to act if things are going in the wrong direction (Ali et al., 2019). Such, technology-based learning provides necessary data for new generation of apps which can illuminate what works and what does not work so that learning outcomes can be enhanced using informed mediation. In this case, the intuition and own perception of a lecturer gets supported with AI enabled systems, providing feedback. Mobile apps developed by HE institutions differ in two main types, including tools *for enhancing learning*, which solidify the content of lectures, self-test students' knowledge of the subject, and allow collaboration with peers and *tools for organising studies*, which easy student transition into university life and assist with various aspects of university experience (Pechenkina, 2017). Such systems rely on data growth and require access to this data across other courses, departments (looking for similarities and average student profiles) and across university itself. Additional challenge is to integrate such distributed data, as it is typically non structured and distributed in thousands of desktops.

To this end, online learning demonstrates the comparability of the in contrast to face-to-face learning (Bernard *et al.*, 2004; Means *et al.*, 2009). The introduction of Massive Opened Online Courses (MOOCs) have changed the earlier perception that the university studies are always held in a formal classroom environment with a physical presence of a lecturer (Young, 2012). They have triggered universities to search for new measures how to attract potential students to more expensive offline format of studies, which included developing new mobile applications supporting online course content and communication of students and lecturers around them. Two main segments of research about online learning exist – the development of good designs and the assessment of students' satisfaction with an online learning platform in comparison to the conventional/traditional face-to-face course (Saadé, He and Kira, 2007).

Students, lecturers, and faculty staff adopt the overarching platform for delivery of the given service, which is often hosted using cloud computing technology. Cloud computing allows access to infrastructure, software, hardware, and platform at any time in any place if there is internet access. Amongst the existent cloud service models, the software-as-a-service (SaaS) model is the most applied service model in HEIs. The studies show that students and tutors utilize also general purpose cloud apps, such as Google Docs/Drive, Calendar, and Sites, and these can be effectively used for communication between academic staff and their students (Owayid and Uden, 2014). These apps have a significant impact on work performance in the higher educational settings, while the administrative staffs is more positive toward using Google Apps than the academics (Al-Emran and Malik, 2016). The early adoption of cloud computing in South

African Universities had the motivation to determine the viability of SaaS adoption (Akande and Van Belle, 2014). SaaS was employed for traditional admin systems including human resource management (HR), customer relationship management (CRM), finance and payroll and asset management, but it proved to be efficient for student management (i.e. student recruitment, enrolment, financial disbursement, graduation, and alumni. This has revealed benefits of SaaS in HEIs.

Specifically, smartphones and app stores have created a foundation for *mobility* trend in higher education which reacted on the way how students prefer accessing learning materials. Current students live in a "*multi-device environment*" and are likely to use mobile apps where this is supported by an app (Glahn, Gruber and Tartakovski, 2015). Consequently, Universities started implementing *BYOD* (Bring Your Own Device) policies, allowing students to access classrooms also virtually from their own mobile devices, even during offline lectures, thus enhancing their learning experience. This creates *blended learning environments* (Osguthorpe and Graham, 2003; Graham, 2006; see also Glahn, Gruber and Tartakovski, 2015) and opportunities to realize Education as a service (Khaddage and Cosío, 2014). The new learning format makes recordings of lectures available anytime, brings new social links between students and fosters collaborative work among students and professors, which was proven by studies in India (Ansari and Tripathi, 2017), Taiwan (Cheng et al., 2017) and Malasia (Masrom, Nadzari and Zakaria, 2016). To this end, students' value mobile applications, developed specifically for university subjects (Vázquez-Cano, 2014). At the same this, this shows that students use mobile learning apps for extending and enriching their learning environment, rather than replacing their campus experience and physical interaction with their peers (Glahn, Gruber and Tartakovski, 2015). Therefore, modern education settings imply mobile learning to blend into classical learning environments, in which paper books, classroom experiences, laptops, and tablets co-exist. This chapter refers to these technologies as EdTechs, which is the practice of utilising technology to support learning and teaching, and effectively manage educational institutions, such as Universities.

In this chapter, we explored EdTechs (Apps) used in the Higher Education Institutions (HEIs) and their impact on teaching and learning processes. In particular, EdTechs used during 2020 Covid-19 pandemic, which resulted in Universities closing and resorting to distance learning tools from home to deliver instruction were also considered. Adopting a qualitative content analysis methodology helped to analyse the impactful EdTechs in HE with support by real-world cases. We analysed the influence of Covid-19 triggered social distancing and the potential of gamification to increase engagement of students into learning processes. Due to recent Covid-19-related events, empirical studies published since 2020 were also considered. The purpose of conducting this study was to address the following research question: What are the opportunities and challenges of EdTechs used in HEIs to deliver learning and teaching during the Covid-19 pandemic?

## EDTECHS IN HE SETTINGS

Many instances of good practice exist across education, particularly in the UK already in which there is a vibrant sector of EdTechs, providing a range of excellent and innovative learning and teaching services via online applications (King et al., 2016). There are various EdTechs used in the UK HE system, and are later used as practical examples to support our theoretical lens of EdTech innovations. For example, Bolton College is currently using Ada, which is a virtual assistant that facilitates teaching and assessment to minimise workload. Also, the Ark Multi Academy Trust has reduced their IT costs by migrating data to cloud-based services. Assistive technology is also being used by the High furlong Special School in Blackpool to allow special needs students to communicate and be active participants in their education. These examples show that technology is supporting progress, leading to improved outcomes (Pellini et al., 2020).

In order to support both HE and the EdTech industry to build on existing good practice and drive further innovation, five key areas need to be considered to help drive such change:

- **Administration processes**: minimising the burden of 'non-teaching' tasks;
- **Assessment processes**: adding effectiveness and efficiency to the assessment process;
- **Teaching practices**: provision of supportive and inclusive educational outcomes for all;
- **Continuing professional development**: supporting teachers, lecturers and education leaders to develop flexibly;
- **Learning throughout life**: supporting decisions to help academics staff and students develop new skills. (Hinds, 2019)

Maximising the opportunities afforded by EdTech calls for a partnership approach that promotes togetherness and the collaboration between academic staff, experts and learners, in addition to tackling the common challenges in the HE domain. The key measures in this strategy intend to support education providers, teachers, leaders and students to be better equipped to adopt EdTech tools, and ensure EdTechs need their individual needs (King et al., 2016). The next sections provide a theoretical basis of EdTechs in HE with support from practical cases in the HE domain. These sections also demonstrate how EdTechs are effective learning and teaching tools, even during challenging times, such as the Covid-19 pandemic. This has resulted in an overreliance on such tools from teachers and learners working from home due to the lockdown, forcing many HEIs to temporarily close.

## Multi-Case of New EdTechs in HE and Covid-19

The recent COVID-19 outbreak has affected all sectors of human endeavour, including disrupted daily routines in Higher Education Institutions (HEIs). This crisis has drastically changed the balance of offline vs. online lecturing content consumption in the blended learning environments. If earlier, the research and practice agreed on blended environment formats as mostly applicable for modern students (Glahn, Gruber and Tartakovski, 2015), the social distancing requirements (enabled by the governments) have called students for self-isolation which has forced conventional/traditional delivery of teaching and learning to be replaced by distance, online, or blended learning styles (prior to the pandemic, only slightly over 25% of all students in UK HEIs received teaching and learning online. This statistic has now grown to 85%). This brought universities to the conclusion that they cannot continue teaching unless they enable students to attend a lecture transmitted from professors' home via utilizing video-conferencing apps. Consequently, the new generation of such tools was integrated into learning process, such as Microsoft teams, and Zoom, which earlier were never applied in education at such a mass scale. Furthermore, according to the UK-based HE institutions such as University of Manchester and the University of Cambridge, the virtual delivery of all courses is extended until summer semester 2021 (Lau J., Yang B. and Dasgupta R., 2020). Such format allows more possibilities in peer-to-peer working with students, in preparing, administrating, and running online lectures, enabling more qualitative sound which is important for students of musicians, for example; and video transmitting algorithms, which allowed less disruptions online. As a result of mass demand for remote work, Zoom has reported a surge in new users, making the company shares value worth $48.8 billion which is more than the World's 7 Biggest Airlines (Ghosh, 2020). Other examples of EdTechs applied in HE and used during the pandemic, include IBM Watson, assistive technologies and 3D visualisation.

Bolton College has utilised IBM to build their virtual assistant called 'Ada' who plays the role of delivering on-demand requests for information, advice and support to its 11,000 plus students. As of last year, Ada has responded to over 2,000 requests and questions regarding general college enquiries, in addition to other specific questions directed at students, such as attendance and curriculum. Although Ada can support students on campus, the system had become unusable in wake of the Covid-19 pandemic. As an alternative, staff and students working from home turned to a similar virtual assistant that could be used off-campus known as 'Amazon Alexa.' This provided the same level of support as Ada, but could be used off-campus. This helped to address the student and staff learning and teaching needs during a global crisis, which in turn saved countless hours on administrative tasks and out of hours teaching, whilst maintaining quality content in an informal learning and teaching environment. (Hinds, 2019)

Similarly, a HEI situated in Blackpool called Highfurlong School have utilised simple assistive technologies that yield positive outcomes for students.

Highfurlong School in Blackpool is a great example of where simple assistive technologies can lead to significant impact on student outcomes. The school is quite special as it mostly caters to student with special needs. The staff have worked strenuously to provide special needs EdTechs for special needs students to communicate and express themselves. Switches and eye-tracking technology or student controlled sensory rooms are just a few examples of the EdTechs used in Highfurlong and they strive to empower disadvantaged students to be active learners. Given the rise of the Covid-19 pandemic, these tools have been unavailable to students, which in turn has impeded their learning experience. Since there are no off-campus solutions, special needs students have been left with no off-campus supportive EdTechs to facilitate their learning. This calls for the development of such tools to cater for all types of students, including disadvantaged students. (Hinds, 2019)

At the same time, the recent transformation of remote learning raised several concerns. First, the virtual attendance of students during online lectures appeared to be less, than the expected physical attendance for such a lecture. This could be explained by the less interaction between students watching the stream online from their bedroom in contrast to what happens during a physical lecture and, the availability of recorded stream after the lecture ends. Unlike a conventional face-to-face classroom teaching/learning, online learning faces a challenge of ensuring that the learner remains engaged. Therefore, it remains challenging to ensure that the learners remain engaged in the learning process. Second, video recordings often included the backgrounds of students and professors' rooms, which broke information privacy of both parties. Third, online lectures that were organised without passwords soon became the target of hackers and internet trolls. For instance, educators from New York City to the University of Southern California have reported multiple cases where the virtual meetings were hijacked by miscreants (Lay, 2020). This usually involves involving somebody who takes over the audio and video controls into public Zoom calls to broadcast inappropriate materials and remarks, such as pornography, racist or sexist jokes to unwitting conference participants. Gharavi, an associate professor in ASU's School of Film, Dance and Theatre, comments on (Redden, 2020): *"I didn't notice it until a student on chat said something about it. Participants were using fake screen names, some of which he said were very offensive. The chat window became incredibly active. Most of the comments were not on topic. They were vulgar, racist, misogynistic toilet humour. I would barely even call it humour"*. Such evidences of *"Zoombombing"* bring disruption to the course and could be a pain for lecturers, especially with low digital skills as they are mostly those who hardly could avoiding trolling in their classes (Redden, 2020). Additionally, as many new users start using Zoom for privacy meetings, information security experts raise confidentiality concerns. The lack of confidentiality in online meetings is reported as the transmission of all meeting encryption keys happens through China and could be potentially controlled by the 3rd party (Marczak and Scott-Railton, 2020).

*Table 1. Drawbacks and Determinants of Flourishing Digital Platforms during Covid-19 Pandemic*

| | Determents | Drawbacks |
|---|---|---|
| **Emergence of EdTechs in wake of Covid-19** | Lack of digital literacy of students | Trolling, zoom bombing |
| | Lack of digital literacy of tutors | Lack of confidentiality |
| | Lack of it infrastructure for students (3rd world countries) | Less privacy than envisioned |
| | Lack of student engagement | Less campus experience for students |
| | Confidentiality fears, information privacy | |

## Better Engagement into EdTechs Through Gamification

As it was recognised in Times Higher Education, switching to online teaching and learning brings economic benefits to the economy of the UK (Grove, 2020), as coronavirus pandemic can increase the scope of educational services that UK universities provide in a long-term perspective, by offering expanded borderless learning measures, including online, blended, and distant learning. Currently, the authors state that Covid-19 has triggered universities to enable remote courses, but it will make them learn technology more and quicker adapt to digitalization trend that is envisioned in world's education in 21st century. Traditionally, many Massive Open Online Courses (MOOCs) report high drop off rates for their students, often explained by the due to "*the lack of motivation, feelings of isolation, and lack of interactivity in MOOCs*" (Krause et al., 2015). The similar way, student engagement in online educational apps is difficult to maintain (McGrath and Bayerlein, 2013; Jang, Park and Mun, 2015). Within the existing relevant literature, there is no consensus about the absolute definition of student engagement. Student engagement is usually explained by "*the accumulation of students in higher educational institutional groups or boards, and their respective active/on-going involvement in the activities that occur in the institutions*" (Kuh and Hu, 2001). Over the past two decades, there has been a constantly increasing research interest towards the definition of a more inclusive understanding of student engagement. Student engagement is described as a field of research"*...concerned with the interaction between time, effort and other resources invested by both students and their HEIs intended to enhance the student experience ...*" (Trowler, 2010), which implies the engagement of a student is into a partnership/collaboration between the tutors and learners in their HEIs.

Prior to the Covid-19 outbreak, 75% of students received their course lectures or teaching instruction offline, however in post-covid settings, we witness that this number has reduced to 15% of offline courses, while the rest being delivered using online. This brings new requirements for preparing new tutors and managers for supporting new era learning processes. For instance, the content must be digitalized, re-assessed before it could be provided online. The key challenge to resolve before this is to develop a strategy how to keep students engaged. There is the need to discover useful relationships between research relating to student engagement and effective online course design and delivery. There are certain benefits for making formal education more informal, social, gamified, and digital.

Research indicates that "every learning and teaching occurs in an environment, or context" (Pittaway, 2012). This environment can refer to where the teaching takes place, for instance, in the classroom, home, work, bus, office, etc. The formation and maintenance of learning environment is typically the responsibility of the lecturer and faculty staff, as they plan the learning processes of a student considering multiple parameters, such as number of course units, teaching spaces, interactions, collaboration and many other aspects. This environment could be driven by lecturer (when the formal course is executed) or driven by expectations of students (when the course is reshaped according to the learning trajectories of the current group). There could be also individual elements embraced for a course for extra flexibility. Moreover, the choice of content that is done by lecturers and faculty members impacts the likelihood of student retention, engagement, and success. Each lecturer has a personalised method for teaching, but there is necessary to ensure the compliance of this diversity of methods to the educational canvas of university and the Key Performance Indicators (KPIs) what determine success or failure of a student. A good context should promote "collaboration, communication, interactivity, participation, and feedback, all using a technologically-advanced online learning environment" (Robinson and Hullinger, 2008). Respecting all this should increase engagement of both students, lecturers, and faculty members to ensure the best learning results. Currently, universities benefit from feedback based on the student scores (Wladis, Conway and Hachey, 2016). In current situation, even lower scores could be explained not by internal problems, but because of external background. Therefore, surveys are widely used by universities to get insights of how lecturers and administrative stuff functions in the online settings.

To this end, there is a potential to increase retention, engagement and learning success of students via a range of social game elements which comprise the recent gamification trend (Krause et al., 2015). Gamification offers to include "*game-like features like points and badges into non-game contexts*", so that that, it increases attention of students and their engagement (Vaibhav and Gupta, 2014). Gamification makes learning, "*a unique and amusing experience*" which drastically increases the user enrolment and user engagement throughout the course (Vaibhav and Gupta, 2014). The need for gamification is explained by interactivity, personalization, and real-time feedback into online courses which is valued by students (Bell, 2014). It is also explained by psychological support which affects learning of a student through opportunity (Landers and Callan, 2011) and motivation (Hansch, Newman and Schildhauer, 2015). Motivation is sometimes limited to *extrinsic* motivation (Xu, 2011) which can be facilitated in the short term after external rewards like badges and points. Competition—either with one's self or with others—also can explain gamification's success (Banfield and Wilkerson, 2014). The positive effects of gamification have been evidenced in computer science (Azmi et al. 2015) and other disciplines (Dicheva et al., 2015). To this end, software might be a promising path to enhance programming education in the 21st century (Olsson, Mozelius and Collin, 2015). A clear potential for its wider application of gamification is envisioned. It serves the purpose to remove education system from "*a grey industrial past ... to enter a bright new technology-driven era*" (Cohen, 2011). To this end, the effect is still being researched to fully examine gamification's effects and determine how to best achieve sustained engagement (Looyestyn et al., 2017). As it was noted in some studies, success of online learning largely depends on "the characteristics of students that are enrolled on the online learning environments" (Leeds et al, 2013).

*Table 2. Drawbacks and Determinants of Gamification Apps used in HE*

| | Determents | Drawbacks |
|---|---|---|
| **Gamification in HE apps** | Unwillingness of students to engage in a game | Less physical interaction between students |
| | Unpredictable reactions of gamification motivation stimuli | Short-term effects, due to *extrinsic* motivation and competition |
| | Lack of gamification method literacy of tutors | Some tutors find inconvenient to work with gamification |

Once the social distancing was put in place, higher education institutions (HEIs) have attempted to identify the factors that may improve or enrich the experience provided to students via eloquent online learning. Although, many academic faculty members are sceptical towards new teaching paradigms, such as gamification, the resent research is promising to explain student engagement in online learning settings via gamification of learning process. These methods have potential to be more effective than traditional/ conventional teaching and learning (see also Shea, Bidjerano and Vickers, 2016; Lederman, 2018).

## RECOMMENDATIONS FROM THEORIES AND PRACTICE

First, new digital technologies can be considered towards better learning analytics for students and related educational ecosystem hosted by cloud computing to increase flexibility and expose HEI users to a broad range of educational resources. The introduction of apps into learning process could be started with general purpose cloud apps, such as Google Docs/Drive, Calendar, and Sites, and these can be effectively used for communication between academic staff and their students (Owayid and Uden, 2014). These apps have a significant impact on work performance in the higher educational settings, while the administrative staffs are more positive toward using Google Apps than the academics (Al-Emran and Malik, 2016).

Second, the learning process should be enabled *blended learning environments* (Osguthorpe and Graham, 2003; Graham, 2006; see also Glahn, Gruber and Tartakovski, 2015), allowing students to enhance their learning experience by accessing online content from their own mobile devices anytime and fosters collaborative work among students and professors.

Third, the learning process must be flexible and engaged with contingency plans. Potential external disruptions, such as financial, health or environmental crisis should not be able to distort the educational service and the variety of scenarios for learning must be modelled in simulated. As an example of such, the reaction to social distancing, weaker retention and engagement and other factors must be considered.

Fifth, to increase retention and student engagement the gamification strategy should be considered to enhance the formal curricula with new techniques embracing generation Z students and their demands. Improving student engagement in online learning environments for HEIs constitutes a critical element that should be addressed in institutional management settings, and therefore and requires a lot of empirical research to contribute to the ever-advancing knowledge base. Besides, given the fact that studies about student engagement are birthing progressively composite questions and issues, there is an anticipated need for additional research that explores how to enhance student engagement within the context of online learning in HEIs.

*Table 3. Current State of EdTech Use in HE*

| | Success | Failure |
|---|---|---|
| **COVID-enabled mass transition to online apps** | Replacement of offline lecturing | Did not enable the same engagement level |
| | Enable exclusive learning channel | Disruptions due to trolls and hackers |
| **Gamification in online apps** | Increases engagement within the course | Is not spread enough for significant results, requires more tutors aware with its methods |
| | Increases popularity of the course among generation Z | less accessible for earlier generations (X,Y) |

## Addressing the Barriers and Lessons Learned

We recognise that teachers and students tend to face a number of barriers to capitalising on the opportunities presented by EdTechs. This calls for appropriate recommendations, which act as a lesson to avoid future problems concerning the development EdTechs to facilitate learning and teaching. Recommendations are as follows:

- Provision of modern infrastructures to address poor internet connections and outdated internal networking and devices;
- Call for better digital capability and skills to use technology effectively;
- Leadership to instigate change and empower students and teachers to be confident users of EdTech, even during unprecedented times such as the Covid-19 pandemic;
- Awareness of available EdTechs and expertise required to compare and contrast different technology options for different types of students with different learning needs e.g. special needs students;
- Need for digital procurement capabilities for better decision making in adopting and implementing EdTechs;
- Consideration for privacy, safety, and data security and how HEIs and their students can be protected.

A lesson learned here is that HEIs should reach a minimum standard of digital maturity, which is an essential pre-cursor to the effective utilisation of EdTechs, on-campus and even off-campus. The effective use of EdTechs, even during unprecedented times follows a proposal of a 'framework for change' (see Fig.1), which calls for a tailored journey that begins with developing a vision, such as determining a key area of importance that EdTechs can support. The framework then moves towards addressing the barriers to accommodate the lessons learned, and ends with implementation and an iteration of how that technology can be maintained to meet teachers and student's needs. This chapter demonstrates our ambition and commitment to support flourishing EdTechs for HEIs, even during a world crisis.

In sum, the absolute consequences of technological development and future apps in HEI cannot be predicted today, but it is highly likely that new apps will be brought by the new disrupting digital technologies allowing virtual reality and personalised education as a service. Consequently, EdTechs have a high potential to provide better education for students, easier teaching process for lecturers, and clearer managerial process for administrators and faculty members.

*Figure 1. EdTech Framework for Educational Technology Reform*

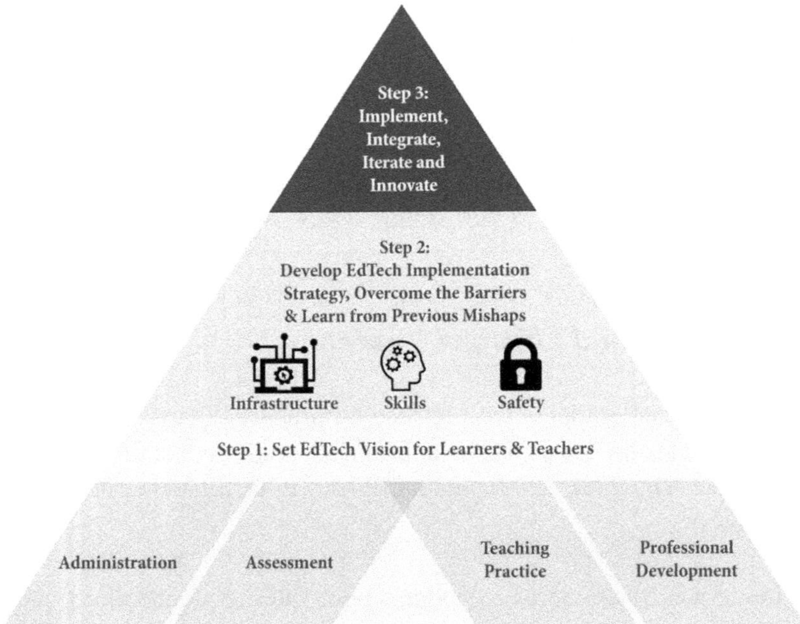


## CONCLUSION

From our analysis of EdTechs in the HE domain, there were successful and unsuccessful experiences. With respect to the Covid-enabled mass transition to online apps showed that it was a great alternative and replacement of online lecturing as this was not possible given the current pandemic. This enables an exclusive learning channel where everyone from different regions could join and collaborate. Despite these benefits, some EdTechs failed to provide the same level of engagement as provided in offline lectures given technological limitations and people talking over one another, which made learning delivery a frustrating experience. Further disruptions in the form of potential attacks from hackers and trolls also hindered the learning experience. On the other hand, gamified online applications showed that engagement did increase with app use, though using the apps was more complex and required more contemporary knowledge to effectively utilise them. Despite this, the gamified apps did increase the popularity of the courses which were being taught.

We reveal that EdTech use often polarizes opinion, meaning that when facing danger, we view it as 'just one more thing to do', though the proper implementation of technology has the ability to transform educational experiences, thereby helping teachers to allocate more of their time on making a real difference to student outcomes and their learning needs. Although there are clear barriers to EdTech use in the higher education domain, government plays a key role in breaking these barriers down, in addition to supporting the sector to capitalise on the opportunities. We are also aware of the huge ambition within the education community and EdTechs have the potential to revolutionise the modern technology approach, even during unprecedented times. Such a strategy can lead to the development of a technology revolution in the higher education domain and promote new and innovative approaches as we embark on a future technological journey.

Based on the above conclusions, future work could incorporate the impact of EdTechs such as cloud-driven gamified apps since these appear to be more successful in providing a more engaging learning experience. Since cloud computing has collaborative tools and features, there is a potential harmony between gamified applications and cloud. Future studies could explore the use of EdTechs to determine its feasibility of providing a better teaching and learning experience and help maintain the lessons learned from previous mishaps. This could be achieved by seeking empirical enquiry about the demand for EdTechs in HEIs, in addition to capturing students' and teachers' perceptions of such innovations to inform future potential adopters of EdTechs and their potential opportunities and barriers.

## REFERENCES

Akande, A. O., & Van Belle, J.-P. (2014). Cloud computing in higher education: A snapshot of software as a service. In *2014 IEEE 6th International Conference on Adaptive Science & Technology (ICAST)*. IEEE. 10.1109/ICASTECH.2014.7068111

Al-Emran, M., & Malik, S. I. (2016). The impact of google apps at work: Higher educational perspective. *International Journal of Interactive Mobile Technologies*, *10*(4), 85–88. doi:10.3991/ijim.v10i4.6181

Ali, M. (2019). Cloud Computing at a Cross Road: Quality and Risks in Higher Education. *Advances in Internet of Things*, *9*(3), 33–49. doi:10.4236/ait.2019.93003

Ali, M. (2020). Multi-Perspectives of Cloud Computing Service Adoption Quality and Risks in Higher Education. In D. B. A. Mehdi Khosrow-Pour (Ed.), Handbook of Research on Modern Educational Technologies, Applications, and Management (2nd ed.). IGI Global.

Ali, M., Wood-Harper, T., & Al-Gahtani, A. S. (2019). Contextual Analysis of Educational Monitoring and Progression as a Service (EMPaaS) System in Higher Education. *Open Journal of Business and Management*, *7*(3), 1525–1542. doi:10.4236/ojbm.2019.73105

Ali, M. B. (2019). Multiple Perspective of Cloud Computing Adoption Determinants in Higher Education a Systematic Review. *International Journal of Cloud Applications and Computing*, *9*(3), 89–109. doi:10.4018/IJCAC.2019070106

Allen, I. E., & Seaman, J. (2017). *Digital Compass Learning: Distance Education Enrolment Report 2017. Babson Survey Research Group*. ERIC.

Ansari, M. S., & Tripathi, A. (2017). An investigation of effectiveness of mobile learning apps in higher education in India. *International Journal of Information Studies and Libraries*.

Azmi, S., Iahad, N. A., & Ahmad, N. (2015). Gamification in online collaborative learning for programming courses: A literature review. *Journal of Engineering and Applied Sciences (Asian Research Publishing Network)*, *10*(23), 1–3.

Banfield, J., & Wilkerson, B. (2014). Increasing student intrinsic motivation and self-efficacy through gamification pedagogy. *Contemporary Issues in Education Research (Online)*, *7*(4), 291–298. doi:10.19030/cier.v7i4.8843

Bell, K. R. (2014). *Online 3.0—the rise of the gamer educator the potential role of gamification in online education*. University of Pennsylvania.

Bernard, R. M. (2004). How does distance education compare with classroom instruction? A meta-analysis of the empirical literature. *Review of Educational Research*, *74*(3), 379–439.

Cheng, H. C., Kung, T. P., Li, C. M., & Sun, Y. J. (2017, February). The current state of mobile apps development of higher education in Taiwan. In *2017 19th International Conference on Advanced Communication Technology (ICACT)* (pp. 780-786). IEEE. 10.23919/ICACT.2017.7890227

Cohen, A. M. (2011). The gamification of education. *The Futurist*, *45*(5), 16.

Crush, M. (2019). Monitoring the PACE of student Learning: Analytics at Rio Salado Community University. *Campus Technology*.

De Wit, H. (2018). Collaborative Online International Learning in Higher Education. In *Encyclopaedia of International Higher Education Systems and Institutions* (pp. 1–3). Springer. doi:10.1007/978-94-017-9553-1_234-1

Dicheva, D., Dichev, C., Agre, G., & Angelova, G. (2015). Gamification in education: A systematic mapping study. *Journal of Educational Technology & Society*, *18*(3).

Ghosh, I. (2020). *Zoom is now worth More Than the World's 7 Biggest Airlines*. https://www.visualcapitalist.com/zoom-boom-biggest-airlines/

Glahn, C., Gruber, M. R., & Tartakovski, O. (2015) Beyond Delivery Modes and Apps: A Case Study on Mobile Blended Learning in Higher Education. The handbook of blended learning: Global perspectives, local designs, 3-21. doi:10.1007/978-3-319-24258-3_10

Grove, J. (2020). *Switch to online teaching can help UK unlock global markets | Times Higher Education (THE)*. Available at: https://www.timeshighereducation.com/news/switch-online-teaching-can-help-uk-unlock-global-markets

Hansch, A., Newman, C., & Schildhauer, T. (2015). *Fostering engagement with gamification: Review of current practices on online learning platforms*. Academic Press.

Hinds, D. (2019). *Realising the potential of technology in education: A strategy for education providers and the technology industry*. Academic Press.

Jang, J., Park, J. J., & Mun, Y. Y. (2015, June). Gamification of online learning. In *International Conference on Artificial Intelligence in Education* (646-649). Springer. 10.1007/978-3-319-19773-9_82

Khaddage, F., & Cosío, J. H. (2014, March). Trends and Barriers on the Fusion of Mobile Apps in Higher Education Where to Next and How? In *Society for Information Technology & Teacher Education International Conference* (pp. 903-909). Association for the Advancement of Computing in Education (AACE).

King, M. R. N., Rothberg, S. J., Dawson, R. J., & Batmaz, F. (2016). Bridging the edtech evidence gap. *Información Tecnológica*, *18*(1), 18–40.

Konert, J., & Lavoué, E. (Eds.). Lecture Notes in Computer Science: Vol. 9307. *Design for Teaching and Learning in a Networked World*. Springer.

Krause, M., Mogalle, M., Pohl, H., & Williams, J. J. (2015, March). A playful game changer: Fostering student retention in online education with social gamification. In *Proceedings of the Second ACM conference on Learning@ Scale* (pp. 95-102). ACM.

Kuh, G. D., & Hu, S. (2001). The effects of student-faculty interaction in the 1990s. *The review of higher education*, *24*(3), 309–332. doi:10.1353/rhe.2001.0005

Landers, R. N., & Callan, R. C. (2011). Casual social games as serious games: The psychology of gamification in undergraduate education and employee training. In Serious games and edutainment applications (pp. 399-423). Springer.

Lau, J., Yang, B., & Dasgupta, R. (2020). Will the coronavirus make online education go viral? *The Higher Education.* https://www.timeshighereducation.com/features/will-coronavirus-make-online-education-go-viral

Lay, J. (2020). *To zoom or not to zoom? That is the question. The Higher Education.* https://www.timeshighereducation.com/news/zoom-or-not-zoom-question

Lederman, D. (2018). Conflicted views of technology: A survey of faculty attitudes. Inside Higher Ed.

Leeds, E. (2013). The impact of student retention strategies: An empirical study. *International Journal of Management in Education*, *7*(1–2), 22–43.

Looyestyn, J., Kernot, J., Boshoff, K., Ryan, J., Edney, S., & Maher, C. (2017). Does gamification increase engagement with online programs? A systematic review. *PLoS One*, *12*(3), e0173403. doi:10.1371/journal.pone.0173403 PMID:28362821

Marczak, B., & Scott-Railton, J. (2020). *Move Fast and Roll Your Own Crypto, A Quick Look at the Confidentiality of Zoom Meetings*. https://citizenlab.ca/2020/04/move-fast-roll-your-own-crypto-a-quick-look-at-the-confidentiality-of-zoom-meetings/

Masrom, M., Nadzari, A. S., & Zakaria, S. A. (2016). Implementation of Mobile Learning Apps in Malaysia Higher Education Institutions. *E-Proceeding of the 4th Global Summit on Education*, 268-76.

McGrath, N., & Bayerlein, L. (2013). Engaging online students through the gamification of learning materials: The present and the future. In *ASCILITE-Australian Society for Computers in Learning in Tertiary Education Annual Conference* (pp. 573-577). Australasian Society for Computers in Learning in Tertiary Education.

Means, B. (2009). *Evaluation of evidence-based practices in online learning: A meta-analysis and review of online learning studies.* Centre for Learning Technology.

Olsson, M., Mozelius, P., & Collin, J. (2015). Visualisation and Gamification of e-Learning and Programming Education. *Electronic Journal of E-Learning, 13*(6), 441-454.

Osguthorpe, R. T., & Graham, C. R. (2003). Blended learning environments: Definitions and directions. *Quarterly Review of Distance Education, 4*(3), 227-33.

Owayid, A. M., & Uden, L. (2014, September). The usage of Google apps services in higher education. In *International Workshop on Learning Technology for Education in Cloud* (pp. 95-104). Springer. 10.1007/978-3-319-10671-7_9

Pechenkina, E. (2017). Developing a typology of mobile apps in higher education: A national case-study. *Australasian Journal of Educational Technology*, *33*(4).

Pellini, A., Hub, E. & Jordan, K. (2020). *Education during the COVID-19 crisis*. Academic Press.

Pittaway, S. M. (2012). Student and staff engagement: Developing an engagement framework in a faculty of education. *Australian Journal of Teacher Education*, *37*(4), 3. doi:10.14221/ajte.2012v37n4.8

Redden, E. (2020). Zoombombing' Attacks Disrupt Classes. *Inside Higher Ed*. https://www.insidehighered.com/news/2020/03/26/zoombombers-disrupt-online-classes-racist-pornographic-content

Robinson, C. C., & Hullinger, H. (2008). New benchmarks in higher education: Student engagement in online learning. *Journal of Education for Business*, *84*(2), 101–109.

Saadé, R. G., He, X., & Kira, D. (2007). Exploring dimensions to online learning. *Computers in Human Behavior*, *23*(4), 1721–1739.

Shea, P., Bidjerano, T., & Vickers, J. (2016). Faculty Attitudes toward Online Learning: Failures and Successes. SUNY Research Network.

Shuler, C., Levine, Z., & Ree, J. (2012). *iLearn II An analysis of the education category of Apple's app store*. Academic Press.

Slade, S., & Prinsloo, P. (2013). Learning analytics: Ethical issues and dilemmas. *American Behavioral Scientist*, *57*(10), 1510–1529.

Stone, C. (2017). *Opportunity through online learning: Improving student access, participation and success in higher education*. National Centre for Student Equity in Higher Education.

Trowler, V. (2010). Student engagement literature review. *The Higher Education Academy*, *11*(1), 1–15.

Vaibhav, A., & Gupta, P. (2014, December). Gamification of MOOCs for increasing user engagement. In *2014 IEEE International Conference on MOOC, Innovation and Technology in Education (MITE)* (pp. 290-295). IEEE. 10.1109/MITE.2014.7020290

Vázquez-Cano, E. (2014). Mobile distance learning with smartphones and apps in higher education. *Educational Sciences: Theory and Practice*, *14*(4), 1505–1520.

Wladis, C., Conway, K. M., & Hachey, A. C. (2016). Assessing readiness for online education—Research models for identifying students at risk. *Online Learning*, *20*(3), 97–109.

Xu, Y. (2011). *Literature review on web application gamification and analytics*. Honolulu, HI: University of Hawaii. CSDL Technical Report 11–05.

Young, J. R. (2012). Inside the Coursera contract: How an upstart company might profit from free courses. *The Chronicle of Higher Education*, *19*(7).

## ADDITIONAL READING

Ali, M. (2019). Cloud Computing at a Cross Road: Quality and Risks in Higher Education. *Advances in Internet of Things*, *9*(3), 33–49. doi:10.4236/ait.2019.93003

Ali, M. (2020). Multi-Perspectives of Cloud Computing Service Adoption Quality and Risks in Higher Education. In D. B. A. Mehdi Khosrow-Pour (Ed.), Handbook of Research on Modern Educational Technologies, Applications, and Management (2nd ed.). IGI Global.

Ali, M. B. (2019). Multiple Perspective of Cloud Computing Adoption Determinants in Higher Education a Systematic Review. *International Journal of Cloud Applications and Computing*, *9*(3), 89–109. doi:10.4018/IJCAC.2019070106

Ali, M. B., Wood-Harper, T., & Ramlogan, R. (2020). A Framework Strategy to Overcome Trust Issues on Cloud Computing Adoption in Higher Education. In Modern Principles, Practices, and Algorithms for Cloud Security (pp. 162-183). IGI Global. doi:10.4018/978-1-7998-1082-7.ch008

Askari, S. H., Ahmad, F., Umair, S., & Khan, S. A. (2018). Cloud Computing Education Strategies: A Review. In Exploring the Convergence of Big Data and the Internet of Things (pp. 43-54). IGI Global. doi:10.4018/978-1-5225-2947-7.ch004

Sanders, N. R. (2014). *Big Data Driven Supply Chain Management: A Framework for Implementing Analytics and Turning Information Into Intelligence*. Pearson Education. https://books.google.co.uk/books?id=-b2LAwAAQBAJ

Sundorph, E., & Mosseri-Marlio, W. (2016). Smart campuses: how big data will transform higher education. Accenture, 1-8.

## KEY TERMS AND DEFINITIONS

**Big Data:** Large data sets that are analysed using a computer to reveal patterns, trends, and relations pertaining to human behaviour and interactions.

**Cloud Computing:** The delivery of online storage, applications and platforms that are highly ubiquitous and flexible in nature.

**COVID-19:** A 2020 virus that caused a world-wide pandemic.

**Digital Applications:** Software that are used and accessed via an online platform.

**Higher Education:** Tertiary-level education taught within universities.

**Learning Engagement:** The degree of participation and concentration of learners when learning.

**MOOCs:** Massive open online courses designed to provide an affordable and flexible way to learn and provide better learning experiences.

# Chapter 8
# Aspectual Analysis of Digital Transformation and New Academic Professionals:
## A Case of Saudi Arabia

**Alaa Abdulrhman Alamoudi**
*Prince Nourah University, Saudi Arabia*

## ABSTRACT

*Higher education institutions (HEIs) are currently developing a significant research interest in transferring from traditional to novel practices in teaching and learning through the use of modern technological tools and platforms. The integration of digital technologies in higher education has tended to focus on improving academic professionals in developing countries like Saudi Arabia. This chapter was driven by a desire to understand ICT implementation in higher education institutions (HEIs) by professionals using digital transformation in Saudi Arabia. This chapter discusses the implementation of digital transformation in teaching and learning at HEIs in Saudi Arabia. This aim is achieved throughout several objectives, beginning by reviewing the related literature and presenting theoretical frameworks. The literature review will provide the possibility of identifying the focal trends related to the topic.*

## INTRODUCTION

Delivery of contemporary high education is based on modern views of learning. While most of the effective research in learning was school-based, higher education has currently developed a significant research interest in transferring from traditional to novice practices in teaching. Integration of digital technologies in higher education has tended to focus on improving academic professionals in the developing countries such as Saudi Arabia.

The rationale of this chapter is to understand the current state of ICT implementation in higher education institutions (HEIs) using digital transformation. Hence, the aim of this article is to discuss implementation of digital transformation in teaching and learning at HEIs in Saudi Arabia. This aim is

DOI: 10.4018/978-1-7998-4846-2.ch008

achieved through the literature review and development of the theoretical framework for future work. The literature review identifies focal trends of the topic for emergence of new academic programs. This chapter contributes to substantiating the conceptual discussion on digital transformation and ICT to enhance design of the higher educational systems in Saudi Arabia.

## LITERATURE REVIEW

### Overview of Technology Integration in Saudi Arabia

With an increasing attention to higher education in Saudi Arabia, higher education institutions and universities rely on technologies to provide a high-quality of learning and teaching experience. Among the technological tools used in HEIs in KSA, there are collaborative eLearning, ICTs (information and Communication Technologies), and CTS (Correspondence Tracking System) for monitoring student enrolment at universities and administrative procedures. The modern learning and teaching trends are mandatory to support faculty members with IT skills to overcome the new challenges. With the Kingdom's 2030 vision, Saudi Arabia implements the National Plan for Information Technology (NPIT) to empower Saudi with e-learning in lifelong education. To this end, the Kingdom established the National Centre for E-Learning & Distance Learning (NCeDL) in Riyadh (Mirza, 2007).

The use of computers at universities in Saudi Arabia began in the 1996. The Ministry of Higher Education (MOHE) established the Computer and Information Centre (CIC) that provided ICT services for educational institutions. MOHE started the project in 2000 that sought to provide schools in KSA with e-content to facilitate learning and teaching (Oyaid, 2009). This project was followed by the establishment of WATANI Schools' Net project in 2001, to connect educational directorates and schools KSA-wide with the wide area network (WAN). With the partnership of Intel, Semanoor – a local software company – created an electronic curriculum, Semanoor browser, e-classroom systems, digital library for all government K-12 public and private schools.

In addition, Al-Khalifa (2009) points out other projects such as Obeikan Education with the web platform "Skoool" for over 250 interactive lessons for K-12 students. The Jehazi project targets at enhancement of teachers' technological competence in KSA and provision of teachers with laptops. In 2008, MOHE in Saudi Arabia launched the initiative of Google Educational Program which equipped 1,200 schools and 20,000 teachers with personal emails to access office applications programs and personal websites. Moreover, MOHE along with Intel and Microsoft launched various educational, training and e-learning projects for Saudi students and teachers. Consequently, KSA became the largest ICT market in the Middle East, with a special focus on science and mathematics (Al-Asmari, 2005).

### Emerging ICT in KSA

To cope up with the trend of higher education digitalization in KSA, the universities incorporated e-learning and launched all curricula online. For instance, the universities of King Saud University (KSU), King Abdul Aziz University (KAU), Al-Baha University, Taiba University, Qassim University, King Khalid University (KKU) and Madinah Islamic University agreed with the NCeDL to incorporate e-learning in study curricula (Al-Khalifa, 2009).

The e-Learning Centre in the Academic Development at King Fahad University of Petroleum and Minerals (KFUPM) granted access to more than 80 online resources through OpenCourseWare Consortium. The same Consortium was utilised by Alfaisal University in 2006. The Deanship of Distance Learning delivered print/correspondence-basis for courses. Furthermore, Saudi universities implemented language management system (LMS) and virtual classrooms to improve learning (Al-Nuaim, 2019). KSU also created the Deanship for e-Learning and Distance

Learning in 2007, whereas e-Learning Unit at King Faisal University was launched in 2008. Additionally, Prince Mohammed bin Fahad University and Effat University in Jeddah, also designed e-learning centers and utilized augmented educational experiences (Mirza, 2008).

Al-Draiby (2010) states that the lecture rooms are fully equipped with data shows, whiteboards, e-podiums, polycom video conferencing, and multi-media centers in KSA universities. Besides LMS, universities provide access to virtual classrooms, collaboration tools, content authoring and capturing tools, along with digital repository systems. In 2007, the Knowledge International University (KIU), was established to fully use of e-learning resources. Furthermore, the MOHE set up a repository for e-learning material to equip universities and students with e-learning materials for different fields of study such as engineering, medicine, computer sciences and humanities; and provided essential training for academics to deal with the technologies (Al-Kahtani, 2001).

However, there are many obstacles that hinder effective use of ICT in KSA. For example, material and financial resources for new learning system operation require considerable networking infrastructure (Al-Asmari, 2005) and budget planning; therefore is a financial constraint to the Saudi government. In addition, a lack of administrative support for e-learning remains challenging since instructional designers in KSA nor educational theory or design are available at universities. Hence, sufficient training in e-learning will need to come from outside the Kingdom. Academic institutions in KSA do not have a basic understanding of e-learning with a lack of basic tools for e-learning education (Alkhalaf, 2012).

## Definitions of ICT in HE

Digital transformation refers to the "deep transformation of business activities and processes, and the organization of processes, competences and models to fully exploit the differences and opportunities of a mix of digital technologies and their accelerating impact across society in a strategic and priority manner at present and at future shifts" (Perkin & Abraham 2017, Higher Education Policy Institute, 2017). Hence, by developing competencies and innovations, and utilizing the potentials to provide more user-oriented and efficient services (Hinchcliffe, 2017). Conceptions of digital transformation in HE refers to ICTs defined as a "diverse set of technological tools and resources used to communicate, create, disseminate, store, and manage information" (Blurton, cited in Hoque & Alam, 2010, p.97. Technologies involved in ICTs include Radio and Television (broadcasting technology), Telephony, Computers, and the Internet. Additionally, there is "e-learning" yet known as online learning- for formal and informal "information network—the Internet, an intranet (LAN) or extranet (WAN) for course delivery, interaction and/or facilitation".

In the context of higher education, the technological trends encompass: Infrastructure, Models, Augmented Reality / Virtual Reality and Gamification (Forbes, 2017). Hence, "digital transformation" of higher education implies changes and reorganization of behaviours, using advances in technological development (Perkin & Abraham, 2017). Through digital transformation, instructors radically change their institutions by using platforms for communication and activity-planning with students, sourcing of study materials, exams assessment, as well as in classes planning (Limani, Hajrizi, Stapleton & Retkoceri, 2019).

For example, to make the content available online, "E-Modules" or modules are written and digitally stored in a computer using word processor for learners. Additionally, teleconferencing is widely used in HE and refers to "interactive electronic communication among people located at two or more different places." (Hoque & Alam, 2010, p.98). They also listed four types of teleconferencing: 1) audio conferencing (live real-time exchange of voice messages); 2) audio-graphic conferencing (used to send texts and images besides voice messages), 3) videoconferencing (used to exchange voice, graphics and moving images); and 4) Web-based conferencing (transmits images, texts, audio and visual media via internet).

Furthermore, open and distance learning is defined by the Commonwealth of Learning (2002) as "a way of providing learning opportunities that is characterized by the separation of teacher and learner in time or place, or both time and place; learning that is certified in some way by an institution or agency; the use of a variety of media, including print and electronic; two-way communications that allow learners and tutors to interact; the possibility of occasional face-to-face meetings; and a specialized division of labour in the production and delivery of courses."

## Herman Dooyeweerd Model

The Dooyeweerd model provides a theory of meaning and modal aspects of human relationship to the Divine. It analyses human's deepest presuppositions in terms of 'ground motives' and links the four motives through the three dualistic ones (Form-Matter, Nature- Grace and Nature-Freedom) to create the antinomies in theoretical thinking and a spectrum of Meaning (Wilson, 1997).

Dooyeweerd's theory of modal aspects shows that all Meaning, Being, Doing, Knowing and norms exist within this temporal realm and are enabled by modal aspects. Each aspect has a kernel meaning that is part of the spectrum of Meaning. Aspects are "the very enablers of the Being, Occurring and Knowing of the whole of temporal reality - which includes all of us" (Basden, 2000). He proposed this final list (Basden, 2002):

- Numeric aspect: amount
- Spatial aspect: continuous extension
- Kinematic aspect: flowing movement
- Physical aspect: energy, matter
- Biotic aspect: life functions
- Sensitive aspect: feeling and response
- Analytical aspect: distinction
- Creative aspect: formative power
- Lingual aspect: symbolic communication
- Social aspect: social interaction
- Economic aspect: frugal use of resources
- Aesthetic aspect: harmony
- Juridical aspect: what is due (rights, responsibility)
- Ethical aspect: self-giving love
- Pistic aspect: faith, vision, commitment

Table 1 summarizes Herman Dooyeweerd's aspects of temporal reality. What makes this model especial for diversity is that the aspects are irreducible, so that no aspect can be derived from the others; which Dooyeweerd called 'sphere sovereignty'. But sphere sovereignty on its own can lead us to fragmentation. He also stressed 'sphere universality': which means that the aspects are closely intertwined with one another, leading to a coherence and harmony. Each aspect of these aspects involves 'echoes' of all the others, and each is involved in a mutual inter-dependency with others.

*Table 1. A presentation of Herman Dooyeweerd's aspects of temporal reality*

| Aspect | Meaning | Good | Dooyeweerd's mode |
|---|---|---|---|
| Quantitative | One, several many; more and less | Reliable amount | Discrete amount |
| Spatial | Here, there, between, around, inside and outside | Simultaneity, continuity | Continuous extension |
| Kinematic | Going, continuous flowing | Change | Mathematical movement; continuous flowing |
| Physical | Forces, energy and matter | Irreversibility, persistence and causality | Energy |
| Biotic / Organic | Living as organisms in an environment | Distinct entities that sustain themselves and reproduce | Life functions |
| Sensitive / Psychic | Feeling, sensing, responding | Interactive engagement with world | Feeling |
| Analytical | Conceptualising, clarifying, categorising and cogitating | Thinking independently of the world; Theoretical thinking | Distinction |
| Formative | Deliberate creative shaping of things | Achievement, innovation | Formative power |
| Lingual | Expressing, recording and interpreting | Externalisation of our intended meaning; Referring beyond to whole web of meaning | Symbolic signification |
| Social | We, us and them; Associating, agreeing, appointing | Company: togetherness, respect, courtesy | Intercourse |
| Economic | Managing limited resources frugally | Sustainable viability / prosperity | Frugality |
| Aesthetic | Harmonising,, enjoying, playing, beautifying | Delight that seems non-necessary | Harmony |
| Juridical | Appropriateness, Due | Due for all, Responsibility; Infrastructures of policy, law, enforcement | Retribution |
| Ethical | Attitude: self-giving love, vulnerability, sacrifice | Extra goodness; Generous attitude pervading society | Love |
| Pistic | Vision, commitment, certainty and belief | Courage, loyalty, hope, meaningfulness, openness to the Divine; changed direction of society | Faith |

The above table is taken from the IJMAP paper a presentation of Herman Dooyeweerd's aspects of temporal reality.

## THEORETICAL FRAMEWORKS AND LITERATURE

This section includes 25 studies that discuss the implementation of digital transformation in HEIs and highlights the aspectual factor analysis in lights of Herman Dooyeweerd Model.

Curran et al. (2019) investigated effects of digital technologies on self-directed learning habits among adult learners. The researchers explored perspectives of learners on the effect of digital and mobile technologies for continuing professional education activities. Semi-structured interviews were administered with 55 adult students from four professional groups. Findings showed that digital and mobile technologies support self-directed learning of health and human services professionals and improve their perceptions of self-directed learning, self-directed learning resources, key triggers, and barriers to undertaking self-directed learning. The researchers introduced a conceptual model to highlight the main factors defining the self-directed learning patterns and practices of adults in a digital age.

Similarly, Limani, Hajrizi, Stapleton and Retkoceri (2019) discussed challenges of implementing digital transformation in higher education public and private institutions and their effects on academic organizations and business processes. Case studies and survey research were conducted to analyse relevant trends in the field of digital transformation at the national higher education institutions and their readiness to employ digital technologies in academic processes. The results showed that digital transformation process depends on digital literacy, professionalism in the classroom or workspace, and challenge value recognition. It was also found that although all institutions reported possession of such strategy, not all eventually held the same extent of knowledge and expertise for this, with the private institutions utilising more media than the public establishments.

In addition, Liu, Zha and He (2019) explored administrators and faculty members' experiences and expectations of MOOC in 50 higher education institutions in China. The result revealed that the government as well as institutions held either sole or joint leadership in MOOC development and operation. Universities followed specific mechanisms to operate MOOCs; however, there were some challenges including insufficient technical support, inadequate curriculum/instructional design training, and a lack of national curriculum/instructional design along with development and platform standards.

Tekic and Koroteev (2019) identified digital transformation strategies in usage of digital technologies and readiness of a business model for digital operation. The study developed a typology of four generic strategies that differ in the primary motivation and target of transformation, leadership style, importance of skills like creativity and entrepreneurial spirit among employees, risks and challenges encountered in the process, consequences of expected failure, and available tactics for improvement.

Furthermore, Bond et al. (2018) investigated face-to-face educational technology use at a mid-sized German university. The results revealed that teachers required professional development, in order to improve their academic digital literacy. This study also showed that although students were willing to use technological tools and digital media for academic purposes, their access to such technologies depended on the teachers' ability to use digital media and the university policies.

To improve the quality of English teaching at the tertiary level in China, Gao (2012) used a CECR policy to focus on student-centered approaches and the use of a computer-based multimedia teaching model. This study investigated the opinions of higher education teachers, administrators and policy makers about the use of educational technology in the policy and whether the policy achieved this goal. The study also explored the responses of teachers towards the requirements of CECR 2004 by ensuring their understanding of ICT, the requirements of CECR 2004 concerning ICT, the present consensus on ICT in pedagogy and the perceptions of policy makers and administrators about these issues. The findings showed that there was a gap between the policy and the reality in terms of ICT pedagogy in tertiary English teaching in China. The researcher used surveys and interviews with higher education teachers, administrators and policy makers across China, to explore their understandings of the policy, their expectations on the current state of implementation and the effectiveness of the implementation.

Gouseti (2017) highlighted the digital practices of doctoral students and their perceptions of the nature of digital scholarship. The researcher conducted a qualitative, in-depth interviews with 12 students in a UK higher education institution. The findings showed 7 types of engagement with digital technologies and identified the issues that underpin digital scholarship practices.

Agbatogun (2013) in his study explored faculty members' use of digital technologies in Nigerian Universities. A Technology Use Scale was carried out for collecting the data and descriptive statistics analysis showed that the majority of faculty members adopted emerging digital technologies for teaching and learning. In addition, some factors influenced faculty members' use of digital technologies in their classrooms including academic status, gender, academic qualification, motivating and discouraging factors. All these variables had significant effects on professionals' use of technologies except gender.

Moreover, Buzzard et al. (2011) reported the findings of the two research studies that showed that students and instructors were eager to use digital technologies in learning and teaching. The findings highlighted issues and concerns in three areas: disciplinary differences, meta-teaching demands, and tool sophistication. While students prefer more traditional instructional technology, faculty members prefer the use of course-learning technology offered by their universities or publishers. Findings also showed that there are huge differences in preferences and usage across disciplines, in particular, business and economics professionals and students having stronger technology preferences than teachers and students of the fine arts and life sciences.

To investigate the impact of digital technologies on academic entrepreneurship, Rippa and Secundo (2019) created a novel concept of Digital Academic Entrepreneurship. The researchers conducted a qualitative literature review to propose an interpretative framework for Digital Academic Entrepreneurship comprised these components: the rationale for the adoption of digital technologies for academic entrepreneurship (why), the emerging forms of digital academic entrepreneurship (what), the stakeholders involved through the digital technologies to achieve the academic entrepreneurship goal (who), and the processes of academic entrepreneurship supported by digital technologies (how). The researchers provided a research agenda for field.

Greener (2012) sought to explore resistance of academic staff to the use of technology affordances in HE teaching and learning. The study was conducted to explore why do staff avoid ICTs and virtual learning environments (VLEs) and of Web 2.0. With the help of a marketing model to adopt digital technologies, the researcher identified the potential personal factors that led to this resistance. The researcher analysed unstructured interviews with staff to explore the possible learning and teaching affordances of ICTs. The staff surveyed showed an interest in using digital technologies in learning and teaching to empower students, and enhance creativity and innovation. Teaching beliefs were the controlling factor, followed by teachers' role. However, staff lack of use of technology was due to the need for last minute preparation, which could be explained by an attitude or belief about pedagogy.

Balyer and Oz (2018) in their qualitative study explored academics' views on digital transformation in education programs and management processes. The sample consists of 20 faculty members working at 9 universities in the Department of Educational Sciences. The semi-structured interviews showed that in the digital transformation process, managers must create a vision to manage an effective learning environment. School shareholders are involved in this transformation by engaging them access to the place and time by providing content and infrastructure which is technologically appropriate.

Ali, WoodHarper and Mohamad (2018) examined (CC) adoption in higher education institutions (HEIs). A systematic literature review of empirical studies was conducted to explore the CC adoption levels in HEIs and the benefits and challenges. 20 articles were included and findings showed that a number of Universities have a keen interest in using CC in their institutions. In conclusion, the review identified a clear literature gap in this research area: limited empirical studies focusing on CC implementation in HEIs.

Despite the wide use of CC (Cloud Computing) in HEIs, there are a few research that addressed the issue of trust in cloud adoption in the UK HEI context, and identifying more efficient strategies to overcome the existing CC trust issue. Ali et al. (2020) created a five-stage strategic roadmap to address the trust issues influencing the uptake of cloud services across UK universities. The researchers found that IT and management participation and support are the essential to the success of the strategic framework.

Ali (2019a) used the Multiview 3 (MV3) model to explore the main qualities and risks that contribute to the adoption or rejection of CC by UK HEIs from multiple perspectives. After conducting an exploratory qualitative study on 32 University staff in 2 UK Universities, findings showed that security, privacy and trust are the key determinants to non-adoption of CC. Determinants to CC adoption include promoting relationships between students and teachers via collaborative tools. Proposing cloud apps for mobile devices to access virtual learning materials and email securely off-campus is another factor. University staff are still at a cross-road when it comes to cloud adoption, but future advances of the cloud may help to make the decision to adopt CC technology.

In addition, Ali, Wood- Harper, and Al-Gahtani (2019) explored the characteristics of an information system to facilitate the teaching practices in UK HEIs from multiple stakeholder perspectives. The researchers evaluated the "MyPGR" system to identify the technical problems UK Universities are facing, with the support of a soft systems approach (CATWOE). The proposed solution is the Educational-Monitoring-and-Progression-as-a-Service (EMPaaS), which is based on the Cloud Computing model. EMPaaS could monitor students' progression and enable students to use free cloud applications to keep track of milestones and progressions (Ali et al., 2019). The highly accessible nature of cloud applications provides the cost-effectiveness of adopting cloud services, which saves additional funds for UK Universities to pursue other investments.

Similarly, Ali (2019b) conducted a qualitative study to investigate the potential barriers and enablers of CC adoption by HEIs from a doctoral student perspective at a University in North-west England. Interview results showed that the most significant enablers of the educational CC were cost efficiency, scalability, flexibility and mobility, and especially collaboration among students. Additionally, the most significant challenges of the educational cloud were security and cultural resistance. The adoption rate of CC is increasing gradually in UK HEIs, due to cost efficient and collaborative nature of the educational cloud.

Lapidos and Ruffolo (2017) identified the structure, content, digital approach, and outcomes of IBHPC (integrated behavioural health and primary care) education program, housed in a school of social work at a major university. The challenges of interprofessional digital education in balancing depth and breadth, continue to merit consideration as quality improvement continues. Digital technologies makes the program accessible to professionals with peer-to-peer chat.

Furthermore, He et al. (2018) investigated the factors that influence students' digital informal learning (DIL). The researchers proposed a model based on decomposed theory of planned behaviour to investigate learners' behavioural intention to DIL. Different aspects of DIL behaviour were explored through examining cognitive learning, metacognitive learning, and social and motivation learning. The researchers also integrated digital competence as a way into the model, besides other variables to test the proposed model. 335 university students selected from 3 universities in China. Findings showed that support and better understanding for the importance of motivation factors such as digital competence and compatibility to explain students' DIL.

Ali (2019c) conducted a systematic review of studies on cloud adoption from a technological, organizational, environmental and personal perspectives. 17 studies in the HEI context from 2012 to 2017 are reviewed and analysed. The findings recommended more studies on cloud adoption in the HEI domain from multiple perspectives, especially in relation to the socio-technical contexts related to cloud adoption.

Likewise, Belichenko, Davidovitch and Kravchenko (2017) utilized methodological aspects of structuring knowledge and effective usage of information resources designed for the scientific and methodological study of practical recommendations in Digital learning implementation. The researchers identified knowledge representation as one of the most serious problems that face the knowledge construction and processing. To enhance the efficiency of learning process, the researchers identified applications and rational structuring knowledge through using information resources of Digital Learning. This model is based on the idea of using the principles of abstraction, encapsulation, modularity, hierarchy, typing, concurrency preservation and implementation. Digital learning was implemented in multidisciplinary aspects: education, mathematics, and statistics.

Ali, Wafer, and Ramlogan (2019) aimed to formulate a model that gives a comprehensive framework about possible factors affecting e-government adoption by citizens. To achieve this goal, an aspectual analysis of Dooyeweerd theory was conducted to overcome the limitations of adoption theories. The research contributes to available literature by providing aspectual method to investigate e-government factors to support understanding of citizens' adoption barriers from a different perspective.

Quaicoe and Pata (2017) proposed a model to explain the situation of Digital Teaching and Learning (TD-TaL) in Ghanaian schools from the perceptions of school teachers. The (TD-TaL) model was developed based on the theories of Valsiner's Zone of Free Movement (ZFM) and Zone of Promoted Action (ZPA) and Vygotsky's Zone of Proximal Development (ZPD). The model aims at exploring the effects of ZFM in schools (comprising Digital environment factors and Personal attitudinal and Digital Culture factors) and ZPA (comprising Teacher Training factor) on the Teachers' Digital Knowledge, Competence and Action (TDKCA) factors to impact teachers in their Zone of Proximal Development. The model was examined in Ghana using the survey data collected from 256 teachers from 45 schools across six districts in the Western Region of Ghana. The findings showed that Personal and Digital Culture factors, but most of all teachers' Digital Attitudes effected directly on Teachers' Digital Activities they claimed to be doing, while from Environmental factors only Schools' Digital Agenda was influencing Teachers' Digital Action both directly and indirectly through Teachers' Digital Training (ZPA). The model showed that in Ghanaian schools the ZFM factors Digital Infrastructure and Digital Support to Digital Teaching did not associate with the ZPA factor Digital Teacher Training and overall to Teachers' Digital Knowledge, Competence and Action factors.

*Table 2. Displays the aspectual factor analysis of the reviewed studies based on Herman Dooyeweerd Model*

| | Aspects | Author | Factors | Description of Aspectual Factors |
|---|---|---|---|---|
| Human Aspects | Analytical (distinction, conceptualization) | Ylber et al. (2019)<br>Ali et al. (2019) | Distinguishing between digital transformation dimensions, issues, implications, and trends<br>Formulating a model that gives a comprehensive view about possible factors affecting e-government adoption by citizens | Analytical aspect helps to distinguish between different digital transformation dimensions, issues, implications, and trends in higher education settings<br>Aspectual analysis of Dooyeweerd theory, which is used as a method to overcome the limitations of adoption theories. |
| | Formative (deliberate shaping: history, culture, technology, goals, achievement) | Zeljko et al. (2019)<br>Pierluigi Rippa<br>Giustina Secundo<br>2019 | Importance of digital transformation skills like creativity<br>Impact of digital technologies on the components of Digital Academic Entrepreneurship | Formative aspect refers to the digital transformation skills like creativity and how and why they are important to higher education settings<br>An interpretative framework for Digital Academic Entrepreneurship and how, what and why processes of academic entrepreneurship supported by digital technologies |
| Social Aspects | Social ('we': sociality, relationships, roles, respect) | Ali et al. (2019)<br>Adrienne Lapidos &<br>Mary Ruffolo (2017) | Student and faculty participation and support<br>Description of the structure, content, digital approach, and outcomes of a continuing education program in integrated behavioural health and primary care, housed in a school of social work at a major university. | Impact of stakeholder support and participation on the digital transformation process in higher education settings<br>The IBHPC program is an interprofessional educational experience that mirrors the collaborative team based care that is expected in integrated care settings. It emphasizes specific techniques—particularly the peer-to-peer chats—help facilitate mutual learning, networking, and sharing resources. |
| | Economic (frugal management of resources) | Aydın Balyer<br>Ömer Öz<br>2019 | IT infrastructure<br>Cost effectiveness<br>Digital transformation benefits<br>Effect of digital transformation, educational management, 21st century pedagogy | Degree of IT usage among higher education stakeholders based on availability of IT resources, IT costs and service efficiency<br>Determining academics' views on digital transformation in education in terms of program and management processes. |
| | Aesthetic (harmony, surprise, fun, play, enjoyment) | Greener (2012) | Business-IT alignment | Impact of IT usage on stakeholder perceptions of digital transformation and whether technologies align with the needs of higher education stakeholders |
| Societal Aspects | Juridical (due: responsibilities + rights) | Gao (2010)<br>Dolch et al. (2018) | Policy and regulations related to the pedagogical use of digital technologies<br>Different policies, initiatives and strategies addressing educational technology innovations in HE. | IT policies and regulations regarding technologies impacting teaching and learning outcomes |
| | Ethical (self-giving love, generosity) | Greener (2012)<br>Ali (2019b) | Attitude or likeness towards the use of digital technologies<br>Exploring the potential barriers and enablers of CC adoption by HEIs from a doctoral student perspective | Likeness towards the use of digital technologies to improve teaching and learning outcomes<br>Discovering the most significant enablers of the educational cloud (cost efficiency, scalability, flexibility and mobility, and collaboration among students) and barriers (security and cultural resistance). |
| | Pistic (vision, aspiration, commitment, belief) | Ali et al. (2019)<br>Gousti (2017) | Trust in digital technology<br>Belief in digital technology<br>Doctoral students engage with digital technologies | Teaching and learning development depends on stakeholders' trust and confidence in technology to deliver pedagogical outcomes and meeting their specific needs e.g. students' learning and teachers' effective delivery of digital classroom sessions<br>Types of doctoral students' engagement and practices with digital technologies to change stereotyping and wrong perceptions. |

*continues on following page*

*Table 2. Continued*

| | Aspects | Author | Factors | Description of Aspectual Factors |
|---|---|---|---|---|
| Other Uncategorised | Quantitative (discrete amount) | Belichenko, et al. (2017) | Combining methodological aspects of structuring knowledge and effective usage of information resources which are designed for the scientific and methodological study of practical recommendations in Digital learning implementation. | Increasing the efficiency at the university learning process on the basis of a possible applications and rational structuring knowledge. The proposed concept of using information resources of Digital Learning is based on the idea of using the principles of abstraction, encapsulation, modularity, hierarchy, typing, concurrency preservation and implementation in such stages of this process as algorithmic support of knowledge structuring and structured transfer of knowledge to students. |
| | Spatial (continuous space) | Adrienne Lapidos & Mary Ruffolo (2017) | | The IBHPC program is an interprofessional educational experience that mirrors the collaborative team based care that is expected in integrated care settings. This collaborative digital approaches may help organizations sustain changes that are made to their workflow and practice. One outstanding example of inter-agency digital collaboration is Project ECHO (see http://echo.unm.edu/), which links specialist teams at academic hubs to primary care physicians in local communities to support the care of complex patients. |
| | Kinematic (movement) | Timmis, Sue; Muhuro, Patricia (2019) | Longitudinal study across three universities, and employing Holland's theory of figured worlds, we highlight rural students' experiences of digital transitions across different cultural worlds. | Students improvise to decode the digital university and figure out new practices. Decolonisation of universities involves rethinking the 'technocratic consciousness' (both colonialist and neoliberal) and its apparatus including digital systems and structures. For rural students to become successful digital practitioners in higher education, universities should acknowledge prior digital experience and forms of knowledge and focus on expanding individual and collective agency in supporting transitions, as mechanisms for shaping a decolonised digital education. |
| | Physical (energy + mass, forces) | He, et al. (2018)<br>Subrahmanyam, Kaveri; Renukarya, Bhavya (2015) | To understand better university students' digital informal learning (DIL), this study proposed a model based on decomposed theory of planned behaviour to investigate students' behavioural intention to DIL. This study also integrated digital competence as a new construct into the model, along with other variables to test the proposed model.<br>The article proposes that different aspects of game features and game play might influence learning in different ways. | Different aspects of DIL behaviour were explored, through examining behaviours of cognitive learning, metacognitive learning, and social and motivation learning.<br>The article identifies 4 potential pathways of digital game influence: time, formal features, content, and context of use. Research findings from games and other technologies are presented to provide support for each pathway. |
| | Biotic / Organic (life functions + organisms) | Alaba Olaoluwakotansibe Agbatogun 2013 | Predicting faculty members' use of digital technologies | Indicate some environmental factors motivate and frustrate faculty members' use of digital technologies in the classroom |
| | Sensitive / Psychic (sense, feeling, emotion) | Curran et al. (2019)<br>Liu, el al. (2019)<br>Buzzard, et al (2011)<br>Ali (2019a) | Effect of digital and mobile technologies on continuing professional education activities.<br>Challenges faced by administrators and faculty when using operating MOOCs<br>Capture usage of technological tools from the perspectives of both students and faculty members<br>Exploring the key qualities and risks that determine the adoption or non-adoption of CC | Impact of technologies in the self-directed learning habits and activities of adult learners.<br>Identifying the experiences and expectations from MOOC administrators and faculty in higher education institutions<br>Differences in preferences and usage across disciplines between instructors and students<br>Determinants to cloud adoption include improving relationships between students and teachers via collaborative tools, |
| | Lingual (meaning carried by symbols) | Belichenko, et al. (2017) | Combining methodological aspects of structuring knowledge and effective usage of information resources which are designed for the scientific and methodological study of practical recommendations in Digital learning implementation. | Increasing the efficiency at the university learning process on the basis of a possible applications and rational structuring knowledge. The proposed concept of using information resources of Digital Learning is based on the idea of using the principles of abstraction, encapsulation, modularity, hierarchy, typing, concurrency preservation and implementation in such stages of this process as algorithmic support of knowledge structuring and structured transfer of knowledge to students. |

Subrahmanyam and Renukarya (2015) identified 4 four pathways of digital game influence: time, formal features, content, and context of use. The conceptual framework presented can ensure learning from, with, and within games. Finally, Timmis and Muhuro (2019) used Holland's theory of figured worlds to describe rural students' experiences of digital transitions across different cultural worlds, prior to university and once they arrive, including the bewildering technocratic systems and practices and resulting conflicts and positioning encountered. To enable rural students to become successful digital practitioners in higher education, universities should acknowledge prior digital experience and forms of knowledge and stress expanding individual and collective agency in supporting transitions, to create a decolonized digital education.

## CONCLUSION

Referring to the literature review in this chapter and the Herman Dooyeweerd Model, it can be concluded that there is a gap in literature in ICT and digital transformation studies in Saudi Arabia in terms of examining the perceptions and practices of students and professionals when using ICT in HEIs in Saudi universities. More studies are needed to explore the barriers and challenges of implementation of effective e-learning systems in learning and teaching.

Therefore, improving research skills, integrating digital transformation in teaching and learning, and providing administrative support are crucial for effective HEIs. Strategic planning and using modern infrastructure allow all students and professionals to communicate effectively and share information successfully. Creating a framework to enhance the implementation of the projects and improve service delivery to empower professionals, students and staff to use IT systems to improve their digital literacy is essential in HEIs in Saudi Arabia. Universities should analyse new digital trends and integrate them in tertiary education and identify the risks and costs to incorporate these technologies.

## REFERENCES


Agbatogun, A. (2013). Interactive digital technologies' use in Southwest Nigerian universities. *Educational Technology Research and Development*, *61*(2), 333–357. Advance online publication. doi:10.100711423-012-9282-1

Al-Asmari, A. (2005). *The use of internet among EFL teachers at the colleges of technology in Saudi Arabia* (Dissertation). Ohio University.

Al-Draiby, O. (2010). *E-learning and Its Effectiveness in Saudi Arabia. Faculty of Computer and Information Technology*. KAU.

Al-Kahtani, S. A. (2001). *Computer-assisted language learning in EFL, instruction at selected Saudi Arabian Universities* (PhD Dissertation). Indian University of Pennsylvania.

Al-Khalifa, H. S. (2009). *E-Learning and ICT integration in colleges and universities in Saudi Arabia*. E-learn Magazine.

Al-Nuaim, H. A. (2019). The use of virtual classrooms in E-learning: A case study in King Abdul-Aziz University, Saudi Arabia. *E-Learning and Digital Media*, *9*(2), 211–222. doi:10.2304/elea.2012.9.2.211

Ali, M. (2019a). Cloud Computing at a Cross Road: Quality and Risks in Higher Education. *Advances in Internet of Things*, *9*(03), 33–49. doi:10.4236/ait.2019.93003

Ali, M. (2019b). The Barriers and Enablers of the Educational Cloud: A Doctoral Student Perspective. *Open Journal of Business and Management*, *7*(01), 1–24. doi:10.4236/ojbm.2019.71001

Ali, M. (2019c). Multiple Perspective of Cloud Computing Adoption Determinants in Higher Education a Systematic Review. *International Journal of Cloud Applications and Computing*, *9*(3), 89–109. doi:10.4018/IJCAC.2019070106

Ali, M., Wood-Harper, T., & Al-Gahtani, A. S. (2019). Contextual Analysis of Educational Monitoring and Progression as a Service (EMPaaS) System in Higher Education. *Open Journal of Business and Management*, *7*(3), 1525–1542. doi:10.4236/ojbm.2019.73105

Ali, M., Wood-Harper, T., & Ramlogan, R. (2020). A-Framework-Strategy-to-Overcome-Trust-Issues-on-Cloud-Computing-Adoption-in-Higher-Education. In B. B. Gupta (Ed.), *Modern Principles, Practices, and Algorithms for Cloud Security* (pp. 162–182). IGI Global. doi:10.4018/978-1-7998-1082-7.ch008

Alkhalaf, S., Drew, S., AlGhamdi, R., & Alfarraj, O. (2012). E-Learning system on higher education institutions in KSA: Attitudes and perceptions of faculty members. *Procedia: Social and Behavioral Sciences*, *47*, 1199–1205. doi:10.1016/j.sbspro.2012.06.800

Balyer, A., & Oz, O. (2018). Academicans' views on digital transformation in education. *International Online Journal of Education and Teaching*, *5*(4), 809–830.

Basden, A. (2000). Aspects of Reality as We Experience It (online). *Andrew Basden 2000-today*. http://dooy.info/aspects.html

Basden, A. (2002). The critical theory of Herman Dooyeweerd? *Journal of Information Technology*, *17*(4), 257–269. Advance online publication. doi:10.1080/0268396022000017770

Belichenko, M., Davidovitch, N., & Kravchenko, Y. (2017). Digital learning characteristics and principles of information resources knowledge structuring. *European Journal of Educational Research*, *6*(3), 261–267. doi:10.12973/eu-jer.6.3.261

Bond, M., Marín, V., Dolch, C., Bedenlier, S., & Zawacki-Richter, O. (2018). Digital transformation in German higher education: Student and teacher perceptions and usage of digital media. *International Journal of Educational Technology in Higher Education*, *15*(48), 1–20. doi:10.118641239-018-0130-1

Buzzard, C., Crittenden, V., Crittenden, W. F., & McCarty, P. (2011). The Use of Digital Technologies in the Classroom: A Teaching and Learning Perspective. *Journal of Marketing Education*, *33*(2), 131–139. doi:10.1177/0273475311410845

Curran, V., Gustavson, D., Simmons, K., Lannon, H., Wang, C., & Garmsiri, M. (2019). Adult learners' perceptions of self-directed learning and digital technology usage in continuing professional education: An update for the digital age. *Journal of Adult and Continuing Education*, *25*(1), 74–93. doi:10.1177/1477971419827318

Forbes.com. (2017). *Forbes Welcome*. https://www.forbes.com/sites/danielnewman/2016/08/30/top-10-trends-for-digital-transformation-in-2017/#22d263ca47a5

Gao, L. (2012). Digital technologies and English instruction in China's higher education system. *Teacher Development: An International Journal of Teachers' Professional Development, 16*(2), 161-179. DOI: doi:10.1080/13664530.2012.667967

Gouseti, A. (2017). Exploring doctoral students' use of digital technologies: What do they use them for and why? *Educational Review, 69*(5), 638–654. doi:10.1080/00131911.2017.1291492

Greener, S. (2012). Using Marketing Models to Review Academic Staff Acceptance of Digital Technology to Enhance Learning in Higher Education. *DIVAI 2012 - 9th International Scientific Conference on Distance Learning in Applied Informatics*, 111-126.

He, T., Zhu, C., & Questier, F. (2018). Predicting digital informal learning: An empirical study among Chinese University students. *Asia Pacific Education Review, 19*(1), 79–90. Advance online publication. doi:10.100712564-018-9517-x

Higher Education Policy Institute. (2017). *Rebooting learning for the digital age: What next for technology enhanced higher education?* Oxuniprint.

Hinchcliffe, D. (2017). *Five emerging technologies for rapid digital transformation*. ZDNet. Available at: http://www.zdnet.com/article/five-emerging-technologies-for-rapid-digital-transformation

Hoque, S., & Alam, S. (2010). The Role of Information and Communication Technologies (ICTs) in Delivering Higher Education – A Case of Bangladesh. *International Education Studies, 3*(2). Available at SSRN: https://ssrn.com/abstract=1630526

Lapidos, L., & Ruffolo, M. (2017). Access to Interprofessional Continuing Education in Integrated Care through Digital Instructional Technology. *Journal of Social Work Education, 53*(S1), S40-S46. DOI: do i:10.1080/10437797.2017.1288596

Limani, Y., Hajrizi, E., Stapleton, L., & Retkoceri, M. (2019). Digital Transformation Readiness in Higher Education Institutions (HEI): The Case of Kosovo. *IFAC PapersOnLine,* 52-57.

Liu, M., Zha, S., & He, W. (2019). Digital Transformation Challenges: A Case Study Regarding the MOOC Development and Operations at Higher Education Institutions in China. *TechTrends, 63*(5), 621–630. doi:10.100711528-019-00409-y

Mirza, A. A. (2007). Utilizing distance learning technologies to deliver courses in a segregated educational environment. *World conference on educational multimedia, hypermedia and telecommunications.* 1855–1860.

Mirza A. A. (2008). Is E-Learning finally gaining legitimacy in Saudi Arabia? *Applied Computing and Informatics, 6*(2).

Oyaid, A. A. (2009). *Education policy in Saudi Arabia and its relation to secondary school teachers. ICT Use, Perceptions, and Views of the Future of ICT in Education* (Ph.D. Thesis). University of Exeter, UK.

Perkin, N., & Abraham, P. (2017). *Building the Agile Business through Digital Transformation*. Kogan Page Stylus.

Quaicoe, J., & & Pata, K. (2017). Basic school teachers' perspective to digital teaching and learning in Ghana. *Education and Information Technologies*. Advance online publication. doi:10.100710639-017-9660-8

Rippa, P., & Secundo, G. (2019). Digital academic entrepreneurship: The potential of digital technologies on academic entrepreneurship. *Technological Forecasting and Social Change, Elsevier*, *146*(C), 900–911. doi:10.1016/j.techfore.2018.07.013

Subrahmanyam, K., & Renukarya, B. (2015). Digital Games and Learning: Identifying Pathways of Influence. *Educational Psychologist*, *50*(4), 335–348. doi:10.1080/00461520.2015.1122532

Tekic, Z., & Koroteev, D. (2019). From disruptively digital to proudly analog: A holistic typology of digital transformation strategies. *Business Horizons*, *62*(6), 683–693. doi:10.1016/j.bushor.2019.07.002

The Commonwelath of Learning. (2002). *An Introduction to Open and Distance Learning*. Available from http://www.col.org/ODLIntro/introODL.htm

Timmis, S., & Muhuro, P. (2019). De-coding or de-colonising the technocratic university? Rural students' digital transitions to South African higher education. *Learning, Media and Technology*, *44*(3), 252–266. doi:10.1080/17439884.2019.1623250

Wilson, F. (1997). The truth is out there: The search for emancipatory principles in information systems design. *Information Technology & People*, *10*(2), 187–204. doi:10.1108/09593849710178207

## ADDITIONAL READING

Dooyeweerd, H. (2016). *A New Critique of Theoretical Thought*. Paideia Press. https://books.google.co.uk/books?id=p7KwQgAACAAJ

## KEY TERMS AND DEFINITIONS

**Aspectual Analysis:** A multi-aspectual analysis technique that promotes black and white thinking of a given system.

**Cloud Computing:** An innovation of ubiquitous and simplified access to data.

**Digital Transformation:** Using digital technologies to develop new or modify existing business processes to meet the changing needs of an organisation.

**Dooyeweerd Model:** The model of aspectual analysis which covers 15 unique aspects to analyse a system or process.

**E-Learning:** Learning via online applications and technologies.

**Higher Education:** Universities in which tertiary level courses are taught.

**Personal Development:** The process of improving individual skills, knowledge and experiences to meet a common goal (e.g., better job prospects).

# Chapter 9
# An Interactive System Evaluation of Blackboard System Applications:
## A Case Study of Higher Education

**Abubakar Albakri**
*Birmingham City University, UK*

**Ahmed Abdulkhaleq**
https://orcid.org/0000-0002-6618-0644
*University of Bradford, UK*

## ABSTRACT

*Online learning today demonstrates comparability with face-to-face learning. New digital technologies provide an improved and immersive learning experience for students and related educational ecosystem. A virtual learning environment (VLE), for example, is an online-based platform that provides digital solutions for teachers and students that enhance the learning experience. This chapter observes the main elements of virtual learning environments, together with an evaluation of the VLE blackboard system design, and discusses how blackboard facilitates teaching, learning, and communication in HEIs. Findings suggest that the weaknesses of blackboard could be compensated by the opportunities, whilst threats should be considered by the policymakers to enrich the teaching and learning experience. Recommendations and future potential research are also provided.*

## INTRODUCTION

Nowadays, online learning demonstrates comparability with face-to-face learning (Bernard et al., 2004; Means et al., 2009). New digital technologies allow for a better learning experience for students and the related educational ecosystem. The introduction of Massive Opened Online Courses (MOOCs) have changed the earlier perception that the university studies are always held in a formal classroom

DOI: 10.4018/978-1-7998-4846-2.ch009

environment with a physical presence of a lecturer (Young, 2012). The integration of technology into the learning process could be initiated with general purpose cloud applications, such as Google Docs or Drive, Calendar, and Sites, which can be used effectively for collaboration between academic staff and their students (Owayid and Uden, 2014). Altogether, this transform learning process to either *blended learning environment* (Osguthorpe and Graham, 2003; Graham, 2006; see also Glahn, Gruber and Tartakovski, 2015) or *virtual learning environment* (Dillenbourg et al., 2002). This allows students to enhance their learning experience by accessing online content from their own mobile devices anytime and fosters collaborative work among students and professors. The *virtual learning environment* differ from *blended learning environment* by extending online components in overall student learning. If for *virtual learning environment*, students interact and learn online, *blended learning environment* calls for a mixture of online and face-to-face learning for a student.

Both environments enable Blackboard systems to support learning process, which enables virtual representation of the course content. Initially planned to enhance face-to-face teaching with course details, syllables, web links, study instructions that are available online, Blackboard system has enabled academic staff, technical staff and students to engage in new form of online interaction, to form groups with different access rights and to contribute to the learning process in almost all modern universities. One of the main barriers impeding utilisation of virtual learning environment is the lack of digital skills, poor design of modern blackboards and incorrect utilisation of a blackboard. In contrast to generation Z of modern students, which cannot imagine the world without IT, the earlier generations of tutors, lecturers and professors may find themselves in a disadvantaged position towards new educational technologies, especially in humanities and mainly due to their previous educational background. As a result of this, many professors find challenging to interact with students online, especially in terms of speed of reaction, timings, format of answers and prefer the conventional ways of interaction. At the same time, many students find the blackboard systems confusing. Their conservative human-machine interface design, which was implemented mainly following the conventional requirements of tutors (Web 1.0), often is less suitable than the one applied in popular apps, marketplaces and social networks that are used by students (Web 2.0). Additional case is the situation in the 3rd world countries, where the access to computer and computer literacy skills is constrained. This implies reflection on how students and lecturers perceive the arrangements of educational activities: (1) engaging in discussion, (2) submitting assignments, and (3) delivering course content. Altogether, this calls for evaluation of potential mass application of interactive virtual learning environments, such as blackboard systems, in higher education institutions (HEIs).

In this chapter we observe the main elements of virtual learning environments, evaluate design of a blackboard system as an example of such, discuss how blackboard facilitates teaching, learning and communication in HEIs and derive recommendations how to avoid or overcome the known barriers impeding utilisation of these digital technologies. The chapter finishes with recommendations and future potential research.

## VIRTUAL LEARNING ENVIRONMENTS (VLE)

A virtual learning environment (VLE) refers to an online-based platform that "offers students and professors digital solutions that enhance the learning experience". Such settings could be defined by the seven elements (Dillenbourg et al., 2002).

First, this is a designed *online* space, for instance, a website or an educational portal. Second, any VLE is a designed *social* space, where students face learning in "educational interactions". A good example of a social space is a real classroom, where discussion and partial interpretation contribute to the "melting pot" of the shared knowledge (In contrast to that, when students read a book, this is not an example of social space). In VLEs all students get their profiles and social media services (chats, forums) which enables better learning. Third, the virtual space is realised in a *variety of designs*: from text-based interfaces to sophisticated 3D graphical outputs. What important here is, that it impacts student's behaviour and the way they work even being described by text (Dillenbourg et al., 1999). Forth, VLE enables students to be *active participants* in learning: they co-construct the virtual space, add content to the topics, engage in simulations and discussions for problem solving. The difference is mainly in transforming 1:1 connection between a teacher and a student to 1: N connection between then, where all students can read the outputs of others and co-create knowledge. Fifth, Virtual learning environments are not *limited to distance learning*: they enrich classroom experiences that make them a blended environment. For instance, face-to-face learning could be supported by the digital representation online, where students can go back to slides, ask questions, which could be partially answered by other students themselves, and scroll the additional course materials. Furthermore, as lots of students do not actually live far away from the campus, they could compensate missing classes due to daily work obligations by utilising virtual learning tools, necessary in educational process online. Same students may enjoy face-to-face discussions, social meetings, kick-off events and other educational activities if they wish. Sixth, Virtual learning environments *integrate heterogeneous technologies* and a *variety of pedagogical approaches in information, communication, collaboration, learning and management.* (see also Peraya et al., 1999). Like face-to-face learning, which combines classes, libraries, class formal communication and informal communication over time, virtual learning digitalises all of these features, incorporates them on the web and makes them available to students.

## OVERVIEW OF BLACKBOARD SYSTEM

Blackboard Systems (BBS) is known to be a virtual learning environment (VLE), and is specifically designed to facilitate the learning process. There are three perspectives that focus on the VLE as an information system within an organisation of implementation. These are (1) implementation as technology acceptance, (2) implementation as diffusion of innovations and (3) implementation as a learning process (Keller, 2005). This software is produced by Blackboard Inc., and was founded in 1997. At that time, Blackboard Company had a vision of introducing new, friendly online resources to provide students with essential details, such as course outlines, syllables, web links, study directions and other relevant information.

Academic staff, technical staff and students are classes that use this method. However, students and academic staff are important users of this programme. Whereas technical staff are responsible for co-ordinating and discussing technical problems such as the issue of usernames and passwords to students and academic staff. Universities are dealing with thousands of students and have staff connected to many colleges, such as finance, computer science, law, and others. In fact, this chapter evaluates the Blackboard system from a student and staff perspective due to the ability to access this part of the system. The Blackboard program requires a username and password to be used, and provides administration tools that help to change the VLE and make learning and sharing information easier online.

The Blackboard program offers a range of features to create a comfortable learning atmosphere for both learners and teachers. These features may be identified as:

- **Assessments**: In this case, teachers will delegate assignments to students. Nonetheless, in this field and within the Blackboard system, students are provided with the Turnitin tool to check the originality of their assignments;
- **Availability control**: Course instructors have the opportunity to track student access to course content, discussion areas, tasks, and other Blackboard program paths;
- **Calendar**: this room enables teachers to decide the dates of significant events, such as tests and day of submission;
- **Communication tools**: The Blackboard program helps students to send emails to each other and to tutors as well. Teachers also have the option to open discussion boards to address classroom subjects in more depth and to share ideas. Furthermore, the latest version of Blackboard (V.9) allows students to receive updates of new material that has been added to the course space. In the blackboard system, students will obtain these alerts on their devices, which is an innovative technical innovation;
- **Course content**: the introduction, alteration and updating of course materials, including posts, assignments and learning media, can be done here;
- **Course management**: allow teachers to add, change and upgrade the features of the course. Teachers have a significant ability to modify the functionality of the program according to their needs;
- **Designing courses**: tutors can complete the initial setup of their course. Students will be automatically registered for their courses in accordance with their curriculum and level of study;
- **Grade centre**: This function includes a record of student grades, item weighting, and performance feedback.

Nevertheless, the Blackboard portal has been related to useful services and websites such as the Student Self-Service Plan, the Marketing Field and the Student Network Webpage. The efficiency and advantages of the Blackboard platform have increased. The Course Section is the main area in which students and teachers exchange information and includes most of the features listed in the previous section.

## CONTEMPORARY BLACKBOARD SYSTEM FEATURES

Lawrence (2006) explains the creation of The Blackboard Academic Suite, which consists of three separate but integrated products. The Blackboard Learning System is the CMS, which offers an online learning platform that includes course management and content development resources, e-mail, chat, discussion forums, task features, evaluation tools, grade book, and course statistics. The other two software – Blackboard Community System and Blackboard Content System – support and add features to the Learning System. The feature that allows more system creation and improvement is “Building Blocks.” Software Development Kit (SDK) may be used to build local Building Blocks that require additional features or connections between Blackboard and external systems or applications, such as plagiarism search or alternative services.

Modern blackboard-like systems offer "a modern, intuitive, completely responsive interface" that "provides a simpler, more efficient teaching and learning experience that goes beyond the conventional learning management system (LMS)." E-learning effectiveness can be affected by digital teaching, immersive learning experiences and consistency of the e-learning program (Liaw, 2008). These systems build new technological foundations, such as Bayesian machine learning settings, using agents (i.e. students and lecturers) to add and remove Bayesian network nodes (Fox et al., 2011). Blackboard systems also incorporate into large-scale smart systems with annotation of media content and "automating parts of conventional social science analysis" (Flaounas et al. 2014). In this area, various AI algorithms could be merged into a single smart network, so that Blackboard can be used to collect "distributed, modular natural language processing algorithms for each annotation of data in a central space without the need to organise their actions".

Altogether, current realities suggest that using advances in information technology, Blackboard can elaborate on these breakthroughs and deliver "personalised, learner-focused contents and activities", promoting interactivity, and engaged learning with immediate feedback (Bradford et al. 2007), which is sometimes constrained in how lecturers utilise the system from their end (Alokluk, 2018). This goes along with mass customisation trend enabled in other domains by the means of IT.

## EVALUATION OF BLACKBOARD SYSTEM DESIGN

Because Blackboard systems are massive, it is necessary to define different sections that will be analysed in this study, such as user groups, targeted activates and contexts. This is also essential for the reader to clarify and understand the assessment process.

As mentioned above, the Blackboard program user groups are academic staff and business school students. Students are identified as young educated students who are currently studying Business Information Technology in the second year of their undergraduate program. In addition to having a strong English language, these students have a high amount of computer and internet skills. However, this level of IT literacy may not be the same for all students, because some of them are international students, and they still need more time and practice to be effective in using the Blackboard system. Since students are young people, they have more potential than most to try out new IT technologies. It will help the university implement emerging learning technologies. As far as academic personnel are concerned, most of the tutors in the Business and Information Technology Course are trained in IT and Business fields. In addition, the age of business school teachers varies from the end of the twenties to over four teenagers. Therefore, their degree of IT literacy should be high and there should be no major obstacles to the use of the Blackboard program. Instead, it is understood that senior staff appear not to have a strong desire to implement emerging technology, and this may affect the extent of successful use of all blackboard apps.

In terms of targeted activities, three commonly used tasks are chosen for evaluation. These tasks are to engage in discussion forums, submit assignments, and deliver course content to students. Typically, students are expected to engage in a discussion after class to discuss the topics of the lecture in more depth and to share their expertise. This discussion space is generated and managed by the professor, and aims to encourage more students who might feel nervous or welcomed to talk to other students about the subject of the lecture. It will allow the teacher to see the conversation and have more information about his / her students, as well as get input on their level of comprehension of his / her face to face lectures. Thanks to its online access, students who have not attended the classroom face-to-face can partake in and benefit from these discussions. As far as the submission of assignments is concerned, this task is primarily carried out by students in order to meet the evaluation requirements of the courses. Blackboard system offers an "Assessment" space to submit the required assignment to the respective tutors.

It is clear that students have two places to submit: one for the draft to test the originality of the assignment, and the other for the submitted assignment. It happens that students do not know where to submit their assignment or may submit their required assignment to the proposed site. In addition, the distribution of course material to students is done through the instructor and the Blackboard material feature of the course. Teachers are expected to upload course materials and make them accessible online, such as PowerPoint slides, Course Guide, and Reading List. This activity is achieved through three spaces on the course page, which are "Module Information," "Learning Materials" and "Reading List." Ironically, the Blackboard program can also be used by web browsers and mobile apps, making online access more convenient for targeted users. They will receive Blackboard alerts, engage in group discussions, and review the content of the course while their smartphones are online.

SWOT analysis is a strategic planning tool used to help an individual or company recognize strengths, vulnerabilities, opportunities and risks relevant to market competition or project planning.

- *Strengths: organisational characteristics that raise a clear advantage;*
- *Weaknesses: organisational characteristics that raise a clear disadvantage;*
- *Opportunities: environmental factors used to the benefit the organisation;*
- *Threats: environmental factors that present clear problems and risk to the organisation.*

*Table 1. SWOT Matrix of Blackboard VLE*

| | |
|---|---|
| **Strengths**<br>Blackboard framework has a range of features intended for VLE<br>Blackboard device interface helps users to switch through a number of connected systems<br>Blackboard Program allows its users to connect anywhere | **Weaknesses**<br>Blackboard system needs more clarification to make better use of it<br>Does the Blackboard system protect the privacy of users when using it?<br>Inefficient design of the Blackboard website could waste the time and energy of users |
| **Opportunities**<br>Consumers agree that using the Blackboard program is a positive idea for them<br>Blackboard users are more in tune with their new design<br>Users feel exciting when using their smartphones to access the Blackboard system<br>Users may participate in the Blackboard Program Discussion Forums via smartphones<br>Appropriate Blackboard system design is required to achieve better user acceptance<br>Blackboards offers ways to set up a variety of social experiences | **Threats**<br>User cells are impaired when using the Blackboard method<br>Consumers need substantial programming skills to make successful use of the Blackboard program<br>Users should understand the symbols and the written words on the blackboard program<br>Users are spending their time on coping with the Blackboard program |

SWOT matrix (Table 1) suggests that the Strengths of Blackboard systems make them favourable for creating VLEs in the current educational settings, despite the significant weaknesses and threats identified during the analysis. Data suggests that the Weaknesses of blackboard could be compensated by the Opportunities, whilst Threats should be considered by the policy makers.

Blackboard system needs more clarifications to reach better usage, it implies "meta-learning" (or "learning how to use learning system") initiatives among tutors and students to explain them the purpose, functionality, and constraints of blackboard systems, preferably before the start of studies. This will enable their better engagement with the System, and eventually better utilisation rate and learning experience. Users' privacy should be protected whist using the systems; all users' data are compliant to GDPR requirements. Universities must engage in vendor engagement programs to influence the way Blackboards are organised. Especially, the requirements of students, as the key target audience of blackboards must be considered. Doing so appropriate design of Blackboard system will reach better users' (i.e. students and lecturers) adoption. Blackboards should be accessible through mobile devices to respect mobility trend. This includes support of both Android and Apple applications, managing notifications, integration of social media tools and the maintenance of database system that supports many users working at the same time.

There are significant threats that are external by the definition, so they could be compensated by the external stakeholders, such as governments or society. First, in term of social dimension, computer literacy should be supported for the target group of students and lecturers. This implies work of supra-national bodies, such as European Union, United Nations and Council of Europe in the areas disadvantaged in terms of IT. Second, the environmental dimension suggests further investigation in the energy consumption of blackboard system and their impacts of spending of energy by the individual (student) and organisational (university) levels. Again, in the 3rd world countries, where access to electricity and internet is constrained, this is a strong barrier to overcome. Third, further investigation is required about the impacts of blackboard systems and VLEs on students' cognitive abilities.

## PEDAGOGIC SUPPORT OF BLACKBOARD SYSTEM

In the Situated Learning Theory (Lave, 1991; Lave and Wenger, 1991), it was established that learning is essentially a social process that is not confined solely to the head of the learner. Training seen as a local practice has as its core distinguishing characteristic a "legitimate peripheral engagement" that encourages learners to participate in the culture of practitioners. Such participation makes the educational process look like the process of entering a new culture. By planning pedagogic support, one must consider that any discipline requires not only specific knowledge or skills about the main subjects, but also acquiring the jargon, values, biases, and other socio-ethical norms. Therefore, the question "how to design learning environments in which the culture that will emerge closely matches the culture to be acquired?" is of primary importance not only for virtual learning environments but for face-to-face learning settings as well. Especially in virtual learning environments, however, it must be envisaged in advance how students would absorb the known elements of culture embracing thematic areas, ethical norms as well as spaces where they might co-construct new culture(s) or at least find an opportunity to extend the current culture of their interest (Cole and Engestrom, 1993). Therefore, because communities are growing, we need to understand how they can enhance education. The main response is culture, taken here in its cognitive sense, i.e. the mental context that mediates the way students perceive situations.

Specifically, with regard to the blackboard system in use, earlier studies suggest that perceived usefulness and perceived satisfaction both contribute to learners' behavioral intention to use the e-learning system (Liaw, 2008). According to Liaw and Huang (2007), five elements should be considered in the planning of the e-learning system: (1) environmental characteristics, (2) environmental satisfaction, (3) learning or collaboration activities, (4) learning characteristics and (5) environmental acceptance. As Dillenbourg et al. (2002) mentions the effectiveness of blackboard system application is bound to "the pedagogical context of use", which comprises "the pedagogical scenario in which the courseware is integrated, the degree of teacher involvement, the time frame, the technical infrastructure, and so forth". As this context is rather technology agnostic, it triggers the same difficulty in scaling up blackboard systems for education. The primary consideration is the extension of social interactions to enable, which is an obvious Opportunity within virtual learning environments (see the SWOT matrix earlier). Such exchange can take place in many ways: synchronous versus asynchronous, text-based versus audio or video, one-to-one versus one-to-many. For example, Universities are using a feature in the Blackboard system known as "Blackboard Collaborate." This provides staff and students a simple, convenient and reliable online collaborative learning solution. This one-to-one and even one-to-many capable feature can offer a degree of dedication that makes learners and teachers feel like they're together in the same classroom through video conferencing devices (Blackboard, 2020).

Planning interactions allows better time and effort distribution within a communicating activity. Grouping of communication threads on forums or networks provides means to structure thematical areas, pull similar questions together and therefore not to overload lecturers answering them. To this end, it resolves the popular lecturers concern who believe that, since their students use a direct communication to them, students will ask frequently the same questions. In addition, administrative faculties must ensure that learning management is transparent, such as questions about seeking resources, negotiating deadlines, asking for appointments are not posed instead of thematic questions about the content of the course (which overloads both lecturers and students who are only interested in thematic areas). The same applies to educational forums, in which it is exceedingly difficult to sustain the flow of messages due to the variety of educational context (Dillenbourg et al., 2002), so that new forms of social interaction like chatbots could be tested and further applied.

Overall, the use of the Blackboard Learning Method will strive to achieve the goals of online education, which have been defined as seven principles of successful teaching (Graham et al., 2001; Alokluk, 2018):

- **Principle 1**: Lecturers should have specific instructions for interactions with students;
- **Principle 2**: Lecturers should organize assignments to facilitate constructive dialogue and cooperation between students;
- **Principle 3**: Lecturers should allow for active learning instead of passive learning;
- **Principle 4**: Lecturers need to provide input and feedback on the information in a timely manner;
- **Principle 5**: Faculty personnel will make it easy to schedule / time support activities, online courses and other timeframes;
- **Principle 6**: Lecturers should require high expectations, demanding assignments, sample cases and recognition for quality work;
- **Principle 7**: Lecturers should value diverse skills and forms of learning, enabling students to select project themes that integrate different viewpoints into online courses.

## UNIVERSITY CASES

### University of Westminster: Modern Blackboard Features

The University has been using Blackboard for quite some time, but more recently, they have expanded the system to include contemporary features. Nowadays, the University uses a variant of Blackboard known as Blackboard Ultra, which is used as a main platform for learning, as well as the addition of other digital tools like Collaborate, Panopto and Padlet. These features allow students to listen to lectures on the go and participate in discussions (Univiersity of Westminster, 2020).

The new and improved Blackboard system also caters to teachers with features such as exams and assessment pages and feedback. Likewise, students can use library facilities, which now incorporate virtual tools and enhanced online library chat capabilities. The University also uses home drive, which is a personal file storage facility for students to upload their work. The modern Blackboard system now comes with enhanced interactive features that promote collaboration between students and staff on a course. These features include discussion board facilities to allow students to ask questions about their work, share ideas and discuss thoughts with tutors, which all part of the University's supportive learning environment. The contemporary Blackboard system also helps students to establish their own personal learning network. This is similar to social media, but in a learning setting in which students can keep in touch with their colleagues and even integrate it with their personal social media accounts. This provides an alternative avenue for students to share ideas, resources and voice their concerns or opinions about a given situation.

Tied in with the University's Blackboard system are the additional software to complement their learning experience. These includes adobe creative cloud that enables students to access a range of adobe software on the cloud, such as Photoshop among other useful software. Other software include AutoCab, MATLAB, Nvivo, SPSS and Microsoft 365, which are all readily available to students (Univiersity of Westminster, 2020).

## Bangor University: Integration of Lecture Capture System into Blackboard

Staff and students today make full use of a lecture capture system known as Panopto. This system enables staff to record lectures and tutorials, as well as upload pre-existing video material, stream the content to students and the option to download the content for online viewing. Today, Panopto is deployed in all teaching spaces and enables staff to install and use the software on many computer or device that has internet access off-campus. Staff can even give students the permission to make their own recordings on the system (HEFCW, 2019).

The need for a lecture capturing system was recognised as a prerequisite to foster new methods of course delivery that were shifting from the traditional classroom approach to a more interactive classroom. The deployment of Panopto enriched the student experience at Bangor, offering a popular and effective student support system on the Blackboard platform. Panopto also encourages distance learning in which it is used to deliver lectures over long distances.

The future developments of Panopto are looking promising given the high demand for distance learning courses today. For this to work, more options and features need to be added to the system such as offline viewing through providing a download feature and also multi-lingual capabilities given the potential language barrier among foreign and international students. All in all, the lecture capture system at Bangor has enabled staff to meet student demand for the provision of richer resources and pedagogical support (HEFCW, 2019).

## Aberystwyth University: Blackboard Exemplary Course Programme Systems

Aberystwyth University have utilised an exemplary course programme system which is deployed on Blackboard to help staff redesign their modules to enhance the student learning experience. The system is known as "Rubric", which aims to provide good practice in learning and teaching, thereby placing learning processes ahead of technology. The attractiveness of Rubric is the evidence-based approaches it promotes via the higher education academy (HEA) as well as other bodies that look to enhance deep learning and reflective practice. Rubric helps to implement these approaches in a clear and easy way (Aberystwyth University, 2019).

Rubric also services as a form of benchmarking in order to redevelop their Blackboard Required Minimum Presence (RMP), which is a common standard for the appropriate use of the Blackboard system and integrates technology for learning and teaching within an interactive space. The University also wants to empower staff to utilise Blackboard to its fullest potential. Rubric's Exemplary Course Program (ECP), which is developed for Blackboard's Catalyst Awards, offers an effective tool for changing pedagogical practice and encourages staff to explore effective use of Blackboard. This was achieved through the provision of staff training to use the Rubric system. This training proved effective since it helped teachers to reflect on how they use Blackboard to interact with students and deliver teaching. This was evidenced by students' enhanced learning experience through the ECP Rubric system. The system also helped teachers to design courses in a student-centered way, which eventually led to a better overall and immersive learning experience for students (Aberystwyth University, 2019; HEFCW, 2019).

Rubric had a far-reaching impact within a short time frame, since the system not only promotes technology, but promotes good practice in learning and teaching within an interactive learning space. The design of the training sessions also made the system popular because all staff wanted the training to use Rubric and it is demonstrated through the improved pedagogical support the University has received in recent years (Aberystwyth University, 2019).

## CONCLUSION

Current blackboard-like systems offer a "current, intuitive, completely sensitive interface" that "provides an easier, more efficient teaching and learning experience" that responds to situated learning theories (Lave, 1991; Lave and Wenger, 1991). Learners engage in the community of professionals, moving towards full involvement in the socio-cultural environment, which makes the educational process look like the process of joining a society.

A modern blackboard is a useful device that facilitates educational benefit and constructivist viewpoints on e-learning effectiveness that can be further informed by digital teaching, immersive learning experiences and e-learning system efficiency (Liaw, 2008). The blackboard system provides a collaborative and user-friendly learning environment for communication, assessment and all information management systems. Both blended learning and virtual learning environments allow Blackboard systems to support learning processes that require virtual representation of course content. Blackboard systems are known to be a simulated learning environment, the main purpose of which is to facilitate the learning process including teaching personnel, technical staff and students, who are classes that use this program.

SWOT matrix suggests that the Strengths of Blackboard systems make them favourable for creating VLEs in the current educational settings, despite the significant weaknesses and threats identified during the analysis. Data suggests that the Weaknesses of blackboard could be compensated by the Opportunities, whilst Threats should be considered by the policy makers.

Further research could follow responding the threats identified in SWOT matrix, so that it could open discussions in newer fields. For instance, medical research can answer if blackboard systems impact cognitive processes? Information systems and humanitarian research might design the courses needed to improve computer literacy to achieve effective use of Blackboard system in 3rd world countries and respond to the question if education in computer literacy can increase the adoption of blackboard systems? Sustainability research could investigate if the energy generation in 3rd world countries could enable access to virtual learning environments and application of Blackboard system as it is perceived by default in the western world? It should also answer the question if application of blackboards is reasonable around the globe, or it remains only a practice of universities in advanced economies.

## REFERENCES

Aberystwyth University. (2019). *Exemplary Course Award*. Retrieved 24th June from https://www.aber.ac.uk/en/is/it-services/elearning/blackboard/blackboard-exemplary-course-award/

Alokluk, J. A. (2018). The Effectiveness of Blackboard System, Uses and Limitations in Information Management. *Intelligent Information Management*, *10*(06), 133–149. doi:10.4236/iim.2018.106012

Barajas, M., & Owen, M. (2000). Implementing virtual learning environments: Looking for holistic approach. *Journal of Educational Technology & Society*, *3*(3), 39–53.

Bernard, R. M. (2004). How does distance education compare with classroom instruction? A meta-analysis of the empirical literature. *Review of Educational Research*, *74*(3), 379–439.

Blackboard. (2020). *Virtual Learning with Web Conferencing*. Retrieved 24th June from https://www.blackboard.com/teaching-learning/collaboration-web-conferencing

Bradford, P., Porciello, M., Balkon, N., & Backus, D. (2006-2007). The Blackboard Learning System: The Be All and End All in Educational Instruction? *Journal of Educational Technology Systems*, *35*(3), 301–314. doi:10.2190/X137-X73L-5261-5656

Cole, M., & Engeström, Y. (1993). A cultural-historical approach to distributed cognition. *Distributed cognitions: Psychological and educational considerations*, 1-46.

Dillenbourg, P., Mendelsohn, P., & Jermann, P. (1999) Why spatial metaphors are relevant to virtual campuses. In Learning and instruction in multiple contexts and settings. Bulletins of the Faculty of Education, 73. University of Joensuu, Finland, Faculty of Education.

Dillenbourg, P., Schneider, D., & Synteta, P. (2002). *Virtual learning environments*. 3rd Hellenic Conference Information & Communication Technologies in Education, Rhodes, Greece.

Flaounas, I., Lansdall-Welfare, T., Antonakaki, P., & Cristianini, N. (2014). *The anatomy of a modular system for media content analysis*. arXiv preprint arXiv:1402.6208

Fox, C. W., Evans, M. H., Pearson, M. J., & Prescott, T. J. (2012). Towards hierarchical blackboard mapping on a whiskered robot. *Robotics and Autonomous Systems*, *60*(11), 1356–1366. doi:10.1016/j.robot.2012.03.005

Glahn, C., Gruber, M.R., & Tartakovski, O. (2015). *Beyond Delivery Modes and Apps: A Case Study on Mobile Blended Learning in Higher Education*. Academic Press.

Graham, C., Cagiltay, K., Lim, B. R., Craner, J., & Duffy, T. M. (2001). Seven principles of effective teaching: A practical lens for evaluating online courses. *The Technology Source*, *30*(5), 50.

Graham, C. R. (2006). Blended learning systems. The handbook of blended learning: Global perspectives, local designs, 3-21.

Grodzinsky, F., & Griffin, J. (2002, June). Blackboard: A web-based resource in the teaching of a multidisciplinary/multi-institutional computer ethics course. In *IEEE 2002 International Symposium on Technology and Society (ISTAS'02). Social Implications of Information and Communication Technology. Proceedings (Cat. No. 02CH37293)* (pp. 126-131). IEEE.

HEFCW. (2019). Enhancing Learning and Teaching through Technology. *Higher Education Funding Council for Wales*, 1-37. https://www.hefcw.ac.uk/documents/policy_areas/learning_and_teaching/ELTT%20-%20showcase%20case%20studies.pdf

Heirdsfield, A., Walker, S., Tambyah, M., & Beutel, D. (2011). Blackboard as an online learning environment: What do teacher education students and staff think? *Australian Journal of Teacher Education (Online)*, *36*(7), 1. doi:10.14221/ajte.2011v36n7.4

Keller, C. (2005). Virtual learning environments: Three implementation perspectives. *Learning, Media and Technology*, *30*(3), 299–311. doi:10.1080/17439880500250527

Lave, J. (1991). *Situating learning in communities of practice*. Academic Press.

Lave, J., & Wenger, E. (1991). *Situated learning: Legitimate peripheral participation*. Cambridge University Press. doi:10.1017/CBO9780511815355

Lawrence, D. H. (2006). Blackboard on a shoestring: Tying courses to sources. *Journal of Library Administration*, *45*(1-2), 245–265. doi:10.1300/J111v45n01_14

Liaw, S. S. (2008). Investigating students' perceived satisfaction, behavioural intention, and effectiveness of e-learning: A case study of the Blackboard system. *Computers & Education*, *51*(2), 864–873. doi:10.1016/j.compedu.2007.09.005

Liaw, S. S., & Huang, H. M. (2006, May). Developing a collaborative e-learning system based on users' perceptions. In *International Conference on Computer Supported Cooperative Work in Design* (pp. 751-759). Springer.

Martin, F. (2008). Blackboard as the learning management system of a computer literacy course. *Journal of Online Learning and Teaching*, *4*(2), 138–145.

Means, B. (2009). *Evaluation of evidence-based practices in online learning: A meta-analysis and review of online learning studies*. Centre for Learning Technology.

Mohsen, M. A., & Shafeeq, C. P. (2014). EFL Teachers' Perceptions on Blackboard Applications. *English Language Teaching*, *7*(11), 108–118.

Osguthorpe, R. T., & Graham, C. R. (2003). Blended learning environments: Definitions and directions. *Quarterly Review of Distance Education*, *4*(3), 227–233.

Owayid, A. M., & Uden, L. (2014, September). The usage of Google apps services in higher education. In *International Workshop on Learning Technology for Education in Cloud* (pp. 95-104). Springer. 10.1007/978-3-319-10671-7_9

Peraya, D., Piguet, A., & Joye, F. (1999) Rapport d'information sur les mondes virtuels. Rapport rédigé pour l»office fédéral de la formation professionnelle et le la technique, Berne, Suisse.

Petimani, M. S., & Adake, P. (2015). Blackboard versus PowerPoint presentation: Students opinion in medical education. *International Journal of Educational and Psychological Researches*, *1*(4), 289. doi:10.4103/2395-2296.163935

Univiersity of Westminster. (2020). *Using Blackboard*. Retrieved 24th June from https://www.westminster.ac.uk/current-students/studies/online-learning

Yeh, H. T., & Lahman, M. (2007). Pre-Service Teachers' Perceptions of Asynchronous Online Discussion on Blackboard. *Qualitative Report*, *12*(4), 680–704.

Young, J. R. (2012). Inside the Coursera contract: How an upstart company might profit from free courses. *The Chronicle of Higher Education*, *19*(07).

## ADDITIONAL READING

Hegazy, A. F., Khedr, A. E., & Al Geddawy, Y. (2015). An Adaptive Framework for Applying Cloud Computing in Virtual Learning Environment at Education a Case Study of "AASTMT". *Procedia Computer Science*, *65*, 450–458. doi:10.1016/j.procs.2015.09.121

Park, S., Jeong, S., & Ju, B. (2018). Employee learning and development in virtual HRD: Focusing on MOOCs in the workplace. *Industrial and Commercial Training*, *50*(5), 261–271. doi:10.1108/ICT-03-2018-0030

Stricker, A., Calongne, C., Truman, B., & Arenas, F. (2017). *Integrating an Awareness of Selfhood and Society into Virtual Learning*. IGI Global. https://books.google.co.uk/books?id=0JvgDQAAQBAJ

## KEY TERMS AND DEFINITIONS

**Blackboard:** A virtual learning environment that provides course management and personal assessment capabilities.

**Blended Learning:** An educational approach which combines online learning materials with traditional classroom methods.

**Higher Education:** A system of education that provides academic courses at the university level.

**Interactive Systems:** Systems that promote interactions between humans and computers.

**Massive Open Online Course:** Affordable and effective online courses that facilitate teaching learning experiences and develop skills and knowledge.

**Pedagogic Support:** Students' learning supported by effective teaching practices.

**Virtual Learning Environment:** An online environment in which learning materials are delivered to students.

# Chapter 10
# Enhancing Student Engagement in Online Learning Environments Post-COVID-19:
## A Case of Higher Education

**M. Kabir Hossain**
https://orcid.org/0000-0002-6342-0681
*University of Bolton, UK*

**Bob Wood**
*University of Manchester, UK*

## ABSTRACT

*The COVID-19 pandemic has significantly affected all sectors of human endeavour worldwide. This has forced a paradigm shift by disrupting 'normal' human life, introducing what is now seen as a 'new normal', which can also be seen as an opportunity rather than a threat. HEIs have equally been affected by this situation, which has forced conventional delivery of teaching and learning to be replaced by distance, online, or blended learning styles. Prior to the pandemic, only slightly over 25% of all students in UK HEIs received teaching and learning online. This statistic has now grown to 85%. This concerns learners' engagement with online learning. Unlike traditional classroom teaching/learning, online learning faces challenges of ensuring the engagement of learners. This chapter aims to explore and discuss measures to enhance student engagement in online learning settings within HEIs. The main objectives are two-fold. First, the study describes what measures exist to enhance student engagement and, second, presents an enhanced framework in online learning in HEIs.*

DOI: 10.4018/978-1-7998-4846-2.ch010

## INTRODUCTION

The pandemic, caused by the novel Coronavirus (Covid-19), has impacted all facets of the economy, the world over. Consequently, a unique approach to pedagogy has emerged as a global norm in the first quarter of the year 2020. Online learning and teaching, distance education, blended learning and teaching are not novel teaching styles or approaches to curriculum design, but they have taken on renewed adoption. There are already many arguments and discussions about whether to classify these recent practices (forced by the emergence of the pandemic) as 'emergency education', within the confines that recognize the extraordinary circumstances in which they have been developed and deployed. These 'pandemic pedagogies' have also become the focus for the education technology industry.

The advent of the world wide web (www) over two decades now has resulted in a rapid increase in online education across secondary and tertiary institutions all over the world (Allen and Seaman, 2017). Recently, many studies have shown the promise of online learning in HEIs (Stone, 2017; de Wit, 2018), as well as demonstrating that learning outcomes in online settings are comparable to face-to-face learning (Bernard *et al.*, 2004; Means *et al.*, 2009). Research has also shown that the majority of academic faculty members hold a skepticism towards new teaching and learning paradigms, with many expressing concerns about the possibility of maintaining student engagement in online learning settings, which are less rigorous and (arguably) effective than traditional/conventional teaching and learning (Shea, Bidjerano and Vickers, 2016; Lederman, 2018).

Prior to the Covid-19 pandemic, just over 25% of the total number of students in HEIs received their course lectures or teaching instruction online, in line with the increasing number of student enrolment. However, the post Covid-19 statistic shows a massive 60% increase, resulting in over 85% of courses in HEIs being delivered using online, distance, or blended learning styles (Sandars et al., 2020). As a direct consequence of this, higher education institutions (HEIs) have constantly and continually attempted to identify the factors that may improve or enrich the experience provided to students via eloquent online learning. This means that there will be modifications by tutors and executives to assist in realising positive outcomes. For instance, tutors or course content developers must improve their content to migrate from existing content to be leaning towards enhanced content (online) delivery thereby creating a learning environment the meets students' learning requirements.

To give an example, the Times Higher Education, which is the recognized spearhead in university rankings, recently published an article discussing the potential benefit – to the economy of the UK – of switching to online teaching and learning (Grove, 2020). According to the article, the coronavirus pandemic can be leveraged to benefit UK universities long-term, by offering expanded borderless learning measures, including online, blended, and distant learning. The authors added that the pandemic has forced the university management to prepare and deliver courses remotely. In other words, universities that leverage on technology to deliver their courses remotely will thrive in and post Covid-19 pandemic. The direct result of this is that, many universities are currently expanding their offerings about potential online teaching and learning in terms of the provision of advice and feedback based on the student scores (Wladis, Conway and Hachey, 2016). This is typically achieved using surveys, which are widely used by HEIs (for instance, the times, guardian, etc.) to get an indication about the performance of the university, lecturers, location.

A critical component that affects the dissemination of information about online learning is that, despite the many studies that have articulated the benefits of successful online learning (Wang and Newlin, 2002; Kerr, Rynearson and Kerr, 2006; Abbitt, 2007; Wang, 2007; Kauffman, 2015), there has, nevertheless, been unexpectedly very little methodical research on this topic, especially compared to studies that have researched about conventional face-to-face classes. Given that the fundamental motivation for the rapid growth in online education has been the consideration of accessibility and elasticity that is offered to student by this learning format, the existing trend is likely to linger for the anticipatable future, resulting in an increased accessibility of higher education to a vast audience of students, consequently forcing a radical transformation.

However, the success of online learning largely depends on the characteristics of students that are enrolled on the online learning environments (Leeds *et al*, 2013). Besides, it is also very evident that members of the academic faculty and course material developers can adopt deliberate and purposeful content that can impact upon the likelihood of student success. Typically, the material should promote collaboration, communication, interactivity, participation, and feedback, all using a technologically-advanced online learning environment (Robinson and Hullinger, 2008). The key challenge for the successful implementation of online or distant learning in HEIs relate to keeping the students engaged. Consequently, there is the need to discover useful relationships between research relating to student engagement and effective online course design and delivery.

An example of such research is obtainable in Saadé, He and Kira (2007), where it was discussed that two main segments of research about online learning exist – the development of good designs and the assessment of students' satisfaction with an online learning platform in comparison to the conventional/traditional face-to-face course.

In light of the foregoing, this study seeks to, possibly rather ambitiously, link these two research paradigms by proposing a concluding framework for fostering online learning – referred to as "An Enhanced Framework for Student Engagement in Online Learning in HEI (EFSEOL)". EFSEOL does not represent a model for the design of online learning materials, but can be rather deployed as a technical and systemic framework that can be used to provide answers to the questions of what are the typical steps to be carried or what are the best practices for enhancing and fostering student engagement in online learning environments within HEIs. Furthermore, the EFSEOL framework is not claimed to be a novel one but represents a fusion of existing studies obtained in the literature that can be used to provide online instructors with an easy-to-use framework that is applicable to practice. In these unprecedented times, the topical context of student engagement in online learning is gaining popularity as a research topic that, however, requires a lot more empirical research in order to advance the knowledge base. In this chapter, a practical framework – the EFSEOL structure - will provide a short synthesis of related extant literature on student engagement, which comprises the conceptual base, and describe the sequential procedures elucidated in the EFSEOL framework, thereby demonstrating how the framework can be used to shape online learning course materials in tandem with recent findings and knowledge obtained in online student engagement literature.

## REVIEW OF RELATED LITERATURE

This section presents a systematic review of existing literature relating to online learning and its impact on teaching and learning. Adopting a qualitative content analysis methodology, there is a review of 59 studies in the literature about online learning ranging from 2008. The review is synthesized using existing theories in order to describe how these impact on online teaching and learning. In addition, there is also an articulation of student engagement in online courses, using key indicators of the NSS student survey in the UK.

## Review Design

The primary sources of data were published journal articles. Given that part of the objectives of this review was to scrutinise the evolution of online education, how it was impacted post 2008 economic crisis, there is a systematic, three-stage literature search. The most important sources of data collection was the Google Scholar. The selection criteria included web-based queries using the descriptors relating to online teaching, online learning, and online instruction searching through empirical studies published since 2008. Additional keywords included in the screening criteria include online courses; e-learning, computer-based courses; teaching; web-based teaching and learning, and virtual and blended learning and teaching.

From the above criteria, 59 articles were selected to answer our research questions: (1) How can online education be characterised? (2) What are the research-led effective practices in online teaching that can foster student engagement?

## What Characterises Effective and Successful Online Education?

The expansion of online education over time has seen a rapid increase in research interest. Comparing online learning to traditional/conventional face-to-face classrooms, McIsaac and Gunawardena (1996), define online education as "no more than a hotchpotch of ideas and practices taken from traditional classroom settings and imposed on learners who just happen to be physically separated from an instructor" (p.5). Besides, the elements of technology and organization are critical, as described by Moore and Kearsley (2012), where distance/online education is defined as "teaching and planned learning in which teaching normally occurs in a different place from learning, requiring communication through technologies as well as special institutional organization" (p.2).

In order to understand the need for distance education, the authors in Moore and Kearsley (Moore and Kearsley, 2012) elucidated the following reasons for justifying the need for distance education:

- Increasing access to learning and teaching
- Providing prospects for updating workforce skills
- Improving the cost efficiency of educational resources
- Improving the quality of existing educational structures
- Balancing disparities between age groups
- Catering for pace of learning between individuals
- Deliver educational campaigns to specific target audiences
- Provide emergency training for key target areas
- Expand the capacity for education in new subject areas
- Offer combination of education with work and family life
- Add an international dimension to the educational experience

The advent and rapid development of the Internet and the World Wide Web (www) has resulted in many benefits to teaching and learning in higher education institutions of learning. Online learning provides opportunities to expand the borders as well as open new markets for higher education institutions, as presented in the introductory section. For instance, in terms of learning, a lot of adult or advanced-age learners can very conveniently enjoy flexibility obtained in learning especially in instances when they have to balance work, study, and family responsibilities. The rapid advancement in technology adopted by online learning programmes in universities has the potential to enhance collaboration, interaction, and engagement between students and tutors, as well as amongst themselves (Bell and Federman, 2013). In addition, the aspect of the obscurity in the online learning environment and ecosphere can easily permit or may allow more students, who, in normal circumstances, would not need to join traditional or conventional face-to-face classes due to being shy in their individual personality, or refusing to partake in online learning where there is no physical contact (i.e. they do not physically meet with each other). In conclusion, the technology and software obtainable in online learning settings can permit the teachers, lecturers, seminar leaders, students, and university administrators to collect, manipulate, and analyse data, feedback, and evaluation in order to provide personalised learning regimes, which can help improve the experience of the learners (Bell & Fedeman, 2013).

## Research-Led Effective Practices in Online Teaching to Foster Student Engagement

In teaching, learning and pedagogy for HEIs, the objective assessment of the student's learning ability, including knowledge and learning is a vital component and requirement for all stakeholders – the students or learners, instructors or teachers/seminar leaders, the educational institution or HEI and the society at large (Valenti, Cucchiarelli and Panti, 2001). However, in order to present an objective evaluation of the online learning needs of a student, there is a need to go beyond objectivity measures and consider the inherent quality of the learning experience as a whole. The most adopted of such measure is referred to as student engagement. Student engagement generally refers to the time and somatic vigour that students expend on activities within their academic experience (Kuh, 2003). In other words, engagement relates to the activities of the student to study a course, practice, obtain feedback, analyse, and apply the same towards problem solving (Kuh, 2003). Improving student engagement can be achieved using three aspects, described in the next three subsections.

## What is Student Engagement?

Within the existing relevant literature, there is not a consensus about the absolute definition of student engagement. Consequently, there exists manifold elucidations of what student engagement can be referred to. Conventionally, student engagement typically denoted the accumulation of students in higher educational institutional groups or boards, and their respective active/on-going involvement in the activities that occur in the institutions (Kuh and Hu 2001). In other words, student engagement should not be only described by something that can be measured using the subjective descriptives that are assessed only on the basis of the form of learning outcomes. Over the past two decades, however, there has been a constantly increasing research interest towards the definition of a more inclusive understanding of student engagement. A recursive definition of student engagement can be found in Trowler (2010), where the author described student engagement as the field of research "...concerned with the interaction between time, effort and other resources invested by both students and their HEIs intended to enhance the student experience ..." This definition implies that student engagement is the product of a partnership/collaboration between the tutors and learners in their HEIs.

### Tutor-Learner partnership

It is essential to improve the interaction between the student and tutors, as this enhances student engagement, even in online learning environments. Tutor-learner partnership relates to the type and regularity of contact that the learners have with their tutors. When referring to contact or interaction, this refers to interactions such as faculty feedback, pointers, and discussion of grades and assignments, ideas, careers, and collaborative projects (Kuh, 2003). Providing feedback to students from assessments represents the most frequent type of interaction between the student and tutors or academic staff. According to a recent survey, findings showed that with the exception of 4%, all students mentioned that they received feedback at least often. Besides, it is also reported that over 60% agreed with the statement that the level of feedback very regular. This can be attributed to the advancement in technology, as it allows various media for which the feedback can be disseminated to the students, for instance on BlackBoard.

### Promoting Active and Collaborative Learning Amongst Learners

Enhancing interactive and collaborative learning involves all efforts by the students to engage in group or class activities, personalised work with other students (Kuh, 2001). The terminology referred to as collaboration is vital to fostering student engagement and learning in the online classroom (Conrad and Donaldson, 2004). In all fairness, the online learning environment (i.e. classroom) has been typically denoted as a learning community, suggesting the expectation that it represents an environment that should promote collaborative energies to promote learning between learners and from learners to tutors. Consequently, the findings from a recent study established the fact that online learners collaborated better when they worked together on projects fairly regularly. In other words, about 80% of students agreed to the fact that there were frequent collaborations amongst themselves, while over 40% agreed to work together frequently. To conclude, group exercises and tasks that require the input or multiple perspectives by engaging in sharing ideas have been proven to be effective learning techniques (Conrad and Donaldson, 2004; Benbunan-Fich, Hiltz and Harasim, 2005). Despite this, a recent survey revealed that a whopping 62% of students had never made a presentation online. It is acclaimed that there is benefit that contributes towards growing their potential to work effectively with others. Palloff and Pratt (2001) advocated that collaborating between students in class work authorises and involves the learner to the extent that it affects subsequent learning situations.

## ENHANCED FRAMEWORK FOR STUDENT ENGAGEMENT IN ONLINE LEARNING IN HEI (EFSEOL)

In HEIs, many methods, prototypes and structures can be used in the design and delivery of online learning environments. Generally speaking, these approaches aim to support and guide course content developers via analysis, design, development, delivery and evaluation of the pedagogical processes. Within literature, there exist these pedagogical design frameworks, which typically focus on student engagement, many of which are motivated by ensuring that the students succeed. There are some factors that may influence active engagement of a student to a certain degree, but the focus of this section is the presentation of the EFSEOL framework to design online instruction that promotes a high level of student engagement. This framework is developed from the result of a far-reaching literature review about student engagement, as presented in the previous section. For online learning design and development to achieve success, online material designers and tutors need better approaches to enhancing student engagement and it is the expectation that the proposed EFSEOL framework will provide such an approach.

In literature, existing studies have analysed many studies about online learning material design, such as in Lee and Jang (2014), where the authors present an qualitative analysis of 20 studies relating to the design of online learning material to develop learning design models (p. 746). The authors extracted four key dimensions for such model development, which are: function, origin (research-driven, practice-led or hybrid), source (literature, existing theories, practice and experience) and analysis (p. 757). The authors combined these critical dimensions to synthesize a sequence of 10 procedures that form a procedural framework for online learning material development (p. 761).

*Figure 1. EFSEOL Student Engagement Framework*

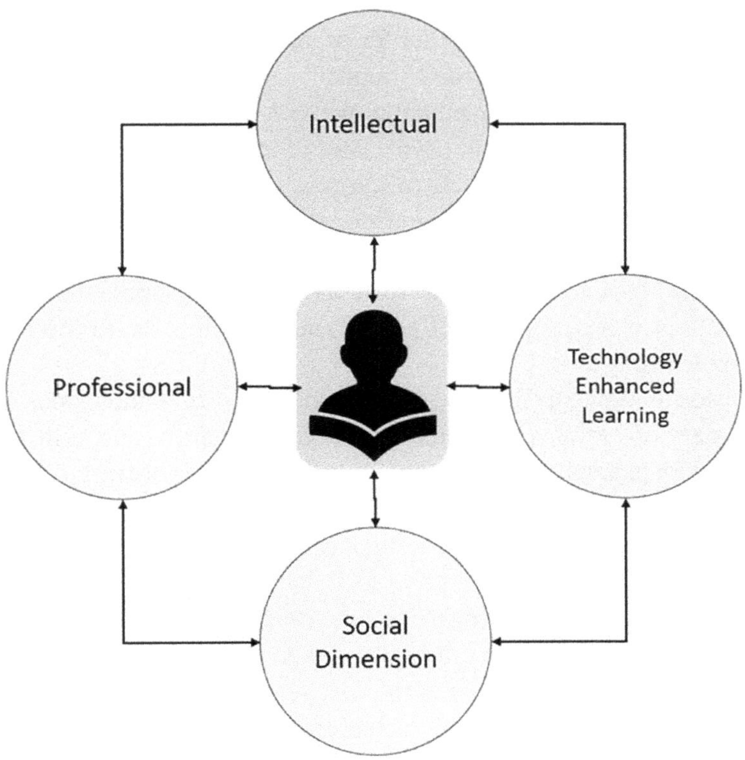


It is important to, at this point, mention that the EFSEOL framework is in no way or form a 'magic wand' that represents a rigid system, but rather a framework or structure that can be used to provide guidance to tutors or course content developers that adopts a research-led or literature-based contexts about enhancing student engagement in online learning environments. In other words, the EFSEOL framework can be a starting point and that represents an organizational schematic representation towards developing and delivering online learning, whilst enhancing student engagement. The framework is presented in Figure 1, and is described as both a practical and abstract framework. In other words, the EFSEOL framework presented in Figure 1 can both provide a structure to follow for enhanced student engagement,

*Table 1. Summary of EFSEOL Dimensions*

| Dimension | Description |
|---|---|
| Intellectual Engagement | Stimulant of student engagement that encompass ideas, notions, and idiosyncrasies relating to pedagogy and education, including political, civic, moral, and ethical issues associated with learning and teaching |
| Social Engagement | This is impacted by the diversity of students enrolling in universities, leading to a variety of views, viewpoints, knowledge, intellect, skill level, confidence and competence |
| Professional Engagement | This relates to pedagogy, which refers to Professional Experience (PE) and the contacts that tutors establish with the course managers or pre-service teachers, management executives, and others occupying managing roles |
| Technology Enhanced Learning | This refers to the analytics of big data providing higher education institutions an opportunity to strategically apply their IT resources to improve the quality of educational services, guide students to provide student experience, deliver higher completion rates, and improve student persistence |

as well as a recommended (rather flexible) order for designing online learning course materials. Table 1 summaries the key dimensions of the EFSEOL model.

In the framework, the intellectual engagement dimension encompasses the items that stimulate student engagement with ideas, notions, and idiosyncrasies relating to pedagogy and education, as well as political, civic, moral, and ethical issues relate to learning and teaching and formal education. According to Junco et al. (2011), intellectually engaging the students represents arguably the most powerful motivating factor for students and tutors alike. Consequently, effective tutors in HEIs should be passionate about pedagogical ideas. In other words, their actions should kindle the interest of their learners by channelling their actions using properly defined structures such as the EFSEOL framework, thereby revealing their own interests.

The social dimension is typically impacted by the diversity of students enrolling in universities, which results in a variety of views, viewpoints, knowledge, intellect, and skill level, confidence and competence. Although independent learning using online learning is critical to university life, it is also pertinent to identify the role that this diversity plays in augmenting individual student learning ability. Collaborating socially between peers presents an opportunity for students to meet other perspectives or viewpoints of seeing the world (in the eyes of their peers), which can develop and outspread their personal views, principles and orientations. According to Krause (2005), social engagement between students and their peers is vital for academic success in university and is "nearly equally as important as intellectual pursuits" (2005, p. 9), especially when one is in the first year (i.e. first-year students). In another study, Masters and Donnison (2010), the authors are of the opinion that in order to succeed in a university, there is a great reliance on the social networks that have been developed in the first year of study (p. 88). The notion of engaging socially refers to a collective effort at getting to know other students, be it in an online or physical class. This requires establishing new friendships with fellow students and partaking in social events with them. Furthermore, social engagement also comprises the formation of positive relations with tutors and learning managers (Pascarella and Terenzini, 2005), and this embroils taking a proactive practicable effort in emerging as an integral part of the overarching learning community in the HEI (Stanford-Bowers, 2008). In another perspective, social engagement can also be perpetrated by formal groups and societies planned and developed by students, which can aid in inter-connecting each other and providing prospects for networking and professional learning.

In terms of professional engagement, relating to the context of Education or pedagogy, this refers to Professional Experience (PE) and the contacts that tutors establish with the course managers or pre-service teachers, management executives, and others occupying managing roles. These relationships extend outside PE, however, as it also encompasses classroom involvement, as well as on a more consistent and continued foundation rather than PE permits, which also includes the membership of professional and developmental associations, for instance the British Association of Management (BAM), IEEE, etc. Furthermore, attending professional learning opportunities, workshops and conferences, sharing experiences concerning student placement ideas as well as pedagogical concepts involving other students are also welcome. Finally, post-graduation, the networks developed by the student during their schooling days can help nurture them as early career tutors and the skills acquired by establishing these networks can permit the graduates from the HEI to advance highly effective teachers.

According to Pittaway (2012), every learning and teaching occurs in an environment, or context. The learning environment is typically the responsibility of the tutor or teaching staff and this environment can refer to where the teaching takes place, for instance, in the classroom, home, work, bus, office, etc. From Figure 1, it can be seen that the student is at the centre of the engagement framework. The entire framework is representative of the contained environment, which is determined by the tutor or learning manager. They have a great deal influence, within their internal course units or lessons, as well as their teaching spaces, wherein they make thoughtful decisions to develop an environment favourable for learning. This environment will be tutor-specific – in other words, each tutor has a personalised teaching method and not all tutors teach in the same way or have the same expectations of themselves and learners but, permitting the differences, there is a great need to ensure that the environment is safe, respectful and supportive for teaching and learning, whilst enhancing student engagement. Therefore, it is essential to acknowledge that the online learning environment plays a vital role in the nature and frequency of interaction between each element of the EFSEOL Framework, and also worth mentioning that the individual dimensions or elements cannot be separated from these environmental factors (see Figure 1).

In terms of technology-enhanced learning, the analytics of big data provides higher education institutions an opportunity to strategically apply their IT resources to improve the quality of educational services, guide students to provide student experience, deliver higher completion rates, and improve student persistence. Over the past decade, Big Data has attracted the interest of academia. Consequently, academic institutions are migrating to cloud architectures and, with the increased adoption of digital devices by users in these ecosystems, is resulting in a situation where more data is being generated in these institutions than ever before (Ali, 2020; M. B. Ali, 2019). Therefore, this creates significant opportunities for using Big Data analytics techniques to find patterns in the data that can enhance decision-making. Big data analytics has been employed in higher education to provide academic, management and administrators the liberty to observe and obtain more insight about their respective institutions and learners and transform that knowledge into insight for informed decision-making. Two instances are discussed in the following paragraphs.

First, technology can be applied towards learning analytics for academic student tracking. The rapid advancement in the volume and veracity of data obtained by HEIs has resulted in a spike in the flow of data. Through learning analytics, HEIs can improve understanding of their learners' challenges and apply the resultant insight to emphatically enhance the improvement (Slade and Prinsloo, 2013). The ability to understand the learning needs of individual students should comprise the motivating factor for the adoption of learning analytics in HEIs. A successful case of implementing learning analytics in a HEI is the Rio Salado University in Arizona, which developed a learning analytics software for tracking student progress in courses, and the resultant analytics of the collected data in order to drive decision-making. The university enrols over 41,000 students in both online and in-campus courses. The application was developed to centre on personalisation, which involves providing assistance to non-traditional students to achieve academic goals through personalised intermediations (Crush, 2019).

Second, cloud computing has the potential to increase flexibility and expose HEI users to a broad range of educational resources (M. B. Ali, 2019; Ali et al., 2020). This includes providing them with access to infrastructure, software, hardware, and platform at any time in any place provided there is internet access. Within HEIs, the users of cloud computing (i.e. students, lecturers, admin staff, developers, programmers and researchers) all adopt the overarching platform for delivery of the given service. Amongst the existent cloud service models, the software-as-a-service (SaaS) model is the most commonly applied service model in HEIs. The authors in Akande and Van Belle (2014) explored the adoption of SaaS cloud computing in South African HEIs, having the main motive of determining the viability of the adoption of SaaS in HEIs. The paper also articulated the benefits and limitations of SaaS in HEIs (M. Ali, 2019).

This findings from the study revealed that most South African HEIs were sensitive to the existence of SaaS and are typically employing public and hybrid cloud services, with none using community cloud services. Furthermore, in South African HEIs, SaaS is mainly applied towards student management (i.e. student recruitment, enrolment, financial disbursement, graduation, and alumni. SaaS is also employed for admin systems including human resource management (HR), customer relationship management (CRM), supply chain management, finance and payroll and asset management. In summary, the study supported the claim that cloud computing was beneficial to HEIs. In HEIs, when tutors are provided with insight into the individual progression of their students, they are able to take action if things are going in the wrong direction. Consequently, technology-based learning provides data that, when analysed can provide this intuition, illuminating what works and what does not work so that learning outcomes can be enhanced using informed mediation. Within HEIs, there is increasing data growth, although most of it is distributed across desktops in departments, faculties, or schools, and typically come in different formats, increasing the difficulty of retrieving nor consolidating it.

## CONCLUSION

Improving student engagement in online learning environments for HEIs constitutes a critical element that should be addressed in institutional management settings, and therefore and requires a lot of empirical research to contribute to the ever-advancing knowledge base. Besides, given the fact that studies about student engagement are birthing progressively composite questions and issues, there is an anticipated need for additional research that explores how to enhance student engagement within the context of online learning in HEIs. This chapter has contributed towards delineating and addressing this research lacuna.

The consequence of the Coronavirus (Covid-19) pandemic has served as an eye-opener in the prospect of disrupting the statuesque in terms of traditional or conventional teaching paradigms. Consequently, universities have been forced to shift their classes from face-to-face to online, distance or blended learning styles. This chapter presented the EFSEOL framework for enhanced application of technology-driven moments towards improving student engagement in online learning. The threat of technological innovation and the attendant job 'transposition' and replacement implies that there is need for equipping students with requisite skillsets to thrive and remain relevant. Consequently, this calls for a reconsideration of teaching curricula and pedagogical underpinnings. The use of technological solutions to detect plagiarism, provide feedback, etc. already contribute to questioning who is responsible for the teaching and learning agenda. In summary, the time is now right for universities to reconsider their core teaching and pedagogical models with relation to technology-led learning solutions and their proprietors. Additionally, higher education institutions should explore the plethora of opportunities (and challenges) opened by the prospect to embrace technology-driven concepts in teaching and learning. These elucidations can present new opportunities for teaching and learning in education, while encouraging long-term learning in a reinforced pedagogical model that can retain the integrity of core values and strengthen the cause for higher education.

The absolute consequences of technological development cannot be predicted today, but it appears to be very probable that software applications will turn out to be a critical enabler for educational adoption of technology for the foreseeable future. Consequently, technology-based systems have a high potential to provide extensive support to students, lecturers and administrators throughout the student lifecycle. Future studies could look into more ubiquitous technologies such as cloud computing to facilitate teaching and learning practice from a technical, institutional and personal lens as these are a growing trend in higher education, which is changing pedagogical landscape in terms of teaching and learning engagement. The EFSEOL framework could be used to analyse cloud driven pedagogy to determine whether it can improve student engagement and learning.

## REFERENCES

Abbitt, J. (2007). Exploring the educational possibilities for a user-driven social content system in an undergraduate course. *Journal of Online Learning and Teaching*, *3*(4), 437–447.

Akande, A. O., & Van Belle, J.-P. (2014). Cloud computing in higher education: A snapshot of software as a service. In *2014 IEEE 6th International Conference on Adaptive Science & Technology (ICAST)*. IEEE. 10.1109/ICASTECH.2014.7068111

Ali, M. (2019). Cloud Computing at a Cross Road: Quality and Risks in Higher Education. *Advances in Internet of Things*, *9*(3), 33–49. doi:10.4236/ait.2019.93003

Ali, M. (2020). Multi-Perspectives of Cloud Computing Service Adoption Quality and Risks in Higher Education. In D. B. A. Mehdi Khosrow-Pour (Ed.), Handbook of Research on Modern Educational Technologies, Applications, and Management (2nd ed.). IGI Global.

Ali, M. B. (2019). Multiple Perspective of Cloud Computing Adoption Determinants in Higher Education a Systematic Review. *International Journal of Cloud Applications and Computing*, *9*(3), 89–109. doi:10.4018/IJCAC.2019070106

Ali, M. B., Wood-Harper, T., & Ramlogan, R. (2020). A Framework Strategy to Overcome Trust Issues on Cloud Computing Adoption in Higher Education. In *Modern Principles, Practices, and Algorithms for Cloud Security* (pp. 162–183). IGI Global. doi:10.4018/978-1-7998-1082-7.ch008

Allen, I. E., & Seaman, J. (2017). *Digital Compass Learning: Distance Education Enrollment Report 2017. Babson Survey Research Group*.

Bell, B. S., & Federman, J. E. (2013). E-learning in postsecondary education. *The Future of Children*, 165–185.

Benbunan-Fich, R., Hiltz, S. R., & Harasim, L. (2005). The online interaction learning model: An integrated theoretical framework for learning networks. *Learning together online: Research on asynchronous learning networks*, 19–37.

Bernard, R. M. (2004). How does distance education compare with classroom instruction? A meta-analysis of the empirical literature. *Review of Educational Research, 74*(3), 379–439.

Conrad, R., & Donaldson, A. (2004). *Engaging the on line learner*. Jossey-Bass.

Crush, M. (2019). Monitoring the PACE of student Learning: Analytics at Rio Salado Community University. *Campus Technology*.

de Wit, H. (2018). Collaborative Online International Learning in Higher Education. In *Encyclopedia of International Higher Education Systems and Institutions* (pp. 1–3). Springer. doi:10.1007/978-94-017-9553-1_234-1

Grove, J. (2020). *Switch to online teaching can help UK unlock global markets | Times Higher Education (THE)*. Available at: https://www.timeshighereducation.com/news/switch-online-teaching-can-help-uk-unlock-global-markets

Junco, R., Heiberger, G., & Loken, E. (2011). The effect of Twitter on college student engagement and grades. *Journal of Computer Assisted Learning, 27*(2), 119–132.

Kauffman, H. (2015). A review of predictive factors of student success in and satisfaction with online learning. In Research in Learning Technology. Association for Learning Technology. doi:10.3402/rlt.v23.26507

Kerr, M. S., Rynearson, K., & Kerr, M. C. (2006). Student characteristics for online learning success. *The Internet and Higher Education, 9*(2), 91–105.

Krause, K. (2005). *Understanding and promoting student engagement in university learning communities*. Paper presented as keynote address: Engaged, Inert or Otherwise Occupied.

Kuh, G. D. (2003). What we're learning about student engagement from NSSE: Benchmarks for effective educational practices. *Change: The Magazine of Higher Learning, 35*(2), 24–32.

Lederman, D. (2018). Conflicted views of technology: A survey of faculty attitudes. Inside Higher Ed.

Lee, J., & Jang, S. (2014). A methodological framework for instructional design model development: Critical dimensions and synthesized procedures. *Educational Technology Research and Development. Springer, 62*(6), 743–765. doi:10.100711423-014-9352-7

Leeds, E. (2013). The impact of student retention strategies: An empirical study. *International Journal of Management in Education, 7*(1–2), 22–43.

Masters, J., & Donnison, S. (2010). First-Year Transition in Teacher Education: The Pod Experience. *Australian Journal of Teacher Education, 35*(2), 87–98.

McIsaac, M. S., Gunawardena, C. N., & Jonassen, D. (1996). Handbook of research for educational communications and technology. New York: Simon & Schuster Macmillan.

Means, B. (2009). *Evaluation of evidence-based practices in online learning: A meta-analysis and review of online learning studies*. Centre for Learning Technology.

Moore, M. G., & Kearsley, G. (2012). *Distance education: A systematic view of online learning*. Wadsworth Cengage Learning.

Palloff, R. M., Pratt, K., & Stockley, D. (2001). Building learning communities in cyberspace: Effective strategies for the online classroom. *The Canadian Journal of Higher Education*, *31*(3), 175.

Pascarella, E. T., & Terenzini, P. T. (2005). *How College Affects Students: A Third Decade of Research* (Vol. 2). ERIC.

Pittaway, S. M. (2012). Student and staff engagement: Developing an engagement framework in a faculty of education. *The Australian Journal of Teacher Education*, *37*(4), 3. doi:10.14221/ajte.2012v37n4.8

Robinson, C. C., & Hullinger, H. (2008). New benchmarks in higher education: Student engagement in online learning. *Journal of Education for Business*, *84*(2), 101–109.

Saadé, R. G., He, X., & Kira, D. (2007). Exploring dimensions to online learning. *Computers in Human Behavior*, *23*(4), 1721–1739.

Shea, P., Bidjerano, T., & Vickers, J. (2016). Faculty Attitudes toward Online Learning: Failures and Successes. SUNY Research Network.

Slade, S., & Prinsloo, P. (2013). Learning analytics: Ethical issues and dilemmas. *American Behavioral Scientist*, *57*(10), 1510–1529.

Stanford-Bowers, D. E. (2008). Persistence in online classes: A study of perceptions among community college stakeholders. *Journal of Online Learning and Teaching*, *4*(1), 37–50.

Stone, C. (2017). *Opportunity through online learning: Improving student access, participation and success in higher education*. National Centre for Student Equity in Higher Education.

Valenti, S., Cucchiarelli, A., & Panti, M. (2001). A framework for the evaluation of test management systems. *Current Issues in Education (Tempe, Ariz.)*, *4*(6).

Wang, A. Y., & Newlin, M. H. (2002). Predictors of performance in the virtual classroom: Identifying and helping at-risk cyber-students. *THE Journal*, *29*(10), 21.

Wang, T.-H. (2007). What strategies are effective for formative assessment in an e-learning environment? *Journal of Computer Assisted Learning*, *23*(3), 171–186.

Wladis, C., Conway, K. M., & Hachey, A. C. (2016). Assessing readiness for online education—Research models for identifying students at risk. *Online Learning*, *20*(3), 97–109.

# Chapter 11
# Exploring the Impact of Digital Learning Platforms on Distance Learning Amidst the COVID-19 Pandemic:
## A Case of Higher Education Institutions

**Omar Mohamed Ali Albakri**
*Birmingham City University, UK*

**Abubakar Albakri**
*Birmingham City University, UK*

## ABSTRACT

*Higher education has been shifting to learning management systems (LMS) for decades. Some universities, like the Open University, have managed to gain international recognition by providing undergraduate degrees to students in different countries. However, in moments of emergency and international disruption higher education institutions need to adapt at unprecedented speed. This chapter focuses on the use of technology in moments of extreme internationalised interference. Using the COVID-19 pandemic as a ground for change, students enrolled in presential courses in Spain, Malta, and the United Kingdom were interviewed in order to understand how they are coping with having contact with their academic life exclusively online. The students' impressions, LMS software, and results (assignments and exams) were also discussed. Finally, the chapter analyses the solutions provided by lecturers and students.*

## INTRODUCTION

In 1971 Suppes (1971) published his findings on an experimental project being developed by the Institute for Mathematical Studies in the Social Sciences at the Stanford University (California, USA), initiated in 1963 with second grade students and finished in 1970 with the authors' predictions for the upcom-

DOI: 10.4018/978-1-7998-4846-2.ch011

ing decade. This report represents one of the first analyses of computer-assisted instruction by a higher education institution and one of the main findings revolves around the student psychological model with social and cultural implications on the evolution of the research. Since 1963 computer sciences has evolved immensely. For instance, the internet, created in the 60s started assuming its current format in the 90s, and computer as a whole became widely accessible later in that decade (Leiner et al., 2009). With its wider adoption came a wider range of usages to the online environment. Higher education has always been seen as a privilege to be the world's wealthy men (Carnevale & Strohl, 2013; Tisdell, 1993; Waters & Brooks, 2010). Affluent families based in the new world's colonies would send their sons to Europe for centuries. A practice which suffered a shift over the centuries considering Times Higher Education has evaluated universities globally and placed North America at the top of the rank with 64 of the world's top 100 universities, followed by Europe with 21 (Baty, 2017; Times Higher Education, 2020). However, the wealth and higher education ratio remained, as the wealthiest countries in the world are still the countries housing the world's top universities.

The ill distribution of top universities versus the world's population has led to several issues with access to a high quality higher education institution to those living in other countries and even to those who cannot afford these top universities. This chapter is grounded on the issues related to distance learning software, with a focus on periods of extreme disrupt. Research on the importance, best practices, benefits and challenges of online and distance learning in higher education has been widely published. However, the emphasis tends to be on the adoption process, investments or the transition/comparison between face-to-face learning and online alternatives.

Dealing with a worldwide pandemic in prosperous times is unprecedented. According to the United Nations (UNAIDS), the HIV/AIDS pandemic, which started in the 80s, is somehow managed through sex education and other precautions. However, throughout history there were four widely studied pandemics: the Antonine and Justinian plagues, the Black Death and the Spanish Flu, chronologically (Hays, 2005; Little, 2006). Excluding the HIV/AIDS pandemic, the other occurred before the advent of digital learning software and had various influences on higher education.

It is well-known that Sir Isaack Newton had to return to his family house due to the plague in 1666 when he formulated his gravity theory (Rickey, 1987; Westfall, 1993). However, apart from discoveries related to the outbreaks, little has been research and published on their impact on higher education. This chapter was developed with one main concern: to understand the impact of a pandemic on enrolled university students during the ongoing quarantine period. The international academic community in the fields related to technology have a particularly important role to play in a disruptive moment such as this: to ensure communication, improvements and guarantee useful systemic change.

Thus, the chapter commences with a critical analyses of Learning Management Systems (LMS) and exploring the most popular software available (Canvas, BlackBoard and Moodle), finally, approaching the on-going issue of physical higher education institutions having to close their doors due to quarantine impositions and migrating towards online classes, seminars, assignments and exams.

## Globalised World and Globalised Learning

Learning Management Systems (LMS) are means to an end: they work as platforms, which connect the university administration, students and academics. It can be used for management, training, to track payments, exam results, to monitor participation in classes, to submit assignments and much more. These systems usually provide means for lecturers to complement their classes and discipline curricula, some including alternatives for online quizzing and testing (James & Gardner, 1995; Valentine & Doug, 2002).

Aligned with LMS, Distance learning (DL) is an excellent method of teaching adult learners due to its malleability and freedom. The student can access and interact with the material as they please according to their priorities (Distefano et al., 2012). Flexibility and freedom which in turn can lead to disengagement, loss of motivation and in some cases, lack of faculty support for simple questions which might arise and for students who rely on the human interaction to learn (James & Gardner, 1995; Lewis, 2010; Moore et al., 2011; Valentine & Doug, 2002). Additionally there are practical difficulties faced in distance learning, from teaching methods, to software cost and complexity and, course curriculum (Diaz & Cartnal, 1999; Distefano et al., 2012; Galusha, 1997).

Additionally, the field of distance learning can vary considerably due to different environments, users, universities, teaching methods; which in turn can have different impact according to the user's social, cultural and economic upbringing (Moore et al., 2011). The learning environment can be levelled depending on the university teaching framework, on the topic being approached or by the student's entry requirements when enrolling.

The acclaimed Open University recently celebrated its 50th anniversary. Based in the United Kingdom, the university is known for offering undergraduate and certification level courses through televised broadcasts, specifically developed brochures and online classes, thus enabling students to undergo their studies from home, across over 157 (The Open University, 2019). Similarly, over the year, other countries have created accessible technical courses which can be learnt through videos posted to the students, books, or other postal services, never however including higher education degrees (Valentine & Doug, 2002). The main reason for distance education to begin was to reach those who could not otherwise acquire more qualified education, starting as a sort of mass education tool (James & Gardner, 1995; Lewis, 2010; Tisdell, 1993; Valentine & Doug, 2002).

Technology has a been a growing source of investments in education, in 2020 the education technology market is expected to reach $252 billion globally (Alton, 2018). According to Doran and Herold (2016), these investments have led to personalised materials e a thorough new method of educating, improving communication, in-class relationship between teacher and student, and student engagement as the digital content is easily assimilated (Herold, 2016).

Considering today's higher education students were also raised in a technological environment, opting for interactive digital media seem to be a useful alternative. Universities in the United Kingdom have opted for a blend between physical and online content for several years. Studies have been done on the reasons why students drop-out of physical and online universities and how students might feel embraced by blended methods (Rovai, 2003).

## Learning Management Systems

From data gathered by the Directors of Online and Distance Learning Environments (DOODLE, 2011) and by Hill (2017), there are several LMS available in the market and focused on higher education, however the most popular are Moodle, BlackBoard, Canvas and Brightspace Desire to Learn (D2L). As the first report focused on practicalities for their students (already used to distance learning) and the second focused on the market share of each software, there are few critical points in regards to universities which are using LMS as an additional tool for in-class learning.

### Moodle

Completely open source, this platform was designed to support teaching and learning through a highly customisable integrated system. Responsible for 49% of the LMS in higher education and adaptable for both blended and strictly online courses, the main features of the platform are its scalability, ease of use and cost. However, being free it relies on partners which can infringe privacy policies in some institutions (Moodle.org, 2020).

### BlackBoard

With nearly 100 million students registered, this platform is the largest education technology and services company in the world, serving higher and further education as well as governments and businesses. Created as a tool for the future of education by undergraduate students, Blackboard was founded in 1997 at Cornell University (USA). Its main features are in line with being privately owned: strong customer services, customisation and available in different media (Blackboard.com, 2020).

### Canvas

Part of the Instructure group, this platform focuses on learning and personal development being present from the first years of education to the work environment where it can also function as a project management tool. By converging academia and business this tool gained power as a holistic option mainly in North America (Canvas, 2020).

### BrightSpace D2L

Also known as Desire to Learn, this platform divides itself on to three fronts: K-12, Higher Education and Corporate Learning. Within the higher education front, Brightspace stands out in the market for promoting expert learning experience which can be crucial for new educational institutions and/or those transitioning to an online existence (d2l.com, 2020).

Considering the literature, personal teaching experience and interviews carried out, the author was able to portray the main benefits and challenges for faculty and for students on table 1.

After analysing the literature and the main software some questions became blatant, why universities have their own LMS instead of using those provided freely by the companies above, and what really defines the quality of software. Considering the study published by the Directors of Online and Distance Learning Environments (Ketcham et al., 2011) and their analyses of software from an institutional perspective, the author deemed more important, at the present time, to analyse learning management from a human-centred perspective through the eyes of the most affected parties of higher education: the students.

Undergraduate and post-graduate students have very different views of the educational system than those of universities or academics. By evaluating LMS and distance learning through the students, the author believes that future endeavours to improve systems and grow might potentially lead to more fruitful and adequate software, thus providing richer results and discussions.

*Table 1. Comparative analysis of the software*

| Learning Management Software | FACULTY | | STUDENTS | |
|---|---|---|---|---|
| | **Benefits** | **Challenges** | **Benefits** | **Challenges** |
| **Moodle** | Free, open access software with a simple and objective user interface | Development and support rely on their 'community' and faculty finds the software limited and in some occasions prefer not to use it | Easy to use | Some of the user interface can be confusing and it is easy to get overwhelmed |
| **Blackboard** | Personalised support service, proprietary product, broadly adopted (which leads to high familiarity) | Biggest of the software companies it might not divide its attention equally between big famous universities and smaller ones | Contains a lot of resources including Library, finances and other administrative functions | It has too many functions, tabs and divisions so simple things might get lost or hard to find |
| **Canvas** | Can be a solution widely available, easy to use and provides a large variety of services | Relatively new and business oriented compared to the others | Might be the same software as the one used in a professional environment | Daily usability, depends on how much the faculty will rely on it |
| **Brightspace D2L** | Highly focused on education and in means of delivering content effectively | Relatively new and small company which might not be able to satisfy all of the faculty's expectations | Visual appeal and ease of use | Daily usability, depends on how much the faculty will rely on it |

## LEARNING THROUGH A SOFTWARE

Universities can be divided into two categories of distance learning: those using software as a complement to presential classes (blended teaching) or those using it as the only mean of learning between the university and the student (online teaching). Barely 2020 has started and thus far, society has faced the unprecedented COVID-19 pandemic. With the spread of the disease and inexistence of a vaccine the need to self-isolate became the most effective solution for people in various countries (World Health Organisation, 2020).

The Russel Group (which represents 24 leading universities in the United Kingdom) along with the British, Italian, Spanish and Maltese Ministries of education have declared their support to the "Stay at Home" movement.

Unprecedented in the modern history international students were repatriated by their home countries and physical universities had to adapt not only to closing its doors, but also to using their LMS software as a solution to avoid losing the semester. Guidelines vary between countries; however, the overall idea is the suspension of face-to-face teaching and closure of non-essential facilities on campus. Professor Dame Nancy Rothwell, President and Vice-Chancellor of the University of Manchester also included on her message to the university's students that "These are challenging times and unprecedented arrangements. I am very proud of the way our University community is rallying together in these difficult circumstances."

The International Association of Universities, member of the European University Association, has released a global survey to monitor and gather data about the impact of COVID-19 on higher education. Composed of 31 questions the questionnaire is collecting data until mid-April and should have its results released by July 2020.

While the survey results are not published, universities that already used to a strong online presence continued to use their software as before, just ensuring students presence and avoiding plagiarism. The other universities however had to find alternatives for teaching, creating suitable environment for discussions and assessing the student's understanding of many topics using communication tools (Skype, Microsoft Teams, Zoom, etc.) alongside the LMS software.

## ON-CAMPUS STUDENTS DEALING WITH ONLINE DISTANCE LEARNING

Higher education online teaching platforms were introduced as means to ensure learning, guarantee universal access to educational materials and connect students and faculty (Herold, 2016; Ketcham et al., 2011; Lewis, 2010; Valentine & Doug, 2002; Vayre & Vonthron, 2019). Consequently, "online learning is a new social process that is beginning to act as a complete substitute for both distance learning and the traditional face-to-face class" (Hiltz & Turoff, 2005 p.60).

Classes, assignments, exams, student's assessments can easily be done online or face-to-face so physical universities changed the format of teaching blending the two. Providing videos of the presential classes on the online platform; accepting the submission of assignments online, etc. However, the physical and digital universities remained separated. The first requiring for most of its activities to be developed locally (within the university), and the second allowing students to enrol from different locations (Hiltz & Turoff, 2005).

According to Bolliger and Wasilik (2009) there are three main factors considered to affect satisfaction of faculty in regards to teaching I an online environment: student-related, instructor-related, and institution-related factors. Moreover, Robinson and Hullinger (2008) associate student engagement to four elements: active and collaborative learning; enriching educational experience; level of academic challenge; and student–faculty interaction. The interaction between students and faculty is highlighted twice as a valuable indicator of the quality and engagement within an online environment (Table 2).

*Table 2. Frequency distribution in Percentage for Engagement Factors[1] (extracted from Robinson & Hullinger, 2008)*

| Benchmark | Very little or Never | Some or Sometimes | Quite a bit or Often | Very much or Very often |
|---|---|---|---|---|
| LEVEL OF ACADEMIC CHALLENGE | | | | |
| a) Mental Activities | | | | |
| Memorising facts, ideas or methods | 12.44 | 40.80 | 33.83 | 12.94 |
| Analysing an idea, experience or theory | 3.48 | 41.79 | 41.29 | 13.43 |
| Synthesising and organizing ideas or experiences | 12.44 | 49.25 | 30.35 | 7.96 |
| Making judgement about the value of information, arguments or methods | 14.43 | 40.30 | 35.82 | 9.45 |

*continues on following page*

*Table 2. Continued*

| Benchmark | Very little or Never | Some or Sometimes | Quite a bit or Often | Very much or Very often |
|---|---|---|---|---|
| Applying theories or concepts | 9.45 | 42.29 | 36.32 | 11.94 |
| c) Expectations and evaluations | | | | |
| Worked harder than you thought you could | 6.47 | 35.32 | 41.29 | - |
| d) Skill development | | | | |
| Write clearly and effectively | 23.88 | 41.79 | 24.88 | 9.45 |
| Speak clearly and effectively | 46.77 | 34.33 | 14.43 | 4.48 |
| Think critically and analytically | 11.44 | 46.27 | 28.36 | 13.93 |
| Analyse quantitative problems | 25.87 | 39.80 | 26.87 | 7.46 |
| **STUDENT-FACULTY INTERACTION** | | | | |
| Discussed ideas from readings or class notes | 18.91 | 56.22 | 16.42 | 8.46 |
| Discussed grades or assignments | 8.46 | 52.24 | 29.35 | 9.95 |
| Received prompt feedback | 4.48 | 29.85 | 47.26 | 18.41 |
| Discussed career plans | 39.80 | 41.79 | 15.92 | 2.49 |
| **ACTIVE AND COLLABORATIVE LEARNING** | | | | |
| Worked with other students | 17.41 | 40.80 | 29.85 | 11.94 |
| Tutored or taught other students | 47.76 | 35.82 | 11.94 | 4.48 |
| Made a class presentation online | 61.69 | 23.38 | 12.44 | 2.49 |
| Visited online library resources to meet class assignments | 9.45 | 43.78 | 29.35 | 17.41 |
| Work effectively with other | 35.32 | 37.81 | 17.91 | 8.96 |
| **ENRICHING EDUCATIONAL EXPERIENCE** | | | | |
| a) Technology competency | | | | |
| Used computer technology to analyse data | 20.90 | 38.81 | 29.85 | 10.45 |
| Developed a webpage or multimedia presentation | 34.83 | 40.80 | 18.41 | 5.97 |
| Use computing and Information technology | 9.95 | 30.85 | 37.31 | 21.89 |
| b) Life enrichment | | | | |
| Regular communication with other students on matters unrelated to the course | 21.39 | 31.84 | 27.36 | 19.40 |
| Visited online library resource, not related to class assignment | 31.84 | 44.78 | 14.93 | 8.46 |
| Learn effectively on your own | 5.47 | 18.91 | 41.79 | 33.83 |
| c) Work enrichment | | | | |
| Participated in online class discussions | 23.88 | 33.83 | 21.39 | 20.90 |
| Acquire job or work-related knowledge and skills | 27.86 | 39.80 | 25.87 | 6.47 |
| Solve complex real-world problems | 22.89 | 45.77 | 22.39 | 8.46 |

In order to promote learner and assessment validity and reliability LMS requires student engagement (Gikandi et al., 2011) for that Young (2006) proposed seven key solutions: i) adapting to student needs; ii) using meaningful examples; iii) motivating students to do their best; iv) facilitating the course effectively; v) delivering a valuable course; vi) communicating effectively and; vii) showing concern for student learning. Physical universities forced to completely shift their teaching profile to online methods have to deal with these well-researched issues in a matter of weeks.

## Teaching Impressions

To investigate how effectively this transition is being done the author interviewed undergraduate students from Spain and postgraduates in Malta and Italy, all countries, which are currently struggling with the COVID-19 pandemic and have their population under quarantine and social-isolation.

The interviewed undergraduates were the most immediately impacted as their semester had just started. In Spain, lecturers chose two formats for classes and to ensure engagement. The first was having the lectures online using Microsoft Teams™ and requesting all the students to submit the solution of an exercise by the beginning of the next class. The second method did not require an online lecture, the student would access the university's LMS and watch a pre-recorded lesson supplied with slides. At the time of the scheduled class, students were expected to send an email to the lecturer with name and student number, this email was replied with an exercise related to the slides, as the student finished each exercise they would send the results and logic back to the lecturer for a follow up exercise.

For masters' students in Malta and Italy, the pressure of closing the universities was faced with a more mild intensity due to the two years programmes and the Easter break. However, for students interviewed there were activities pre-scheduled which had to be done online. One of the students had a seminar scheduled with a professor from Spain to a group of 25 students. The Seminar was then done on Zoom™ with 27 different participants on the call.

In Italy, the students had mid-term assignments and exams, which were all done online with the university's LMS. For the undergraduates in Spain however, the exams were either done orally through individual calls, or transformed into assignments to be submitted through the LMS. In both situations, the main issue for the faculty was dealing with the students' commitment to do the activities individually and without consulting other materials (plagiarising or cheating the results). Solutions varied considerably from universities using software such as Turnitin™ to find obvious plagiarism, to creating personalised exams per student or to requiring the rationale of the resolution to be explained as well as the exercise.

When enquired about satisfaction with the abrupt change answers varied considerably. As happened with Young (2006) the level of involvement of the lecturer motivated the students as well as the trust already established with the faculty in question. Structure and a flexible classroom environment also helped, especially for disciplines which were seem as complicated or those, which required discussion.

The shift to an online environment incurred several challenges and benefits. International students were able to return to their countries to spend the period in quarantine with their families and universities did not have to lose a whole semester (which would lead to issues with tuition payments, delayed graduations, etc.). For lecturers on the other hand, the move meant changing many teaching aspects, classes and assignments already planned for the semester, not only having to change the content, but also the presentation and format, to ensure commitment and motivation in an increasingly complicated and psychologically demanding situation.

Another crucial factor to be considered is that university students are not necessarily adults. Galusha (1997) previously stated that online learning is the best method to teach adults, but the students interviewed all agreed that the hardest part of "leaving" the face-to-face format is to be disciplined and organised in order to still manage to thrive during the semester. Some of these students are used to attending classes, studying informally and eventually taking exams. The time required to follow the classes and still answer exercises with the rationale behind can be time demanding activities and some students are not prepared for, risking failing some of the disciplines.

Arguments on the future of online teaching and learning in higher education can vary. Kim and Bonk (2006) propose that key skills for a high quality online course should also involve the programme coordinator, student counsellor, technology trainer and others; however, what happened in 2020 was unprecedented and did not allow the time for such developments. It had then to rely mainly on the discipline leader and their expertise with online classes and their subjects.

## Students Opinions

In order to understand the level of concern with the pandemic, geographical location and area of study the students were asked their degrees, universities and if they had been repatriated by their countries or privately. Half of the students returned to their home countries privately and half stayed because either they chose to or because their residence is in the same city they study in. Even though the main focus were students who were dislocated by the pandemic, all the students, regardless of geographic location, were currently having classes exclusively online and dealing with learning software.

Shifting from face-to-face classes to online calls has affected students differently. Most undergraduates believe the course content was well organised and planned by the academic, as well as the workload expected. However, one of the masters' student pointed out that "*in the case of my particular masters, in which the theme is people and human contact, online courses are a huge downfall in relation to content learning. Debates and experience exchange becomes limited and there is also a problem in relation to internet connection and time zones*".

The interviewed students were also asked how they feel studying from home. One of the students believes to have more time from home, having to worry less; others that the pandemic situation has added a toll to the concerns of the semester, one even adding, "*both students and teachers have to show themselves open and adaptable to make it work*". The most distinct answer came from the student based in Malta who said: *"On one side, I feel safer and less anxious by being back in my home country, surrounded by family and a support system. At the same time, I can't help but remember that I should be having the time of my life in the experience of this exchange semester, especially since my specialisation was on migration and Malta is basically the hotspot for this in Europe".*

In regards to potential delays to the graduation, opinions varied even more, with students claiming that the change is forcing them to be more organised and independent, whereas others believe all measures are being taken to avoid delays, especially considering the fact that the students need to pay tuition fees or have to deal with visa expiration issues. Overall, one of the undergraduate exchange student based in Spain was advised by the university to remain in her country of residence and finish the semester online, with the support from the university regarding possible issues and documentation required. In Malta however, the spring term is expected to happen as planned, starting in May.

Finally, when asked about the improvements the students considered pertinent to distance learning, the undergraduates focused on matters such as having a dedicated space in the house to keep their concentration and having more time for the assignments. Masters' students on the other hand seemed more understanding of the situation and the critical issues involved with closing a university due to a pandemic. One of them pointing out that: "*I understand that universities currently are dealing with this in an expected way, so it is hard to criticize knowing that it is a difficult moment for all. I guess teachers could in the future be more prepared to use technological tools when needed*".

The level of preparation of the lecturers was pointed out more than once, especially in regards to the interaction with the students and familiarity with online tools; which in turn led to a sense of nostalgia towards university life and the traditional format of classes.

In agreement with Dame Nancy Rothwell, the author believes the university community has been dealing superbly with the current seclusion scenario, creating alternatives for students and, in some cases for lecturers. The Polytechnic University of Turin, in Italy, has prepared guidelines for the faculty to deal with online teaching, including easy links to virtual classrooms and to the information technology support personnel. In Spain, *CRUE Universidades Españolas* - main higher education organisation in the country, has developed an online platform to support the transition to online teaching.

The biggest outcome of this sudden change in higher education is the speed of response from higher education organisations, especially in countries strongly affected by the pandemic (Spain and Italy). Harvard University (USA) and the University of Sao Paulo (Brazil), both based in countries, which are slowly embracing quarantine measures, are discouraging events with more than 10 people and heavily investing on research to stop the pandemic. The United Nations University, based in Tokyo – Japan, on the other hand, focused on adapting operations and leaving the network of institutes to declare their own measures.

## CONCLUSION

The unprecedented pandemic generated by the COVID-19 has led to several global consequences, disrupting the international community on not only a health perspective but also forbidding transit and shutting down countries. Higher education institutions were in turn faced with an unexpected new challenge: change from a face-to-face learning environment to an online learning tool, which would in turn ensure the continuity of the semester. With the potential to last for many months, the pandemic also affected students who had deliberately chosen presential universities instead of online institutions for various reasons. This chapter analysed the evolution of learning technologies and the incidence of learning management systems and software designed for higher education, assessing the effectiveness of this sudden transition from traditional methods to those online. In many ways, this shift empowered students who can now have stronger participation on the pedagogical techniques used as the lecturers also have to adapt to the change.

The literature has proposed that techniques such as collaborative tasks, problem-based learning, online discussions and numerous case studies and exercises could represent crucial grounds to ensure a trustful relationship with the students who in turn will be more likely to stay motivated and learn. With these details in mind and the limitation faced in this research, the material provided by Kim and Bonk (2006) is the closest analyses to provide useful predictions for these results, as they were able to survey 562 different people on the quality of online learning (Table 3). The analyses of LMS and Distance

Learning through students' perspectives provided richer and more objective results than those proposed and found by academics or universities. Undergraduates tend to be less independent and rely strongly on strict schedules and precise information. Choosing a physical course is a reflexion of that. Postgraduate students on the other hand, tend to be more interested in interacting with their peers and lecturers in order to have new and broad perspectives of the same issue. The software on the other hand, tends to place all students under one single category. The same can be said in regards to the needs of different disciplines, social courses rely on discussion and argumentation, whereas architecture and engineering tend to require specific formulae, exercise resolution, etc.

*Table 3. Predictions About How the Quality of Online Learning will be measure (extracted from Kim & Bonk, 2006)*

| Response | Number of respondents | Response rate (%) |
|---|---|---|
| Comparison of student achievement with those in live or face-to-face classroom settings | 237 | 43.8 |
| Student performance in simulated tasks of real-world activities | 80 | 14.8 |
| Student course evaluations | 47 | 8.7 |
| Course completion rates | 36 | 6.6 |
| Course interactivity ratings and evaluations | 24 | 4.4 |
| Other | 24 | 4.4 |
| Student placement into jobs | 23 | 4.3 |
| Student satisfaction questionnaires | 12 | 3.1 |
| Computer log data of student usage and activity | 1 | 0.2 |

All considered, this chapter presents an objective and summarised empirical evaluation of the usage of Learning Management Systems and Distance Learning Software in higher education through the perspective of students, presenting their difficulties and potential means of improving said software to adapt better to the different need of undergraduates, postgraduates, engineers, social scientist, architects, etc. Also noticing that none of the physical-university students interviewed would like to change to online courses.

This chapter was also faced with two main limitations. One, the fact that this chapter is being published whilst the COVID-19 pandemic is still on going without predictions to an end. Second, the interviews were very limited due to the previously mentioned quarantine most countries are imposing and the student's availability due to coursework, classes and different time zones.

These issues however, also offer grounds for future research on the topic, potentially revisiting the topic once the pandemic is over, or evaluating the results with the students interviewed, thus aligning the predictions described here with the outcomes of this event. A comparative study could therefore reveal some interesting trends of pre and post covid-19 distance learning interventions. Many distance-learning interventions are also relying on ubiquitous technologies such as cloud computing and big data to share information and perform teaching learning activities online in a collaborative interactive environment (Ali, 2019; Ali, 2020; Ali et al., 2020). The role of ubiquitous technologies in the use distance learning interventions amidst the covid-19 pandemic could also be another area of research to explore.

## REFERENCES

d2l.com. (2020). *LMS Platforms: Brightspace LMS*. https://www.d2l.com/products/

Alemán, A., & Renn, K. (2002). Women in Higher Education: An Encyclopedia. ABC-CLIO.

Ali, M. (2019). Cloud Computing at a Cross Road: Quality and Risks in Higher Education. *Advances in Internet of Things*, *9*(3), 33–49. doi:10.4236/ait.2019.93003

Ali, M. (2020). Multi-Perspectives of Cloud Computing Service Adoption Quality and Risks in Higher Education. In D. B. A. Mehdi Khosrow-Pour (Ed.), Handbook of Research on Modern Educational Technologies, Applications, and Management (2nd ed.). IGI Global.

Ali, M. B., Wood-Harper, T., & Ramlogan, R. (2020). A Framework Strategy to Overcome Trust Issues on Cloud Computing Adoption in Higher Education. In Modern Principles, Practices, and Algorithms for Cloud Security (pp. 162-183). IGI Global. doi:10.4018/978-1-7998-1082-7.ch008

Alton, L. (2018). *By the Numbers: A Deep Dive into Technology and Education*. Connected IT Blog. https://community.connection.com/numbers-deep-dive-technology-education/

Baty, P. (2017). *These maps could change how we understand the role of the world's top universities*. Times Higher Education. https://www.timeshighereducation.com/blog/these-maps-could-change-how-we-understand-role-worlds-top-universities

Blackboard.com. (2020). *Blackboard*. https://www.blackboard.com/en-uk

Bolliger, D. U., & Wasilik, O. (2009). Factors influencing faculty satisfaction with online teaching and learning in higher education. *Distance Education*, *30*(1), 103–116. doi:10.1080/01587910902845949

Canvas. (2020). *Instructure.com*. https://www.instructure.com/en-gb

Carnevale, A. P., & Strohl, J. (2013). *Separate and Unequal How Higher Education Reinforces the Intergenerational Reproduction of White Racial Privilege*. Georgetown University Center on Education and the Workforce.

Carter, P. (2018). *The first women at university: remembering 'the London Nine.'* Times Higher Education. https://www.timeshighereducation.com/blog/first-women-university-remembering-london-nine

Diaz, D. P., & Cartnal, R. B. (1999). Students' Learning Styles in Two Classes: Online Distance Learning and Equivalent On-Campus. *College Teaching*, *47*(4), 130–135. doi:10.1080/87567559909595802

Distefano, A., Rudestam, K., Silverman, R., & Long, P. D. (2012). Learning Management Systems (LMS). In *Encyclopedia of Distributed Learning*. SAGE Publications, Inc.

Doran, L., & Herold, B. (2016). 1-to-1 Laptop Initiatives Boost Student Scores, Study Finds. *Education Week*. https://www.edweek.org/ew/articles/2016/05/18/1-to-1-laptop-initiatives-boost-student-scores-study.html

Galusha, J. (1997). Barriers to Learning in Distance Education. *Interpersonal Computing and Technology*, *5*, 6–14.

Gikandi, J. W., Morrow, D., & Davis, N. E. (2011). Online formative assessment in higher education: A review of the literature. *Computers & Education, 57*(4), 2333–2351. doi:10.1016/j.compedu.2011.06.004

Hays, J. N. (2005). *Epidemics and Pandemics: Their Impacts on Human History* (S. Danver, L. Esterman, & G. Rossi, Eds.). ABC-CLIO, Inc.

Herold, B. (2016). Technology in Education: An Overview. *Education Week*. https://www.edweek.org/ew/issues/technology-in-education/

Hill, P. (2017). *Academic LMS Market Share: A view across four global regions*. ELiterate. https://eliterate.us/academic-lms-market-share-view-across-four-global-regions/

Hiltz, S. R., & Turoff, M. (2005). Education goes digital: The evolution of online learning and the revolution in higher education. *Communications of the ACM, 48*(10), 59. doi:10.1145/1089107.1089139

James, W. B., & Gardner, D. L. (1995). Learning styles: Implications for distance learning. *New Directions for Adult and Continuing Education, 1995*(67), 19–31. doi:10.1002/ace.36719956705

Ketcham, G., Landa, K., Brown, K., Charuk, K., Defranco, T., Heise, M., Mccabe, R., & Youngs-Maher, P. (2011). Learning Management. *Systematic Reviews*.

Kim, K.-J., & Bonk, C. J. (2006). The Future of Online Teaching and Learning in Higher Education: The Survey Says.... *EDUCAUSE Quarterly*.

Leiner, B. M., Cerf, V. G., Clark, D. D., Kahn, R. E., Kleinrock, L., Lynch, D. C., Postel, J., Roberts, L. G., & Wolff, S. (2009). A brief history of the internet. *Computer Communication Review, 39*(5), 22–31. doi:10.1145/1629607.1629613

Lewis, G. S. (2010). I Would Have Had More Success If…: Student Reflections on Their Performance in Online and Blended Courses. *American Journal of Business Education, 3*(11), 13–22. doi:10.19030/ajbe.v3i11.58

Little, L. K. (2006). Plague and the end of antiquity: The pandemic of 541-750. In Plague and the End of Antiquity: The Pandemic of 541-750. Cambridge University Press.

Moodle.org. (2020). *Moodle - Open-source learning platform*. https://moodle.org/

Moore, J. L., Dickson-Deane, C., & Galyen, K. (2011). E-Learning, online learning, and distance learning environments: Are they the same? *Internet and Higher Education, 14*(2), 129–135. doi:10.1016/j.iheduc.2010.10.001

Parker, P. (2015). The Historical Role of Women in Higher Education. *Administrative Issues Journal: Connecting Education, Practice, and Research, 5*(1), 3–14. doi:10.5929/2015.5.1.1

Rickey, V. F. (1987). Isaac Newton: Man, Myth, and Mathematics. *The College Mathematics Journal, 18*(5), 362–389. doi:10.1080/07468342.1987.11973060

Robinson, C. C., & Hullinger, H. (2008). New Benchmarks in Higher Education: Student Engagement in Online Learning. *Journal of Education for Business, 84*(2), 101–109. doi:10.3200/JOEB.84.2.101-109

Rovai, A. P. (2003). In search of higher persistence rates in distance education online programs. *The Internet and Higher Education*, *6*(1), 1–16. doi:10.1016/S1096-7516(02)00158-6

Suppes, P. (1971). *Computer-Assisted Instruction at Stanford* (Technical Report 174). Stanford.

The Open University. (2019). *50 Years: a movement of millions, a mission of one*. www.50.open.ac.uk

Times Higher Education. (2020). *World University Rankings 2020*. Times Higher Education - World University Rankings. https://www.timeshighereducation.com/world-university-rankings/2020/world-ranking#!/page/0/length/25/sort_by/rank/sort_order/asc/cols/stats

Tisdell, E. J. (1993). Interlocking Systems of Power, Privilege, and Oppression in Adult Higher Education Classes. *Adult Education Quarterly*, *43*(4), 203–226. doi:10.1177/0741713693043004001

Valentine & Doug. (2002). Distance Learning: Promises, Problems, and Possibilities. *Online Journal of Distance Learning Administration, 5*(3).

Vayre, E., & Vonthron, A. M. (2019). Relational and psychological factors affecting exam participation and student achievement in online college courses. *Internet and Higher Education, 43*(May), 100671.

Waters, J., & Brooks, R. (2010). Accidental achievers? International higher education, class reproduction and privilege in the experiences of UK students overseas. *British Journal of Sociology of Education*, *31*(2), 217–228. doi:10.1080/01425690903539164

Westfall, R. S. (1993). *The Life of Isaac Newton*. Cambridge University Press.

World Health Organisation. (2020). *Coronavirus (COVID-19) events as they happen*. https://www.who.int/emergencies/diseases/novel-coronavirus-2019/events-as-they-happen

Young, S. (2006). Student Views of Effective Online Teaching in Higher Education. *International Journal of Phytoremediation*, *21*(1), 65–77.

## ADDITIONAL READING

Wilson, K. B., Tete-Mensah, I., & Boateng, K. A. (2014). Information and communication technology use in higher education: Perspectives from students. *European Scientific Journal, ESJ, 10*(19).

## KEY TERMS AND DEFINITIONS

**COVID-19:** A virus that led to a worldwide pandemic in 2020.
**Digital Learning Platforms:** Systems and technologies that foster learning development.
**Distance Learning:** Studying remotely, giving the freedom to learn at any convenient time.
**Higher Education:** Academic education taught within universities.

**Learning Management Systems:** Systems that manage and deliver educational services ranging from courses to training programs.

**Online Learning:** The process of learning via online platforms and technologies.

**Pedagogy:** The practice of teaching in a classroom environment.

## ENDNOTE

1 N=201

# Chapter 12
# Deploying Knowledge Management for Effective Technologies in Higher Education Partnerships

**Enis Elezi**
https://orcid.org/0000-0001-5031-6415
*Teesside University, UK*

**Christopher Bamber**
https://orcid.org/0000-0001-8555-0690
*Organisational Learning Centre, UK*

## ABSTRACT

*The Higher Education sector is rapidly changing and is in a current state of flux because of the changing global demand of students. To cope with this dynamism, Higher Education Institutions (HEIs) are entering into partnerships to combine competences and market presence. The purpose of this chapter is to provide a better understanding of Knowledge Management (KM) in HEIs and discuss the role of communication and organisational learning when working in partnerships. The authors present developmental stages of a higher education partnership so that deployment of underutilised KM technologies can be identified at each stage. The chapter then identifies KM factors specifically useful for the evaluation stage of a higher education partnership; thus, measurement of those factors could foster organisational learning more easily. The chapter also provides a discussion of underutilised technologies in HEIs and explains how improving utilisation would enhance institutional and cross-institutional performance.*

DOI: 10.4018/978-1-7998-4846-2.ch012

## INTRODUCTION

The Higher Education sector's current collaborative culture is aimed at building resilience and coping with the dynamics of global educational change. However, there are many underutilised technologies in Higher Education Institutions (HEIs), especially when considering the stages of partnership development and the potentially significant role of technology in communication and learning across institutions. Even though, communication and learning practices are well rooted within UK HEIs there is indication that existing practices could be further developed and as a result that would enhance knowledge creation capacities. The following sections further point out that although embedded KM practices and activities support social capital development, it is expected that HEIs could exploit their available underutilised technologies better to improve their impact on social capital from partnership ventures.

HEI executives, governors and leadership teams should explicitly include KM training in staff Continuing Professional Development strategies and should promulgate an understanding of their institute's Social Impact as these will not only benefit themselves but will also benefit HE partnership development. Scholars, HE policy makers and HE practitioners of KM can gather a range of insights, presented through the following sections, pointed at fostering communication and learning, with underutilised technologies in the Higher Education context.

Therefore the objectives of this chapter are to:

- Identify the developmental stages of a Higher Education Partnership so that deployment of underutilised knowledge management technologies can be identified at each stage.
- Propose Knowledge Management factors specifically useful for the evaluation stage of a Higher Education Partnership thus, if those factors where measured organisational learning could be fostered more easily.
- Provide discussion of underutilised technologies in Higher Education Partnerships and explain how improving utilisation would enhance institutional and cross-institutional performance.

## BACKGROUND TO THE HEI CONTEXT

The crucial purpose of Knowledge Management (KM) in Higher Education is to make certain that performance is maintained at desired results through knowledge creation. The modern context of global Higher Education is such that, HEI collaborative ventures are widespread and becoming normal. Many HEIs are developing sustainability, resilience and growth through partnership development (Bamber & Elezi, 2020a; Bordogna, 2019; Guerrero et al., 2019). For high performance of partnerships it is essential that knowledge management factors are managed to effectively maintain and transfer knowledge to all partnership staff. Empirical research by Bamber & Elezi (2020b) focused on the three important factors of evaluation associated with performance management and knowledge creation with respect to social capital; monitoring and review meetings and; continuing professional development. The following sections build on that research, which was particularly helpful, as evaluation in Higher Education has been underutilised and often misunderstood. The focus of this chapter is therefore the fostering of communication and learning with underutilised technologies in Higher Education.

## THE NEED FOR FOSTERING COMMUNICATION AND LEARNING WITHIN EDUCATIONAL PARTNERSHIPS

Developing a knowledge based strategy at an institutional level allows HEIs to take appropriate measurements against the uncertainty posed in the external environment and be able to capitalise on market opportunities (Bordogna, 2019; Caniglia et al., 2017). Shams & Belyaeva (2019) highlight that having established a knowledge based strategy allows HEIs to display a more proactive market behaviour which contributes to strengthening the competitive advantage of an HE establishment. Studies undertaken by Feiz et al. (2019), Suomi et al. (2014) and Gibbs & Knapp (2002) discuss that in such a complex and uncertain business environment, HEIs should develop resilience and institutional capabilities that would allow these institutions to adapt to a changing environment. Likewise, Iqbal et al. (2019) and Abubakar et al. (2019) argue that resilience and institutional capabilities are developed through a robust understanding of institutions' strategic intent and capabilities and resources available to HE management and staff. Institutional resilience and capabilities are promoted and consolidated through institutional communication, willingness and ability of learning, sharing and transferring institutional and individual knowledge. A structured institutional communication flow, supported with learning, sharing and transferring knowledge initiatives not only enhances the effectiveness of institutional operations but contributes to developing a strategic advantage that allows HEIs to develop institutional capabilities and demonstrate resilience. The fostering of communication and learning culture within the HE sector helps education establishments to enhance the working practices in respect to communication channels and assist with the knowledge exchange flow, thus contributing to institutional resilience.

Market competitiveness can be strengthened, as discussed by scholars (Bordogna, 2019; Guerrero et al., 2019) who have elaborated on the challenges that HEIs experience in strengthening market share. They have highlighted that competitive forces are continuously changing, particularly when it comes to accessing scarce resources and ensuring support from a range of stakeholders. Market experts (Altbatch et al., 2019; Gibbs & Knapp, 2002) comment that due to the internationalisation of HE education and a significant role that technological developments have had on the education of societies, HEIs are dealing with much more informed prospective students. Student demographics continue to change and prospective student are seeking flexibility and value for money in selecting their educational programmes. However, Elezi & Bamber (2018) explain that due to lack of resources and access to different student demographics HEIs consider the development of partnerships a strategy to minimise market uncertainty and make the most of opportunities. In the context of market uncertainties and opportunities, Elezi & Bamber (2018) conclude that if applied effectively, KM assists HEIs with minimising external risks that are commonly related to new undertakings between HEIs. Collaborations between HEIs may result in a range of outcomes, including new programmes or courses which may have been possible to achieve individually however, help HEIs to expand and consolidate their market share as a result of responding to expectations of prospective students. Hence HEIs, working collaboratively, have an opportunity to exchange best practices, expand their individual institutional knowledge repositories, and enhance intellectual capacities through continuous learning. As HEIs work collaboratively in generating new educational related products and services, it is important to acknowledge that focus remains on developing institutional intellectual capacities and expand knowledge repositories which are deemed essential when it comes to managing change (Yang & Zhang, 2019). Bamber & Elezi (2020b) and Elezi & Bamber (2018) indicate that working collaboratively allows HEIs to share risks and resources, including institutional infrastructure and also provides the opportunity to absorb new knowledge and skills when it comes to recruiting students. Collaboration facilitates access to wider combined intellectual capacities and capabilities which are utilised to diversify the product portfolio and increase educational offers and student population (Guerrero et al., 2019; Feiz et al., 2019; Elezi & Bamber, 2018). Additionally, using partnerships as a mechanism of dealing with market uncertainties and opportunities, HEIs are therefore able to strengthen their institutional capabilities and intellectual capacities thus demonstrating greater degree of resilience for institutions involved in the partnership.

## Successful Educational Partnerships Embrace Collaborative Technologies

The critical importance of identifying and understanding KM factors has been discussed by numerous scholars as important in designing a partnership and ensuring its functionality. Moreover, Feiz et al. (2019) and Mahdi et al. (2019) suggest that, senior management teams of HEIs should give an equal importance to scanning the external environment as well inspecting internal capabilities in order to compile relevant KM factors that will allow the partnership to respond to market uncertainties and opportunities. Partnership development research undertaken by Reid et al (2001) elaborating on the formation stages of alliances was used by Elezi & Bamber (2018) to identify key factors that are present in different stages of educational partnerships development. Elaborating on such theories, case study research undertaken by Elezi & Bamber (2018) identified and grouped the KM factors in five categories of a partnership development process as initially suggested by Reid et al (2001). Essential to this discussion, figure 1, illustrates the KM factors identified in respect to each of the categories of partnership development which include Motivation to Collaborate, Partner Characteristics, Operating Structure and Norms, Structural Choice and Performance. Understanding the stages of a partnership formation accompanied by the KM factors that impact each stage supports HEIs in developing a collaborative strategy that fosters clear communication and learning initiatives. The significant role of technologies, for HE partners involved in a partnership, is to develop a robust understanding of the developmental stages their institutions will go through. Once there is a clear understanding on the expectations between HEI partners, then fostering communication and learning with underutilised technologies used in HE becomes an operational matter that may be guided by a knowledge based strategy designed at institutional and partnership levels. The application of technologies, particularly those underutilised, have a positive impact on teaching and learning practices as well as research outputs which as discussed by Ahalt & Fecho (2015) could be some of the outcomes HE partnerships may generate when seeking to expand market share through collaborative work.

Virtual Learning Environment (VLE) and Learning Management Systems (LMS) are very important communication platforms that contribute to the attainment of strategic objectives set amongst HEI partnerships (Huda et al., 2018; Kirkwood & Price, 2013). Furthermore, Becnel (2019) and Adi & Scotte (2016) elaborate on how technology has promoted innovative approaches for HE staff and students to collaborate, learn and communicate effectively regardless of time and location. The major importance of audio-visual technologies where educators, in a virtual environment, could share information with learners as and when required is discussed by Ziegler, G. (2019) and Liu et al. (2019). Hence, teaching and learning development, as considered by many authors (Costello, 2020; Becnel, 2019; Cassidy et al., 2014) must adapt to using virtual technologies. Hence, Virtual Reality (VR) and Augmented Reality (AR) are underutilised technologies in HE and according to Costello (2020) provide opportunities for educators to promote a hands on approach and engage their learners in problems they may experience in their relevant industries. Having fully explored the stages of partnership formation accompanied by

*Figure 1. Knowledge Management factors in HE partnership development stages (adapted from Elezi & Bamber, 2018)*

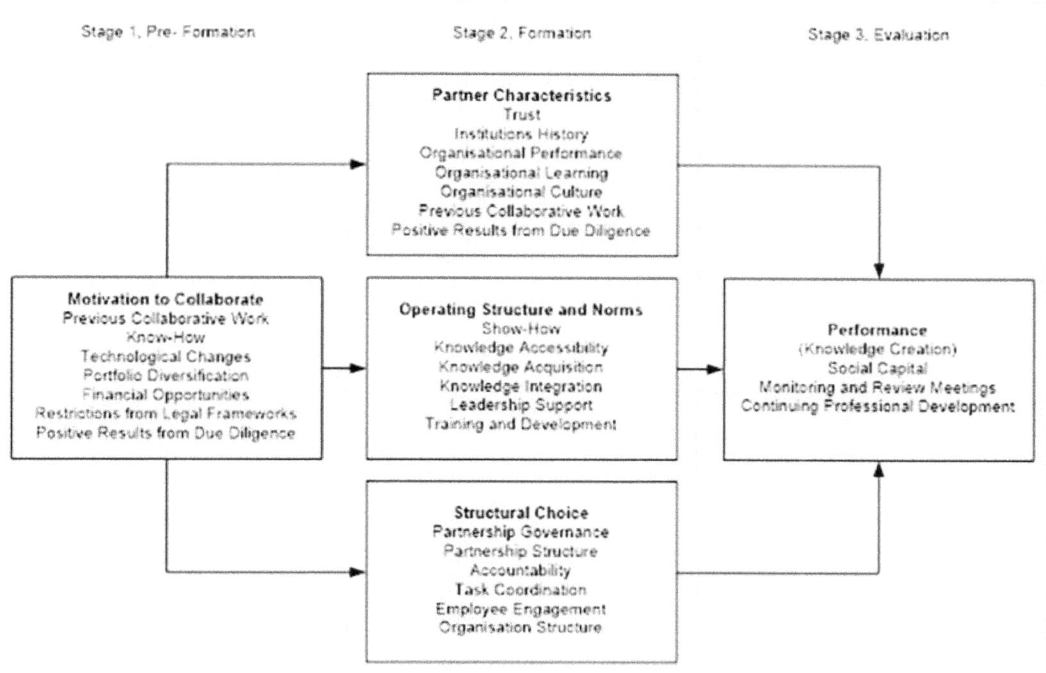


the KM factors supporting each formation stage as shown in figure 1, HEIs will be able to adequately plan, implement and monitor the necessary steps needed to foster communication and learning through underutilised technologies in HE. Nevertheless, the success of an HE partnership, is assessed on the evaluation stage as shown in figure 1, which will be further elaborated in the following sections of this chapter.

## Fostering Communication and Learning in HEIs

Comprehensible consideration and explicit adoption of HEI collaborative communication and learning technologies helps HEIs to detect the type of knowledge partners may need in different stages of a partnership. Hence, identification of knowledge needs at departmental and institutional levels becomes prominent. Management thus need to undertake the appropriate KM initiatives to support the dissemination of knowledge across partners through institutional strategies that demonstrate clarity in respect to communication channels and learning capabilities.

Effective communication allows HEIs to share and transfer knowledge constructively across partnerships. Work presented by Feiz et al. (2019) and Guerrero et al. (2019) highlight that effective partnership communications increase the opportunities to learn, thus, supporting educational institutions in aligning their managerial practices in accordance to stakeholder expectations. Effective cross functional and cross institutional communication facilities learning, which from a KM perspective relates with absorptive capacities and the ability of HEIs to absorb new knowledge. Tsai et al. (2019) and Elezi & Bamber

(2018) explain that ability to absorb new knowledge and generate new products or services is amongst the main metrics that management may use to assess the financial implications of exchanging knowledge in partnership settings. Nevertheless, Elezi & Bamber (2018) highlight the lack of commitment as one of the main reasons that compromises partnership functionality and success and may delay its progress or even lead to a termination of collaboration. Under these circumstances, it will be challenging to discuss the role of KM initiatives in supporting knowledge exchange across partners due to poorly structured communication channels that do not support institutional learning when working collaboratively. The three stages of partnership development, presented in figure 1 include the KM factors that partners will need to manage individually, as well as collaboratively, in order to progress a partnership successfully. The next section will discuss in more detail the factors relating to KM evaluation in HE partnerships that aim to foster communication with underutilised technologies.

## CRITICAL EVALUATION OF PERFORMANCE IN THE HEI CONTEXT

A considerable part of the literature in organisational learning (Yan & Zhang, 2019; Mahdi et al., 2019; Secolsky & Denison, 2012; Saunders, Trowler and Bamber, 2011) and HE discusses the importance of performance evaluation in assessing the impact of new initiatives, or any changes, that have taken place with the purpose of adding value to the existing HE products or services. Although, evaluation of performance is acknowledged as a constructive measurement that allows HEIs to further enhance their institutional capabilities, literature in HE (Elezi & Bamber 2018; Secolsky & Denison, 2012) point out that evaluating performance is underutilised. Work undertaken by Secolsky & Denison (2012) and Hodson & Thomas (2001) discuss issues related to quality, measurements and evaluations in the context of HE partnerships which shed light on somewhat limited literature on evaluation of performance. The evaluation of performance, the third stage of partnership development is an uncharted area of research, in the context of HE partnerships, but it is also deemed important from regulatory authorities and governmental institutions in assessing the quality and impact of HEIs in societies (Bamber and Anderson, 2012). Consequently, Elezi (2020) comments that evaluating performance provides opportunities for HEIs to reflect individually as well as collectively on the strategy and actions undertaken in order to identify areas for improvement and be able to continue to add value to their educational portfolios.

Evaluating the performance of a partnership through KM lenses offers the opportunity to gather feedback from different managerial levels and sources internal and external to institutions involved in a partnership. As illustrated by TEQSA (2018) common metrics used to evaluate performance relate to measuring institutional risk factors of financial performance, market share, quality and the overall competitiveness that an HEI might have developed as a result of knowledge exchange with partners and that has led to diversification of educational portfolio. Furthermore, evaluating performance provides partners with an opportunity to assess cohesion between partners regarding managerial practices and initiatives as well as examine the extent to which communication channels and learning capabilities have supported knowledge exchange and knowledge integration required to deliver partnership expectations. Elezi & Bamber (2018) argue that creation of knowledge and income generated will be the initial metrics HEIs' management will be interested to assess. Therefore, table 1 presents the key issues regarding the evaluation stage of a partnership that Elezi & Bamber (2018) identified through case study research.

*Table 1. The identified Knowledge Creation issues discussed by Bamber and Elezi (2020b)*

| Stage of the Partnership | Key Issue | The Identified KM Factors |
|---|---|---|
| Evaluation | Performance (Knowledge Creation) | · Social capital<br>· Monitoring and review meetings<br>· Continuing professional development of staff |

Evaluating the performance of a partnership may be a complex process that withdraws information from numerous individuals, teams and processes. Assessing the effectiveness of collaborative practices in the context of the needs and intended outcomes that initially instigated the need of a partnership, Elezi & Bamber (2018) suggest that evaluation of performance should be structured on the basis of the motivation to collaborate, the first stage of the partnership development, (see figure 1). The following section focuses on discussing the key issues of performance which from a KM perspective is inherently related to the concept of knowledge creation as that is aligned with the added value deriving from entering into a partnership agreement. More specifically, the following section will elaborate on the KM factors of social capital, monitoring and review meetings and continuing professional development of staff.

## SOCIAL CAPITAL IN THE CONTEXT OF HEI AVAILABLE TECHNOLOGIES

With reference to social capital theory Harris et al. (2019), Sander (2002) and Uslaner (2003) discuss that humans realise the complexity of the world and acknowledge their individual limitations which in response encourages them to develop relationships and networks with likeminded individuals driven by reciprocity and norms. Bordogna (2019) and García-Sánchez et al. (2019) explain that a higher degree of social capital is noted in better established societies which often reflect a higher ability to create jobs, clear career development opportunities and structured promotional pathways across different industries. Social capital in the context of a partnership emphasises the importance of social interactions between individuals and teams involved in a partnership with regards to knowledge sharing and transferring with the purpose of adding value to their collaborative efforts. With the development of technologies, HEIs have the opportunity to use social media metrics to assess their performing in respect to social capital. For instance, Lemoine & Richardson (2019) and Liu et al. (2019) argue that the appropriate use of technological platforms allow HEIs to assess social capital on the basis of retention rates, graduation rates and employability rates.

Also, the Learning Management Systems (LMSs) used by HEIs to develop their Virtual Learning Environments (LVEs) give the opportunity to assess enrolment awards, graduation rates to specific student populations, and student engagement with teaching and learning materials. Lemoine & Richardson (2019) argue that using data gathered through the LMSs or VLEs of HEI partners while working collaboratively allows management and educators to monitor students' progress on regular basis and be able intervene in time if needed. By intervening in time, HEIs increase the chances of improving student retention rates and student learning experience. Another important point is made by Fadil & Khaldi (2020) and Costello (2020) who argue that utilising technology allows HEIs to better identify student's individual learning needs, thus being able to offer a personalised student learning experience that encourages a higher level of student engagement with the institution during the academic studies. HIEs' executives are involved in numerous decisions relating to course and programme development, validation and administration and student services thus making use of appropriate technologies to extract data from graduating classes, employability rates or other relevant metrics HEIs are able to enhance their decision making process and consequently have a better institutional and partnership performance.

Moreover, Fadil & Khaldi (2020) and Tsai et al. (2019) explain that embedding analytics in cloud based student information systems allows HEIs to study patterns from previous academic years and student cohorts which helps with the identification of trends or tendencies in terms of student demand. Doing so, allows HEIs to assess their institutional and partnership capabilities and resources in being able to respond to the projected student demand. Being able to store, access and analyse data at departmental, institutional and partnership levels, allows HEIs to enhance their ability of matching students with the right courses and facilitating student's academic journey leading to graduation and later on, employment thus contributing to the development of social capital (Fadil & Khaldi, 2020; Costello, 2020). In addition to gathering data about students, application of technologies can help the HEI senior management teams to gather data regarding faculty and enhance the planning of academic year by providing more detailed information on institutional resources and capabilities necessary to contribute to social capital development. For instance, data on faculty turnover rate, number of classes per faculty, number of faculties per study programme or subject, number of publications and grants received helps HEIs to structure the allocation of resources and increase the efficiency of their operations. Importantly, data collected in respect to faculty helps HEIs to calculate the cost per faculty and education of each student thus providing valuable insights information that will be used to evaluate the performance of HEI partners.

## MONITORING AND REVIEW MEETINGS IN THE CONTEXT OF HEI TECHNOLOGIES

Measuring success of a partnership is an ongoing process and is suggested to be carried out at various stages of evaluation however it is essential that monitoring success and failure and regular review meetings are explicit and documented. One of the reasons that collaborative efforts tend to end unsuccessfully relates to cohesion between partners which has implications on establishing a shared vision, and identifying and agreeing on a set of expectations. Lack of cohesion also negatively impacts planning and allocation of resources which compromises institutional capabilities to respond to partnership challenges and opportunities. Hence, Elezi & Bamber (2018) suggest when assessing the performance of a partnership, it is important to take into account the KM factor of monitoring and review meetings. By doing so, HEI partners will be able to reflect on the usefulness and effectiveness of institutional policies, procedures and initiatives dedicated to sharing, transferring, applying and creating knowledge at partnership levels. Contemporary technological developments provide innovative and flexible alternatives in supporting interested parties in their collaborative endeavours regardless of location, boundaries and time zones. Becnel (2019) and Ryan & Grubbs (2017) discus that technological platforms dedicated to supporting remote meetings for collaborative work purposes are becoming more prevalent as they facilitate social interaction and monitoring of social behaviour.

In addition to platforms like Skype, and Google Hangouts which have been used extensively, Zoom is another platform that has become very popular as it provides the option of cloud recording, meaning that video, audio and chat text can be stored in Zoom cloud. From a KM perspective, knowledge storage is a crucial activity in ensuring effective KM and the cloud system plays a significant role in supporting with knowledge accessibility and knowledge availability (Ziegler, 2019). Considering the dynamics of the business environment and the complexity of collaborative work being able to access the available information and knowledge allows partners to develop cohesion and clarity while working towards a common purpose. Contemporary developments in technology support important operational managerial concepts related to tractability of ideas, thoughts, discussions and opinions where members have access to written records that help with planning and monitoring. Furthermore, representatives across different HEI partners have the opportunity to make use of cloud based systems to share data and documents and importantly work collaboratively at the same time thus helping partners to develop cross-institutional team synergy (Ali, 2018; Ali, 2019a; Ali, 2020; Ali, 2019b). Tsai et al. (2019) explain that application of such technologies helps partners to access a wider pool of information in a shorter space of time and in a more cost effective manner due to lees travelling associated with collaborative projects. Nevertheless, Bordogna (2019) explains that while having access to a wider pool of information may be fruitful, partners should clarify roles and responsibilities and structure their communication and actions on the basis of expectations agreed between partners. Aligning actions with the expectations allows partners to assess their progress, and efficiency and effectiveness of joint decisions and importantly contribute to the development of trust among partners which as discussed by Elezi & Bamber (2018) and Bamber & Elezi (2020a; 2020b) leads to better communication flows and learning opportunities. Elezi (2020) highlight that in a partnership context trust is an evolving concept and its progress will depend on the ability of partners to deliver the agreed outcomes. Therefore, application of technologies to assist HEI partners in monitoring and review meetings supports the exchange of knowledge through quicker and flexible communication channels that lead to a better team cohesion, enhances ability to learn and develops trust.

## CONTINUING PROFESSIONAL DEVELOPMENT IN THE CONTEXT OF HEI TECHNOLOGIES

Table one infers that knowledge creation is the key issue associated with performance measurement of a KM system and that is why continuing professional development (CPD) of staff, within the partnership context, is shown as a KM factor. Working collaboratively indicates that HEI staff will need to be prepared to reflect the changes occurring at institutional and partnership levels, therefore it is vitally important to design appropriate CPD programmes that are aligned with the partnership objectives. Depending on the partnership stage, CPD programmes should address training and development needs of staff at strategic and operational levels (Richman & Parrish, 2017). The critical understanding of legal frameworks, policies and procedures used to govern HEIs is essential in facilitating collaborative work across partners that may have different expertise or capabilities. The development of partnerships between HEIs is complex as it involves various roles that are characterised from different interests, capabilities and decision making processes that tend to vary throughout different stages of collaborative work (Edgar, 2020; Harris et al., 2019). For instance senior executive teams focus on strategic decisions, while HE educators mainly are responsible for overseeing teaching and learning practices and ensure that strategic decisions are delivered in accordance to the partners' expectations. In addition, administrative staff play an important part on developing, maintaining and updating institutional repositories thus playing a crucial role in governance compliance. Considering workload of HE educators and administrative staff and the importance of training and development, Chou & Ramser (2019) highlight that HEIs are increasingly making use of technology to deliver CPD programmes. CPD plays an important role in knowledge creation which is crucial when assessing the performance of partnerships. Applying technology allows

HEIs to provide continuous learning and development opportunities for staff who have to adjust their professional practices in flexible, personalised and cost efficient means. As a result of technological developments most of institutional compliance related training takes place via e-learning platforms and the challenge for CPD developers remains the development of engaging content. Digital learning, in many cases adapted to be delivered through various devices, reduces resistance to learning because of flexibility and personalisation of training programmes. Flexibility of CPD programmes contributes to employee engagement by allowing them to develop a sense of autonomy and ownership which according to Stewart et al. (2019) are essential in developing a high performing team. From a KM perspective employee engagement is essential in allowing partners to exchange, absorb and apply knowledge as well as unlearn and learn new procedural, operational and commercial knowledge.

Furthermore, utilisation of technology in developing CPD programmes for HE staff could also benefit from gamification concepts. Using gamification techniques CPD developers have the opportunity to make use of metrics related to programme knowledge, completion time and achievements to deliver learning badges as acknowledgments for their commitment to CPD programmes. It is important to encourage a sense of achievement which is expected to have a positive impact in increasing employee motivation and participation (Richman & Parrish, 2017; Ng'ambi et al., 2013a; 2013b) and consequently institutional knowledge capabilities and competitiveness. Although still at early stages, because of technological development CPD programmes may take into account the application of virtual world immersion where HE staff could undergo training field in a virtual environment, which in the context of HEIs would be particularly beneficial for student support related services. While technological platforms may not necessarily be suitable for all the training needs of HEI staff entering and working in partnerships, they offer the opportunity of scaling training and developing programmes, reducing delivery costs and increase flexibility and personalisation of content.

## FOSTERING UNDERUTILISED TECHNOLOGIES IN HIGHER EDUCATION

It is widely agreed that utilisation of technology facilities knowledge exchange and supports KM initiatives. However, while technology is an important facilitator, emphasis should be placed on HE governors and leadership teams which are responsible for designing institutional strategies, dealing with budget planning and allocation of resources and development of infrastructure (Rehman & Iqbal, 2020; Chou & Ramser, 2019). Working collaboratively can be challenging due to the differences noted amongst institutions nevertheless, application of technologies will help individuals, teams and institutions to exchange larger amounts of information and knowledge and be able to use metrics for improving decision making process. Fostering underutilised technologies in HEIs requires the support of HE governors and leadership teams who must promote and support a collaborative culture, based on mutual respect and encourages learning across different managerial levels. Underutilised technologies allow HE executives to make better use of data for performance measurement purposes as well as enhance the efficiency of operational strategies at institutional and partnership levels.

Scholars and HE policy makers can give a significant contribution in understanding communication and learning technologies available to HEIs and provide the necessary guidance and technical direction required for successful implementation. As technology continues to evolve in a fast pace, it is important to explore its impact on the development and management of educational programmes and courses. Gathering research based insights on aspects of teaching and learning practices and measuring students' outcomes will help HEIs to adjust and amend important strategic actions that relate mainly to marketing and recruitment of students but also with planning and allocation of resources. HE practitioners could also give an important contribution regarding KM initiatives. Knowledge is dynamic and multidisciplinary, therefore its management becomes challenging particularly when working collaboratively. Hence, HE practitioners emphasis should focus on developing KM systems that are intertwined with institutional systems across partnerships and make an effective use of communication and learning technologies with the purpose attaining partnership expectations.

An HEI's vision and strategic intent will require the fundamental support of academic and administrative staff, hence the role of governors and leadership teams is important in promoting a collaborative culture with a shared vision. Technology has provided HEIs with opportunities to diversify their educational portfolios, expand students' population through a wider reach, and reduce operational costs related to teaching and learning practices. Importantly, utilisation of emerging technologies allows educators and administrative staff to communicate and exchange necessary information related to student engagement and performance which can be reviewed and adjusted as needed in order to enhance student learning experience.

## CONCLUSION

This chapter has shown that within the context of the global economy Higher Education Institutes have appropriately taken to collaborating in Higher Education partnerships to remain competitive and cope with market dynamism. The very construct of partnerships means that communication is much more complex than a single organisation. Higher Education Partnerships develop through five stages and need to improve existing and implement new communication technologies in order to foster learning.

The final stage, albeit the stages are iterative, is evaluation of the partnerships performance. Essential for improving performance of HE Partnerships is the adoption of communication and learning technologies at this evaluation stage, hence three key KM factors that HEIs should measure have been described as Social Capital; Monitoring and Review Meetings and; Continuing Professional Development of Staff Communication. Without embracing technology, particularly for evaluation of performance, there will be no competitive advantage for HEIs. It is therefore essential for HEIs to identify and adopt or adapt communication and learning technologies through structured evaluation of the partnership performance.

## REFERENCES

Abubakar, A. M., Elrehail, H., Alatailat, M. A., & Elçi, A. (2019). Knowledge management, decision-making style and organizational performance. *Journal of Innovation & Knowledge*, *4*(2), 104–114. doi:10.1016/j.jik.2017.07.003

Adi, A., & Scotte, C. G. (2016). Barriers to emerging technology and social media integration in higher education: Three case studies. In Professional Development and Workplace Learning: Concepts, Methodologies, Tools, and Applications (pp. 1161-1182). IGI Global.

Ahalt, S., & Fecho, K. (2015). Ten emerging technologies for higher education. *RENCI White Paper Series, 3*(1), 1-18.

Ali, M. (2018). The Barriers and Enablers of the Educational Cloud: A Doctoral Student Perspective. *Open Journal of Business and Management*, *7*(1), 1–24. doi:10.4236/ojbm.2019.71001

Ali, M. (2019). Cloud Computing at a Cross Road: Quality and Risks in Higher Education. *Advances in Internet of Things*, *9*(3), 33–49. doi:10.4236/ait.2019.93003

Ali, M. (2020). Multi-Perspectives of Cloud Computing Service Adoption Quality and Risks in Higher Education. In D. B. A. Mehdi Khosrow-Pour (Ed.), Handbook of Research on Modern Educational Technologies, Applications, and Management (2nd ed.). IGI Global.

Ali, M. B. (2019). Multiple Perspective of Cloud Computing Adoption Determinants in Higher Education a Systematic Review. *International Journal of Cloud Applications and Computing*, *9*(3), 89–109. doi:10.4018/IJCAC.2019070106

Altbach, P. G., Reisberg, L., & Rumbley, L. E. (2019). *Trends in global higher education: Tracking an academic revolution*. Brill.

Bamber, C., & Elezi, E. (2020b). *Knowledge Management Evaluation in British Higher Education Partnerships. Journal of Information and Knowledge Management*. Ahead-of-print.

Bamber, C. J., & Elezi, E. (2020a). *What culture is your university? Have universities any right to teach entrepreneurialism? Higher Education Evaluation and Development*. Ahead-of-print.

Becnel, K. (Ed.). (2019). *Emerging Technologies in Virtual Learning Environments*. IGI Global. doi:10.4018/978-1-5225-7987-8

Bordogna, C. M. (2019). The effects of boundary spanning on the development of social capital between faculty members operating transnational higher education partnerships. *Studies in Higher Education*, *44*(2), 217–229. doi:10.1080/03075079.2017.1349742

Caniglia, G., Luederitz, C., Groß, M., Muhr, M., John, B., Keeler, L. W., & Lang, D. (2017). Transnational collaboration for sustainability in higher education: Lessons from a systematic review. *Journal of Cleaner Production*, *168*, 764–779. doi:10.1016/j.jclepro.2017.07.256

Cassidy, E. D., Colmenares, A., Jones, G., Manolovitz, T., Shen, L., & Vieira, S. (2014). Higher education and emerging technologies: Shifting trends in student usage. *Journal of Academic Librarianship*, *40*(2), 124–133. doi:10.1016/j.acalib.2014.02.003

Chou, S. Y., & Ramser, C. (2019). A Multilevel Model of Organizational Learning: Incorporating Employee Spontaneous Workplace Behaviours, Leadership Capital and Knowledge Management. *The Learning Organization*, *26*(2), 132–145. doi:10.1108/TLO-10-2018-0168

Costello, R. (Ed.). (2020). *Gaming Innovations in Higher Education: Emerging Research and Opportunities*. IGI Global.

Edgar, C. O. E. (Ed.). (2020). *Management Training Programs in Higher Education for the Fourth Industrial Revolution: Emerging Research and Opportunities*. IGI Global.

Elezi, E. (2020). Role of Knowledge Management in Developing Higher Education Partnerships: Towards a Conceptual Model. In *Proceedings of the 7th Business Systems Laboratory, International Symposium* (pp. 98-104). Academic Press.

Elezi, E., & Bamber, C. (2018). Knowledge management factors affecting educational partnerships within the British HE/FE sector. *International Journal of Knowledge Management Studies*, *9*(3), 243–259. doi:10.1504/IJKMS.2018.094213

Fadil, O. A., & Khaldi, M. (2020). Learning Management Systems: Concept and Challenges. In Personalization and Collaboration in Adaptive E-Learning (pp. 158-175). IGI Global.

Feiz, D., Dehghani Soltani, M., & Farsizadeh, H. (2019). The effect of knowledge sharing on the psychological empowerment in higher education mediated by organizational memory. *Studies in Higher Education*, *44*(1), 3–19. doi:10.1080/03075079.2017.1328595

García-Sánchez, P., Díaz-Díaz, N. L., & De Saá-Pérez, P. (2019). Social capital and knowledge sharing in academic research teams. *International Review of Administrative Sciences*, *85*(1), 191–207. doi:10.1177/0020852316689140

Gibbs, P., & Knapp, M. (2002). *Marketing Further and Higher Education Research: an educator's guide to promoting courses, departments and institutions*. Kogan Page.

Guerrero, M., Urbano, D., & Herrera, F. (2019). Innovation practices in emerging economies: Do university partnerships matter? *The Journal of Technology Transfer*, *44*(2), 615–646. doi:10.100710961-017-9578-8

Harris, C. M., Wright, P. M., & McMahan, G. C. (2019). The emergence of human capital: Roles of social capital and coordination that drive unit performance. *Human Resource Management Journal*, *29*(2), 162–180. doi:10.1111/1748-8583.12212

Huda, M., Maseleno, A., Atmotiyoso, P., Siregar, M., Ahmad, R., Jasmi, K., & Muhamad, N. (2018). Big data emerging technology: Insights into innovative environment for online learning resources. *International Journal of Emerging Technologies in Learning.*, *13*(1), 23–36. doi:10.3991/ijet.v13i01.6990

Iqbal, A., Latif, F., Marimon, F., Sahibzada, U. F., & Hussain, S. (2019). From knowledge management to organizational performance. *Journal of Enterprise Information Management*, *32*(1), 36–59. doi:10.1108/JEIM-04-2018-0083

Kirkwood, A., & Price, L. (2013). Examining some assumptions and limitations of research on the effects of emerging technologies for teaching and learning in higher education. *British Journal of Educational Technology*, *44*(4), 536–543. doi:10.1111/bjet.12049

Lemoine, P. A., & Richardson, M. D. (2019). Creative disruption in higher education: Society, technology, and globalization. In Educational and social dimensions of digital transformation in organizations (pp. 275-293). IGI Global.

Liu, Y., Fan, X., Zhou, X., Liu, M., Wang, J., & Liu, T. (2019). Application of Virtual Reality Technology in Distance Higher Education. In *Proceedings of the 2019 4th International Conference on Distance Education and Learning* (pp. 35-39). 10.1145/3338147.3338174

Mahdi, O. R., Nassar, I. A., & Almsafir, M. K. (2019). Knowledge management processes and sustainable competitive advantage: An empirical examination in private universities. *Journal of Business Research*, *94*, 320–334. doi:10.1016/j.jbusres.2018.02.013

Ng'ambi, D., & Bozalek, V. (2013b). Leveraging informal leadership in higher education institutions: A case of diffusion of emerging technologies in a southern context. *British Journal of Educational Technology*, *44*(6), 940–950. doi:10.1111/bjet.12108

Ng'ambi, D., Bozalek, V., & Gachago, D. (2013a). Empowering educators to teach using emerging technologies in higher education: A case of facilitating a course across institutional boundaries. In *Proceedings of the International Conference on e-Learning* (pp. 292-301). Cape Town, South Africa: Academic Press.

Rehman, U. U., & Iqbal, A. (2020). *Nexus of knowledge-oriented leadership, knowledge management, innovation and organizational performance in higher education. Business Process Management Journal*. Ahead-of-print.

Reid, D., Bussiere, D., & Greenaway, K. (2001). Alliance formation issues for knowledge-based enterprises. *International Journal of Management Reviews*, *3*(1), 79–100. doi:10.1111/1468-2370.00055

Richman, L. J., & Parrish, A. (2017). Introduction to Themed Issue: Technology to Support and Enhance Professional Development Schools. *School-University Partnerships*, *10*(3), 1–4.

Ryan, S. M., & Grubbs, W. T. (2017). *Curricular Collaborations: Using Emerging Technologies to Foster Innovative Partnerships. In 3D Printing: Breakthroughs in Research and Practice*. IGI Global.

Sander, T. H. (2002). Social capital and new urbanism: Leading a civic horse to water? *National Civic Review*, *91*(3), 213–234. doi:10.1002/ncr.91302

Secolsky, C., & Denison, D. B. (Eds.). (2012). *Handbook on measurement, assessment, and evaluation in higher education*. Routledge. doi:10.4324/9780203142189

Shams, S. R., & Belyaeva, Z. (2019). Quality assurance driving factors as antecedents of knowledge management: A stakeholder-focussed perspective in higher education. *Journal of the Knowledge Economy*, *10*(2), 423–436. doi:10.100713132-017-0472-2

Stewart, S. C., Witte, J. E., & Witte, M. M. (2019). Workforce Development and Higher Education Partnerships: Transdisciplinarity in Practice. In Handbook of Research on Transdisciplinary Knowledge Generation (pp. 369-382). IGI Global.

Suomi, K., Kuoppakangas, P., Hytti, U., Hampden-Turner, C., & Kangaslahti, J. (2014). Focusing on dilemmas challenging reputation management in higher education. *International Journal of Educational Management*, *28*(4), 461–478. doi:10.1108/IJEM-04-2013-0046

TEQSA. (2018). *The Tertiary Education Quality & Standards Agency*. Regulatory Risk Framework, Tertiary Education Quality and Standards Agency.

Tsai, Y. S., Poquet, O., Gašević, D., Dawson, S., & Pardo, A. (2019). Complexity leadership in learning analytics: Drivers, challenges and opportunities. *British Journal of Educational Technology*, *50*(6), 2839–2854. doi:10.1111/bjet.12846

Uslaner, E. M. (2003). Volunteering and social capital: how trust and religion shape civic participation in the United States. In Social capital and participation in everyday life (pp. 104-117). Routledge.

Yan, Y., & Zhang, Z. (2019). Knowledge Transfer, Sharing, and Management System Based on Causality for Requirements Change Management. In *Proceedings of the 2019 3rd International Conference on Information System and Data Mining* (pp. 201-207). 10.1145/3325917.3325947

Ziegler, G. (2019). Knowledge Management System: Designing a Virtual Community of Practice for Higher Education. In *Intelligent Computing-Proceedings of the Computing Conference* (pp. 1009-1029). Springer.

## ADDITIONAL READING

Annabi, C. A., & Wilkins, S. (2016). The use of MOOCs in transnational higher education for accreditation of prior learning, programme delivery, and professional development. *International Journal of Educational Management*, *30*(6), 959–975. doi:10.1108/IJEM-05-2015-0057

Hasani, K., & Sheikhesmaeili, S. (2016). Knowledge management and employee empowerment: A study of higher education institutions. *Kybernetes*, *45*(2), 337–355. doi:10.1108/K-04-2014-0077

Sulisworo, D. (2012). Enabling ICT and knowledge management to enhance competitiveness of higher education institutions. *International Journal of Education*, *4*(1), 112. doi:10.5296/ije.v4i1.1207

Tilchin, O., & Kittany, M. (2016). Adaptive knowledge management of project-based learning. *Journal of Education and Training Studies*, *4*(6), 137–144. doi:10.11114/jets.v4i6.1461

## KEY TERMS AND DEFINITIONS

**Academic Partnerships:** A partnership between several universities to collaboratively facilitate the delivery of learning opportunities.

**Collaboration:** The act of working together cooperatively.

**Communication:** An exchange of information between people or systems.

**E-Learning:** Learning facilitated by online technologies.

**Higher Education:** University education in which courses are taught at the undergraduate, postgraduate, and doctor level.

**Knowledge Management:** The process of managing information and resources efficiently within an organisation.

**Learning Performance:** A measure of how well students are learning in terms of knowledge and skills development.

# Chapter 13
# A Text Mining Analysis of Faculty Reflective Narratives on Their Participation in the TeachTech Program at The University of Texas at El Paso:
## Implications for Integrating IT Technologies Into College Pedagogy

**Kenneth C. C. Yang**
https://orcid.org/0000-0002-4176-6219
*The University of Texas at El Paso, USA*

**Yowei Kang**
https://orcid.org/0000-0002-7060-194X
*National Taiwan Ocean University, Taiwan*

## ABSTRACT

*The University of Texas at El Paso has launched the TeachTech Program to help its instructors to learn and implement the applications of new instructional technologies in the university classrooms. The objectives of this chapter are to examine what faculty members have experienced after taking part in the TeachTech Program. This study employed an online interview method to solicit past and present TeachTech Program participants (N=17) to share their experiences. Participants responded to a questionnaire hosted at QuestionPro. Faculty recurrent keywords and key phrases were collected from participants' experiential narratives. Using the key phrase extraction functions from QDA Miner and WordStat has found the following phrases related to their experiences: "incorporate technology," "collaborate sessions," "hybrid version," "desire to learn," and "solve problems." Implications and discussions were provided.*

DOI: 10.4018/978-1-7998-4846-2.ch013

# INTRODUCTION

## The Integration of Technology into College and University Classrooms

Technology has increasingly played an important role in today's pedagogy in college and university classrooms around the world (Davis, 2019). Three billion dollars have been spent on procuring digital contents (Herold, 2016). Over 8 billion dollars have also been invested in software and hardware to enhance the technology capability of classrooms (Herold, 2016). For example, renowned higher education institutes such as the Cronkite School of Journalism at Arizona State University, Harvard Business School, and Queensland University of Technology (in Australia) have all eagerly embraced these innovations into their teaching (Davis, 2019). The integration of new technologies into college and university classrooms is particularly essential to their core functions (McCallum, Schultz, Sellke, & Spartz, 2015) because, according to the National Center for Educational Statistics, there are around 19.9 million students in higher education institutes in the U.S. (Davis, 2019). Their academic success will have significant impacts on the nation's future.

The integration of new educational technologies into college and university classrooms has been identified as a vital part to improve students' learning and ultimate academic success (Zhang, Dang, Amer, 2016). According to the Department of Education report (2006, p. 25), colleges and universities are encouraged to "evaluate student learning through the development of 'pedagogies, curricula, and technologies to improve learning" (cited in McCallum et al., 2015, p. 42). The Office of Educational Technology, under U.S. Department of Education, has developed its *2020 National Educational Technology Plan* (NETP) that will integrate new educational technologies into education to improve students' equity and opportunity across the nation (Office of Educational Technology, 2019). More specific, this new NETP initiative, aims to present "a vision of equity, active use, and collaborative leadership to make everywhere, all-the-time learning possible" (Office of Educational Technology, 2019, n.p.).

To respond to this call for action, many colleges and universities have been enthusiastically developing and launching initiatives to introduce educational technologies into their classrooms (Yang & Kang, 2020). For example, the Center for Teaching and Learning at University of Washington is set up to offer faculty members to integrate technologies into their pedagogy and instructional materials (Center for Teaching and Learning, n.d. https://www.washington.edu/teaching/teaching-resources/engaging-students-in-learning/teaching-with-technology-2/; Yang & Kang, 2020). Harvard Business School has also designed a state-of-art 1,000 seat stadium (lecture hall) with a 61.8-foot-wide curved LED display to allow students and the instructor to engage in meaningful dialogues (Davis, 2019). Similarly, the University of Texas at El Paso has launched its Blackboard Institute to help faculty members transform their courses to the platform (UTEP, n.d., https://campusedge.utep.edu/browse-by-unit/technology-support-services). Other initiatives include Teaching with Videos series to help instructors to tailor their teaching materials to integrate audio-visual technologies into their pedagogies (UTEP, n.d., https://campusedge.utep.edu/browse-by-unit/technology-support-services).

There are various types of educational technologies available for teachers interested in adopting a technologized classroom; they include *White Noise*, *Cold Turkey*, *Kahoot*, *Venngage*, *Trello*, *Plickers*, *Nearpod*, *Prezi*, and *Class Dojo* (McQuire, 2016; Yang & Kang, 2020). Other technologies include *Google Apps*, *PowerPoint*, *Canvas*, *Clickers*, *Smartphone*, *Panopto*, etc. (Center for Teaching and Learning, n.d. https://www.washington.edu/teaching/teaching-resources/engaging-students-in-learning/teaching-with-technology-2/; Yang & Kang, 2020). In a chart describing the component of the 21st century classroom

(Eldrige, 2015), to prepare students for the real world, the futuristic classroom will include tablets, open-source textbooks, social media, mobile apps, gamifications, and learning analytics to enhance students' overall learning experiences.

The popularity of educational technologies in the college and university classrooms has been attributed to their many potential benefits claimed by their advocates among academic researchers, educators, and government policy-makers (Office of Educational Technology, 2017, 2019; Yang & Kang, 2020). For example, benefits discussed among academic researchers often emphasize the technology's capabilities to help both students and instructors in fostering an empowering educational environment. For example, Saxena (2013) points out the following benefits of incorporating educational technologies into faculty's pedagogy in the higher education context in terms of the followings: 1) allowing faculty members to share resources and ideas online; 2) enabling students to be exposed to technologies and research skills when they are young; 3) allowing both teachers and students to access to a variety of online resources; 4) creating an environment for a technology-enabled flipped classroom; 5) taking advantage of the growing online learning market (Yang & Kang, 2020). For many educators, their reasons to adopt technologies in their classroom are to help diversify their teaching styles (such as teaching through face-to-face, online, or hybrid modes), to motivate students through creating relevance, engagement, and fun, and to enhance course materials and their effectiveness (Eldrige, 2015). Among policy-makers, educational technologies are claimed to create more engaging and personalized learning and experiences and to help students deal with real-world problems through project-based learning (Office of Educational Technology, 2017). Furthermore, technology also help educators to collaborate beyond school and geographical boundaries (Office of Educational Technology, 2017).

The widespread applications of educational technologies in college and university classrooms have led educators to improve their instructional methods and materials fundamentally to ensure students' academic success. This technology also increase the entertaining experiences that students have with the teaching materials. Another example is the integration of augmented reality into history classes to enable students to virtually "field visit" the historical sites that may have been destroyed and create a stronger engagement with the course contents (Office of Educational Technology, 2017).

Among the separate technological integration into college and university classrooms, a flipped classroom method is heavily dependent on technology (Zuber, 2016). As an innovative technology-enabled pedagogy, a flipped classroom, also known as flipped, hybrid or blended learning (Zhang et al., 2016), usually involves students to watch lecture videos before attending each face-to-face class session (Zuber, 2016). This new pedagogical approach has been empirically tested to be more effective than traditional face-to-face class and e-learning (Zhang et al., 2016). Many have also claimed that the technology-enhanced flipped learning can improve students' critical thinking ability, enhance collaborative learning, facilitate personalized learning, and taking into consider students' individual learning styles (Zhang et al., 2016). However, as Zuber (2016) has summarized from previous flipped classroom method literature, this requires students to have critical abilities to process a large amount of information to ensure the effective use of technology. Existing research in flipped learning has mainly focused on students' academic improvement, student perception, student engagement, motivation to learn (Refer to Zhang et al., 2016, p.264 for a review). There are some earlier study on studying factors predicting why instructors decide to adopt e-learning, web-based, or gamified learning system (Thowfeek & Hussein, 2008; Motaghina, Hassanzadeh, & Moghadam, 2013; Li & Wang, 2016). Unfortunately, little has been done in studying the experiences of college and university instructors when they are faced with the challenges of learning and implementing educational technologies in their classrooms. To fill the gap in this area, this study employed a text mining analysis of faculty members' experiential narratives after taking part in the TeachTech Program at the University of Texas at El Paso.

## BACKGROUND

### The TeachTech Program at the University of Texas at El Paso

The TeachTech Program aims to recruit faculty members ranging from tenured, tenure-track, to adjunct to work collaboratively with its university technology experts to deploy, develop, evaluate, and implement innovative strategies to integrate new educational technologies into their teaching (TeachTech Program, n.d., https://campusedge.utep.edu/event/2319-teach-tech-research-cohort). Preference of cohort selection is given to faculty instructors that adopt a flipped and blended classroom approach in their pedagogy (TeachTech Program, n.d., https://campusedge.utep.edu/event/2319-teach-tech-research-cohort). The program focuses on selecting faculty members who have little or no experience in using technology to enhance their pedagogy and students' learning (TeachTech Program, n.d., https://campusedge.utep.edu/event/2319-teach-tech-research-cohort). Since its initial launch in 2018, the program has trained over 20 faculty members who have successfully integrating technologies into their courses. Some examples of their projects include gamification in nursing courses, gamification in advertising and communication classes, and virtual reality technology in training interview, among other interesting faculty-developed projects (Yang & Kang, 2020). **The** TeachTech Program is designed to answer two questions related to the applications of new educational technologies in the college and university classrooms:

**Q1:** "What role can instructional technology take to facilitate integrative and applied learning?"
**Q2:** "Which instructional technology tools can best support faculty and student success?"

In 2019, the program launched its third cohort to focus on OER/Affordable Materials (TeachTech Program, n.d., https://www.utep.edu/technologysupport/_Files/docs/The-TeachTech-Research-Program-Full-Description1.pdf). This initiative is a response to the Texas Higher Education Coordinating Board's 60x30 Texas Initiative that encourages colleges and universities to transform their teaching materials to OER (TeachTech Program, n.d., https://www.utep.edu/technologysupport/_Files/docs/The-TeachTech-Research-Program-Full-Description1.pdf). As part of the Open Educational Resources Grant Program by the State of Texas, the objectives of TeachTech's OER Initiative aim to ensure that students will have access to affordable and easily accessible course materials on the first day of the class (TeachTech Program, n.d., https://www.utep.edu/technologysupport/_Files/docs/The-TeachTech-Research-Program-Full-Description1.pdf). Other objectives include the decreased reliance on commercial publishers and increased localization of course contents to meet the accessibility requirements of each institution (TeachTech Program, n.d., https://www.utep.edu/technologysupport/_Files/docs/The-TeachTech-Research-Program-Full-Description1.pdf).

In addition to the TeachTech Program that trains faculty cohorts to promote the use of technologies, UTEP has also launched several initiatives (such as Large Size Active Learning Classroom, Dean and Faculty Dashboard on Faculty Engagement with Blackboard, Video Content Management System for

Academics) to help faculty members integrate these educational technologies into their classrooms (Technology Support, n.d., https://www.utep.edu/technologysupport/Initiatives/All_Initiatives.html).

## Research Objectives and Questions

This chapter aims to examine what faculty members have experienced after taking part in the TeachTech Program. The researcher aims to use a text mining software to identify topics from faculty participants' experiential narratives. The study aims to collect experiential narratives from over 20 faculty participants of the Program in the past 2 years to provide answers to the following seven research questions:

The study aims to collect experiential narratives from over 20 faculty participants of the TeachTech Program in the past 2 years to provide answers to the following seven research questions:

**Q1**: What motivates these participants to apply and take part in the TeachTech Program?

**Q2**: What do these participants think the impacts of TeachTech Program on their own teaching, learning, and life as a faculty?

**Q3**: What have these faculty participants done to transform their own courses during and after taking part in the program?

**Q4**: What best practice recommendations would they provide upon reflecting their own applications of instructional technologies in their pedagogy

**Q5**: What instructional technologies have been integrated in their pedagogy after completing the TeachTech Program?

**Q6**: What difficulties have they experienced in the retooling process?

**Q7**: Did the participation in the TeachTech Program change what the faculty's perception over technology, digitalized course contents, and their own pedagogical philosophy?

# MAIN FOCUS OF THE CHAPTER

## The Importance of Faculty Reflections

Despite the hyperbole of the educational technologies in college and university classrooms, faculty acceptance and involvement have been found to be lukewarm (Natriello, 2005, cited in Baran, Correia, & Thompson, 2001). Furthermore, the majority of existing research that examines how faculty members respond to the integration of new technologies into their courses often focuses on the time and efforts required to develop course materials in the technology-enabled teaching methods (Tiaht & Porter, 2016). Increasingly, researchers in technology-enhanced teaching methods (such as online teaching or blended/flipped classroom pedagogy) has begun to study how instructors experience in a post-graduate online teaching curriculum (Baran et al., 2001; Gonzalez, 2016). Through a phenomenographic interview approach, seven instructors have expressed that institutional influence, nature of students, and subject of curriculum often influence their own strategies in teaching online courses (Gonzalez, 2016). Baran et al. (2001) find through their extensive literature review that the roles and competencies of the online teachers are critical to the success of its implementation. Instructors who adopt educational technologies in their classrooms often serve as a content facilitator, advisor/counsellor, assessor, manager/administrator, process facilitator, researcher, and technologies (Goodyear et al., 2001 cited in Baran et al., 2001 for a detailed review). To serve these roles effectively, instructors need to have technology-, communication-, and assessment-competencies (Baran et al., 2001). Because the roles of instructors and their associated competencies are considered to be important to the effectiveness of technology-enhanced pedagogies, it is also critical to study what their experiences are when they take part in the TeachTech Program, or other similar programs, that help college and university instructors to become familiar with educational technologies and technology-enhanced pedagogies.

In Baran et al. (2001) study, they propose the importance of using a critical reflection approach to help instructors to improve their own teaching practices. Critical reflection is defined as 'the process by which adults identify the assumptions governing their actions, locate the historical and cultural origins of the assumptions, question the meaning of the assumptions, and develop alternative ways of acting' (Stein, 2000, p. 3). Many guidebooks on how to succeed in integrating educational technologies often tell instructor what should be done and what routines should be taken (Baran et al., 2001). Baran et al. (2001) criticize such an internalization of so-called "best practices" through mere replication often prevents instructor to explore and discover their own pedagogical approaches. Therefore, the critical reflection approach will helps these instructors to empower themselves by questioning many well-accepted assumptions of current pedagogical practices (Baran et al., 2001). Therefore, collecting what college and university instructors have experienced in the TeachTech Program is vital to the future success of educational technologies in their classrooms. To collect experiential narratives, the authors follow Schön's (1988) approach to collect both "reflection in action" (during the experience) and "reflection on action" (after the experience) narratives. Many TeachTech Program fellows have used technologies in their classrooms (i.e., "reflection in action"); however, what they have learned through the program also helps them to improve their current implementation (i.e., "reflection on action").

## RESEARCH METHODS

Data mining on text has been gaining attention among academic researchers and business practitioners in recent years (Trilling & Jonkman, 2018; Yang & Kang, 2018). This research method has been used to discover and extract "interesting, non-trivial knowledge from free or unstructured text" (Kao & Poteet, 2007, p. 1). As a methodology, all text mining techniques are known to allowed researchers to identify recurrent keywords, phrases, topics in the document corpus and to explore relationships among these recurrent concepts (Yang & Kang, 2018). The authors employ *QDA Miner* and *WordStat* suite that offers an easy-to-use tool to extra key phrases in the unstructured texts from the document corpus. *QDA Miner* allows the identification of keywords with the highest number of frequencies from the document corpus and to reflect the most important and salient keywords, key phrases, and topics (Touri & Koteyko, 2015). Researchers who employ text-mining methods usually follow the steps; that is, text pre-processing, applications of text mining software, and post-processing (Zhang, Chen, & Liu, 2015). The pre-processing step includes the collection of media corpus to compile the database for later analyses. The pre-processing of raw data (Lin, Ha, & Liao, 2016) aims to ensure the integrity and relevance of the extracted texts in the collected corpus.

## Sampling Method

Seventeen participants of this study are recruited from two cohorts of TeachTech Program between 2017 and 2018. Questionnaire and interview research methods are commonly used when studying instructors' responses in technology-enhanced pedagogies (Baran et al., 2001; Gonzalez, 2016; Tokmak, Yakin, & Dogusoy, 2019). For example, Tokmak et al. (2019) survey 36 teachers who take part in a computer literacy program to understand their experiences in digital storytelling technologies. Their study includes a list of demographic, three open-ended, and semi-structured interview questions (Tokmak et al., 2019).

The intended cohort size for the TeachTech Program is 10 per recruitment. The sample is thus 20 participants. However, some faculty members drop out of the program. In the end, eight participants are from Cohort 1 (2017) and includes six associate professors, one lecturer, and one clinical professor. Their departments include Entering Student Program, Teacher Education, Political Science, Electrical and Computer Engineering, Chemistry, English (Literature), Mathematical Sciences, and Civil Engineering. Their gender distribution includes three males and five females. Seventeen participants were from Cohort 2 (2018) and they include 4 males and 5 females. Their department affiliations include civil engineering, pharmacy, BUILDING Scholars Post-Doc Program, history, speech and language pathology, English, biological sciences, art, and communication. Email solicitations have been sent to the participants three times to invite them to complete an online questionnaire hosted at the university's QuestionPro service.

The IRB-approved questionnaire includes the IRB consent form, a brief introductory statement, and open-ended questions to inquire their motivation to take part in the TeachTech Program (Q1), the reflective assessment of the program on their own teaching, learning and professional life as a faculty (Q2), whether the TeachTech Program has helped transformed their courses (Q3), faculty's reflective assessment on whether best practice examples helps their pedagogy (Q4), types of technologies that are integrated into their pedagogy (Q5), reflective narratives on difficulty encountering in the integration process (Q6), impacts on faculty's own perceptions with educational technologies and their applications (Q7), pre- and post-participation integration of technology into faculty's own teaching (Q8), and reflections on technology adoption due to their TeachTech participation (Q9).

## RESEARCH FINDINGS

To answer nine research questions, several text-mining techniques that extract recurrent words and phrases in the document corpus are used. After the extraction of keywords, phrases, or terms, another procedure is used to estimate their relative importance by examining the frequency statistics, called Term-Frequency (TF) or TF-IDF (Term-Frequency-Inverse document Frequency) (Tesoa, Olmedillab, Martínez-Torresc, & Toral, 2018; Yang & Kang, 2020). To understand the meaning of TF-IDF, Kobayashi, Mol, Berkers, Kismihók, and Hartog (2018) claim that an extracted word or a phrase with a low IDF can often be removed because they have little discriminatory power and can be discarded in the analysis. TF-IDF is a statistics that take into consideration both the importance of a word or a phrase and their specificity (Also refer to Yang & Kang, 2020). Furthermore, QDA Miner and WordStat programs also allow researchers to identify extracted keywords, phrases, and patterns in context through its KWIC (or Keyword-in-Context) function, so these extracted terms can be accurately interpreted.

This chapter first began with a Word Cloud analysis procedure that has been a widely used text mining technique to represent frequency of keywords, phrases, and terms (Srivastava, 2014). The next ten figures attempt to present the visually relative importance of extracted keywords, phrases, and terms in the faculty participants' experiential narratives from the questionnaire survey. The larger the words, the more important they are. The authors also report TF-IDF statistics to represent the importance of the extracted words and key phrases.

In terms of participants' motivation to apply and take part in the TeachTech Program (Q1), important words as shown in Figure 1 include "technology" (TF-IDF=0.9), "adopters" (TF-IDF=1), "incorporate" (TF-IDF=0.4), "online" (TF-IDF=0.5), "engage" (TF-IDF=0.5), and "innovative" (TF-IDF=0.5). To better understand these extracted keywords, the authors also attempt to interpret them in context. One of the respondents says, "I am teaching online courses and wanted to enhance my interaction with the students." Another respondent has expressed that, "I wanted to incorporate technology into my course and teach in an innovative way." Another respondent has written, "I wanted to use technology as a way to engage students."

*Figure 1. Q1: Please share what motivates you to apply and take part in the TeachTech Program?*
*Source: The Authors*

In terms of participants' perceptions of overall impacts of TeachTech Program on their teaching, learning (Q2), and professional life as a faculty, the recurrent words include "technology" (TF-IDF=0.7), "technologies" (TF-IDF=1.4), "colleagues" (TF-IDF=0.4), "Edupuzzle" (TF=IDF=0.4), "Qualtric" (TF-IDFD=0.4) "Blackboard" (TF-IDF=0.4), and "tools" (TF-IDF=1) (Refer to Figure 2).

These extracted keywords appear in the following experiential narratives. For example, one respondent points out the importance of learning from other colleagues about their technology adoption decisions: "It was absolutely fantastic. I was not only able to learn about various teaching tools but also to interact

*Figure 2. Q2: What do you think the overall impacts of TeachTech Program on your own teaching, learning, and professional life as a faculty? Please share both positive and negative, if any, impacts.*
*Source: The Authors*

and discuss with other colleagues sharing the same passion. I wasn't able to utilize the selected tool fully but it encouraged me to look for similar tools and enhanced my interaction with students."

Another respondent clearly points out what technologies they have learned in their experiential narratives below: "I found that the overall impact of the Teach Tech program was positive with no negative impacts. 1. I learned how to use new technology. In addition to Qualtrics and Blackboard, I used Second Life Virtual Simulation software. 2. I learned about additional technology during our Teach Tech meetings. Not only from the Teach Tech staff but from the participating faculty. Through these meetings, I learned how to use technology as a way to measure student outcomes (EdPuzzle, Quizlet). 3. I stepped out of my comfort zone and found that a non-traditional way of teaching course material can make teaching and learning stimulating. It kept me "on my toes" in a sense that I knew the Teach Tech Program was expecting me to bring my experience to the table."

The integration of educational technologies into the classroom also requires faculty users to progress from simply being aware to gain confidence of their decision to adoption as shown in the narratives below: "I gained more awareness of the different technologies available and the various support and services offered to faculty by UTEP Acadamic Technologies. I gained more confidence and incorporated more technology such as Blackboard, Survey Monkey and Qualtrics, Poll Everywhere and REEF Polling, EdPuzzle, and Doodle Poll."

In terms of participants' reflective experiential narratives when on action (Schön, 1988), several recurrent words have emerged to highlight faculty participants' experiences as how the TeachTech Program has transformed their own teaching during and after their participation (Q3). These salient themes include "simulation" (TF-IDF=1.4), "technology" (TF-IDF=1), "project" (TF-IDF=1), "collaborate" (TF-IDF=0.5) (Refer to Figure 3). One of the respondents describes how Blackboard has been integrated into their teaching as part of resources available to students: "I have added blackboard collaborate sessions as a resource for my students." Another respondents provides a detailed list of technologies adopted and rationale behind their adoption: "In addition to the virtual simulation project, have used Qualtrics and Quizlet. The virtual simulation project (Second Life Software) helped assess student clinical decision making and course content. The students also rated their level of confidence using pre and post-tests (Qualtrics). I hope to use virtual simulation with graduate students as a way to expose them to various real patient-case scenarios prior to their external clinical practicums."

Similarly, another respondent also provides their experiences to integrate these technologies for a variety of class activities:

*My homework assignments include appropriate math videos where students watched via EdPuzzle and answer embedded questions. I use classroom voting via REEF polling more often. I always use Qualtrics for survey to get students input. Since I teach math, I use online manipulatives and GeoGebra (free software) in some of my courses. I use Blackboard to post the PowerPoint slides, homework, course materials, and link to resources. I would say I now use technology strategically and with confidence. On the other hand, I am not an early adopter in new technology. There are probably a lot out there that are useful for my courses but I am not aware.*

*Figure 3. Q3: What have you done to transform your own courses during and after taking part in the TeachTech Program to help students learn better?*
*Source: The Authors*

In terms of participants' own reflections on their own technology integration experiences (Q4). Keywords and key phrases from their best practice recommendations include "technology" (TF-IDF=1), "objectives" (TF-IDF=1), "effective" (TF-IDF=0.5), "communicative" (TF-IDF=0.4), and "feedback" (TF-IDF=0.5) (Refer to Figure 4 below). These extracted words point out a successful plan to integrate technologies in college and university classrooms requires the faculty adopters to monitor students' feedback, to communicate to students about what technologies could help their learning and to accomplish learning objectives, and to ensure the effective use of technology throughout the process.

As one of the respondents says, "If you are introducing a new tool it platform in your courses, you should ask for student feedback during the semester." Similarly, another respondent points out, "Practice using the new technology on other faculty to reduce margin of error with students. Communicate with your assigned Teach Tech advisor. They are always willing to help and are an amazing resource." The willingness to adapt and openness for failure are also critical as shown in the following narratives: "Don't use technology for the sake of using technology. One's use of technology must be driven by one's learning objectives for students. On the other hand, one should be flexible to adjust one's learning objectives as technology is incorporated. One must be patient with oneself because it take time to learn how to incorporate technology effectively. Also, willingness to fail and persevere is a highly desirable attribute."

*Figure 4. Q4: What best practice recommendations would you provide upon reflecting you own applications of instructional technologies in their pedagogy?*
*Source: The Authors*

In terms of participants' reflective narratives on what instructional technologies have been included in their pedagogy after completing the TeachTech Program (Q5). Some of the keywords that have appeared include "assignment" (TF-IDF=1.4), "Edupuzzle" (TF-IDF=0.5), "online" (TF-IDF=0.4), and "Blackboard" (TF-IDF=0.5) (Refer to Figure 5 below). For example, one of the respondents share their experiential narratives below:

*I tried flipping instruction in one of my undergraduate courses in two consecutive semesters. I taught that course as a 50-50 hybrid course so that students will learn on their own by watching videos via Edpuzzle.com in which they have to answer embedded questions while watching the video. For the self-learning class, they had to answer the questions in an assignment and turn in via Blackboard. During class meetings, students will apply the math knowledge gained through self-study to solve problems, discuss challenges and questions they have on assignment and homework, and be introduced to the next topic they would be self-learning. They have to turn in a problem-solving homework, in addition to the online self-learning assignment, each week. I shared these resources with another instructor who taught the hybrid version in the following semester. We stopped implementing this hybrid version so that we have face time for students to solve problems in class.*

*Figure 5. Q5: What instructional technologies have been integrated in your own pedagogy after completing the TeachTech Program?*
*Source: The Authors*

In terms of difficulties that faculty participants have encountering in the retooling process (Q6), recurrent words include "discontinued" (TF-IDF=0.5), "time" (TF-IDF=0.5), and "Microsoft" (TF-IDF=0.5) (Refer to Figure 6). One of the respondents says the technology he/she intends to adopt has be discontinued by Microsoft.

In terms of whether taking part in the TeachTech Program has changed faculty participants' perceptions over technology, course content digitalization, and their own pedagogical philosophy (Q7). Recurrent words include "cohort" (TF-IDF=1.0), "technology" (TF-IDF=0.5), "desire" (TF-IDF=1), "collaborative" (TF-IDF=0.5), "attitude" (TF-IDF=0.5), "incorporate" (TF-IDF=0.5), and "novice" (TF-IDF=0.5) (Refer to Figure 7 below).

*Figure 6. Q6: What difficulties have you experienced in the retooling process?*
*Source: The Authors*

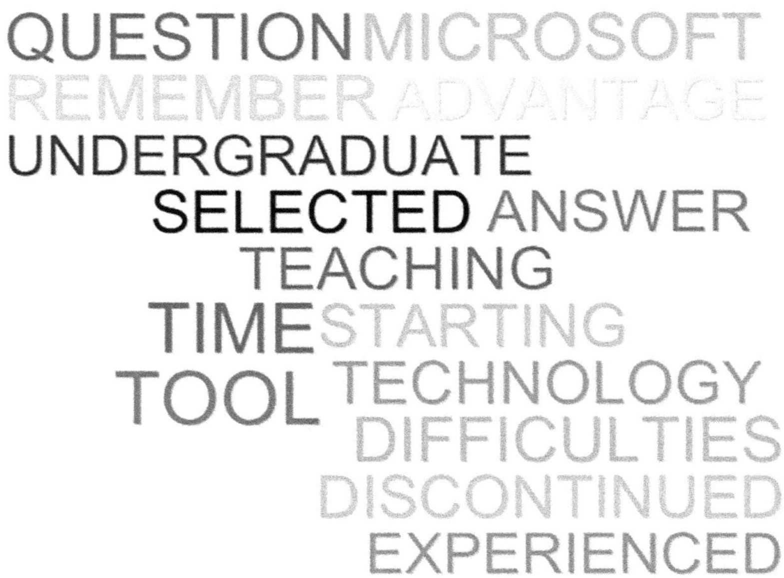


*Figure 7. Q7: Did the participation in the TeachTech Program change what the faculty's perceptions over technology, digitalized course contents, and their own pedagogical philosophy?*
*Source: The Authors*

Respondents have expressed the positive experiences of taking part in the TeachTech Program. For example, the collaborative learning environment created by a cohort with different levels of technology experience has been perceived to beneficial to foster a long-term commitment to integrate technologies. For example, one of the respondents says, "I believe it did. Our cohort had various levels of technological experience. Some were novices, while others were more experienced. I found that we all had a genuine desire to learn something new and incorporate it into our courses. After our presentations at the end of our term, we had an attitude of accomplishment. I personally had a continued desire to learn more. I would love to be a part of another cohort in the future."

Furthermore, the TeachTech Program also provides a supportive environment to help faculty members become familiar and open with these technologies as expressed by another respondent: "I think this platform encouraged all of us to do something outside our comfort zone and timely help was provided to all of us to solve any problems. I learnt about new tools and digital resources that Academic Technology has to offer." The supportive environment provided by the TeachTech Program is also described by another respondent in the narrative below: "I would say I am even more open to technology and more patient with myself in incorporating new technology. I would like to use Blackboard Collaborate one day (I haven't because I am only teaching face-to-face courses)."

In terms of participants' own technology integration experiences before taking part in the TeachTech Program (Q8), "Blackboard" (TF-IDF=0.4), "clickers" (TF-IDF=0.5), "PowerPoint" (TF-IDF=0.5), and "YouTube" (TF-IDF=0.5) (Refer to Figure 8)

*Figure 8. Q8: Before you participated in the TeachTech Program, what types of technologies have you used in your classes? These technologies may include Blackboard, the Internet, PowerPoint, Online Conferencing, etc.*
*Source: The Authors*

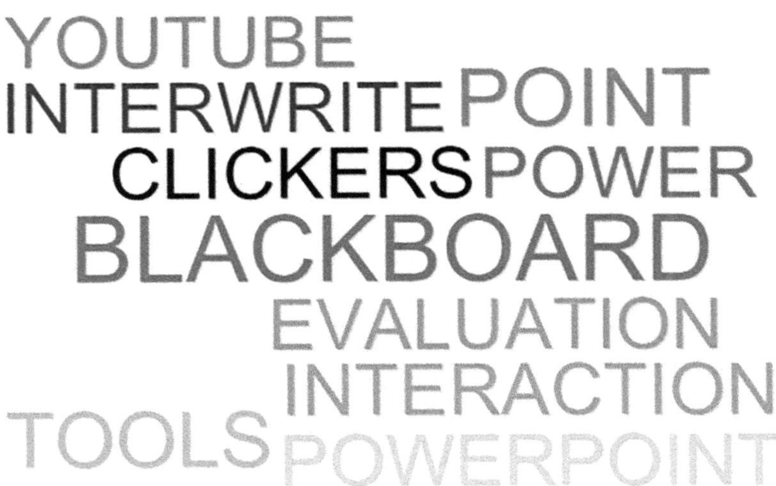

In terms of new technologies learned from the TeachTech Program, participants have expressed that their adoption of the following technologies (Q9): "Qualtrics" (TF-IDF=1.0), "Camtasia" (TF-IDF=0.5), "editing" (TF-IDF=0.5), "Quizlet" (TF-IDF=0.5), and "video" (TF-IDF=0.5) (Refer to Figure 9). The following experiences from the respondents also provide detailed description about how these technologies have been used in the classroom: "I learnt about some of new tools like second life and VR and how we can incorporate those in our courses"; "As previously mentioned, I learned how to use Quizlet and Qualtrics. I used Quizlets to review content in class. Qualtrics was use in pre and post surveys regarding the students' level of confidence"; "Camtasia for video editing."

*Figure 9. Q9: What new technologies have you learned from the TeachTech Program?*
*Source: The Authors*

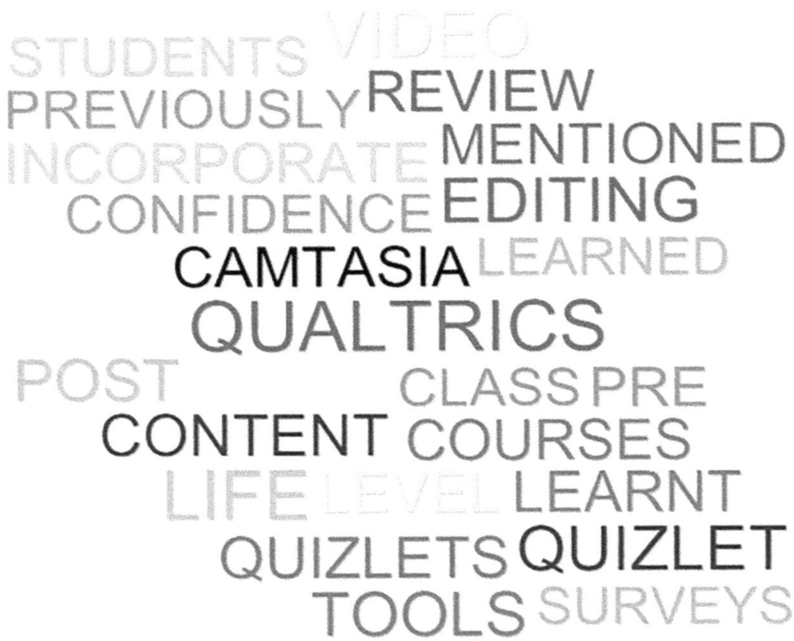


To summarize what faculty participants' overall experiences with the TeachTech Program, the authors have also run key phrase extraction (with a minimum frequency of 3) that will best summarizes their experiential narratives. The data has identified the following key phrases: "incorporate technology" (TF-IDF=0.5), "answer embedded question" (TF-IDF=1), "Blackboard collaboration" (TF-IDF=0.4), "collaborative session" (TF-IDF=1.0), "desire to learn" (TF-IDF=1), "level of confidence" (TF-IDF=1), "selected tool" (TF-IDF=1), "simulation project" (TF-IDF=1), "solve problems" (TF-IDF=1) (Refer to Figure 10)

*Figure 10: Overall Experience Participating in TeachTech Program: Key Phrase Extraction (Q1-Q9)*
*Source: The Authors (Frequency= minimum 3)*

## DISCUSSION

With the rapid diffusion of educational technologies in today's college and university classrooms, many faculty members have eagerly embraced these technologies in their pedagogical approaches. Many of these efforts are also supported by encouraging empirical results that confirm the effectiveness of technology-enhanced instruction (Fador, Aldamen, & Saadullah, 2018; Tomak et al., 2019). For example, Fador et al. (2018) empirically validates the improvement on students' improvement and perception among online, flipped, and traditional management classes. Their results confirm online and flipped classrooms have fewer absenteeism, and access to online course materials help students' performance in both online and flipped classrooms (Fador et al., 2018). Tokmak et al. (2019) survey 36 prospective teachers in a computer literacy class and conclude that students perceive a technology-enhanced flipped classroom to be challenging, entertaining, and instructive.

Recently, scholars have begun to shift their focus to better understand what faculty adopters feel and think about these technologies and their pedagogical implications (Dumont & Raggo, 2018; Li & Wang, 2016; Motaghian et al., 2013). Dumont and Raggo (2019) study what faculty members think about teaching a hybrid class in non-profit management. Their study confirms some of the findings reported above about the innovativeness and location-freedom of technology-enhanced instructions (such as hybrid, online, and flipped classrooms). However, many faculty members have also become aware that the lack of face-to-face interactions with students are a key drawback when teaching online. The lack of personal interactions with students has been mentioned multiple times in the experiential narratives of the TeachTech participants that technologies should be integrated into the classroom to enhance interactions with students.

To motivate faculty members to adopt educational technologies, their perceptions about these technologies are critical to their adoption decisions. Motaghian et al. (2013) survey of 115 university instructors in Iran confirms that favourable perceived usefulness, perceived ease of use, and system quality about these technologies will lead to their adoption by instructors. Perceived usefulness of technologies is also found to be the most important predictor (Motaghian et al. 2013). The text mining data reported in this chapter lend further support to the importance of how educational technologies will be perceived by the faculty members. Many of the respondents have expressed that they are motivated to take part in the TeachTech Program because they believe technologies will be beneficial to students' learning and engagement. Furthermore, many faculty participants have said that the TeachTech Program somehow helps them to become aware of the availability and usefulness of these technologies. Once technologies are favourably perceived, their attitudes toward their actual applications will also be enhanced and actual integration will be made possible (Thowfeek & Hussein, 2008).

Finally, as pointed out in Dumont and Raggo (2018), the lack of clarity of policies and rules in the higher education institute about technology-enhanced teaching could also interfere with the effectiveness of its implementation. Launching a university-sponsored TeachTech Program is a clear signal that the initiative is supported and encourage by the administration and will help those faculty members who are interested to continue their commitment. In the experiential data reported above, many of the TeachTech program participants have expressed the importance of working in a cohort and receiving continual technology support from the school to facilitate their integration process. A clear commitment from the college and university administration is also critical because several of the TeachTech participants have mentioned the importance of stepping out their comfort zone (to learn new technologies) and become confident to accept trial and errors in the technology adoption process.

## RECOMMENDATIONS, LIMITATIONS, AND FUTURE DIRECTIONS

The findings reported in this chapter are limited by the methodology and the sample recruited to answer the interview questions. As an interview study, the study is not able to produce quantitative inferential statistics to identify relationships among variables. Furthermore, because the text mining analyses are based on the experiential narratives from the TeachTech Program participants, the researchers are not able to explore the relationships between participants' demographics, perceptions of technologies, and their adoption behaviours in a large scale survey (Li & Wang, 2016). Li and Wang's (2016) quantitative survey may offer a next step to explore the relationships between participants' gender, perceptions of technologies, lifestyle variables, and their technology adoption behaviours. Furthermore, text-mining techniques have their innate methodological limitation in terms of the processing of words, keywords, phrases, and dictionaries in identifying recurrent linguistic patterns and trends to generate findings (Tesoa et al., 2018). The sole reliance on a single word may ignore the diversity of word meanings as warned by many scholars using text mining methods (Tesoa et al., 2018). They also caution that the use of keywords and key phrases similarly runs into problems of reducing their importance in different contexts (Tesoa et al., 2018; Yang & Kang, 2018).

## REFERENCES

Baran, E., Correia, A.-P., & Thompson, A. (2011, November). Transforming online teaching practice: Critical analysis of the literature on the roles and competencies of online teachers. *Distance Education*, *32*(3), 421–439. doi:10.1080/01587919.2011.610293

Davis, C. (2019, December). AV tech that recruits. *AV Technology*, 28-43.

Dumont, G., & Raggo, P. (2018). Faculty perspectives about distance teaching in the virtual classroom. *Journal of Nonprofit Education & Leadership*, *8*(1), 41–61. doi:10.18666/JNEL-2018-V8-I1-8372

Eldridge, C. (2015, July 14). *Education technology - A competitive landscape that is a diamond in the rough for new startups.* The Startup Ecosystem. Retrieved on December 19, 2019 from https://startupecosystem.blogspot.com/2015/2007/education-technology-competitive.html

Fadol, Y., Aldamen, H., & Saadullah, S. (2018, July). A comparative analysis of flipped, online and traditional teaching: A case of female Middle Eastern management students. *International Journal of Management Education*, *16*(2), 266–280. doi:10.1016/j.ijme.2018.04.003

Gonzalez, C. (2009). Conceptions of, and approaches to, teaching online: A study of lecturers teaching postgraduate distance courses. *Higher Education*, *57*(3), 299–314. doi:10.100710734-008-9145-1

Herold, B. (2016, February 5). Technology in education: An overview. *Education Week*. Retrieved on December 19, 2019 from https://www.edweek.org/ew/issues/technology-in-education/index.html

Kao, A., & Poteet, S. R. (2007). *Natural language processing and text mining*. Springer. doi:10.1007/978-1-84628-754-1

Kobayashi, V. B., Mol, S. T., Berkers, H. A., Kismihók, G., & Hartog, D. N. D. (2018). Text mining in organizational research. *Organizational Research Methods*, *21*(3), 733–765. doi:10.1177/1094428117722619 PMID:29881248

Li, S.-C. S., & Huang, W.-C. (2016). Lifestyles, innovation attributes, and teachers' adoption of game-based learning: Comparing non-adopters with early adopters, adopters and likely adopters in Taiwan. *Computers & Education*, *96*, 29–41. doi:10.1016/j.compedu.2016.02.009

Lin, F.-R., Ha, D., & Liao, D. (2016, January 5-8). *Automatic content analysis of media framing by text mining techniques.* Paper presented at the 49th Hawaii International Conference on System Sciences. 10.1109/HICSS.2016.348

McCallum, S., Schultz, J., Sellke, K., & Spartz, J. (2015). An examination of the flipped classroom approach on college student academic involvement. *International Journal on Teaching and Learning in Higher Education*, *27*(1), 42–55.


McCallum, S., Schultz, J., Sellke, K., & Spartz, J. (2015). An examination of the flipped classroom approach on college student academic involvement. *International Journal on Teaching and Learning in Higher Education*, *27*(1), 42–55.


McGuire, S. (2016, August 5). *9 Technology tools to engage students in the classroom. TeachThrough: We Grow Teachers.* Retrieved on June 11, 2019 from https://www.teachthought.com/technology/2019-technology-tools-engage-students-classroom/

Motaghian, H., Hassanzadeh, A., & Moghadam, D. K. (2013, January). Factors affecting university instructors' adoption of web-based learning systems: Case study of Iran. *Computers & Education*, *61*(1), 158–167. doi:10.1016/j.compedu.2012.09.016

Office of Educational Technology. (2017). Reimagining the Role of Technology in Education. Retrieved on January 1, 2020 from https://tech.ed.gov/files/2017/01/NETP17.pdf.

Office of Educational Technology. (2019). 2020 National Educational Technology Plan. Retrieved January 1, 2020 from https://tech.ed.gov/files/2017/01/NETP17.pdf.

Saxena, S. (2013, October 8). How Important is use of Technology in Education. *EdTech Review*. Retrieved on June 11, 2019 from http://edtechreview.in/news/2681-technology-in-education

Schön, D. (1988). Educating the reflective practitioner. San Francisco, C.A.: Jossey-Bass.

Srivastava, T. (2014, May 7). Build a word cloud using text mining tools of R. *Analytics Vidhya*. Retrieved on Apri 25, 2019 from https://www.analyticsvidhya.com/blog/2014/2005/build-word-cloud-text-mining-tools/

Stein, D. (2000). *Teaching critical reflection* (Myths and realities No. 7). Columbus, OH: ERIC Clearinghouse on Adult, Career, and Vocational Education. (ED445256)

Tesoa, E., Olmedillab, M., Martínez-Torres, M. R., & Toral, S. L. (2018, April). Application of text mining techniques to the analysis of discourse in eWOM communications from a gender perspective. *Technological Forecasting and Social Change*, *129*, 131–142. doi:10.1016/j.techfore.2017.12.018

Thowfeek, M. H., & Hussin, H. (2008). Instructors' perspective on e-learning adoption in Sri Lanka: A preliminary investigation. *Communications of the IBIMA*, *6*, 124–129.

Tiahrt, T., & Porter, J. C. (2016). What do I do with this flipping classroom: Ideas for effectively using class time in a flipped course. Elm Street Press.

Tokmak, H. S., Yakin, I., & Dogusoy, B. (2019, January). Prospective English teachers' digital storytelling experiences through a flipped classroom approach. *International Journal of Distance Education Technologies*, *17*(1), 78–99. doi:10.4018/IJDET.2019010106

Touri, M., & Koteyko, N. (2015). Using corpus linguistic software in the extraction of news frames: Towards a dynamic process of frame analysis in journalistic texts. *International Journal of Research Methodology*, *18*(6), 601–616. doi:10.1080/13645579.2014.929878

Trilling, D., & Jonkman, J. G. F. (2018). Scaling up content analysis. *Communication Methods and Measures*, *12*(2-3), 158–174. doi:10.1080/19312458.2018.1447655

Yang, K. C. C., & Kang, Y. W. (2020). The effectiveness of gamification on students' engagement, learning outcomes, and learning experiences. In Handbook of Research Creating Meaningful Experiences in Online Courses (pp. 286-305). Hershey, PA: IGI-Global Publisher.

Yang, K. C. C., & Kang, Y. W. (2018, October 27-29). *Global communication educators' responses to the new media landscape: A text mining approach to understand trends and future developments in communication curricula around the world.* Paper Presented at The New Paradigms in Communication Education Stream, The Asian Congress for Media and Communication (ACMC) 2018 International Conference, National Chengchi University, Taiwan.

Zhang, Y., Chen, M., & Liu, L. (2015). A review on text mining. In *2015 6th IEEE International Conference on Software Engineering and Service Science (ICSESS)* (pp. 681-685). New York, NY: IEEE. 10.1109/ICSESS.2015.7339149

Zhang, Y., Dang, Y., & Amer, B. (2016, November). A large-scale blended and flipped class: Class design and investigation of factors influencing students' intention to learn. *IEEE Transactions on Education*, *59*(4), 263–273. doi:10.1109/TE.2016.2535205

Zuber, W. J. (2016). The flipped classroom, a review of the literature. *Industrial and Commercial Training*, *48*(2), 97–103. doi:10.1108/ICT-05-2015-0039

## ADDITIONAL READING

Berrett, D. (2012). How 'flipping' the classroom can improve the traditional lecture. The Chronicle of Higher Education, Retrieved October 6, 2019 from https://www.chronicle.com/article/How-Flipping-the-Classroom/130857

Çakıroğlu, Ü. (2014). Analyzing the effect of learning styles and study habits of distance learners on learning performances: A case of an introductory programming course. *The International Review of Research in Open and Distributed Learning*, *15*(4). Advance online publication. doi:10.19173/irrodl.v15i4.1840

Caligaris, M., Rodrígueza, G., & Laugero, L. (2016). A first experience of flipped classroom in numerical analysis. *Procedia: Social and Behavioral Sciences*, *217*, 838–845. doi:10.1016/j.sbspro.2016.02.158

Cheng, B., Wang, M., Moormann, J., Olaniran, B. A., & Chen, N.-S. (2012, April). The effects of organizational learning environment factors on e-learning acceptance. *Computers & Education*, *58*(3), 885–899. doi:10.1016/j.compedu.2011.10.014

Dexter, J. (2017, January 25). The global phenomenon of E-Learning courses. Training Industry, Retrieved on August 14, 2019 from https://trainingindustry.com/blog/e-learning/the-global-phenomenon-of-e-learning-courses/

Eom, S. (2010, July 5-7). Relationships between e-learning systems and learning outcomes: A path analysis model. Paper presented at the 2010 IEEE 10th International Conference on Advanced Learning Technologies (ICALT), Sousse, Tunisia. 10.1109/ICALT.2010.147

Fichten, C. S., Ferraro, V., Asuncion, J. V., Chwojka, C., Barile, M., Nguyen, M. N., & … . (2009). Disabilities and e-learning problems and solutions: An exploratory study. *Journal of Educational Technology & Society*, *12*(4), 241–256.

Katz, S. M. (2008, January). Assessing a hybrid format. *Journal of Business and Technical Communication*, *22*(1), 92–110. http://jbt.sagepub.com. doi:10.1177/1050651907307710

Keller, J. H., Hassell, J. M., Webber, S. A., & Johnson, J. N. (2009, September). A comparison of academic performance in traditional and hybrid sections of introductory managerial accounting. *Journal of Accounting Education*, *27*(3), 147–154. doi:10.1016/j.jaccedu.2010.03.001

Keramati, A., Afshari-Mofrad, M., & Kamrani, A. (2011, May). The role of readiness factors in e-learning outcomes: An empirical study. *Computers & Education, 57*(3), 1919–1929. doi:10.1016/j.compedu.2011.04.005

Kohli, C., Lancellotti, M. P., & Thomas, S. (2017, Winter). Student attitudes towards hybrid business classes: lessons for implementation. Journal of the Academy of Business Education, 387-395.

Lancellotti, M., Thomas, S., & Kohli, C. (2015). online video modules for improvement in student learning. *Journal of Education for Business, 91*(1), 1–4.

Marcelo, C., Yot, C., & Mayor, C. (2015). University teaching with digital technologies. *Media Education Research Journal, 13*(45), 117–124.

Megan, M. L., Bessie, L., & Anita, F. (2017, January). Measuring the impact of course modality on student knowledge, performance and communication apprehension in public speaking pedagogy. *Media Watch, 8*(1), 7–19.

Minović, M., Štavljanin, V., Milovanović, M., & Starčević, D. B. (2008). Usability issues of e-learning systems: Case-study for Moodle learning management system. In R. Meersman, Z. Tari, & P. Herrero (Eds.), *On the move to meaningful internet systems: OTM 2008 Workshops* (pp. 561–570). Springer. doi:10.1007/978-3-540-88875-8_79

Murray, M., & Jackson, P. (2009, December 12-14). Web 2.0 in the classroom: The possibilities. Paper presented at the Proceedings of the 2009 International SIGED: IAIM Conference, Phoenix, AZ.

Rahimi, E., Van Den Berg, J., & Veen, W. (2014). Facilitating student-driven constructing of learning environments using Web 2.0 personal learning environment. *Computer Education, 81*, 235–246. doi:10.1016/j.compedu.2014.10.012

Ramey, K. (2012, November 6). Types of technology used in the classroom. Retrieved on October 5, 2019 from https://www.useoftechnology.com/types-technology-classroom/

Thowfeek, M. H., & Salam, M. N. A. (2014, August). Students' assessment on the usability of e-learning websites. *Procedia: Social and Behavioral Sciences, 141*, 916–922. doi:10.1016/j.sbspro.2014.05.160

Von Heupt, N. (2018, September). Hybrid classrooms: Removing barriers to face-to-face training. *Training & Development*, 10–11.

Yang, K. C. C., & Kang, Y. W. (2017). (2018, July 5-8). Representing the Internet and World Wide Web in mass media: A comparative text mining study of mass media in the Greater China Region and the U.S. Paper Presented at the *24th International Conference of the International Association for Intercultural Communication Studies (IAICS)*, De Paul University, Chicago, U.S.A.

## KEY TERMS AND DEFINITIONS

**Blended Learning:** A term that is synonymous to flipped learning. It refers to the use of a combination of learning delivery approaches, such as face-to-face synchronous or online asynchronous method to allow students to learn either online or offline.

**Critical Reflection:** A term to describe the process by which people identify the assumptions to guide their actions, locate the cultural and historical contexts of these assumptions, inquire the meaning of these assumptions, and develop different ways of actions.

**EdTech:** Abbreviated from educational technology. A term often refers to different types of instructional technologies (such as the Internet, mobile devices, streaming technologies, cloud storage, digital games, etc.) that are applied in classrooms ranging from K12 to higher education institutes.

**Experiential Narratives:** A term that refers to written or spoken account of what a person has experienced in a specific event. This type of narratives can be from a first-person or third-person perspective when describing their personal account of a particular event.

**Flipped Classroom/Learning:** It refers to an instructional strategy that has recently gained prominence among educational community. The innovative strategy focuses on the integration of instructional and EdTech technologies to allow the instructor to offer online resources and to gamify a class to allow students to learn actively. The strategy allows instructors to transform homework assignments to activities that student can actively participate and engage during the face-to-face class meetings.

**Gamification:** Gamification refers to the applications of game design principles and the inclusion of game elements in non-gaming contexts. The gamification practice is also considered to be an informal umbrella term to describe the inclusion of game design elements in non-game applications such as business, education, health care, human resources, to name a few.

**Hybrid Classroom/Learning:** A term that describes a technologized classroom where students study course materials delivered through connected pedagogical platforms (such as the Internet) and then interact with the instructors during the face-to-face meetings to clarify what they have learned online.

**Interactivity:** An important dimension of information-communication technologies (or ICTs). This term refers to the process ICT users are provided with the technical capabilities to modify communication contents and to have real-time interactions with participants in a communication process.

**Online Learning:** A term to describe an emerging pedagogical approach to learn at students' premise and at students' own pace through the integration of advanced information-communication technologies (such as Blackboard, Moodle, YouTube) either asynchronously or synchronously.

**Pedagogy:** This term refers to a systematic instructional method employed by an instructor to convey core subject matters to students. This term can also refer to the study of teaching methods to help an instructor to choose the most effective approach after taking into consideration students' motivation, learning styles, social, economic, and cultural background.

**Text Mining:** A term that refers to a growingly popular research method to process and analyse a large of textual data. This research method include the pre-processing, text categorization, clustering of documents, and extraction of keywords, key phrases, or topics. Text mining techniques also involve the use of text visualization where word clouds, graphs, and maps can be used to represent the relationships among extracted information from the corpus.

**TF-IDF:** Abbreviated from Term-Frequency-Inverse document Frequency. TF-IDF is a popular statistical term that take into consideration both the importance of a word or a phrase and their specificity.

**Topic Modelling:** A text mining procedure, also commonly found in machine learning and natural language processing methods, to discover hidden semantic structure from the collection of documents through statistical procedures.

**Word Cloud:** A text visualization technique that is used to graphical represent the importance of a word or a key phrase on the basis of their importance in relation to the whole corpus. A larger image of a specific word or phrase denotes its relative importance among the documents in the corpus.

# Chapter 14
# Technological Impact on Public Engagement in Alternative Educational and Heritage Institutions:
## Portraying Minorities Through Interactive Exhibits

**Natalia Moreira**
https://orcid.org/0000-0002-1031-3508
*School of Materials, University of Manchester, UK*

**Eleanor C. Ward**
*University of Manchester, UK*

## ABSTRACT

*Cultural institutions and higher education establishments in the UK face significant challenges and uncertainties in the present and foreseeable future, particularly in terms of securing ongoing funding in a period of austerity. In an era of constricting budgets, institutions are encouraged to find creative solutions to generating revenue streams and demonstrating impact, which in turn, offers ample opportunities for innovation and mutual benefit through collaboration between the academic and heritage sectors. This chapter focuses on the 'REALab' consultancy programme, piloted and funded by the University of Manchester, which allowed a group of multidisciplinary researchers to address representation and inclusion of underrepresented groups at the Museum of Science and Industry in Manchester. The chapter is presented as a case study into the collaboration process between academic and heritage institutions. It will discuss the methods and success of the project and evaluate the importance of the interactive and innovative profile of the museum in the process.*

DOI: 10.4018/978-1-7998-4846-2.ch014

## INTRODUCTION

In recent years, universities throughout across the globe have engaged in an impressive number of institutional initiatives and activities that promote multiculturalism in higher education (Tierney & Lanford, 2018). In an effort to promote research and cultivate ties with business communities, Universities have been given the backing of private donors and entrepreneurial partnerships with various corporate entities. Nurturing global networks and attracting talented students calls for Universities to explore the viability of establishing branch campuses globally (Lanford & Tierney, 2016). In particular, online education has changed the way many institutions think about how to deliver effective learning and teaching through innovative practices. Meanwhile, national governments have devoted much of their attention towards improving individual skillsets to meet the challenges of a knowledge economy, which in turn as persuaded tertiary institutions to develop new degree programs and promote inclusion through expanding access to students from previously underrepresented ethnic and socioeconomic backgrounds (Jongbloed et al. 2008). However, it is often not as simple when defining the identity of a university campus, especially since the institution's culture is subjective depending on individuals' perspectives and motivations. Therefore, the topic of institutional culture has garnered much attention recently special, particularly in higher education studies.

Cultural institutions and higher education establishments, particularly those in the United Kingdom, face significant challenges and uncertainties, particularly in terms of securing ongoing funding in a period of austerity (Summers, 2009). In an era of constricting budgets, it is more essential than ever that these organizations can demonstrate appreciable public impact and value for money in their activities. However, the current climate offers many opportunities for innovation and mutual benefit through collaboration between technology and heritage sectors. In summer 2015, the Museum of Science and Industry (MSI) embarked upon an experimental project with REALab, a pilot consultancy programme made up of PhD students from the University of Manchester. The groups that joined REALab were in competition with each other, working towards a 'Dragon's Den'[1] formatted pitch. The program, founded by Rosalinda Quintieri, a PhD student at the Department of Art History and Visual Studies of the University of Manchester, aimed "to provide engagement and consultancy skills training and opportunities for PhD candidates and provide non-Higher Education institutions [...] with access to appropriate and targeted research expertise to support sustainability, cultural innovation and social value" (Quintieri, 2015).

This pilot tested the benefits of student PhD-led consultancies as an innovative approach to consultancy work. Quintieri notes during an interview:

*When I thought about REALab my main priorities were to allow interfaculty/interdisciplinary work, provide professional training not easily accessible to PhDs through the main internal providers, work with an array of different organisations (cultural, third sector, social enterprises) and allow the possibility through the program for the organic development of a trustworthy professional relationship between partners and researchers.*

The positives of this approach are reflected in the number of projects initially proposed by different organisations interested in having students with this specific knowledge profile. The novelty of this combination of interdisciplinary work and training provides a rich environment for development.

## REALab: The Project's Cradle

The Manchester Museum of Science and Industry's brief described as a project that:

*In order to enrich their collections and the stories that they tell, they aim to diversify the content of their galleries so that they had better represent their audiences. They would like to reveal stories relating to people that are currently under-represented in their museum. For example, this could include the role of women, Black, Asian and Minority Ethnic (BAME) people, Lesbians, Gay, Bisexual and Transgender (LGBT) people and people with disabilities in the history and contemporary practice of science and industry in Manchester. (Quintieri, 2015)*

They also required the following deliverables be met: "*(1) Review and report on available literature and archive resources; (2) Identify key diverse stories/people that relate to the museum's core themes; and (3) Identify possible academic and community partners for future collaboration." (Quintieri, 2015).* This initial brief would be constantly reviewed with the MSI's staff represented by Jan Hicks (Archives and Information Manager) and Meg McHugh (Senior Curator).

In addition, the PhD students involved in the REALab project underwent a training programme to introduce them to the basics of consultancy and project management. The first session, called 'Consultancy Process and Problem Analysis' was an introduction to the consultancy process and the project to be worked on. The second training session was a workshop with the different partners, at this session the groups had a chance to network with the staff representatives facilitating the communication between both parties.

After meeting the representative from MSI (Jan Hicks), the authors discussed the brief and then presented this preliminary consultation to the other student researchers. Because of this meeting, the group identified the key needs and wishes, which were not clearly described in the brief, focussing mainly on a deliverable report on how other museums have approached similar issues as well providing essential ways to implement the findings locally.

The following training session (3) was 'Project Management' with Yvonne McLean, a management coach from Inkling Training, which helped demonstrate the structure of a successful project and how to deal with unexpected issues. This session facilitated the students foresee how additional planning could be useful in the conception of our projects. The fourth and final training, carried out by Caroline Clegg, director and performance coach, was focussed on the presentation and pitching skills in preparation for the Dragon's Den.

## Contributions

The group working with MSI won the competition and proceeded to the next stage of the project: producing a written report, in which the findings and recommendations were presented. This article will analyse the success of the partnership, and the achievement of interdisciplinary researchers. The project represented an example of the expectations and ideas associated with consultancy, how outreach is helpful to museum projects, including collaboration and education through placements. The contribution of this chapter and REALab is the opportunity to collaborate with other researchers, and the chance to work outside particular research groups. The group has diverse backgrounds, which meant they approached research in distinct ways. Due to the presence of scientists, engineers, writers and historians the approaches varied from highly analytical disseminations of research to exploring creative approaches of extrapolating these ideas. These differences turned into opportunities for growth. The strengths of this diverse group identified specific improvements for MSI, which would not be identified by a lone researcher, or a team lacking the diversity of approaches and subject-knowledge. This chapter focuses on the 'REALab' consultancy programme, piloted and funded by the University of Manchester, School of Humanities. It will use the project as a case study into the collaboration process between academic and heritage institutions within a technological and interactive environment. The documented project will discuss how it met objectives for collaboration and impact for both the MSI and The University of Manchester. The chapter will explore the methods and success of relationship and network building between specialists in diverse fields of research and enterprise.

## PROJECT BACKGROUND

Research collaboration between museums and universities or other heritage institutions has long formed an intrinsic part of the way that museums work (Hooper-Greenhill et al., 2000). Relationships now include paid consultancy projects and the trend for the use of freelancers and contractors. Yet this new approach retains the strata of expert and non-expert research collaborations. The general public, on the other hand, normally form the subjects of exhibitions, provide feedback, or help curate temporary exhibitions heavily guided by members of the museum staff (Govier, 2009; Graham, 2016). The impetus behind collaboration, consultancy projects and public engagement is often the recognition that an institution needs to change. In particular, consultants are often associated with change, for example the introduction of a new method of working or a new area in which to work, compared to contractors, freelancers or interns who take on work within the existent portfolio of an institution. Within this frame of reference, the stratification of expert and non-expert may become challenging.

### Consultancies

The core activity of a consultant is advising or problem solving (Will, 1997). It can be used in varied ways: (1) *temporary* project where the workload exceeds the capacity of permanent staff or for which expertise is required that falls outside that of the current staff; (2) the addressing of a problem that the current staff have been unable to solve; (3) the facilitation of a change in the organisational structure; (4) or mode of operation of the organisation (Fischer, 2001; Wulff & Palacios, 1991). Successful consultancy projects in a museum can lead to long-term engagement with new audiences, developing new skills and ways of working for existent staff (Fischer, 2001), and in the most extreme cases turn around a failing organisation. In all the instances detailed above, the organisation that hires a consultant will expect to pay a high fee, which for many heritage or cultural institutions, may be prohibitive when a project is not considered essential. Within the museum and heritage sector, one can find spinout consultancy firms from both higher education institutions (HEIs) and groups of cultural institutions (CIs), in which the research and professional expertise of the researcher or museum professional is harnessed in a way that goes beyond traditional collaboration.

## Student Consultancies

The formation and use of student consultancies provides a mode of collaboration between HEIs and CIs that sit outside traditional collaborations, student placements or research projects. Student consultancies demonstrate the impact of educational and cultural institutions on the wider heritage landscape. The human capital of the university provides knowledge transfer, both in terms of students' skills and expertise, and the final outcome of the project (Gilmore & Comunian, 2016). Consequently, student consultancy projects may provide research or advice on areas that sit outside of the frame of knowledge or skills provided by the museum staff. Any successful consultancy project rests on its ability to be reciprocal, both concerning how communicative and accommodating an institution is during the project, but also in the formulation of the original brief and concerning the expectations regarding its outcome.

The concept of student consultancies has been around for at least two decades[2,3]. These consultancies tend to focus on undergraduate development. Additionally, universities such as Leicester and Oxford have successfully produced reports and developed rich research on the topic. While the REALab programme bears many similarities with other student consultancies, its difference is that the programme specifically targets PhD students, and therefore students with experience and a substantially higher level of education than undergraduate student consultancies. The inclusion of students from any discipline means that the knowledge-base and research skills is higher than that of an undergraduate who studies in the specific discipline that a project focuses on. REALab focused on teaching general skills and methods that a consultant has in their toolkit, while the provision of guidance on the specifics of the museum was provided by MSI's representatives.

In this instance, the group who worked on the project for MSI reflected the diversity of the programme. These skills were particularly beneficial to the project. The group included researchers in the areas of nanoscience, identity and gender in contemporary poetry about disability, consumer involvement in sustainable fashion development, and social, economic, labour and gender history. Encapsulating the Schools of Pharmacy, Humanities, Engineering and Physics, the researcher's communication and discussions were at points confusing and circular. Even when arguing the same points, the manner of approaching this problem and reaching a solution proved not as linear as expected. Usually projects such as this, are developed within a cultural dimension which is shared by the team members (Hofstede, 2010). However, in this context, part of the solution to the project was mediating the way we each approached the brief. From this standpoint, programmes such as REALab can be viewed as creating a melting pot of expertise, personal profiles and academic approaches.

## Museum of Science and Industry

The city of Manchester is known mainly for one reason: being the cradle of the Industrial revolution and pioneering many of the ground breaking innovations which followed, from the first weaving machines powered by water or steam, to the development of the world's first stored-programme computer in 1948, 'Baby' (Carter, 2012; Jivraj, 2011; Beckert, 2014; Anderson and Carden-Coyne, 2007). As part of this scenario and based in a city proud of its rich ethnic diversity, the Manchester Museum of Science and Industry is constantly singled out due to several reasons. These include the museum's interactive and creative approach to presenting the history of science, technology and industry, and portraying how this fields have evolved and what might lay in the future (Museum of Science and Industry, 2014). Thus, the MSI aims to be internationally recognised for their perspective regarding the influence of science, industry and innovation on the creation and maintenance of modern society.

## METHODOLOGICAL DESIGN

The project required a specific approach to combine the researcher's expertise and the interests of the client. The group considered the different ways to approach this research as can be seen on Table 1.

*Table 1. Relevant situations for different research methods (modified from (Creswell, 2013; Yin, 2013).*

| METHOD | Major strength | Major weakness | Why it was not chosen? |
|---|---|---|---|
| **Experiment** | Cause-effect relationship (can draw conclusions about causality) | Artificiality and Feasibility | Because it often does not represent true learning environments |
| **Archival Analysis** | Establishes facts and draw conclusions about past events | Relies on external resources what can be time consuming and bias (information can be incomplete, obsolete, may not identify the cause of the problem, etc.) | Based exclusively in past situations (even if they are related to current facts) |
| **Ethnography** | Investigates a culture through an in-depth study of the members of the culture | Depends on human observations and responses | Focussed on a specific cultural background or ethnographic group |
| **Action research** | Great interaction between practical and theoretical stances ('on the spot' procedure) | Little or no control over independent variables | Cannot fulfil the scientific requirement for generalisability ('antithesis of experimental research') |
| **Grounded theory** | Discover what problems exist in a given social environment and how the persons involved handle it | Time consuming (only concluded once a theory is built and proven generalisable) | It analysis the current situation and creates a theory out of it, testing and reformulating the propositions until a theory is developed |
| **Narrative enquiry** | Observation as a mean of data collection (analyses repeatability of fact – the 'normal') | Depends on human observations and responses | Distortions in data occur in biased questions in interviews, questionnaires, selective observation of events, etc. |

'Action Research' was considered the best solution to meeting the brief, due to its focus on disseminating research and implementing it. This form of research constantly adapts to the specific need of the client and other researchers, thus providing an innovative solution. Additionally, this methodology raises the importance of research independence. In order to guarantee the interaction between all the involved parties, the use of action research and its constant review of the client's needs was required in order to achieve success. This entails the strengthening of the relationship between client and solution finder. To do so, it is very important to constantly review the project brief and adjust the theory found in the data being analysed.

## Market Analysis

Due to the museum's strong experience with market research and analysis, the need to expand the data collection into a fieldwork became unnecessary. However, the understanding of previous projects, which looked into similar underrepresented groups within national or local contexts proved essential. This meant that the Group required a systematic review of the literature, as summarised in the Figures below (Fig.1 and Fig.2).

*Figure 1. The focuses we found in other museums*

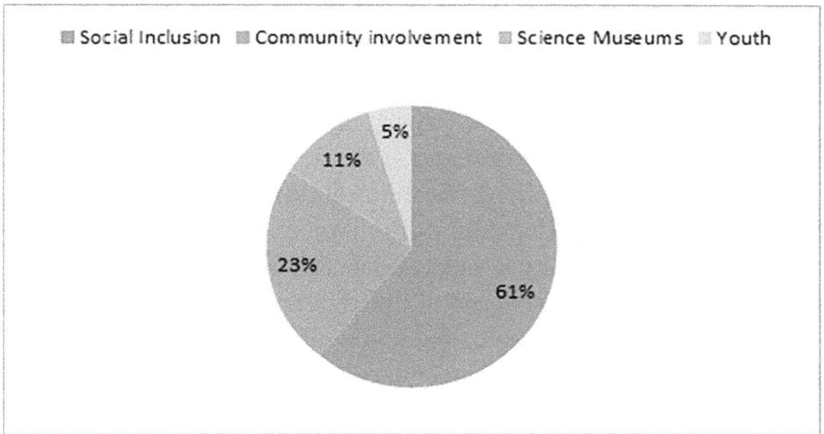


*Figure 2. The main minorities other museums focused on*

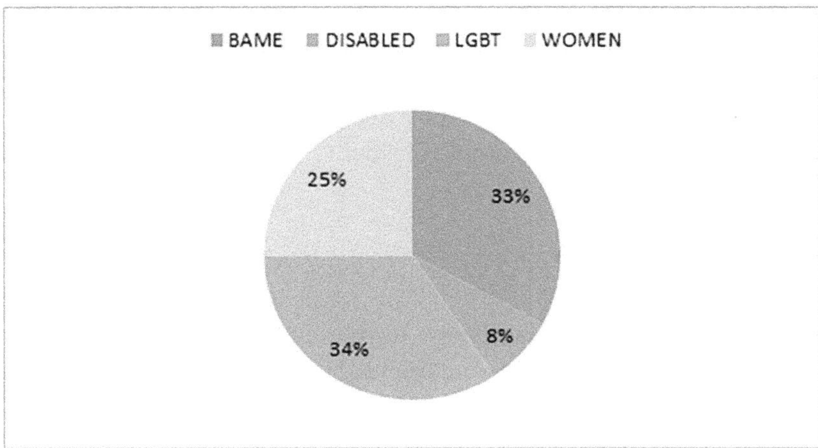


A discussion of the implementation of the project, utilising the skills of action research within the cultural sector, based on data found in the literature, follows.

## Implementation of the Project

One of the unique selling points of the REALab programme was the series of training sessions in project management and business analysis methods delivered to the students involved, which were intended to build skills in consultancy. REALab provided vast business skills. One of the first skills used when analysing what MSI required from their project was a 'Strengths, Weaknesses, Opportunities and Threats' (SWOT) analysis. This SWOT initially examined MSI as a whole, acknowledging their positioning within the museum industry, its online presence and the importance of an interactive and innovative solution.

From their feedback, we identified their need for the focus on an analysis of the museum communities and how they consider inclusiveness in their collections, not the make-up of their audience. The team, focused on identifying how MSI's characteristics of Manchester as "diverse, radical and global"[4] could be reproduced in the project brief. Subsequently, further research was undertaken, starting with the MSI itself. The project observed how they currently engage with the community, leading to the realisation that many of their projects were infrequent attempts at engaging with individual parts of communities instead of incorporating all minorities within the museum as a whole. This meant evaluating how critical it was to avoid prejudiced judgements or further isolation of the disadvantaged communities being considered.

During the five months of the development of the project, both parties met multiple times. Each meeting improved the interaction and encouraged collaboration and constant reassessing of the goals. This unique characteristic of action research and this kind of project was widely praised by MSI's Staff. The final report took three months to compile, and was a substantial piece of research. These included case studies of the best practices, but also recommendations for implementation, pointing out where MSI could make small but substantial changes to improve the levels of inclusivity. Eventually leading to the final deliverable (which was not accounted for initially) a meeting with the MSI Senior Management, presenting the full and final results.

As a final consequence, some of the suggestions were immediately implemented, such as books being purchased for the library. As a group of researchers, this experience and final presentation to the full team of curators and interested parties from within the museum demonstrated the difference between academia and the world of the museum. This made it difficult to implement the findings first considered by the group to be the simplest, such as adding images to the existing exhibitions, which required copyright permission, which the authors did not consider.

## FINDINGS

Thoroughly researching the field of inclusiveness in museums, the authors went through 82 papers, books, websites and other publications that were relevant to the subject (Anderson, 2009; Anderson et al., 2007; Arnot, 2007; Aspinall, 2009; Baptist, 2014; etc.), considering other cases of implementation. Even though the researched museum is located in the United Kingdom, which has a different and universal access to museums and culture in general, the cases ranged from studies in the UK, Europe and The United States of America. The combination of the systematic research of the literature and action research produced a list of findings including what was called 'quick wins', ideas the authors considered faster and cost efficient to implement. They were divided into four categories:

## Diversifying the Museum

This section focused on the personnel of the museum.

- **QUICK WIN** - The formation of working groups of existing MSI staff and volunteers to address the issue of underrepresentation, using the presented LGBT Working Group from the Victoria & Albert Museum[5] as a model of best practise for re-analysing and reinterpreting collections and communicating with other staff and the wider public.
- Devise an action plan to ensure that opportunities for volunteers and staff are not limited by economic or social factors. Whilst a programme like the Science and Heritage Career Ladder has great advantages, this obviously requires staffing provision and funding, the sourcing of which, from charitable or governmental sources may or may not be a short-term priority, but as a starting point an action plan. This identified key improvements or changes of focus in recruitment and training policy could be highly effective.
- A consultation project, ideally in collaboration with professional and/or community organisations such as Manchester Disabled People's Access Group, to provide a holistic assessment of MSI's facilities, resources, and exhibitions to ensure that the museum is providing a welcoming, safe, and accessible experience for all visitors with impairments.

## Diversifying Content

These were suggestions targeting the museum's content:

- Devise a collections policy for underrepresented groups, perhaps in tandem with working groups, which considers a number of key proposals:
    - The re-evaluation of existing collections to assess hidden or unacknowledged histories and provenances of items.
    - The collection of objects, images, and oral histories related to science, scientists, and industry from links cultivated with, among others: local community organisations working with underrepresented groups, trade union LGBT, BAME, and disabled members groups, local university alumni associations, and national Science, Technology, Engineering and Maths (STEM) organisations such as WISRNet, the STEM Disability Committee, and the Campaign for Science and Engineering.
    - Ensuring that the archival database and any online resources created are catalogued appropriately and searchable by key themes or keywords reflecting diversity.
    - The launch of a concerted project to re-evaluate existing displays and identify areas where generally white, able-bodied, and heteronormative representations have been chosen, where a more diverse image would be equally as appropriate, including, but not exclusively, the suggestions made above.

## Engaging Communities

This section is unusual as it was intended to generate a longer lasting collaboration between the museum and local communities, which could possibly be misrepresented:

- The commissioning of a project to review the best ways in which to create and nurture long-term and mutually productive relationships with underrepresented communities and local community organisations.
- A market research project to focus on the reasons why non-visitors to museums decide not to visit, with a particular focus on underrepresented demographic and economic groups.
- Development of a permanent programme of events that relates to the inclusion of traditionally marginalised communities, using the working groups as a driver in their conception.

### Engaging With Research and Academia

These suggestions involved strengthening partnerships between MSI and the academic community as the museum concentrates on portraying scientific and industrial accomplishments and notable research developed in the Greater Manchester area.

- **QUICK WIN** - Purchase books suggested above for staff use in the MSI library collection.
- Recruit an advisory panel of key academics, including those named above to ensure that the redevelopment projects on the narrative galleries engage with recent research and represent a diverse array of groups, beginning with the redevelopment of the Textiles Gallery.
- Commission an internal and external consultation project to explore how heritage and academic organisations can foster mutually-beneficial collaboration in the current and future funding and research environment, including, but not limited to the consideration of:
    - Exploring funding avenues to bring more researchers to work with MSI on discrete project work, including those suggested, with REALab, other programmes at the University of Manchester, and more widely.
    - Exploring national and international funding avenues such as research councils and Heritage Lottery Funding as sources for potential projects, perhaps including original academic research, academic conferences, teaching and learning opportunities, and public engagement projects, including using information technology.

## DISCUSSION AND ANALYSIS

The review of relevant museology demonstrates that what is ignored or not included in a collection or exhibition can be of great significance to those who identify as part of underrepresented groups. This inclusion may not always be seen as wholly positive for persons who define themselves as 'other' from the mainstream, and that allowing input and agency on behalf of communities and researchers can bridge the gap between integration and independence. The fact that the museum has identified a lack of representation of women, and BAME, LGBT, and disabled persons as a priority in commissioning the original report strongly suggests that it is a progressive institution, intent on delivering a mission to inspire and educate its public in the history of science and technology. Since 2011 the Museum of Science and Industry has been increasing visitors' visibility within its premises. 'Revolution Manchester' is a 50-screen video wall placed at the main hall where visitors can take pictures of themselves and "become" part of the collection. Strongly committed to its purpose of encouraging younger generations to become members of the STEM (Science, Technology, Engineering and Maths) community, in 2019 the MSI celebrated its 50th anniversary proposing an exhibition using their visitors' experiences as its focal point.

A summary of key themes, recent research, and prominent local and national academics in the history of all four underrepresented groups was compiled as a starting point for curatorial staff in redeveloping the galleries with said inclusiveness in mind. The new, reformulated museum is due to be inaugurated in October 2020. The recommendations and potential projects identified in the report were informed to the curators and together will provide an effective framework to meet the goals of MSI in ensuring that it represents Manchester's radical and global heritage through a dynamic and technological environment. Based on our findings, we drew a conceptual model as part of our practical contribution to illustrate the collaboration process between academic and heritage institutions within a technological and interactive environment (Fig.3).

*Figure 3. Model of academic and heritage institutions within technological/interactive environments*

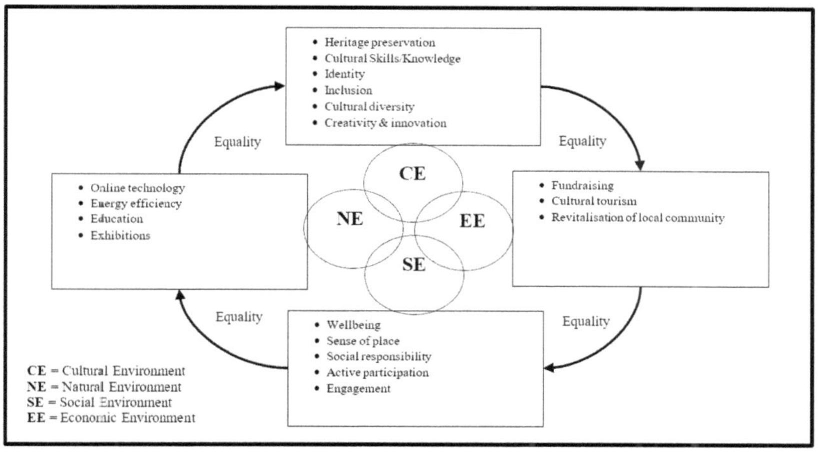


The model reflects four dimensions that must be assessed to promote equality among academic and heritage institutions within technological/interactive environments. These dimensions include cultural, economic, social and natural environments. While cultural environments aim to promote the likes of heritage preservation, inclusion and innovation within academic and heritage institutions, economic environments consider the revitalisation of local communities and cultural tourism. In terms of the social environments, these promote the likes of individual wellbeing, social responsibility, active participation and engagement, all of which are required to promote inclusion of types of individuals within an academic and interactive learning space. Lastly, the natural environment refers to the actual setting such as heritage and academic organisations, as well as the technological infrastructure and educational practice. In sum and as part of our theoretical and practical contribution, these indicators appear to be useful to assess the progress made by a museum in terms of sustainability leading to equilibrium and equality across the four dimensions.

## CONCLUSION

From the beginning of the project in June 2015 to the completion of this chapter approximately five year later, the authors learnt the differences between how research can be undertaken within a consultancy group, but also the difference between academic research and the research being undertaken by cultural institutions such as MSI. Considering the fact that the REALab pilot programme was a success and led to further implementation, there was a need to highlight the benefits of this experience. This research project identified the importance of interdisciplinary work, and the programme was an ideal way to explore how to implement this type of research not just within single faculties, but also throughout the university.

The advantages of MSI as a professional and educational non-profit and their collaboration with the authors as researchers instead of consultants, is the connection offered to the public. The Museum of Science and Industry plans to improve interaction with underrepresented public as well as utilising the skillset of highly qualified academic researchers. This interaction led to the dissemination and extrapolation of the issues surrounding inclusivity in the museum sector. The authors were able to create a personal approach to the problem, acknowledging the difficulties in changing how the museum operates.

Considering the previously explained differences between professional consultants and PhD-led consultancy, the project identified a different set of future projects. This provided grounds for discussion on what was currently practical for the museum to implement immediately, and other projects that could be seen as long-term ideas. Now, the authors are excitingly awaiting for the new projects to be unveiled in order to appreciate the usage of the findings presented here and how will they embrace the diverse Mancunian community. Although this can be seen as a limitation given the lack of industry cases, it does provide an opportunity to exploit a potential knowledge gap through empirical enquiry. Future studies could research the prospects of such projects where stakeholders and project owners provide their views about non-profit museum projects for educational purposes to determine their feasibility and whether they are needed. In addition, future researchers could adopt our proposed model to analyse the previously proposed study to understand the role of sustainability in non-profit museum environments in terms of social, economic, natural and cultural perspectives, which were found to be a significant theoretical finding.

## REFERENCES

Anderson, J. (2009). Voices in the dark: Representations of disability in historical research. *Journal of Contemporary History*, *44*(1), 107–116. doi:10.1177/0022009408098649

Anderson, J., & Carden-Coyne, A. (2007). Introduction: Enabling the past. *European Review of History*, *14*, 447–457. doi:10.1080/13507480701752102

Arnot, C. (2007). Stephen Whittle: Body of Work. *The Guardian*. Retrieved from https://www.theguardian.com/society/2007/apr/17/socialcare.highereducationprofile

Aspinall, P. J. (2009). *Estimating the size and composition of the lesbian, gay, and bisexual population in Britain: Equality and Human Rights Commission Research Report*. Retrieved from https://www.equalityhumanrights.com/sites/default/files/documents/research/research__37__estimatinglgbpop.pdf

Baptist, E. (2014) *The Half Has Never Been Told: Slavery and the Making of American Capitalism*. BBC interview with Darwen residents: https://www.youtube.com/watch?v=Fd-8pXP5eNU

Beckert, S. (2014). Empire of Cotton: A Global History. Academic Press.

Brosnan, M. (2015). *The women war workers of the North-West*. Retrieved from https://www.iwm.org.uk/history/the-women-war-workers-of-the-north-west

Brown, D. C., & Webb, C. R. (2007). *Race in the American South: From Slavery to Civil Rights*. Academic Press.

Campaign for Science and Engineering. (2014). *Improving Diversity in STEM: A report by the Campaign for Science and Engineering (CaSE)*. Retrieved from https://sciencecampaign.org.uk/CaSEDiversityin-STEMreport2014.pdf

Carden-Coyne, A. (2014). The Politics of Wounds: Military Patients and Medical Power in the First World War. Oxford.

Carter, H. (2012). *Alan Turing part of Manchester exhibition charting gay rights*. Retrieved from https://www.theguardian.com/uk/the-northerner/2012/aug/17/manchester-gay-rights-alan-turing

Cech, E. A., & Waidzunas, T. J. (2011). Navigating the heteronormativity of engineering: The experiences of lesbian, gay, and bisexual students. *Engineering Studies*, *3*(1), 1–24. doi:10.1080/19378629.2010.545065

Creswell, J. W. (2013). *Research design: Qualitative, quantitative, and mixed methods approaches*. Sage publications.

Fischer, D. (2001). Value-Added Consulting: Teaching Clients How to Fish. *Curator (New York, N.Y.)*, *44*(1), 83–96. doi:10.1111/j.2151-6952.2001.tb00031.x

Gilmore, A., & Comunian, R. (2016). Beyond the campus: Higher education, cultural policy and the creative economy. *International Journal of Cultural Policy*, *22*(1), 1–9. doi:10.1080/10286632.2015.1101089

Govier, L. (2009). *Leaders in co-creation? Why and how museums could develop their co-creative practice with the public, building on ideas from the performing arts and other non-museum organisations*. Academic Press.

Graham, D. H. (2016). The 'co' in co-production. *Science Museum Group Journal, 5*(Spring). http://journal.sciencemuseum.org.uk/browse/issue-05/the-co-in-co-production/

Hofstede, G. (2010). The GLOBE debate: Back to relevance. *Journal of International Business Studies*, *41*(8), 1339–1346. doi:10.1057/jibs.2010.31

Hooper-Greenhill, E., Sandell, R., Moussouri, T., & O'Riain, H. (2000). *Museums and social inclusion: the GLLAM Report*. Academic Press.

Jongbloed, B., Enders, J., & Salerno, C. (2008). Higher education and its communities: Interconnections, interdependencies and a research agenda. *Higher Education*, *56*(3), 303–324. doi:10.100710734-008-9128-2

Quintieri, R. (2015). *What is REALab?* https://uomrealab.wordpress.com/what-is-realab/

Summers, D. (2009). David Cameron warns of 'new age of austerity'. *The Guardian.*

Tierney, W. G., & Lanford, M. (2016). Conceptualizing innovation in higher education. In *Higher education: Handbook of theory and research* (pp. 1–40). Springer. doi:10.1007/978-3-319-26829-3_1

Tierney, W. G., & Lanford, M. (2018). Institutional culture in higher education. Encyclopedia of international higher education systems and institutions, 1-7.

Will, L. (1997). *Opportunities and constraints for the use of consultants in museum documentation.* CIDOC Jahrestagung.

Wulff, R. L., & Palacios, G. (1991). We/They The care and feeding of museum consultants. *Museum International, 43*(4), 188–190.

Yin, R. K. (2013). *Case study research: Design and methods.* Sage publications.

## ADDITIONAL READING

Caulton, T. (2006). *Hands-On Exhibitions: Managing Interactive Museums and Science Centres.* Taylor & Francis. https://books.google.co.uk/books?id=TTf8hctWb24C

Lamas, D., Loizides, F., Nacke, L., Petrie, H., Winckler, M., & Zaphiris, P. (2019). *Human-Computer Interaction – INTERACT 2019: 17th IFIP TC 13 International Conference, Paphos, Cyprus, September 2–6, 2019, Proceedings, Part IV.* Springer International Publishing. https://books.google.co.uk/books?id=-PGrDwAAQBAJ

Tzanaki, K. (2004). *On-line Virtual Museums: an application of on-line VR Museum for the Parthenon Marbles. Internet: a means of cultural repatriation.* Universal Publishers. https://books.google.co.uk/books?id=MU_qsS8wu90C

## KEY TERMS AND DEFINITIONS

**Creative Education:** Learners' ability to use their imagination and critical thinking to produce new ideas.

**Cultural Heritage Institutions:** An organisation that operates under a culture/subculture to preserve or promote cultural heritage.

**Diversity:** The inclusion of many things.

**Higher Education:** An institution in which University or academic level education is taught.

**Inclusiveness:** The quality of handling a series of subjects or areas.

**Interactive Exhibits:** An exhibit that goes beyond the traditional museum to include interactive content.

**Public Engagement:** The inclusion of specialists who interact, engage, and learn from non-specialists.

## ENDNOTES

1 A British BBC TV series in which budding entrepreneurs get three minutes to pitch their business ideas to five multi-millionaires willing to invest their own cash in exchange for equity. First launched in Japan, Dragon's Den is now an international brand with versions airing in countries across the globe. (More information can be found on https://www.bbc.co.uk/programmes/b006vq92).

2 Some examples of this include the European Confederation of Junior Enterprises (JADE – www.jadenet.org) which was founded in 1995, and provides means for students in the Business School to undertake consultancy projects in order to gain experience in both consulting and the maintenance of a self-sustaining company.

3 At the University of Oxford (https://www.ox.ac.uk/research/innovation-and-partnership/expertise-and-knowledge/find-academic-consultant?wssl=1), the Student Consultancy takes in students from all disciplines and year levels and works specifically with non-profits, charities, public institutions or SMEs in the local area. Projects focus on the areas of marketing, revenue, branding, customer awareness or strategy, and all projects are led by a mentor from the careers service.

4 Part of the MSI brief and can be found on the REALab's website: https://uomrealab.wordpress.com/projects2014-2015/mosi/.

5 The V&A LGBTQ working group forms part of a cross-museum network that can be accessed as a means of organising joint or related events and exhibitions. Their online presence is active with a vibrant blog, and the V&A website now includes a dedicated hub to LGBTQ histories at the museum and a guide to objects in the museum that possess a connection or narrative associated with LGBTQ will soon be available online (the original paper version was produced as part of 2015's "Pride in London Parade"). – quoted from the final report presented to MSI.

# Chapter 15
# Future Teaching and Learning Applications in the Smart Campus:
## A Review on Higher Education Institutions

**Trevor Wood-Harper**
https://orcid.org/0000-0002-2246-3191
*Alliance Manchester Business School, UK*

## ABSTRACT

*As the population of cities rise, environmental concerns become a greater issue owing to the exponential increase in the use of natural resources. This raises further issues regarding the sustainability of environments wherein individuals perform different activities. ICT, for example, plays a key role in the sustainability of resources, which presents an obstacle for large areas of a city and its societal structure. University campuses and cities can easily be compared in terms of size and represent environments that are challenging to replicate in another ecosystem. The idea is conceived by transforming a conventional campus into a smart campus based on a smart city model, where the incorporation of technologies or innovative developments meets individual needs (e.g., teaching and learning) with power over resource use. This chapter explores prospective applications for teaching and learning in a scaled environment or university campus.*

## INTRODUCTION

The population of cities as well as migration from rural areas is growing exponentially. The persistent growth in population demonstrates a number of environmental concerns, mostly in terms of an increase in the consumption of natural resources. (Kumar, 2016). Consumption of resources has indeed been extensively studied, with a lot of emphasis on the sustainability of environments wherein individuals perform different activities. Executing a sustainability study assisted by the use of information and communication technologies (ICTs) is a significant obstacle for large areas of the city, and also for variations

DOI: 10.4018/978-1-7998-4846-2.ch015

in the societal structure. This chapter explores prospective applications for teaching and learning in a scaled environment or university campus. University campuses can be as large as cities and represent environments that are usually difficult to recreate in another ecosystem. The idea is conceived by transforming a conventional campus into a smart campus based on the principles and experiences of smart cities, where the incorporation of technologies or innovative developments meets the needs of people with power over resource use.

Smart cities are partly the result of developments in the ICT sector, where, thanks to the Internet of Things (IoT), numerous devices can connect to the Internet and produce information that enables them to communicate effectively with other members. However, moving from a traditional city to an intelligent city requires a great deal of technical and sociocultural effort, as well as a high level of investment in physical and economic resources. Before considering the smart city environment, the problems to be tackled are wide-ranging and require experts in various fields to work together to optimise resources (Morales Lucas et al., 2018).

The university campus conforms to the previous definition, so having this kind of ecosystem is the ideal starting point for this study. Geographical distribution, administration and the number of people who attend them are ideal environments for the demonstration of smart campus techniques or processes (Vasileva et al., 2018). However, the issue of what the "smart and sustainable campus" is and what it contains remains. Other more concrete questions emerge from this initial question: is ICT capable of solving sustainability problems on a smart campus? Which changes does the smart campus give in terms of sustainability over the conventional campus? Moreover, do traditional campuses meet, at least in part, the requirements of smart and sustainable campuses? Not all of these questions can be answered on the basis of a single experience; therefore, they should be addressed in cooperation with the various fields that make up the administrative and academic part of the university campus and on the basis of the experience of related work. Several of these works do not cover a study such as the one proposed, where the objective of creating a smart campus goes hand in hand with the sustainability of the campus and the environment.

The centralisation and analysis of data on the smart campus are essential for their contribution to the process of recognising events and needs, provided that universities make decisions on the basis of the data they have about students and their administrative structures. However, traditional decision-making needs developing methods of data processing and performance in a shorter timeframe. The problem is that the amount of data far exceeds the processing capacities of the traditional research platforms (Villegas-Ch & Luján-Mora, 2017). Having techniques that detect the needs of the university population and produce results on the basis of trends is the basis of a smart campus. The alternative, therefore, which is currently the trend in data science for its superior results, is the use of big data. These platforms offer alternatives for data management and learning about students that are flexible, cost-effective and shorter in duration. Traditional techniques such as business intelligence (BI) and data mining may perform data analysis. However, due to their nature and the limitations of the data, many of them are omitted or eliminated in the preparation process; it is important to keep most of the data on a smart campus while looking for alternative cleaning techniques so that the efficiency of decision-making is not affected (Chen et al., 2012).

This chapter proposes to view smart campus deployments through emerging innovations such as blockchain that have the potential to foster teaching and learning practices in higher education institutions. Adequate usage of resources in a sustainable setting is made possible by being able to handle the different devices from a previous review of the data collected from the setting (Kim & Lim, 2019). The outcomes of this research make it possible to create supportive spaces where students and teachers have fulfilled their needs in complete harmony with the community.

## SMART CAMPUS DEFINITIONS

First, it must be noted that the word "smart campus" has been used in the past to refer to digital media platforms that handle university content (Atif et al., 2015) a selection of strategies aimed at raising the smartness of university students (Bakken et al., 2016). The definition of smart campus in this chapter refers to the hardware and software needed to provide advanced, intelligent context-conscious facilities and applications to university students and staff. In addition, the term "smart university" refers to the hardware and software used to develop tools to fulfil the key dimensions of the university mission.

- Encourage community-based information sharing and mutual vision among the various stakeholders of the university (e.g., teachers, students, administration, non-profit organizations, research institutions, residents, industries, and governments);
- Improve the process of teaching, learning and evaluating higher education;
- Promote research and innovation.

These characteristics make smart campuses and universities unique and make it possible to differentiate them from other concepts such as smart cities. However, smart campuses or universities are similar to smart cities in the way they are organized, which revolves around six smart areas:

**Intelligent governance**: It allows university staff and students to take part in the various decisions that need to be taken at a university or on a specific campus.

**Intelligent mobility**: In the case of a smart campus, this field deals with various issues related to the available transport systems, which should be efficient, green, safe and capable of providing smart services.

**Smart environment**: This area relates to smart solutions that can monitor, protect and act on the environment while also managing available resources in a sustainable manner. For example, smart environmental systems provide solutions for monitoring waste, water or air quality. In addition, this area is usually related to the deployment of systems to control and monitor the energy consumed, generated and distributed throughout the campus.

**Smart People**: It relates to the involvement of university users in teaching and learning processes or their participation in other events.

**Smart living**: It is responsible for monitoring the multiple living factors involved in daily campus activities, including those related to health, safety or user behaviour. Intelligent living services can therefore perform the following (Pompei et al., 2018):

- Estimate the occupation of the room and determine student attendance in the classroom;
- Monitor access to classroom or laboratory equipment;
- Providing interactive teaching services and context-aware applications.

**Smart economy**: This smart sector deals with the competitiveness of a campus in relation to topics such as entrepreneurship or creativity.

The contiguous outer circle refers to some of the most relevant technologies needed to provide solutions for six smart fields, including IoT, Augmented Reality (AR), Cyber-Physical Systems (CPSs) or UAVs (Unmanned Aerial Vehicles). Note that some of these technologies are the same as those proposed by Industry 4.0 (Fernández-Caramés & Fraga-Lamas, 2018), so commercial and industrial deployments are already available in other fields outside smart campuses (Blanco-Novoa, Fernández-Caramés,

Fraga-Lamas, & Vilar-Montesinos, 2018). In addition, vertical fields such as cyber security also have an impact on several of the technologies cited, as their contribution is key to avoiding potential issues (Fernández-Caramés et al., 2017).

In short, smart areas are typically involved in the day-to-day operations of the university. For example, smart plug-and-play objects may be involved in many university activities, while some environmental sensors are essential for the operation of smart buildings (Blanco-Novoa, Fernández-Caramés, Fraga-Lamas, & Castedo, 2018). There are also other fields, such as smart agriculture, which may be specific to smart campuses that include, in their premises, areas for the cultivation of certain crops that may require the use of autonomous decision-making support systems (Pérez-Expósito et al., 2017). So, we can define smart campuses through looking at each component of the smart terminology as pillars. Table 1 summarises the five pillars of smart campuses:

*Table 1. Smart Definition through the Lens of Traditional vs New Innovations*

| SMART Feature | University Systems | Innovation |
|---|---|---|
| **S**elf-directed: | Specific time table | Just in time technology |
| **M**otivated | Lectures or physical classrooms | Expanding teaching methods through communication collaborative learning and experiential learning |
| **A**daptive | Educational content | Improved customisability that focus on user needs |
| **R**esource Enriched | Traditional text sources | Expanding content through better access to online materials and developing creativity skills |
| **T**echnology Embedded | Physical space | Expanding space at the home, mobile, global and local level |

The five pillars summarised in Table 1 address the improvement of universities. It can be argued that all universities are smart and tend to be smart along various paths of development. For example, a self-directed feature of smart universities says that a traditional university system often follows rigid day-to-day time tables, and smart universities can benefit from flexible time extensions via just-in-time or any-time online opportunities. This raises the question of what are the true capabilities of smart campus technology.

## CAPABILITIES OF SMART CAMPUSES

When students decide where to go to university, the campus experience can go a long way towards winning prospects. Schools have recently faced a steep competition for students, as higher education institutions are struggling to meet their enrolment goals, and overall student experience is a key factor (Mulholland & Turner, 2018). Today's students, growing up in a tech-driven, connected world, expect on-demand experience. Savvy universities and colleges are investing in smart campuses to meet the needs of these digital natives. Smart campus uses networked technologies to facilitate collaboration, make more efficient use of resources, improve security, save money and make campus more connected and enjoyable. With a smart campus, institutions can link systems such as lighting, sensors, appliances, cameras, door locks and more to enable seamless and integrated learning for students, faculty members and administrators (Prandi et al., 2019). This represents the capabilities of smart higher education campuses.

Smart campus technology has the potential to improve student retention, resulting in substantial cost savings. But this is the tip of the iceberg, as smart campuses can deliver a lot more. Several other smart campus capabilities follow (Fernández-Caramés & Fraga-Lamas, 2019; Prandi et al., 2019; Valks et al., 2019; Villegas-Ch et al., 2019):

## Lowers Operational Costs

As business decisions are driven by data, operational costs are reduced. Smart campuses use powerful analytical tools and robust reporting capabilities to combine information on:

- Facility management practices;
- Resource utilisation;
- Student preferences;
- Transportation scheduling;
- Travel patterns.

This comprehensive data allows higher education institutions to recognise and realise previously impossible efficiencies. For example, as universities track student travel habits, they may develop campus transit systems to automate routes and increase services more effectively during peak hours. The more universities know about their students, the more precisely they can design systems that reduce costs while still meeting student needs.

## Improves Energy Efficiency

There are several ways a smart campus can use technology to save on resources. For example, a smart university campus can use networked smart lighting to reduce energy use and conserve energy during less busy times. Motion sensors and data in use patterns allow administrators to identify vital lighting banks that must remain in place and which can be left out if needed. Parking is another area that can be improved with smart campus technology. Using campus Wi-Fi, smart sensors and video cameras, students can find available campus parking spaces without driving around the campus in their vehicle. This reduces traffic, reduces accidents and reduces fuel consumption by students looking for parking all over the campus. In addition, campuses can save on power, electricity and other services with the use of data from smart campus software.

## Provides Better Student and Visitor Experiences

Today's students and campus visitors are more tech-savvy than ever before and, thanks to the Amazon Effect, they demand more personalised experiences. Smart campus supports this customisation with features such as built-in tracking and navigation on their smart devices, helping everyone get around more quickly and easily. AR maps overlay real-time, location-specific data (collected by smart campus sensors) using a smartphone or smart-wearable app.

Campus security also benefits from the technology of the smart campus. Connected surveillance cameras provide campus security information in real time, and smart integrations allow students and visitors to quickly report on location information issues that are instantly available. Networked emergency sensors such as smoke detectors, fire alarms and other necessities are automatically controlled to protect students and provide rapid response. In the event of an emergency, universities can use smart campus technology to send instant alerts and even provide directions to the nearest exit or safe area.

Administrators can also use WRLD 3D heat map visualisations to render dense datasets in an intuitive view that make information easier to digest and understand. One potential application includes the use of parking and pedestrian data to model traffic dynamics in 3D, directly overlaid on the virtual campus. You could also map the usage data to visualise which campus areas are most and least used, and then adjust the resources accordingly.

Smart campus technology also improves campus life in many ways. Student collaboration is made simpler and more frequent through integrated communication services that help people to connect in meaningful and useful ways. Payments at campus cafeterias, restaurants and book stores are made easier through near-field technologies and smart cards that automatically deduct funds from student accounts. Students may also use real-time occupancy systems to see the research rooms or advanced facilities are available for use (without walking all the way around the campus to find out).

### Develop Smart Campus Capabilities

Smart campuses are becoming more prevalent, and as technology develops, integrations will become more powerful and more beneficial to students and faculties alike. 3D maps have the power to bring together all smart campus technologies into a single, fully navigable platform that reduces operational costs, increases resource efficiency, improves student and visitor experience, and much more.

These capabilities lead to the potential application of other technologies to facilitate higher education. As an example, this chapter explores blockchain, as it is a technology that is starting to gain traction in higher education, particularly in the deployment of technology on the smart campus.

## POTENTIALS OF BLOCKCHAIN IN SMART CAMPUSES

In 2008, the architecture of the cryptocurrency blockchain application was conceptualised by a person or group of people using the pseudonym, Satoshi Nakamoto, in an online manuscript titled 'Bitcoin: A Peer-to-Peer Electronic Cash System' (Nakamoto, 2008). A year later, the operating rules drafted in this chapter were later used to implement the Bitcoin virtual currency transaction system. The central concept of blockchain is based on a database known as a distributed ledger, the content of which must first be decided upon by network users for inclusion or alteration. Once the information item (or its modified version) has met the consensus standard, the information will be grouped into a block that will be appended to the previous block sequence. The concept of blockchain makes the participation of a trusted third party irrelevant, without losing the trust of the transaction itself. Cryptographic encoding of data in blocks ensures that data is safe from unintentional and malicious tampering, thereby creating trust between network users.

At its core, blockchain technology brings with it an important value of business trust, which at the same time disrupts the accepted practice and necessity of trusted third parties or intermediaries in contractual relationships. The concept of trust in business transactions is well known and critical and has long been recognised by economists (Arrow, 1972 in Phelps, 1975) that almost every commercial transaction has an element of trust within itself. This raises the question: to what extent is blockchain capable of disrupting business activities (such as contracting, data sharing, citizen-identity recording, asset retention, registration of intellectual property, learning, and other notary attestations)? Some authors, such as Lakhani and Iansiti (2017), have considered the "truth about blockchain" technology in terms of hype vs long-term reliability (Pisa & Juden, 2017). Contracts, transactions and documents are among the fundamental mechanisms of our economic, legal and political systems. They protect assets and set organisational boundaries. They establish and verify identities and chronic events, yet these critical tools and bureaucracies formed to manage them have not kept up with the digital transformation of the economy. Blockchain is promising to solve this problem.

Universities as economic people are equally exposed to the risk of data protection and to the lack of internal control mechanisms that are supposed to help. This makes the loss of data records at universities a major concern. In view of other established cost inefficiencies and operational constraints, this in part implies that blockchain has a potential solution (or in part) to these problems, or substantially enhances them (Broggi et al., 2018).

The development and evolution of blockchain technology appears to be driven by its potential ability to deal with issues involving dual spending, consensus, immutability, confidence in transactions, identification, general data protection. Such blockchain applications will vary depending on the design-characteristics, including the content of what is stored in the ledger, the process used to reach a consensus, and the degree to which the ledger is allowed (Pisa & Juden, 2017). Related feasibility studies are therefore named for careful implementations of blockchain by businesses and academia.

Block Application Opportunities for Universities: Table 1 refers to the discussion that follows. The benefits of blockchain implementation for universities are plausible at different levels, including universal applications and academic-specific use. The payment of blockchain applications by universities is likely to be made on an ongoing basis over time with varying positive spill over benefits as outlined in Table 2, which is drawn from Nakamoto (2008), Swan (2015), Pisa and Juden (2017) and Broggi (2018).

In addition, there are real world blockchain usage cases for universities. Universities would benefit from business cooperation as well as from funded graduate training. The University's targeted blockchain exposures include, among others, the Ripple University Blockchain Research Initiative (UBRI), Oxford Blockchain University (Woolf Development) and the Open University's Knowledge Media Institute.

The introduction of blockchain technology is not without obstacles. New technologies are known to face implementation and adaptation challenges. So, blockchain is not going to be different. Analysts (Pinna & Ruttenberg, 2016; Pisa & Juden, 2017) agree that governance issues may have different degrees of impact on each blockchain implementation. Possible implementation issues include: compliance rules for multi-distributed ledgers; conflict resolution between users; delegation of authority for blockchain software changes; access authorisation authority for network users; and monitoring and evaluation of system performance. The obstacles to the large-scale adoption of blockchain technology refer to possibility of non-harmonisation in the global regulatory environment, and the lack of Blockchain Technology and Smart University standards. Other general limitations of blockchain include privacy, initial cost and cultural change issues, as well as system integration processes. However, the implementation of the blockchain in academia is intended to benefit the higher education landscape. The next section delve deeper into smart campus deployment with potential blockchain integration.

*Table 2. Blockchain Applications for Universities*

| Application | Benefit |
|---|---|
| **Blockchain Possibilities for Universities Universal Usage** | |
| Advantages of Data Security through Decentralisation | Decentralised data ledgers eliminate the risk of one stop data failure (malicious or system malfunction) |
| Decentralised Notary | To collect the time-stamped paper attestation. Document not stored but is stored in hash format |
| Digital Identity | Relevant identification details: passports, national identity card, online account registration, birth certificate, proof of residency |
| Disintermediation | Removes the need of a trustworthy middle party with its associated costs, risks and time inefficiencies |
| Preservation of Intellectual Property | Removes the need for intermediaries to manage and conserve personal works of art and innovation |
| Process Integrity and Immutability | Transparency should reduce the risk of dishonesty and tampering |
| Serve as Registry | Provides a time stamped systematic record of assets |
| Smart Contracts | Automatically store and activate transaction contracts when they are due |
| **Blockchain Possibilities for Universities Academic Specific Usage** | |
| Digital Academic Certificate | Provides instant and self-assessment of academic credentials even though the university no longer exists |
| Journal coin | The intuition of bitcoin wallets used as newspaper coins can be used to stimulate and gain academic brown points for newspaper editors, reviewers, and review moderators |
| Learn coin | Institutions or individual students can publish their funding needs and receive coins from spontaneous learning donors, even pseudonymously |
| Learning contract exchanges | Suitable for Continuing Professional Education (CPE) and could benefit institutions offering services to government workers and the private sector |
| Massive Open Online Courses (MOOCs) | Cryptocurrency and blockchain can be used to enable the recording and payment of MOOCs |
| Smart Learning Contract: financial Sponsor to Student (S2S) peers | Smart contracts will be triggered by academic performance or built-in rules for releasing bitcoins, or learning coins, or local fiat from sponsor to student (S2S) |

## SMART CAMPUS DEPLOYMENTS

### Deployment Cases

There are just a few studies in the literature that provide explanations of the actual smart campuses. An example of such a smart campus is the IoT and cloud computing architecture based on the Wuhan University of Technology Smart Campus (China) designed to support a variety of applications (Guo & Zhang, 2015). IoT is also the key to the West Texas A&M University smart campus, which is set up on 176 acres of land that includes 42 different buildings. Such a smart campus focuses on delivering IoT-related and safe infrastructure and has tested systems for smart parking or environmental monitoring (Webb & Hume, 2018). Another notable example of a smart campus is Birmingham City University, located in the United Kingdom. The aim of the proposed smart campus is essentially to create a scalable and flexible service-oriented architecture (SOA) where service integration and orchestration can be easily carried out by using the Enterprise Service Bus (ESB) (Hipwell, 2014).

*Table 3. Summary of Several Key Smart Campus Deployments*

| University | Smart Campus | Country | Size | Application | Blockchain Support |
|---|---|---|---|---|---|
| Birmingham City University **Hipwell (2014)** | Yes | Birmingham, United Kingdom | Two campuses: roughly 18,000 and 24,000m$^2$ respectively | Microsoft's BizTalk Server as ESB | No |
| Wuhan University of Technology **Guo and Zhang (2015)** | Yes | Wuhan, China | Unknown | Smart learning and living | No |
| West Texas A&M University **Webb and Hume (2018)** | Yes | Texas, USA | .71km$^2$ with 42 buildings and a 9.68km$^2$ ranch | Environmental monitoring; water irrigation; and smart parking | No |
| Universidad Politécnica de Madrid **Alvarez-Campana et al. (2017)** | Yes | Madrid, Spain | 5.5km$^2$ with 144 buildings | Smart emergency management and traffic restriction | No |

Table 3 summarises the main characteristics of the most relevant smart campus deployments, together with their location, size, hardware and blockchain-enabled applications. Interestingly, none of the deployment cases showed any support for blockchain, which may indicate that the technology is still in its infancy in the higher education domain. Further exploration into this phenomenon is thus needed.

## Smart Applications

Both indoor and outdoor applications can be deployed on a smart campus or university site. (Muhamad et al., 2017), but such smart applications differ in their requirements. The most significant difference is that IoT can make use of fixed communication infrastructure (e.g. WiFi access points) in indoor environments. On the other hand, outdoors, IoT also relies on batteries and needs to exchange data at relatively long distances (at least several hundred meters, up to 2 km). Below are some of the most applicable frameworks for both scenarios:

**Applications for teaching and learning**: Technologies embedded in a smart campus or university can also help students learn through their mobile phones (Wang & Ng, 2012) or have a ubiquitous user-centered personalised learning and advanced analytics training experience. (Aldowah et al., 2017; Demirer et al., 2017; Maksimović, 2018). These technologies also enable teachers to make use of specific learning services (e.g. online programming contests), sophisticated online teaching platforms, and to implement new teaching paradigms such as Flipped Classroom or amplification (Xu et al., 2019).

**Activities in research and innovation**: Smart campus or university technology can be used to foster collaboration and cooperation between people (e.g., international networks of living laboratories). For example, crowdsourcing can be used to gather data from people with various backgrounds (e.g. students, teachers, researchers and administrative staff) and to create large-scale databases for more analysis and new applications (Adamkó et al., 2014).

**Applications for Community-based knowledge transfer**: Smart campus and university technologies can be explored for the benefit of the global community, either by increasing awareness of sustainability issues or by actively involving citizens as key players in smart environments (Prandi et al., 2019).

## FUTURE CHALLENGES

Despite the evolution of smart campuses and universities in recent years due to technological advances in fields such as IoT, cloud computing and certain communication paradigms, future university planners, IoT vendors and developers will still face significant challenges in the following areas (Ali, 2019a, 2019b; Ali, 2020).

**Scalability**: because a campus can cover a wide area where a large number of users can request smart services, it is important for applications to be easily scalable in order to adapt their output to the number of simultaneous users.

**Service Flexibility**: A smart campus or university should be able to offer various services, which may differ based on the physical environment in which they are delivered (e.g., based on the faculty), on the particular person who needs them (e.g., access rights that differ between student and professor) or on the particular purpose (e.g. moving towards more efficient teaching and learning facilities).

**Long-distance low-power communications**: since campuses usually cover areas of thousands of square meters that often involve monitoring outdoor smart IoT objects (e.g. street lights, irrigation systems), it is important to consider the use of long-distance wireless communication technologies in the smart campus architecture, the energy consumption of which should be as low as possible to maximise IoT node batch.

**New Communication Technologies**: While this chapter focuses on the most important communications technologies currently in use, smart campus designers should be aware of the latest communications innovations in order to incorporate them in the architecture they have developed. For example, some authors are already suggesting possible applications for 6G technologies (Letaief et al., 2019; Rappaport et al., 2019).

**Blockchain integration**: DLTs like blockchain can be very useful to ensure operational efficiency, data transparency, authenticity and security. This aspect is the key to developing new decentralised smart applications (i.e. DApps) and to leveraging new artificial intelligence paradigms such as big data, machine learning, or deep learning. These paradigms need to rely on reliable datasets to achieve their full potential and to generate new data model-based applications. Nonetheless, smart campus designers need to use blockchain with care, taking into account their advantages and disadvantages. Furthermore, the incorrect use of smart contracts can be problematic, since they are capable of triggering certain automatic behaviours that may have serious economic or personal consequences.

**Lack of smart campus standards and public initiatives**: although smart city initiatives have proliferated worldwide in recent years, there are only a few specifically related to smart campuses and universities. In addition, there is no common framework for designing or deploying them, so future developers will need to keep compatibility and interoperability in mind.

**Seamless integration of outdoor and indoor smart campus applications**: due to their communication needs, outdoor and indoor applications may differ in the underlying technologies, making it necessary to design architectures and devices that allow switching between communication transceivers. It ensures that, while the lower layers of the communication protocol that vary, the upper layers are compatible so that they can provide smooth communication between users, IoT artefacts and computer devices distributed across the campus.

## CONCLUSION

This chapter looked at smart campus deployments through emerging innovations such as blockchain that have the potential to foster teaching and learning practices in higher education institutions and how they can leverage the opportunities created by the latest and most relevant IT technologies. Since reviewing the fundamentals of smart campuses and universities, this work centered on exploring the potential of IoT and blockchain for the development of new smart campuses and smart university applications. Furthermore, the new primary implementations as well as their communications technologies have been documented and evaluated. It was found that blockchain has the potential to be integrated into the smart campus via applications for teaching and learning, promote activities in research and innovation and provide applications for community-based knowledge transfer. In spite of these potentials, blockchain integration does hold some potential future challenges, such as scalability and service flexibility problems, long-distance low-power communications, requirement of novel communication technologies, integration issues, lack of smart campus standards and public initiatives and issues with seamless integration of outdoor and indoor smart campus applications. Finally, these key future challenges are identified in order to allow future university planners, IoT vendors and developers to develop a roadmap for the design and deployment of the next generation of smart campuses and universities, and thus future studies could pursue this as a potential research endeavour.

### Recommendations

1. Universities should be aware of future social and cultural demands.
2. University IT practitioners should consider all types of stakeholders when deciding a new IT project.

## REFERENCES

Adamkó, A., Kãdek, T., & Kósa, M. (2014). Intelligent and adaptive services for a smart campus. *2014 5th IEEE Conference on Cognitive Infocommunications (CogInfoCom).*

Aldowah, H., Rehman, S. U., Ghazal, S., & Umar, I. N. (2017). Internet of Things in higher education: A study on future learning. *Journal of Physics: Conference Series.*

Ali, M. (2019a). The Barriers and Enablers of the Educational Cloud: A Doctoral Student Perspective. *Open Journal of Business and Management*, *7*(1), 24. doi:10.4236/ojbm.2019.71001

Ali, M. (2019b). Cloud Computing at a Cross Road: Quality and Risks in Higher Education. *Advances in Internet of Things*, *9*(3), 33–49. doi:10.4236/ait.2019.93003

Ali, M. (2020). Multi-Perspectives of Cloud Computing Service Adoption Quality and Risks in Higher Education. In D. B. A. Mehdi Khosrow-Pour (Ed.), Handbook of Research on Modern Educational Technologies, Applications, and Management (2nd ed.). IGI Global.

Alvarez-Campana, M., López, G., Vázquez, E., Villagrá, V. A., & Berrocal, J. (2017). Smart CEI moncloa: An iot-based platform for people flow and environmental monitoring on a Smart University Campus. *Sensors (Basel)*, *17*(12), 2856. doi:10.339017122856 PMID:29292790

Atif, Y., Mathew, S. S., & Lakas, A. (2015). Building a smart campus to support ubiquitous learning. *Journal of Ambient Intelligence and Humanized Computing*, *6*(2), 223–238. doi:10.100712652-014-0226-y

Bakken, J. P., Uskov, V. L., Penumatsa, A., & Doddapaneni, A. (2016). Smart universities, smart classrooms and students with disabilities. In *Smart Education and e-Learning 2016* (pp. 15–27). Springer. doi:10.1007/978-3-319-39690-3_2

Blanco-Novoa, O., Fernández-Caramés, T. M., Fraga-Lamas, P., & Castedo, L. (2018). A cost-effective IoT system for monitoring Indoor radon gas concentration. *Sensors (Basel)*, *18*(7), 2198. doi:10.339018072198 PMID:29986540

Blanco-Novoa, O., Fernández-Caramés, T. M., Fraga-Lamas, P., & Vilar-Montesinos, M. A. (2018). A practical evaluation of commercial industrial augmented reality systems in an industry 4.0 shipyard. *IEEE Access: Practical Innovations, Open Solutions*, *6*, 8201–8218. doi:10.1109/ACCESS.2018.2802699

Broggi, J., Gallagher, M., Lilly, J., Duquette, J., Nimura, C., Pattenden, M., Richter, F., Arbide, L., Avin, S., & Kelley, K. (2018). *Woolf-Building the first Blockchain University*. White Paper.

Chen, H., Chiang, R. H., & Storey, V. C. (2012). Business intelligence and analytics: From big data to big impact. *Management Information Systems Quarterly*, *36*(4), 1165–1188. doi:10.2307/41703503

Demirer, V., Aydın, B., & Çelik, Ş. B. (2017). Exploring the educational potential of Internet of Things (IoT) in seamless learning. In The Internet of Things: Breakthroughs in Research and Practice (pp. 1-15). IGI Global.

Fernández-Caramés, T. M., & Fraga-Lamas, P. (2018). A review on human-centered IoT-connected smart labels for the industry 4.0. *IEEE Access: Practical Innovations, Open Solutions*, *6*, 25939–25957. doi:10.1109/ACCESS.2018.2833501

Fernández-Caramés, T. M., & Fraga-Lamas, P. (2019). Towards Next Generation Teaching, Learning, and Context-Aware Applications for Higher Education: A Review on Blockchain, IoT, Fog and Edge Computing Enabled Smart Campuses and Universities. *Applied Sciences*, *9*(21), 4479. doi:10.3390/app9214479

Fernández-Caramés, T. M., Fraga-Lamas, P., Suárez-Albela, M., Castedo, L., Crepaldi, P., & Pimenta, T. (2017). A methodology for evaluating security in commercial RFID systems. In *Radio Frequency Identification*. InTech. doi:10.5772/64844

Guo, M., & Zhang, Y. (2015). *The research of smart campus based on Internet of Things & cloud computing*. Academic Press.

Hipwell, S. (2014). Developing smart campuses—A working model. *2014 International Conference on Intelligent Green Building and Smart Grid (IGBSG)*.

Kim, T., & Lim, J. (2019). Designing an Efficient Cloud Management Architecture for Sustainable Online Lifelong Education. *Sustainability*, *11*(6), 1523.

Kumar, T. M. V. (2016). *Smart Economy in Smart Cities: International Collaborative Research: Ottawa, St.Louis, Stuttgart, Bologna, Cape Town, Nairobi, Dakar, Lagos, New Delhi, Varanasi, Vijayawada, Kozhikode, Hong Kong*. Springer Singapore. https://books.google.co.uk/books?id=fhDpDAAAQBAJ

Lakhani, K. R., & Iansiti, M. (2017). The truth about blockchain. *Harvard Business Review*, *95*, 118–127.

Letaief, K. B., Chen, W., Shi, Y., Zhang, J., & Zhang, Y.-J. A. (2019). The roadmap to 6G: AI empowered wireless networks. *IEEE Communications Magazine*, *57*(8), 84–90. doi:10.1109/MCOM.2019.1900271

Maksimović, M. (2018). IOT concept application in educational sector using collaboration. *Facta Universitatis, Series: Teaching. Learning and Teacher Education*, *1*(2), 137–150.

Morales Lucas, C., de Mingo López, L. F., & Gómez Blas, N. (2018). Natural computing applied to the underground system: A synergistic approach for smart cities. *Sensors (Basel)*, *18*(12), 4094. doi:10.339018124094 PMID:30467278

Muhamad, W., Kurniawan, N. B., & Yazid, S. (2017). Smart campus features, technologies, and applications: A systematic literature review. *2017 International Conference on Information Technology Systems and Innovation (ICITSI).*

Mulholland, G., & Turner, J. (2018). *Enterprising Education in UK Higher Education: Challenges for Theory and Practice.* Taylor & Francis. https://books.google.co.uk/books?id=bsuNDwAAQBAJ

Pérez-Expósito, J. P., Fernández-Caramés, T. M., Fraga-Lamas, P., & Castedo, L. (2017). VineSens: An eco-smart decision-support viticulture system. *Sensors (Basel)*, *17*(3), 465. doi:10.339017030465 PMID:28245619

Phelps, E. S. (1975). *Altruism, Morality, and Economic Theory*. Russell Sage Foundation. https://books.google.co.uk/books?id=fIS4BgAAQBAJ

Pinna, A., & Ruttenberg, W. (2016). *Distributed ledger technologies in securities post-trading revolution or evolution?* ECB Occasional Paper 172.

Pisa, M., & Juden, M. (2017). Blockchain and economic development: Hype vs. reality. *Center for Global Development Policy Paper*, *107*, 150.

Pompei, L., Mattoni, B., Bisegna, F., Nardecchia, F., Fichera, A., Gagliano, A., & Pagano, A. (2018). Composite Indicators for Smart Campus: Data Analysis Method. *2018 IEEE International Conference on Environment and Electrical Engineering and 2018 IEEE Industrial and Commercial Power Systems Europe (EEEIC/I&CPS Europe).*

Prandi, C., Monti, L., Ceccarini, C., & Salomoni, P. (2019). Smart campus: Fostering the community awareness through an intelligent environment. *Mobile Networks and Applications*, •••, 1–8.

Rappaport, T. S., Xing, Y., Kanhere, O., Ju, S., Madanayake, A., Mandal, S., Alkhateeb, A., & Trichopoulos, G. C. (2019). Wireless communications and applications above 100 GHz: Opportunities and challenges for 6G and beyond. *IEEE Access: Practical Innovations, Open Solutions*, *7*, 78729–78757. doi:10.1109/ACCESS.2019.2921522

Swan, M. (2015). *Blockchain: Blueprint for a New Economy*. O'Reilly Media. https://books.google.co.uk/books?id=4vFiBgAAQBAJ

Valks, B., Arkesteijn, M., & Den Heijer, A. (2019). *Smart campus tools 2.0 exploring the use of real-time space use measurement at universities and organizations*. Facilities. doi:10.1108/F-11-2018-0136

Vasileva, R., Rodrigues, L., Hughes, N., Greenhalgh, C., Goulden, M., & Tennison, J. (2018). What Smart Campuses Can Teach Us about Smart Cities: User Experiences and Open Data. *Information*, *9*(10), 251. doi:10.3390/info9100251

Villegas-Ch, W., & Luján-Mora, S. (2017). Analysis of data mining techniques applied to LMS for personalized education. *2017 IEEE World Engineering Education Conference (EDUNINE).*

Villegas-Ch, W., Molina-Enriquez, J., Chicaiza-Tamayo, C., Ortiz-Garcés, I., & Luján-Mora, S. (2019). Application of a Big Data Framework for Data Monitoring on a Smart Campus. *Sustainability*, *11*(20), 5552. doi:10.3390/su11205552

Wang, M., & Ng, J. W. (2012). Intelligent mobile cloud education: smart anytime-anywhere learning for the next generation campus environment. *2012 Eighth International Conference on Intelligent Environments.*

Webb, J., & Hume, D. (2018). *Campus IoT collaboration and governance using the NIST cybersecurity framework*. Academic Press.

Xu, X., Li, D., Sun, M., Yang, S., Yu, S., Manogaran, G., Mastorakis, G., & Mavromoustakis, C. X. (2019). Research on key technologies of smart campus teaching platform based on 5G network. *IEEE Access: Practical Innovations, Open Solutions*, *7*, 20664–20675. doi:10.1109/ACCESS.2019.2894129

## ADDITIONAL READING

Fortes, S., Santoyo-Ramón, J. A., Palacios, D., Baena, E., Mora-García, R., Medina, M., Mora, P., & Barco, R. (2019). The Campus as a Smart City: University of Málaga Environmental, Learning, and Research Approaches. *Sensors (Basel)*, *19*(6), 1349. doi:10.339019061349 PMID:30889886

Yan, H., & Hu, H. (2016). A Study on Association Algorithm of Smart Campus Mining Platform Based on Big Data. *2016 International Conference on Intelligent Transportation, Big Data & Smart City (IC-ITBS)* 10.1109/ICITBS.2016.11

## KEY TERMS AND DEFINITIONS

**E-Learning:** Learning via online applications or systems.

**Higher Education:** University level education in which undergraduate, postgraduate, and doctoral courses are taught.

**ICT:** Information communication technologies are systems that promote the use of information sharing and collaboration via a range of software tools.

**Learning Applications:** Software tools that promote teaching and learning.

**Smart Campus:** Similar to smart cities, they are settings in which applications can create new teaching and learning experiences that lead to improved educational outcomes.

**Smart Cities:** Settings in which devices and applications generate new experiences or services that lead to effective and efficient outcomes.

# Compilation of References


Abbitt, J. (2007). Exploring the educational possibilities for a user-driven social content system in an undergraduate course. *Journal of Online Learning and Teaching*, *3*(4), 437–447.

Aberystwyth University. (2019). *Exemplary Course Award*. Retrieved 24th June from https://www.aber.ac.uk/en/is/it-services/elearning/blackboard/blackboard-exemplary-course-award/

Abubakar, A. M., Elrehail, H., Alatailat, M. A., & Elçi, A. (2019). Knowledge management, decision-making style and organizational performance. *Journal of Innovation & Knowledge*, *4*(2), 104–114. doi:10.1016/j.jik.2017.07.003

Acikkar, M., & Akay, M. F. (2009). Support vector machines for predicting the admission decision of a candidate to the School of Physical Education and Sports at Cukurova University. *Expert Systems with Applications*, *36*(3), 7228–7233. doi:10.1016/j.eswa.2008.09.007

Adamkó, A., Kădek, T., & Kósa, M. (2014). Intelligent and adaptive services for a smart campus. *2014 5th IEEE Conference on Cognitive Infocommunications (CogInfoCom).*

Adamson, D., Dyke, G., Jang, H., & Rosé, C. P. (2014). Towards an agile approach to adapting dynamic collaboration support to student needs. *International Journal of Artificial Intelligence in Education*, *24*(1), 92–124. doi:10.100740593-013-0012-6

Adi, A., & Scotte, C. G. (2016). Barriers to emerging technology and social media integration in higher education: Three case studies. In Professional Development and Workplace Learning: Concepts, Methodologies, Tools, and Applications (pp. 1161-1182). IGI Global.

Agbatogun, A. (2013). Interactive digital technologies' use in Southwest Nigerian universities. *Educational Technology Research and Development*, *61*(2), 333–357. Advance online publication. doi:10.100711423-012-9282-1

Ahalt, S., & Fecho, K. (2015). Ten emerging technologies for higher education. *RENCI White Paper Series, 3*(1), 1-18.

Akande, A. O., & Van Belle, J.-P. (2014). Cloud computing in higher education: A snapshot of software as a service. In *2014 IEEE 6th International Conference on Adaptive Science & Technology (ICAST)*. IEEE. 10.1109/ICASTECH.2014.7068111

Al-Asmari, A. (2005). *The use of internet among EFL teachers at the colleges of technology in Saudi Arabia* (Dissertation). Ohio University.

Aldowah, H., Rehman, S. U., Ghazal, S., & Umar, I. N. (2017). Internet of Things in higher education: A study on future learning. *Journal of Physics: Conference Series*.

Al-Draiby, O. (2010). *E-learning and Its Effectiveness in Saudi Arabia. Faculty of Computer and Information Technology*. KAU.

Alemán, A., & Renn, K. (2002). Women in Higher Education: An Encyclopedia. ABC-CLIO.

Al-Emran, M., & Malik, S. I. (2016). The impact of google apps at work: Higher educational perspective. *International Journal of Interactive Mobile Technologies*, *10*(4), 85–88. doi:10.3991/ijim.v10i4.6181

Alfarsi, G. M. S., Omar, K. A. M., & Alsinani, M. J. (2017). A rule-based system for advising undergraduate students. *Journal of Theoretical & Applied Information Technology*, *95*(11).

Ali, M. (2020). Multi-Perspectives of Cloud Computing Service Adoption Quality and Risks in Higher Education. In D. B. A. Mehdi Khosrow-Pour (Ed.), Handbook of Research on Modern Educational Technologies, Applications, and Management (2nd ed.). IGI Global.

Ali, M. B., Wood-Harper, T., & Ramlogan, R. (2020). A Framework Strategy to Overcome Trust Issues on Cloud Computing Adoption in Higher Education. In Modern Principles, Practices, and Algorithms for Cloud Security (pp. 162-183). IGI Global. doi:10.4018/978-1-7998-1082-7.ch008

Ali, M. (2018). The Barriers and Enablers of the Educational Cloud: A Doctoral Student Perspective. *Open Journal of Business and Management*, *7*(1), 1–24. doi:10.4236/ojbm.2019.71001

Ali, M. (2019). Cloud Computing at a Cross Road: Quality and Risks in Higher Education. *Advances in Internet of Things*, *9*(3), 33–49. doi:10.4236/ait.2019.93003

Ali, M. B. (2019). Multiple Perspective of Cloud Computing Adoption Determinants in Higher Education a Systematic Review. *International Journal of Cloud Applications and Computing*, *9*(3), 89–109. doi:10.4018/IJCAC.2019070106

Ali, M., Wood-Harper, T., & Al-Gahtani, A. S. (2019). Contextual Analysis of Educational Monitoring and Progression as a Service (EMPaaS) System in Higher Education. *Open Journal of Business and Management*, *7*(3), 1525–1542. doi:10.4236/ojbm.2019.73105

Al-Kahtani, S. A. (2001). *Computer-assisted language learning in EFL, instruction at selected Saudi Arabian Universities* (PhD Dissertation). Indian University of Pennsylvania.

Alkhalaf, S., Drew, S., AlGhamdi, R., & Alfarraj, O. (2012). E-Learning system on higher education institutions in KSA: Attitudes and perceptions of faculty members. *Procedia: Social and Behavioral Sciences*, *47*, 1199–1205. doi:10.1016/j.sbspro.2012.06.800

Al-Khalifa, H. S. (2009). *E-Learning and ICT integration in colleges and universities in Saudi Arabia*. E-learn Magazine.

Allen, I. E., & Seaman, J. (2017). *Digital Compass Learning: Distance Education Enrollment Report 2017. Babson Survey Research Group.*

Allen, I. E., & Seaman, J. (2017). *Digital Compass Learning: Distance Education Enrolment Report 2017. Babson Survey Research Group*. ERIC.

Al-Nuaim, H. A. (2019). The use of virtual classrooms in E-learning: A case study in King Abdul-Aziz University, Saudi Arabia. *E-Learning and Digital Media*, *9*(2), 211–222. doi:10.2304/elea.2012.9.2.211

Alokluk, J. A. (2018). The Effectiveness of Blackboard System, Uses and Limitations in Information Management. *Intelligent Information Management*, *10*(06), 133–149. doi:10.4236/iim.2018.106012

Altbach, P. G., Reisberg, L., & Rumbley, L. E. (2019). *Trends in global higher education: Tracking an academic revolution*. Brill.

Alton, L. (2018). *By the Numbers: A Deep Dive into Technology and Education*. Connected IT Blog. https://community.connection.com/numbers-deep-dive-technology-education/

Alvarez-Campana, M., López, G., Vázquez, E., Villagrá, V. A., & Berrocal, J. (2017). Smart CEI moncloa: An iot-based platform for people flow and environmental monitoring on a Smart University Campus. *Sensors (Basel), 17*(12), 2856. doi:10.339017122856 PMID:29292790

Anagnostopoulos, D., Rutledge, S. A., & Jacobsen, R. (2013). Mapping the information infrastructure of accountability. *The Infrastructure of Accountability: Data Use and the Transformation of American Education*, 1–20.

Anderson, J. (2009). Voices in the dark: Representations of disability in historical research. *Journal of Contemporary History, 44*(1), 107–116. doi:10.1177/0022009408098649

Anderson, J., & Carden-Coyne, A. (2007). Introduction: Enabling the past. *European Review of History, 14*, 447–457. doi:10.1080/13507480701752102

Andrejevic, M., & Selwyn, N. (2019). Facial recognition technology in schools: Critical questions and concerns. *Learning, Media and Technology*, 1–14. doi:10.1080/17439884.2020.1686014

Andris, C., Cowen, D., & Wittenbach, J. (2013). Support vector machine for spatial variation. *Transactions in GIS, 17*(1), 41–61. doi:10.1111/j.1467-9671.2012.01354.x

Ansari, M. S., & Tripathi, A. (2017). An investigation of effectiveness of mobile learning apps in higher education in India. *International Journal of Information Studies and Libraries.*

Antonopoulos, N., & Gillam, L. (2010). *Cloud computing*. Springer. doi:10.1007/978-1-84996-241-4

Aparicio, F., Morales-Botello, M. L., Rubio, M., Hernando, A., Muñoz, R., López-Fernández, H., Glez-Peña, D., Fdez-Riverola, F., de la Villa, M., Maña, M., Gachet, D., & Buenaga, M. (2018). Perceptions of the use of intelligent information access systems in university level active learning activities among teachers of biomedical subjects. *International Journal of Medical Informatics, 112*, 21–33. doi:10.1016/j.ijmedinf.2017.12.016 PMID:29500018

Aparicio, M., Oliveira, T., Bacao, F., & Painho, M. (2019). Gamification: A key determinant of massive open online course (MOOC) success. *Information & Management, 56*(1), 39–54. doi:10.1016/j.im.2018.06.003

Armbrust, M., Fox, A., Griffith, R., Joseph, A. D., Katz, R., Konwinski, A., Lee, G., Patterson, D., Rabkin, A., Stoica, I., & Zaharia, M. (2010). A view of cloud computing. *Communications of the ACM, 53*(4), 50–58. doi:10.1145/1721654.1721672

Arnot, C. (2007). Stephen Whittle: Body of Work. *The Guardian*. Retrieved from https://www.theguardian.com/society/2007/apr/17/socialcare.highereducationprofile

Aspinall, P. J. (2009). *Estimating the size and composition of the lesbian, gay, and bisexual population in Britain: Equality and Human Rights Commission Research Report*. Retrieved from https://www.equalityhumanrights.com/sites/default/files/documents/research/research__37__estimatinglgbpop.pdf

Atif, Y., Mathew, S. S., & Lakas, A. (2015). Building a smart campus to support ubiquitous learning. *Journal of Ambient Intelligence and Humanized Computing, 6*(2), 223–238. doi:10.100712652-014-0226-y

Azmi, S., Iahad, N. A., & Ahmad, N. (2015). Gamification in online collaborative learning for programming courses: A literature review. *Journal of Engineering and Applied Sciences (Asian Research Publishing Network), 10*(23), 1–3.

Bahadir, E. (2016). Using Neural Network and Logistic Regression Analysis to Predict Prospective Mathematics Teachers' Academic Success upon Entering Graduate Education. *Educational Sciences: Theory and Practice, 16*(3), 943–964.

Bailey, L. W. (2019). *Educational Technology and the New World of Persistent Learning*. IGI Global. https://books.google.co.uk/books?id=3_CBDwAAQBAJ

Baker, T., & Anissa, N. (2019). *Educ-AI-tion rebooted? Exploring the future of artificial intelligence in schools and colleges.* Retrieved 4th Apr from https://media.nesta.org.uk/documents/Future_of_AI_and_education_v5_WEB.pdf

Bakken, J. P., Uskov, V. L., Penumatsa, A., & Doddapaneni, A. (2016). Smart universities, smart classrooms and students with disabilities. In *Smart Education and e-Learning 2016* (pp. 15–27). Springer. doi:10.1007/978-3-319-39690-3_2

Balyer, A., & Oz, O. (2018). Academicans' views on digital transformation in education. *International Online Journal of Education and Teaching*, *5*(4), 809–830.

Bamber, C. J., & Elezi, E. (2020a). *What culture is your university? Have universities any right to teach entrepreneurialism? Higher Education Evaluation and Development.* Ahead-of-print.

Bamber, C., & Elezi, E. (2020b). *Knowledge Management Evaluation in British Higher Education Partnerships. Journal of Information and Knowledge Management.* Ahead-of-print.

Banfield, J., & Wilkerson, B. (2014). Increasing student intrinsic motivation and self-efficacy through gamification pedagogy. *Contemporary Issues in Education Research (Online)*, *7*(4), 291–298. doi:10.19030/cier.v7i4.8843

Baptist, E. (2014) *The Half Has Never Been Told: Slavery and the Making of American Capitalism.* BBC interview with Darwen residents: https://www.youtube.com/watch?v=Fd-8pXP5eNU

Barajas, M., & Owen, M. (2000). Implementing virtual learning environments: Looking for holistic approach. *Journal of Educational Technology & Society*, *3*(3), 39–53.

Baran, E., Correia, A.-P., & Thompson, A. (2011, November). Transforming online teaching practice: Critical analysis of the literature on the roles and competencies of online teachers. *Distance Education*, *32*(3), 421–439. doi:10.1080/01587919.2011.610293

Barata, G., Gama, S., Jorge, J., & Gonçalves, D. (2015). Gamification for smarter learning: Tales from the trenches. *Smart Learning Environments*, *2*(1), 10. doi:10.118640561-015-0017-8

Basden, A. (2000). Aspects of Reality as We Experience It (online). *Andrew Basden 2000-today.* http://dooy.info/aspects.html

Basden, A. (2002). The critical theory of Herman Dooyeweerd? *Journal of Information Technology*, *17*(4), 257–269. Advance online publication. doi:10.1080/0268396022000017770

Baty, P. (2017). *These maps could change how we understand the role of the world's top universities.* Times Higher Education. https://www.timeshighereducation.com/blog/these-maps-could-change-how-we-understand-role-worlds-top-universities

Bayne, S. (2015). Teacherbot: Interventions in automated teaching. *Teaching in Higher Education*, *20*(4), 455–467. doi:10.1080/13562517.2015.1020783

Becker, S. A., Brown, M., Dahlstrom, E., Davis, A., DePaul, K., Diaz, V., & Pomerantz, J. (2019). *NMC horizon report: 2018 higher education edition.* EDUCAUSE. https://library.educause.edu/-/media/files/library/2019/4/2019horizonreport.pdf

Beckert, S. (2014). Empire of Cotton: A Global History. Academic Press.

Becnel, K. (Ed.). (2019). *Emerging Technologies in Virtual Learning Environments.* IGI Global. doi:10.4018/978-1-5225-7987-8

Beer, D. (2016). *Metric power.* Springer. doi:10.1057/978-1-137-55649-3

Belichenko, M., Davidovitch, N., & Kravchenko, Y. (2017). Digital learning characteristics and principles of information resources knowledge structuring. *European Journal of Educational Research*, *6*(3), 261–267. doi:10.12973/eu-jer.6.3.261

Bell, B. S., & Federman, J. E. (2013). E-learning in postsecondary education. *The Future of Children*, 165–185.

Bell, K. R. (2014). *Online 3.0—the rise of the gamer educator the potential role of gamification in online education.* University of Pennsylvania.

Benbunan-Fich, R., Hiltz, S. R., & Harasim, L. (2005). The online interaction learning model: An integrated theoretical framework for learning networks. *Learning together online: Research on asynchronous learning networks*, 19–37.

Bernard, R. M. (2004). How does distance education compare with classroom instruction? A meta-analysis of the empirical literature. *Review of Educational Research*, *74*(3), 379–439.

Biesta, G. (2009). Good education in an age of measurement: On the need to reconnect with the question of purpose in education. *Educational Assessment, Evaluation and Accountability, 21*(1), 33–46.

Blackboard. (2020). *Virtual Learning with Web Conferencing*. Retrieved 24th June from https://www.blackboard.com/teaching-learning/collaboration-web-conferencing

Blackboard.com. (2020). *Blackboard.* https://www.blackboard.com/en-uk

Blanco-Novoa, O., Fernández-Caramés, T. M., Fraga-Lamas, P., & Castedo, L. (2018). A cost-effective IoT system for monitoring Indoor radon gas concentration. *Sensors (Basel)*, *18*(7), 2198. doi:10.339018072198 PMID:29986540

Blanco-Novoa, O., Fernández-Caramés, T. M., Fraga-Lamas, P., & Vilar-Montesinos, M. A. (2018). A practical evaluation of commercial industrial augmented reality systems in an industry 4.0 shipyard. *IEEE Access: Practical Innovations, Open Solutions*, *6*, 8201–8218. doi:10.1109/ACCESS.2018.2802699

Bolliger, D. U., & Wasilik, O. (2009). Factors influencing faculty satisfaction with online teaching and learning in higher education. *Distance Education*, *30*(1), 103–116. doi:10.1080/01587910902845949

Bond, M., Marín, V., Dolch, C., Bedenlier, S., & Zawacki-Richter, O. (2018). Digital transformation in German higher education: Student and teacher perceptions and usage of digital media. *International Journal of Educational Technology in Higher Education*, *15*(48), 1–20. doi:10.118641239-018-0130-1

Boninger, F., & Molnar, A. (2016). *Learning to be watched: Surveillance culture at school.* The Eighteenth Annual Report on Schoolhouse Commercialism Trends. National Center for Education Policy at the University of Colorado at Boulder. Http://Nepc. Colorado. Edu/Files/Publications/RB% 20Boninger-Molnar% 20Trends. Pdf

Booth, A., Sutton, A., & Papaioannou, D. (2016). *Systematic Approaches to a Successful Literature Review.* SAGE Publications. https://books.google.co.uk/books?id=DKj0CwAAQBAJ

Bordogna, C. M. (2019). The effects of boundary spanning on the development of social capital between faculty members operating transnational higher education partnerships. *Studies in Higher Education*, *44*(2), 217–229. doi:10.1080/03075079.2017.1349742

Bradbury, A., & Roberts-Holmes, G. (2018). How data impacts on early years educators. *Early Years Educator*, *19*(10), 38–44. doi:10.12968/eyed.2018.19.10.38

Bradford, P., Porciello, M., Balkon, N., & Backus, D. (2006-2007). The Blackboard Learning System: The Be All and End All in Educational Instruction? *Journal of Educational Technology Systems*, *35*(3), 301–314. doi:10.2190/X137-X73L-5261-5656

Broggi, J., Gallagher, M., Lilly, J., Duquette, J., Nimura, C., Pattenden, M., Richter, F., Arbide, L., Avin, S., & Kelley, K. (2018). *Woolf-Building the first Blockchain University.* White Paper.

Brosnan, M. (2015). *The women war workers of the North-West.* Retrieved from https://www.iwm.org.uk/history/the-women-war-workers-of-the-north-west

Brown, D. C., & Webb, C. R. (2007). *Race in the American South: From Slavery to Civil Rights.* Academic Press.

Brown, M. (2020). Seeing students at scale: How faculty in large lecture courses act upon learning analytics dashboard data. *Teaching in Higher Education, 25*(4), 384–400. doi:10.1080/13562517.2019.1698540

Brunton, F., & Nissenbaum, H. (2015). *Obfuscation: A user's guide for privacy and protest.* Mit Press. doi:10.7551/mitpress/9780262029735.001.0001

Burgers, C., Eden, A., van Engelenburg, M. D., & Buningh, S. (2015). How feedback boosts motivation and play in a brain-training game. *Computers in Human Behavior, 48*, 94–103. doi:10.1016/j.chb.2015.01.038

Burrows, R. (2012). Living with the h-index? Metric assemblages in the contemporary academy. *The Sociological Review, 60*(2), 355–372. doi:10.1111/j.1467-954X.2012.02077.x

Buzzard, C., Crittenden, V., Crittenden, W. F., & McCarty, P. (2011). The Use of Digital Technologies in the Classroom: A Teaching and Learning Perspective. *Journal of Marketing Education, 33*(2), 131–139. doi:10.1177/0273475311410845

Campaign for Science and Engineering. (2014). *Improving Diversity in STEM: A report by the Campaign for Science and Engineering (CaSE).* Retrieved from https://sciencecampaign.org.uk/CaSEDiversityinSTEMreport2014.pdf

Campbell-Kelly, M., Garcia-Swartz, D. D., Aspray, W., & Ceruzzi, P. E. (2008). The rise, fall, and resurrection of software as a service: historical perspectives on the computer utility and software for lease on a network. In *The Internet and American Business* (pp. 201–230). MIT Press Cambridge.

Caniglia, G., Luederitz, C., Groß, M., Muhr, M., John, B., Keeler, L. W., & Lang, D. (2017). Transnational collaboration for sustainability in higher education: Lessons from a systematic review. *Journal of Cleaner Production, 168*, 764–779. doi:10.1016/j.jclepro.2017.07.256

Canvas. (2020). *Instructure.com.* https://www.instructure.com/en-gb

Carden-Coyne, A. (2014). The Politics of Wounds: Military Patients and Medical Power in the First World War. Oxford.

Carlson, J. R., Fosmire, M., Miller, C., & Sapp Nelson, M. (2011). *Determining data information literacy needs: a study of students and research faculty libraries faculty and staff scholarship and research.* Academic Press.

Carnevale, A. P., & Strohl, J. (2013). *Separate and Unequal How Higher Education Reinforces the Intergenerational Reproduction of White Racial Privilege.* Georgetown University Center on Education and the Workforce.

Carter, H. (2012). *Alan Turing part of Manchester exhibition charting gay rights.* Retrieved from https://www.theguardian.com/uk/the-northerner/2012/aug/17/manchester-gay-rights-alan-turing

Carter, P. (2018). *The first women at university: remembering 'the London Nine.'* Times Higher Education. https://www.timeshighereducation.com/blog/first-women-university-remembering-london-nine

Casamayor, A., Amandi, A., & Campo, M. (2009). Intelligent assistance for teachers in collaborative e-learning environments. *Computers & Education, 53*(4), 1147–1154. doi:10.1016/j.compedu.2009.05.025

Cassidy, E. D., Colmenares, A., Jones, G., Manolovitz, T., Shen, L., & Vieira, S. (2014). Higher education and emerging technologies: Shifting trends in student usage. *Journal of Academic Librarianship*, *40*(2), 124–133. doi:10.1016/j.acalib.2014.02.003

Cech, E. A., & Waidzunas, T. J. (2011). Navigating the heteronormativity of engineering: The experiences of lesbian, gay, and bisexual students. *Engineering Studies*, *3*(1), 1–24. doi:10.1080/19378629.2010.545065

Cheng, H. C., Kung, T. P., Li, C. M., & Sun, Y. J. (2017, February). The current state of mobile apps development of higher education in Taiwan. In *2017 19th International Conference on Advanced Communication Technology (ICACT)* (pp. 780-786). IEEE. 10.23919/ICACT.2017.7890227

Chen, H., Chiang, R. H., & Storey, V. C. (2012). Business intelligence and analytics: From big data to big impact. *Management Information Systems Quarterly*, *36*(4), 1165–1188. doi:10.2307/41703503

Chen, J.-F., & Do, Q. H. (2014). Training neural networks to predict student academic performance: A comparison of cuckoo search and gravitational search algorithms. *International Journal of Computational Intelligence and Applications*, *13*(01), 1450005. doi:10.1142/S1469026814500059

Cheong, C., Cheong, F., & Filippou, J. (2013). Quick Quiz: A Gamified Approach for Enhancing Learning. PACIS, Chitra, K. (2020). Adoption of Gamification tool in Higher Education: An empirical study. *Studies in Indian Place Names*, *40*(3), 3132–3146.

Chou, Y. (2013). *Comprehensive List of 90+ Gamification case studies with ROI Stats*. Retrieved 8th Mar from https://gamificationplus.uk/comprehensive-list-90-gamification-cases-roi-stats/

Chou, S. Y., & Ramser, C. (2019). A Multilevel Model of Organizational Learning: Incorporating Employee Spontaneous Workplace Behaviours, Leadership Capital and Knowledge Management. *The Learning Organization*, *26*(2), 132–145. doi:10.1108/TLO-10-2018-0168

Cioffi, R., Travaglioni, M., Piscitelli, G., Petrillo, A., & De Felice, F. (2020). Artificial Intelligence and Machine Learning Applications in Smart Production: Progress, Trends, and Directions. *Sustainability*, *12*(2), 492. doi:10.3390u12020492

Ciolacu, M., Tehrani, A. F., Binder, L., & Svasta, P. M. (2018). Education 4.0-Artificial Intelligence Assisted Higher Education: Early recognition System with Machine Learning to support Students' Success. *2018 IEEE 24th International Symposium for Design and Technology in Electronic Packaging(SIITME)*, 23–30.

Ciolacu, M., Tehrani, A. F., Binder, L., & Svasta, P. M. (2018). Education 4.0-Artificial Intelligence Assisted Higher Education: Early recognition System with Machine Learning to support Students' Success. In *2018 IEEE 24th International Symposium for Design and Technology in Electronic Packaging (SIITME)*. IEEE.

Cohen, A. M. (2011). The gamification of education. *The Futurist*, *45*(5), 16.

Cole, M., & Engeström, Y. (1993). A cultural-historical approach to distributed cognition. *Distributed cognitions: Psychological and educational considerations*, 1-46.

Collins, C., Andrienko, N., Schreck, T., Yang, J., Choo, J., Engelke, U., Jena, A., & Dwyer, T. (2018). Guidance in the human–machine analytics process. *Visual Informatics*, *2*(3), 166–180. doi:10.1016/j.visinf.2018.09.003

Conghuan, Y. (2011). A service computing model based on interaction among local Campus Clouds. In *2011 6th International Conference on Computer Science & Education (ICCSE)*. IEEE. 10.1109/ICCSE.2011.6028668

Connolly, T. M., Boyle, E. A., MacArthur, E., Hainey, T., & Boyle, J. M. (2012). A systematic literature review of empirical evidence on computer games and serious games. *Computers & Education*, *59*(2), 661–686. doi:10.1016/j.compedu.2012.03.004

Conrad, R., & Donaldson, A. (2004). *Engaging the on line learner*. Jossey-Bass.

Costello, R. (Ed.). (2020). *Gaming Innovations in Higher Education: Emerging Research and Opportunities*. IGI Global.

Cózar-Gutiérrez, R., & Sáez-López, J. M. (2016). Game-based learning and gamification in initial teacher training in the social sciences: An experiment with MinecraftEdu. *International Journal of Educational Technology in Higher Education*, *13*(1), 2. doi:10.118641239-016-0003-4

Creswell, J. W. (2013). *Research design: Qualitative, quantitative, and mixed methods approaches*. Sage publications.

Crush, M. (2019). Monitoring the PACE of student Learning: Analytics at Rio Salado Community University. *Campus Technology*.

Curran, V., Gustavson, D., Simmons, K., Lannon, H., Wang, C., & Garmsiri, M. (2019). Adult learners' perceptions of self-directed learning and digital technology usage in continuing professional education: An update for the digital age. *Journal of Adult and Continuing Education*, *25*(1), 74–93. doi:10.1177/1477971419827318

d2l.com. (2020). *LMS Platforms: Brightspace LMS*. https://www.d2l.com/products/

Davis, C. (2019, December). AV tech that recruits. *AV Technology*, 28-43.

De Lange, C. (2015). Welcome to the bionic dawn. *New Scientist*, *227*(3032), 24–25. doi:10.1016/S0262-4079(15)30881-2

De Vries, H., Kremers, S., Smeets, T., Brug, J., & Eijmael, K. (2008). The effectiveness of tailored feedback and action plans in an intervention addressing multiple health behaviors. *American Journal of Health Promotion*, *22*(6), 417–424. doi:10.4278/ajhp.22.6.417 PMID:18677882

De Wit, H. (2018). Collaborative Online International Learning in Higher Education. In *Encyclopaedia of International Higher Education Systems and Institutions* (pp. 1–3). Springer. doi:10.1007/978-94-017-9553-1_234-1

Dede, C. J., Ho, A. D., & Mitros, P. (2016). Big data analysis in higher education: Promises and pitfalls. *EDUCAUSE Review*.

Demirer, V., Aydın, B., & Çelik, Ş. B. (2017). Exploring the educational potential of Internet of Things (IoT) in seamless learning. In The Internet of Things: Breakthroughs in Research and Practice (pp. 1-15). IGI Global.

Demirer, V., Aydın, B., & Çelik, Ş. B. (2017). *Exploring the educational potential of Internet of Things (IoT) in seamless learning The Internet of Things: Breakthroughs in Research and Practice*. IGI Global.

Dennis, M. J. (2018). Artificial intelligence and recruitment, admission, progression, and retention. *Enrollment Management Report*, *22*(9), 1–3. doi:10.1002/emt.30479

Denny, P. (2013). The effect of virtual achievements on student engagement. *Proceedings of the SIGCHI Conference on Human Factors in Computing Systems*.

Dery, K., Kolb, D., & MacCormick, J. (2014). Working with connective flow: How smartphone use is evolving in practice. *European Journal of Information Systems*, *23*(5), 558–570. doi:10.1057/ejis.2014.13

Deterding, S., Dixon, D., Khaled, R., & Nacke, L. (2011). From game design elements to gamefulness: defining gamification. *Proceedings of the 15th International Academic MindTrek Conference: Envisioning Future Media Environments*.

Diaz, D. P., & Cartnal, R. B. (1999). Students' Learning Styles in Two Classes: Online Distance Learning and Equivalent On-Campus. *College Teaching*, *47*(4), 130–135. doi:10.1080/87567559909595802

Dicheva, D., Dichev, C., Agre, G., & Angelova, G. (2015). Gamification in education: A systematic mapping study. *Journal of Educational Technology & Society*, *18*(3).

Dillenbourg, P., Mendelsohn, P., & Jermann, P. (1999) Why spatial metaphors are relevant to virtual campuses. In Learning and instruction in multiple contexts and settings. Bulletins of the Faculty of Education, 73. University of Joensuu, Finland, Faculty of Education.

Dillenbourg, P., Schneider, D., & Synteta, P. (2002). *Virtual learning environments*. 3rd Hellenic Conference Information & Communication Technologies in Education, Rhodes, Greece.

Dillon, T., Wu, C., & Chang, E. (2010). Cloud computing: issues and challenges. In *2010 24th IEEE International Conference on Advanced Information Networking and Applications*. IEEE. 10.1109/AINA.2010.187

Distefano, A., Rudestam, K., Silverman, R., & Long, P. D. (2012). Learning Management Systems (LMS). In *Encyclopedia of Distributed Learning*. SAGE Publications, Inc.

Dodigovic, M. (2007). Artificial intelligence and second language learning: An efficient approach to error remediation. *Language Awareness*, *16*(2), 99–113. doi:10.2167/la416.0

Doran, L., & Herold, B. (2016). 1-to-1 Laptop Initiatives Boost Student Scores, Study Finds. *Education Week*. https://www.edweek.org/ew/articles/2016/05/18/1-to-1-laptop-initiatives-boost-student-scores-study.html

Du, J., Jiang, C., Gelenbe, E., Xu, L., Li, J., & Ren, Y. (2018). Distributed Data Privacy Preservation in IoT Applications. *IEEE Wireless Communications*, *25*(6), 68–76. doi:10.1109/MWC.2017.1800094

Dumont, G., & Raggo, P. (2018). Faculty perspectives about distance teaching in the virtual classroom. *Journal of Nonprofit Education & Leadership*, *8*(1), 41–61. doi:10.18666/JNEL-2018-V8-I1-8372

Dunlosky, J., Rawson, K. A., Marsh, E. J., Nathan, M. J., & Willingham, D. T. (2013). Improving students' learning with effective learning techniques: Promising directions from cognitive and educational psychology. *Psychological Science in the Public Interest*, *14*(1), 4–58. PubMed

Dwyer, C., Hiltz, S., & Passerini, K. (2007). Trust and privacy concern within social networking sites: A comparison of Facebook and MySpace. *AMCIS 2007 Proceedings*, 339.

Eassom, S. (2015). IBM Watson for education. *IBM Insights on Business, 1*.

Edgar, C. O. E. (Ed.). (2020). *Management Training Programs in Higher Education for the Fourth Industrial Revolution: Emerging Research and Opportunities*. IGI Global.

Edwards, J. S., & Taborda, E. R. (2016). Using knowledge management to give context to analytics and big data and reduce strategic risk. *Procedia Computer Science*, *99*, 36–49. doi:10.1016/j.procs.2016.09.099

Eldridge, C. (2015, July 14). *Education technology - A competitive landscape that is a diamond in the rough for new startups*. The Startup Ecosystem. Retrieved on December 19, 2019 from https://startupecosystem.blogspot.com/2015/2007/education-technology-competitive.html

Elezi, E. (2020). Role of Knowledge Management in Developing Higher Education Partnerships: Towards a Conceptual Model. In *Proceedings of the 7th Business Systems Laboratory, International Symposium* (pp. 98-104). Academic Press.

Elezi, E., & Bamber, C. (2018). Knowledge management factors affecting educational partnerships within the British HE/FE sector. *International Journal of Knowledge Management Studies*, *9*(3), 243–259. doi:10.1504/IJKMS.2018.094213

Erl, T., Puttini, R., & Mahmood, Z. (2013). *Cloud computing: concepts, technology & architecture*. Pearson Education.

Eynon, R. (2013). *The rise of Big Data: what does it mean for education, technology, and media research?* Academic Press.

Fadil, O. A., & Khaldi, M. (2020). Learning Management Systems: Concept and Challenges. In Personalization and Collaboration in Adaptive E-Learning (pp. 158-175). IGI Global.

Fadol, Y., Aldamen, H., & Saadullah, S. (2018, July). A comparative analysis of flipped, online and traditional teaching: A case of female Middle Eastern management students. *International Journal of Management Education*, *16*(2), 266–280. doi:10.1016/j.ijme.2018.04.003

Feiz, D., Dehghani Soltani, M., & Farsizadeh, H. (2019). The effect of knowledge sharing on the psychological empowerment in higher education mediated by organizational memory. *Studies in Higher Education*, *44*(1), 3–19. doi:10.1080/03075079.2017.1328595

Feng, S., Zhou, S., & Liu, Y. (2011). Research on data mining in university admissions decision-making. *International Journal of Advancements in Computing Technology*, *3*(6), 176–186. doi:10.4156/ijact.vol3.issue6.21

Fernández-Caramés, T. M., & Fraga-Lamas, P. (2018). A review on human-centered IoT-connected smart labels for the industry 4.0. *IEEE Access: Practical Innovations, Open Solutions*, *6*, 25939–25957. doi:10.1109/ACCESS.2018.2833501

Fernández-Caramés, T. M., & Fraga-Lamas, P. (2019). Towards Next Generation Teaching, Learning, and Context-Aware Applications for Higher Education: A Review on Blockchain, IoT, Fog and Edge Computing Enabled Smart Campuses and Universities. *Applied Sciences*, *9*(21), 4479. doi:10.3390/app9214479

Fernández-Caramés, T. M., Fraga-Lamas, P., Suárez-Albela, M., Castedo, L., Crepaldi, P., & Pimenta, T. (2017). A methodology for evaluating security in commercial RFID systems. In *Radio Frequency Identification*. InTech. doi:10.5772/64844

Fischer, D. (2001). Value-Added Consulting: Teaching Clients How to Fish. *Curator (New York, N.Y.)*, *44*(1), 83–96. doi:10.1111/j.2151-6952.2001.tb00031.x

Fitz-Walter, Z., Tjondronegoro, D., & Wyeth, P. (2011). Orientation passport: using gamification to engage university students. *Proceedings of the 23rd Australian Computer-Human Interaction Conference.*

Flaounas, I., Lansdall-Welfare, T., Antonakaki, P., & Cristianini, N. (2014). *The anatomy of a modular system for media content analysis.* arXiv preprint arXiv:1402.6208

Forbes.com. (2017). *Forbes Welcome*. https://www.forbes.com/sites/danielnewman/2016/08/30/top-10-trends-for-digital-transformation-in-2017/#22d263ca47a5

Forrest, C. (2017). *80% of IoT apps not tested for vulnerabilities, report says.* Retrieved 24th Feb 2019 from https://www.techrepublic.com/article/80-of-IoT-apps-not-tested-for-vulnerabilities-report-says/

Fox, C. W., Evans, M. H., Pearson, M. J., & Prescott, T. J. (2012). Towards hierarchical blackboard mapping on a whiskered robot. *Robotics and Autonomous Systems*, *60*(11), 1356–1366. doi:10.1016/j.robot.2012.03.005

Fraga-Lamas, P., Fernández-Caramés, T. M., Suárez-Albela, M., Castedo, L., & González-López, M. (2016). A Review on Internet of Things for Defense and Public Safety. *Sensors (Basel)*, *16*(10), 1644. doi:10.339016101644 PMID:27782052

Fraile, F., Tagawa, T., Poler, R., & Ortiz, A. (2018). Trustworthy industrial IoT gateways for interoperability platforms and ecosystems. *IEEE Internet of Things Journal*, *5*(6), 4506–4514. doi:10.1109/JIOT.2018.2832041

Fu, F.-L., Su, R.-C., & Yu, S.-C. (2009). EGameFlow: A scale to measure learners' enjoyment of e-learning games. *Computers & Education*, *52*(1), 101–112.

Gallagher, P. (2017, Sept. 24). The University of Warwick launches new department to employ all temporary or fixed-term teaching staff. *The Independent.*

Galusha, J. (1997). Barriers to Learning in Distance Education. *Interpersonal Computing and Technology*, *5*, 6–14.

Gao, L. (2012). Digital technologies and English instruction in China's higher education system. *Teacher Development: An International Journal of Teachers' Professional Development*, *16*(2), 161-179. Doi:10.1080/13664530.2012.667967

García-Sánchez, P., Díaz-Díaz, N. L., & De Saá-Pérez, P. (2019). Social capital and knowledge sharing in academic research teams. *International Review of Administrative Sciences*, *85*(1), 191–207. doi:10.1177/0020852316689140

Garris, R., Ahlers, R., & Driskell, J. E. (2002). Games, motivation, and learning: A research and practice model. *Simulation & Gaming*, *33*(4), 441–467. doi:10.1177/1046878102238607

Gawali, S. K., & Deshmukh, M. K. (2019). Energy Autonomy in IoT Technologies. *Energy Procedia*, *156*, 222–226. doi:10.1016/j.egypro.2018.11.132

Ge, C., & Xie, J. (2015). Application of Grey Forecasting Model Based on Improved Residual Correction in the Cost Estimation of University Education. *International Journal of Emerging Technologies in Learning*, *10*(8), 30. doi:10.3991/ijet.v10i8.5215

Ghosh, I. (2020). *Zoom is now worth More Than the World's 7 Biggest Airlines*. https://www.visualcapitalist.com/zoom-boom-biggest-airlines/

Gibbs, P., & Knapp, M. (2002). *Marketing Further and Higher Education Research: an educator's guide to promoting courses, departments and institutions*. Kogan Page.

Gikandi, J. W., Morrow, D., & Davis, N. E. (2011). Online formative assessment in higher education: A review of the literature. *Computers & Education*, *57*(4), 2333–2351. doi:10.1016/j.compedu.2011.06.004

Gilmore, A., & Comunian, R. (2016). Beyond the campus: Higher education, cultural policy and the creative economy. *International Journal of Cultural Policy*, *22*(1), 1–9. doi:10.1080/10286632.2015.1101089

Giora, R., Fein, O., Kronrod, A., Elnatan, I., Shuval, N., & Zur, A. (2004). Weapons of mass distraction: Optimal innovation and pleasure ratings. *Metaphor and Symbol*, *19*(2), 115–141. doi:10.120715327868ms1902_2

Glahn, C., Gruber, M. R., & Tartakovski, O. (2015) Beyond Delivery Modes and Apps: A Case Study on Mobile Blended Learning in Higher Education. The handbook of blended learning: Global perspectives, local designs, 3-21. doi:10.1007/978-3-319-24258-3_10

Glahn, C., Gruber, M.R., & Tartakovski, O. (2015). *Beyond Delivery Modes and Apps: A Case Study on Mobile Blended Learning in Higher Education*. Academic Press.

Gómez, J., Huete, J. F., Hoyos, O., Perez, L., & Grigori, D. (2013). Interaction system based on internet of things as support for education. *Procedia Computer Science*, *21*, 132–139. doi:10.1016/j.procs.2013.09.019

Gonzalez, C. (2009). Conceptions of, and approaches to, teaching online: A study of lecturers teaching postgraduate distance courses. *Higher Education*, *57*(3), 299–314. doi:10.100710734-008-9145-1

Goralski, M. A., & Tan, T. K. (2020). Artificial intelligence and sustainable development. *International Journal of Management Education*, *18*(1), 100330. doi:10.1016/j.ijme.2019.100330

Görnerup, O., Gillblad, D., Holst, A., & Bjurling, B. (2013). *Big data analytics-a research and innovation agenda for Sweden*. The Swedish Big Data Analytics Network.

Gough, D., Oliver, S., & Thomas, J. (2017). An introduction to systematic reviews. *Sage (Atlanta, Ga.)*.

Gouseti, A. (2017). Exploring doctoral students' use of digital technologies: What do they use them for and why? *Educational Review*, *69*(5), 638–654. doi:10.1080/00131911.2017.1291492

Govier, L. (2009). *Leaders in co-creation? Why and how museums could develop their co-creative practice with the public, building on ideas from the performing arts and other non-museum organisations*. Academic Press.

Graham, C. R. (2006). Blended learning systems. The handbook of blended learning: Global perspectives, local designs, 3-21.

Graham, C., Cagiltay, K., Lim, B. R., Craner, J., & Duffy, T. M. (2001). Seven principles of effective teaching: A practical lens for evaluating online courses. *The Technology Source*, *30*(5), 50.

Graham, D. H. (2016). The 'co' in co-production. *Science Museum Group Journal, 5*(Spring). http://journal.sciencemuseum.org.uk/browse/issue-05/the-co-in-co-production/

Greener, S. (2012). Using Marketing Models to Review Academic Staff Acceptance of Digital Technology to Enhance Learning in Higher Education. *DIVAI 2012 - 9th International Scientific Conference on Distance Learning in Applied Informatics*, 111-126.

Grodzinsky, F., & Griffin, J. (2002, June). Blackboard: A web-based resource in the teaching of a multi-disciplinary/multi-institutional computer ethics course. In *IEEE 2002 International Symposium on Technology and Society (ISTAS'02). Social Implications of Information and Communication Technology. Proceedings (Cat. No. 02CH37293)* (pp. 126-131). IEEE.

Grove, J. (2015). Teach Higher 'disbanded' ahead of campus protest. *Times Higher Education, 2*.

Grove, J. (2020). *Switch to online teaching can help UK unlock global markets | Times Higher Education (THE)*. Available at: https://www.timeshighereducation.com/news/switch-online-teaching-can-help-uk-unlock-global-markets

Guerrero, M., Urbano, D., & Herrera, F. (2019). Innovation practices in emerging economies: Do university partnerships matter? *The Journal of Technology Transfer*, *44*(2), 615–646. doi:10.100710961-017-9578-8

Guilloux, V., Locke, J., & Lowe, A. (2013). Digital business reporting standards: Mapping the battle in France. *European Journal of Information Systems*, *22*(3), 257–277. doi:10.1057/ejis.2012.5

Guo, M., & Zhang, Y. (2015). *The research of smart campus based on Internet of Things & cloud computing*. Academic Press.

Hall, W., & Pesenti, J. (2019). *Growing the Artificial Intelligence Industry in the UK*. Academic Press.

Hammer, J., & Lee, J. (2011). Gamification in Education: What, How, Why Bother. *Academic Exchange Quarterly*, *15*(2).

Hansch, A., Newman, C., & Schildhauer, T. (2015). *Fostering engagement with gamification: Review of current practices on online learning platforms*. Academic Press.

Hansen, J. D., & Reich, J. (2015). Democratizing education? Examining access and usage patterns in massive open online courses. *Science*, *350*(6265), 1245–1248. doi:10.1126cience.aab3782 PMID:26785488

Harris, C. M., Wright, P. M., & McMahan, G. C. (2019). The emergence of human capital: Roles of social capital and coordination that drive unit performance. *Human Resource Management Journal*, *29*(2), 162–180. doi:10.1111/1748-8583.12212

Harwood, T., & Garry, T. (2017). Internet of Things: Understanding trust in techno-service systems. *Journal of Service Management*, *28*(3), 442–475. doi:10.1108/JOSM-11-2016-0299

Hatala, R., Cook, D. A., Zendejas, B., Hamstra, S. J., & Brydges, R. (2014). Feedback for simulation-based procedural skills training: A meta-analysis and critical narrative synthesis. *Advances in Health Sciences Education: Theory and Practice*, *19*(2), 251–272. doi:10.100710459-013-9462-8 PMID:23712700

Haugeland, J. (1989). *Artificial Intelligence: The Very Idea*. MIT Press. https://books.google.co.uk/books?id=zLFSPdIuqKsC

Hays, J. N. (2005). *Epidemics and Pandemics: Their Impacts on Human History* (S. Danver, L. Esterman, & G. Rossi, Eds.). ABC-CLIO, Inc.

Heeks, R., & Stanforth, C. (2007). Understanding e-Government project trajectories from an actor-network perspective. *European Journal of Information Systems, 16*(2), 165–177. doi:10.1057/palgrave.ejis.3000676

HEFCW. (2019). Enhancing Learning and Teaching through Technology. *Higher Education Funding Council for Wales*, 1-37. https://www.hefcw.ac.uk/documents/policy_areas/learning_and_teaching/ELTT%20-%20showcase%20case%20studies.pdf

Heidt, C. T., Arbuthnott, K. D., & Price, H. L. (2016). The effects of distributed learning on enhanced cognitive interview training. *Psychiatry, Psychology and Law, 23*(1), 47–61. doi:10.1080/13218719.2015.1032950

Heirdsfield, A., Walker, S., Tambyah, M., & Beutel, D. (2011). Blackboard as an online learning environment: What do teacher education students and staff think? *Australian Journal of Teacher Education (Online), 36*(7), 1. doi:10.14221/ajte.2011v36n7.4

Hepp, A., Breiter, A., & Friemel, T. N. (2018). Digital Traces in Context| Digital Traces in Context—An Introduction. *International Journal of Communication, 12*, 11.

Herold, B. (2016). Technology in Education: An Overview. *Education Week*. https://www.edweek.org/ew/issues/technology-in-education/

Herold, B. (2016, February 5). Technology in education: An overview. *Education Week*. Retrieved on December 19, 2019 from https://www.edweek.org/ew/issues/technology-in-education/index.html

He, T., Zhu, C., & Questier, F. (2018). Predicting digital informal learning: An empirical study among Chinese University students. *Asia Pacific Education Review, 19*(1), 79–90. Advance online publication. doi:10.100712564-018-9517-x

Higher Education Policy Institute. (2017). *Rebooting learning for the digital age: What next for technology enhanced higher education?* Oxuniprint.

Hill, P. (2017). *Academic LMS Market Share: A view across four global regions*. ELiterate. https://eliterate.us/academic-lms-market-share-view-across-four-global-regions/

Hiltz, S. R., & Turoff, M. (2005). Education goes digital: The evolution of online learning and the revolution in higher education. *Communications of the ACM, 48*(10), 59. doi:10.1145/1089107.1089139

Hinchcliffe, D. (2017). *Five emerging technologies for rapid digital transformation*. ZDNet. Available at: http://www.zdnet.com/article/five-emerging-technologies-for-rapid-digital-transformation

Hinds, D. (2019). *Realising the potential of technology in education: A strategy for education providers and the technology industry*. Academic Press.

Hipwell, S. (2014). Developing smart campuses—A working model. *2014 International Conference on Intelligent Green Building and Smart Grid (IGBSG)*.

Hofstede, G. (2010). The GLOBE debate: Back to relevance. *Journal of International Business Studies, 41*(8), 1339–1346. doi:10.1057/jibs.2010.31

Hooper-Greenhill, E., Sandell, R., Moussouri, T., & O'Riain, H. (2000). *Museums and social inclusion: the GLLAM Report*. Academic Press.

Hoque, S., & Alam, S. (2010). The Role of Information and Communication Technologies (ICTs) in Delivering Higher Education – A Case of Bangladesh. *International Education Studies, 3*(2). Available at SSRN: https://ssrn.com/abstract=1630526

Hsu, C.-L., & Lin, J. C.-C. (2018). Exploring factors affecting the adoption of Internet of Things services. *Journal of Computer Information Systems*, *58*(1), 49–57. doi:10.1080/08874417.2016.1186524

Huang, S.-P. (2018). Effects of using artificial intelligence teaching system for environmental education on environmental knowledge and attitude. *Eurasia Journal of Mathematics, Science and Technology Education*, *14*(7), 3277–3284. doi:10.29333/ejmste/91248

Huda, M., Maseleno, A., Atmotiyoso, P., Siregar, M., Ahmad, R., Jasmi, K., & Muhamad, N. (2018). Big data emerging technology: Insights into innovative environment for online learning resources. *International Journal of Emerging Technologies in Learning.*, *13*(1), 23–36. doi:10.3991/ijet.v13i01.6990

Hwang, K., Dongarra, J. J., & Fox, G. C. (2011). *Distributed and cloud computing: clusters, grids, clouds, and the future internet*. Morgan Kaufmann.

Iqbal, A., Latif, F., Marimon, F., Sahibzada, U. F., & Hussain, S. (2019). From knowledge management to organizational performance. *Journal of Enterprise Information Management*, *32*(1), 36–59. doi:10.1108/JEIM-04-2018-0083

Islam, S. M. R., Kwak, D., Kabir, M. H., Hossain, M., & Kwak, K. (2015). The Internet of Things for Health Care: A Comprehensive Survey. *IEEE Access: Practical Innovations, Open Solutions*, *3*, 678–708. doi:10.1109/ACCESS.2015.2437951

Jackman, S. R., Witard, O. C., Jeukendrup, A. E., & Tipton, K. D. (2010). Branched-Chain Amino Acid Ingestion Can Ameliorate Soreness from Eccentric Exercise. *Medicine and Science in Sports and Exercise*, *42*(5), 962–970. doi:10.1249/MSS.0b013e3181c1b798 PMID:19997002

Jain, L., & Bhardwaj, S. (2010). Enterprise cloud computing: Key considerations for adoption. *International Journal of Engineering and Information Technology*, *2*, 113–117.

James, W. B., & Gardner, D. L. (1995). Learning styles: Implications for distance learning. *New Directions for Adult and Continuing Education*, *1995*(67), 19–31. doi:10.1002/ace.36719956705

Janeček, V. (2018). Ownership of personal data in the Internet of Things. *Computer Law & Security Review*, *34*(5), 1039–1052. doi:10.1016/j.clsr.2018.04.007

Jang, J., Park, J. J., & Mun, Y. Y. (2015, June). Gamification of online learning. In *International Conference on Artificial Intelligence in Education* (646-649). Springer. 10.1007/978-3-319-19773-9_82

Jiang, F., Jiang, Y., Zhi, H., Dong, Y., Li, H., Ma, S., Wang, Y., Dong, Q., Shen, H., & Wang, Y. (2017). Artificial intelligence in healthcare: Past, present and future. *Stroke and Vascular Neurology*, *2*(4), svn-2017–svn-000101. doi:10.1136vn-2017-000101 PMID:29507784

Ji, Y., & Liu, Y. (2016). Development of Intelligent Teaching System Based on 3D Technology in the Course of Digital Animation Production. *International Journal of Emerging Technologies in Learning*, *11*(09), 81–86. doi:10.3991/ijet.v11i09.6116

Johnson, L., Becker, S. A., Cummins, M., Estrada, V., Freeman, A., & Hall, C. (2016). *NMC horizon report: 2016 higher education edition*. The New Media Consortium.

Jonassen, D., Davidson, M., Collins, M., Campbell, J., & Haag, B. B. (1995). Constructivism and computer-mediated communication in distance education. *american. Journal of Distance Education*, *9*(2), 7–26. doi:10.1080/08923649509526885

Jongbloed, B., Enders, J., & Salerno, C. (2008). Higher education and its communities: Interconnections, interdependencies and a research agenda. *Higher Education*, *56*(3), 303–324. doi:10.100710734-008-9128-2

Junco, R., Heiberger, G., & Loken, E. (2011). The effect of Twitter on college student engagement and grades. *Journal of Computer Assisted Learning*, *27*(2), 119–132.

Kao, A., & Poteet, S. R. (2007). *Natural language processing and text mining*. Springer. doi:10.1007/978-1-84628-754-1

Kardan, A. A., Sadeghi, H., Ghidary, S. S., & Sani, M. R. F. (2013). Prediction of student course selection in online higher education institutes using neural network. *Computers & Education*, *65*, 1–11. doi:10.1016/j.compedu.2013.01.015

Katal, A., Wazid, M., & Goudar, R. H. (2013). Big data: issues, challenges, tools and good practices. In *2013 Sixth International Conference on Contemporary Computing (IC3)*. IEEE. 10.1109/IC3.2013.6612229

Kauffman, H. (2015). A review of predictive factors of student success in and satisfaction with online learning. In Research in Learning Technology. Association for Learning Technology. doi:10.3402/rlt.v23.26507

Kaur, R., Sharma, M., & Taruna, S. (2019). Privacy Preserving Data Mining Model for the Social Networking. In *2019 6th International Conference on Computing for Sustainable Global Development (INDIACom)*. IEEE.

Kearney, E., Shemla, M., van Knippenberg, D., & Scholz, F. A. (2019). A paradox perspective on the interactive effects of visionary and empowering leadership. *Organizational Behavior and Human Decision Processes*.

Keller, C. (2005). Virtual learning environments: Three implementation perspectives. *Learning, Media and Technology*, *30*(3), 299–311. doi:10.1080/17439880500250527

Kelly, J. (2014, Feb 5). *Big data: Hadoop, business analytics and beyond* [Blog post]. Wikibon.

Kerr, M. S., Rynearson, K., & Kerr, M. C. (2006). Student characteristics for online learning success. *The Internet and Higher Education*, *9*(2), 91–105.

Ketcham, G., Landa, K., Brown, K., Charuk, K., Defranco, T., Heise, M., Mccabe, R., & Youngs-Maher, P. (2011). Learning Management. *Systematic Reviews*.

Khaddage, F., & Cosío, J. H. (2014, March). Trends and Barriers on the Fusion of Mobile Apps in Higher Education Where to Next and How? In *Society for Information Technology & Teacher Education International Conference* (pp. 903-909). Association for the Advancement of Computing in Education (AACE).

Khan, A., Ahmad, F. H., & Malik, M. M. (2017). Use of digital game based learning and gamification in secondary school science: The effect on student engagement, learning and gender difference. *Education and Information Technologies*, *22*(6), 2767–2804. doi:10.100710639-017-9622-1

Kim, K.-J., & Bonk, C. J. (2006). The Future of Online Teaching and Learning in Higher Education: The Survey Says.... *EDUCAUSE Quarterly*.

Kim, T., & Lim, J. (2019). Designing an Efficient Cloud Management Architecture for Sustainable Online Lifelong Education. *Sustainability*, *11*(6), 1523.

King, M. R. N., Rothberg, S. J., Dawson, R. J., & Batmaz, F. (2016). Bridging the edtech evidence gap. *Información Tecnológica*, *18*(1), 18–40.

Kirkwood, A., & Price, L. (2013). Examining some assumptions and limitations of research on the effects of emerging technologies for teaching and learning in higher education. *British Journal of Educational Technology*, *44*(4), 536–543. doi:10.1111/bjet.12049

Kluger, A. N., & DeNisi, A. (1996). The effects of feedback interventions on performance: A historical review, a meta-analysis, and a preliminary feedback intervention theory. *Psychological Bulletin, 119*(2), 254–284. doi:10.1037/0033-2909.119.2.254

Kobayashi, V. B., Mol, S. T., Berkers, H. A., Kismihók, G., & Hartog, D. N. D. (2018). Text mining in organizational research. *Organizational Research Methods, 21*(3), 733–765. doi:10.1177/1094428117722619 PMID:29881248

Konert, J., & Lavoué, E. (Eds.). Lecture Notes in Computer Science: Vol. 9307. *Design for Teaching and Learning in a Networked World*. Springer.

Kose, U., & Arslan, A. (2016). Intelligent e-learning system for improving students' academic achievements in computer programming courses. *International Journal of Engineering Education, 32*(1), 185–198.

Krause, K. (2005). *Understanding and promoting student engagement in university learning communities*. Paper presented as keynote address: Engaged, Inert or Otherwise Occupied.

Krause, M., Mogalle, M., Pohl, H., & Williams, J. J. (2015, March). A playful game changer: Fostering student retention in online education with social gamification. In *Proceedings of the Second ACM conference on Learning@ Scale* (pp. 95-102). ACM.

Krebs, P., Prochaska, J. O., & Rossi, J. S. (2010). A meta-analysis of computer-tailored interventions for health behavior change. *Preventive Medicine, 51*(3-4), 214–221. doi:10.1016/j.ypmed.2010.06.004 PMID:20558196

Krieger, D. J., & Belliger, A. (2014). *Interpreting Networks: Hermeneutics, Actor-Network Theory & New Media*. Transcript.

Krishna, K. P., Kumar, M. M., & Sri, P. A. (2018). Student information system and performance retrieval through dashboard. *International Journal of Engineering & Technology, 7*(2.7), 682-685.

Kroeze, W., Werkman, A., & Brug, J. (2006). A systematic review of randomized trials on the effectiveness of computer-tailored education on physical activity and dietary behaviors. *Annals of Behavioral Medicine, 31*(3), 205–223. doi:10.120715324796abm3103_2 PMID:16700634

Krotov, V. (2017). The Internet of Things and new business opportunities. *Business Horizons, 60*(6), 831–841. doi:10.1016/j.bushor.2017.07.009

Kuh, G. D. (2003). What we're learning about student engagement from NSSE: Benchmarks for effective educational practices. *Change: The Magazine of Higher Learning, 35*(2), 24–32.

Kuh, G. D., & Hu, S. (2001). The effects of student-faculty interaction in the 1990s. *The Review of Higher Education, 24*(3), 309–332. doi:10.1353/rhe.2001.0005

Kumar, T. M. V. (2016). *Smart Economy in Smart Cities: International Collaborative Research: Ottawa, St.Louis, Stuttgart, Bologna, Cape Town, Nairobi, Dakar, Lagos, New Delhi, Varanasi, Vijayawada, Kozhikode, Hong Kong*. Springer Singapore. https://books.google.co.uk/books?id=fhDpDAAAQBAJ

Lakhani, K. R., & Iansiti, M. (2017). The truth about blockchain. *Harvard Business Review, 95*, 118–127.

Landers, R. N., & Callan, R. C. (2011). Casual social games as serious games: The psychology of gamification in undergraduate education and employee training. In Serious games and edutainment applications (pp. 399-423). Springer.

Lapidos, L., & Ruffolo, M. (2017). Access to Interprofessional Continuing Education in Integrated Care through Digital Instructional Technology. *Journal of Social Work Education, 53*(S1), S40-S46. Doi:10.1080/10437797.2017.1288596

Lau, J., Yang, B., & Dasgupta, R. (2020). Will the coronavirus make online education go viral? *The Higher Education*. https://www.timeshighereducation.com/features/will-coronavirus-make-online-education-go-viral

Lave, J. (1991). *Situating learning in communities of practice*. Academic Press.

Lave, J., & Wenger, E. (1991). *Situated learning: Legitimate peripheral participation.* Cambridge University Press. doi:10.1017/CBO9780511815355

Lawrence, D. H. (2006). Blackboard on a shoestring: Tying courses to sources. *Journal of Library Administration*, *45*(1-2), 245–265. doi:10.1300/J111v45n01_14

Lay, J. (2020). *To zoom or not to zoom? That is the question. The Higher Education.* https://www.timeshighereducation.com/news/zoom-or-not-zoom-question

Lazarus, S. S., Thurlow, M. L., Lail, K. E., & Christensen, L. (2009). A longitudinal analysis of state accommodations policies: Twelve years of change, 1993—2005. *The Journal of Special Education*, *43*(2), 67–80. doi:10.1177/0022466907313524

Lederman, D. (2018). Conflicted views of technology: A survey of faculty attitudes. Inside Higher Ed.

Leeds, E. (2013). The impact of student retention strategies: An empirical study. *International Journal of Management in Education*, *7*(1–2), 22–43.

Lee, J., & Jang, S. (2014). A methodological framework for instructional design model development: Critical dimensions and synthesized procedures. *Educational Technology Research and Development. Springer*, *62*(6), 743–765. doi:10.100711423-014-9352-7

Lee, K., Lee, S., & Yang, H.-D. (2014). Towards on cloud computing standardization. *International Journal of Multimedia & Ubiquitous Engineering*, *9*(2), 169–176. doi:10.14257/ijmue.2014.9.2.17

Lee, S. M., & Chen, L. (2011). An integrative research framework for the online social network service. *Service Business*, *5*(3), 259–276. doi:10.100711628-011-0113-y

Leiner, B. M., Cerf, V. G., Clark, D. D., Kahn, R. E., Kleinrock, L., Lynch, D. C., Postel, J., Roberts, L. G., & Wolff, S. (2009). A brief history of the internet. *Computer Communication Review*, *39*(5), 22–31. doi:10.1145/1629607.1629613

Lemoine, P. A., & Richardson, M. D. (2019). Creative disruption in higher education: Society, technology, and globalization. In Educational and social dimensions of digital transformation in organizations (pp. 275-293). IGI Global.

Letaief, K. B., Chen, W., Shi, Y., Zhang, J., & Zhang, Y.-J. A. (2019). The roadmap to 6G: AI empowered wireless networks. *IEEE Communications Magazine*, *57*(8), 84–90. doi:10.1109/MCOM.2019.1900271

Lewis, G. S. (2010). I Would Have Had More Success If…: Student Reflections on Their Performance in Online and Blended Courses. *American Journal of Business Education*, *3*(11), 13–22. doi:10.19030/ajbe.v3i11.58

Liaw, S. S. (2008). Investigating students' perceived satisfaction, behavioural intention, and effectiveness of e-learning: A case study of the Blackboard system. *Computers & Education*, *51*(2), 864–873. doi:10.1016/j.compedu.2007.09.005

Liaw, S. S., & Huang, H. M. (2006, May). Developing a collaborative e-learning system based on users' perceptions. In *International Conference on Computer Supported Cooperative Work in Design* (pp. 751-759). Springer.

Liberati, A., Altman, D. G., Tetzlaff, J., Mulrow, C., Gøtzsche, P. C., Ioannidis, J. P., Clarke, M., Devereaux, P. J., Kleijnen, J., & Moher, D. (2009). The PRISMA statement for reporting systematic reviews and meta-analyses of studies that evaluate health care interventions: Explanation and elaboration. *PLoS Medicine*, *6*(7), e1000100. doi:10.1371/journal.pmed.1000100 PMID:19621070

Limani, Y., Hajrizi, E., Stapleton, L., & Retkoceri, M. (2019). Digital Transformation Readiness in Higher Education Institutions (HEI): The Case of Kosovo. *IFAC PapersOnLine,* 52-57.

Lin, F.-R., Ha, D., & Liao, D. (2016, January 5-8). *Automatic content analysis of media framing by text mining techniques.* Paper presented at the 49th Hawaii International Conference on System Sciences. 10.1109/HICSS.2016.348

Li, S.-C. S., & Huang, W.-C. (2016). Lifestyles, innovation attributes, and teachers' adoption of game-based learning: Comparing non-adopters with early adopters, adopters and likely adopters in Taiwan. *Computers & Education, 96*, 29–41. doi:10.1016/j.compedu.2016.02.009

Little, L. K. (2006). Plague and the end of antiquity: The pandemic of 541-750. In Plague and the End of Antiquity: The Pandemic of 541-750. Cambridge University Press.

Liu, N., & Li, G. (2011). Research on digital campus based on cloud computing. In *International Conference on Computer Education, Simulation and Modeling*. Springer. 10.1007/978-3-642-21802-6_34

Liu, L. F., Li, Y., Xiong, Y., Cao, J., & Yuan, P. (2018). An EEG study of the relationship between design problem statements and cognitive behaviours during conceptual design. *Artificial Intelligence for Engineering Design, Analysis and Manufacturing, 32*(3), 351–362. doi:10.1017/S0890060417000683

Liu, M., Zha, S., & He, W. (2019). Digital Transformation Challenges: A Case Study Regarding the MOOC Development and Operations at Higher Education Institutions in China. *TechTrends, 63*(5), 621–630. doi:10.100711528-019-00409-y

Liu, Y., Fan, X., Zhou, X., Liu, M., Wang, J., & Liu, T. (2019). Application of Virtual Reality Technology in Distance Higher Education. In *Proceedings of the 2019 4th International Conference on Distance Education and Learning* (pp. 35-39). 10.1145/3338147.3338174

Livingstone, S., & Sefton-Green, J. (2016). *The class: Living and learning in the digital age* (Vol. 1). NYU Press. doi:10.18574/nyu/9781479884575.001.0001

Li, X. (2007). Intelligent agent–supported online education. *Decision Sciences Journal of Innovative Education, 5*(2), 311–331. doi:10.1111/j.1540-4609.2007.00143.x

Lodhi, P., Mishra, O., Jain, S., & Bajaj, V. (2018). StuA: An intelligent student assistant. *IJIMAI, 5*(2), 17–25. doi:10.9781/ijimai.2018.02.008

Lo, J.-J., Chan, Y.-C., & Yeh, S.-W. (2012). Designing an adaptive web-based learning system based on students' cognitive styles identified online. *Computers & Education, 58*(1), 209–222. doi:10.1016/j.compedu.2011.08.018

Looyestyn, J., Kernot, J., Boshoff, K., Ryan, J., Edney, S., & Maher, C. (2017). Does gamification increase engagement with online programs? A systematic review. *PLoS One, 12*(3), e0173403. doi:10.1371/journal.pone.0173403 PMID:28362821

Luckin, R. (2017). The implications of artificial intelligence for teachers and schooling. *Future Frontiers: Education for an AI World*, 109–126.

Luckin, R., Holmes, W., Griffiths, M., & Corcier, L. B. (2016). *Intelligence Unleashed: An Argument for AI in Education.* Pearson. https://books.google.co.uk/books?id=3OZduwEACAAJ

Lupton, D., & Williamson, B. (2017). The datafied child: The dataveillance of children and implications for their rights. *New Media & Society, 19*(5), 780–794. doi:10.1177/1461444816686328

Lustria, M. L. A., Noar, S. M., Cortese, J., Van Stee, S. K., Glueckauf, R. L., & Lee, J. (2013). A meta-analysis of web-delivered tailored health behavior change interventions. *Journal of Health Communication, 18*(9), 1039–1069. doi:10.1080/10810730.2013.768727 PMID:23750972

Mahdi, O. R., Nassar, I. A., & Almsafir, M. K. (2019). Knowledge management processes and sustainable competitive advantage: An empirical examination in private universities. *Journal of Business Research, 94*, 320–334. doi:10.1016/j.jbusres.2018.02.013

Majeed, A., & Ali, M. (2018). *How Internet-of-Things (IoT) making the university campuses smart? QA higher education (QAHE) perspective.* Paper presented at the Computing and Communication Workshop and Conference (CCWC), 2018 IEEE 8th Annual.

Maksimović, M. (2018). IoT concept application in educational sector using collaboration. *Facta Universitatis, Series: Teaching. Learning and Teacher Education, 1*(2), 137–150.

Maksimović, M. (2018). IOT concept application in educational sector using collaboration. *Facta Universitatis, Series: Teaching. Learning and Teacher Education, 1*(2), 137–150.

Malone, T. W. (1982). Heuristics for designing enjoyable user interfaces: Lessons from computer games. *Proceedings of the 1982 Conference on Human Factors in Computing Systems.*

Mani, Z., & Chouk, I. (2018). Consumer Resistance to Innovation in Services: Challenges and Barriers in the Internet of Things Era. *Journal of Product Innovation Management, 35*(5), 780–807. doi:10.1111/jpim.12463

Manolev, J., Sullivan, A., & Slee, R. (2019). The datafication of discipline: ClassDojo, surveillance and a performative classroom culture. *Learning, Media and Technology, 44*(1), 36–51. doi:10.1080/17439884.2018.1558237

Manwaring, K., & Clarke, R. (2015). Surfing the third wave of computing: A framework for research into eObjects. *Computer Law & Security Review, 31*(5), 586–603. doi:10.1016/j.clsr.2015.07.001

Marczak, B., & Scott-Railton, J. (2020). *Move Fast and Roll Your Own Crypto, A Quick Look at the Confidentiality of Zoom Meetings.* https://citizenlab.ca/2020/04/move-fast-roll-your-own-crypto-a-quick-look-at-the-confidentiality-of-zoom-meetings/

Martin, F. (2008). Blackboard as the learning management system of a computer literacy course. *Journal of Online Learning and Teaching, 4*(2), 138–145.

Masrom, M., Nadzari, A. S., & Zakaria, S. A. (2016). Implementation of Mobile Learning Apps in Malaysia Higher Education Institutions. *E-Proceeding of the 4th Global Summit on Education*, 268-76.

Masters, J., & Donnison, S. (2010). First-Year Transition in Teacher Education: The Pod Experience. *Australian Journal of Teacher Education, 35*(2), 87–98.

Mayring, P. (2004). Qualitative content analysis. *A companion to Qualitative Research, 1*, 159–176.

McCallum, S., Schultz, J., Sellke, K., & Spartz, J. (2015). An examination of the flipped classroom approach on college student academic involvement. *International Journal on Teaching and Learning in Higher Education, 27*(1), 42–55.

McGrath, N., & Bayerlein, L. (2013). Engaging online students through the gamification of learning materials: The present and the future. In *ASCILITE-Australian Society for Computers in Learning in Tertiary Education Annual Conference* (pp. 573-577). Australasian Society for Computers in Learning in Tertiary Education.

McGuire, S. (2016, August 5). *9 Technology tools to engage students in the classroom. TeachThrough: We Grow Teachers.* Retrieved on June 11, 2019 from https://www.teachthought.com/technology/2019-technology-tools-engage-students-classroom/

McIsaac, M. S., Gunawardena, C. N., & Jonassen, D. (1996). Handbook of research for educational communications and technology. New York: Simon & Schuster Macmillan.

McStay, A. (2018). Emotional AI: The rise of empathic media. *Sage (Atlanta, Ga.)*.

Means, B. (2009). *Evaluation of evidence-based practices in online learning: A meta-analysis and review of online learning studies*. Centre for Learning Technology.

Middleton, C., Scheepers, R., & Kristiina, V. T. (2014). When mobile is the norm: Researching mobile information systems and mobility as post-adoption phenomena. *European Journal of Information Systems*, *23*(5), 503–512. doi:10.1057/ejis.2014.21

Mirza A. A. (2008). Is E-Learning finally gaining legitimacy in Saudi Arabia? *Applied Computing and Informatics*, *6*(2).

Mirza, A. A. (2007). Utilizing distance learning technologies to deliver courses in a segregated educational environment. *World conference on educational multimedia, hypermedia and telecommunications*. 1855–1860.

Misiejuk, K., & Wasson, B. (2017). *State of the field report on learning analytics*. Academic Press.

Mitcham, C. (2005). *Encyclopaedia of science, technology, and ethics*. Academic Press.

Miwa, K., Terai, H., Kanzaki, N., & Nakaike, R. (2014). An intelligent tutoring system with variable levels of instructional support for instructing natural deduction. *Information and Media Technologies*, *9*(1), 132–140. doi:10.1527/tjsai.29.148

Mohammed Banu, A., Trevor, W.-H., & Mostafa, M. (2018). Benefits and Challenges of Cloud Computing Adoption and Usage in Higher Education: A Systematic Literature Review. *International Journal of Enterprise Information Systems*, *14*(4), 64–77. doi:10.4018/IJEIS.2018100105

Moher, D., Liberati, A., Tetzlaff, J., & Altman, D. (2009). PRISMA Group: Methods of systematic reviews and meta-analysis: preferred reporting items for systematic reviews and meta-analyses: the PRISMA statement. *Journal of Clinical Epidemiology*, *62*(10), 1006–1012. doi:10.1016/j.jclinepi.2009.06.005 PMID:19631508

Moher, D., Liberati, A., Tetzlaff, J., & Altman, D. G. (2009). Preferred reporting items for systematic reviews and meta-analyses: The PRISMA statement. *Annals of Internal Medicine*, *151*(4), 264–269. doi:10.7326/0003-4819-151-4-200908180-00135 PMID:19622511

Mohsen, M. A., & Shafeeq, C. P. (2014). EFL Teachers' Perceptions on Blackboard Applications. *English Language Teaching*, *7*(11), 108–118.

Mollick, E. R., & Rothbard, N. (2014). *Mandatory fun: Consent, gamification and the impact of games at work*. The Wharton School research paper series.

Moodle.org. (2020). *Moodle - Open-source learning platform*. https://moodle.org/

Moore, J. L., Dickson-Deane, C., & Galyen, K. (2011). E-Learning, online learning, and distance learning environments: Are they the same? *Internet and Higher Education*, *14*(2), 129–135. doi:10.1016/j.iheduc.2010.10.001

Moore, M. G., & Kearsley, G. (2012). *Distance education: A systematic view of online learning*. Wadsworth Cengage Learning.

Morales Lucas, C., de Mingo López, L. F., & Gómez Blas, N. (2018). Natural computing applied to the underground system: A synergistic approach for smart cities. *Sensors (Basel)*, *18*(12), 4094. doi:10.339018124094 PMID:30467278

Motaghian, H., Hassanzadeh, A., & Moghadam, D. K. (2013, January). Factors affecting university instructors' adoption of web-based learning systems: Case study of Iran. *Computers & Education*, *61*(1), 158–167. doi:10.1016/j.compedu.2012.09.016

Mueck, M., & Karls, I. (2018). *Networking Vehicles to Everything: Evolving Automotive Solutions*. Walter de Gruyter GmbH & Co KG.

Muhamad, W., Kurniawan, N. B., & Yazid, S. (2017). Smart campus features, technologies, and applications: A systematic literature review. *2017 International Conference on Information Technology Systems and Innovation (ICITSI).*

Mulholland, G., & Turner, J. (2018). *Enterprising Education in UK Higher Education: Challenges for Theory and Practice.* Taylor & Francis. https://books.google.co.uk/books?id=bsuNDwAAQBAJ

Myers, M. D., & Newman, M. (2007). The qualitative interview in IS research: Examining the craft. *Information and Organization*, *17*(1), 2–26. doi:10.1016/j.infoandorg.2006.11.001

Nah, F. F.-H., Zeng, Q., Telaprolu, V. R., Ayyappa, A. P., & Eschenbrenner, B. (2014). Gamification of education: a review of literature. *International Conference on HCI in Business.*

Naidoo, R., & Williams, J. (2015). The neoliberal regime in English higher education: Charters, consumers and the erosion of the public good. *Critical Studies in Education*, *56*(2), 208–223. doi:10.1080/17508487.2014.939098

Neff, R., & Fry, J. (2009). Periodic prompts and reminders in health promotion and health behavior interventions: Systematic review. *Journal of Medical Internet Research*, *11*(2), e16.

Ng'ambi, D., Bozalek, V., & Gachago, D. (2013a). Empowering educators to teach using emerging technologies in higher education: A case of facilitating a course across institutional boundaries. In *Proceedings of the International Conference on e-Learning* (pp. 292-301). Cape Town, South Africa: Academic Press.

Ng'ambi, D., & Bozalek, V. (2013b). Leveraging informal leadership in higher education institutions: A case of diffusion of emerging technologies in a southern context. *British Journal of Educational Technology*, *44*(6), 940–950. doi:10.1111/bjet.12108

Nguyen, J., Sánchez-Hernández, G., Armisen, A., Agell, N., Rovira, X., & Angulo, C. (2018). A linguistic multi-criteria decision-aiding system to support university career services. *Applied Soft Computing*, *67*, 933–940. doi:10.1016/j.asoc.2017.06.052

Nicholas, D., Watkinson, A., Jamali, H. R., Herman, E., Tenopir, C., Volentine, R., Allard, S., & Levine, K. (2015). Peer review: Still king in the digital age. *Learned Publishing*, *28*(1), 15–21. doi:10.1087/20150104

Nimmo, R. (2011). Actor-network theory and methodology: Social research in a more-than-human world. *Methodological Innovations Online*, *6*(3), 108–119. doi:10.4256/mio.2011.010

Njeru, A. M., Omar, M. S., Yi, S., Paracha, S., & Wannous, M. (2017). *Using IoT technology to improve online education through data mining.* Paper presented at the 2017 International Conference on Applied System Innovation (ICASI). 10.1109/ICASI.2017.7988469

Noble, N., Paul, C., Carey, M., Blunden, S., & Turner, N. (2015). A randomised trial assessing the acceptability and effectiveness of providing generic versus tailored feedback about health risks for a high need primary care sample. *BMC Family Practice*, *16*(1), 95. doi:10.118612875-015-0309-7 PMID:26243144

Noura, M., Atiquzzaman, M., & Gaedke, M. (2018). Interoperability in Internet of Things: Taxonomies and Open Challenges. *Mobile Networks and Applications.*

O'Donovan, P., Gallagher, C., Leahy, K., & O'Sullivan, D. T. J. (2019). A comparison of fog and cloud computing cyber-physical interfaces for Industry 4.0 real-time embedded machine learning engineering applications. *Computers in Industry*, *110*, 12–35. doi:10.1016/j.compind.2019.04.016

Oberländer, A. M., Röglinger, M., Rosemann, M., Kees, A., Ågerfalk, P., & Tuunainen, V. (2018). Conceptualizing business-to-thing interactions – A sociomaterial perspective on the Internet of Things. *European Journal of Information Systems*, *27*(4), 486–502. doi:10.1080/0960085X.2017.1387714

Office of Educational Technology. (2017). Reimagining the Role of Technology in Education. Retrieved on January 1, 2020 from https://tech.ed.gov/files/2017/01/NETP17.pdf.

Office of Educational Technology. (2019). 2020 National Educational Technology Plan. Retrieved January 1, 2020 from https://tech.ed.gov/files/2017/01/NETP17.pdf.

Olsson, M., Mozelius, P., & Collin, J. (2015). Visualisation and Gamification of e-Learning and Programming Education. *Electronic Journal of E-Learning, 13*(6), 441-454.

Osguthorpe, R. T., & Graham, C. R. (2003). Blended learning environments: Definitions and directions. *Quarterly Review of Distance Education, 4*(3), 227-33.

Osguthorpe, R. T., & Graham, C. R. (2003). Blended learning environments: Definitions and directions. *Quarterly Review of Distance Education*, *4*(3), 227–233.

Owayid, A. M., & Uden, L. (2014, September). The usage of Google apps services in higher education. In *International Workshop on Learning Technology for Education in Cloud* (pp. 95-104). Springer. 10.1007/978-3-319-10671-7_9

Oyaid, A. A. (2009). *Education policy in Saudi Arabia and its relation to secondary school teachers. ICT Use, Perceptions, and Views of the Future of ICT in Education* (Ph.D. Thesis). University of Exeter, UK.

Ozturk, Z. K., Cicek, Z., & Ergul, Z. (2017). Sentiment Analysis: An Application to Anadolu University. *Acta Physica Polonica A*, *132*(3), 753–755. doi:10.12693/APhysPolA.132.753

Palloff, R. M., Pratt, K., & Stockley, D. (2001). Building learning communities in cyberspace: Effective strategies for the online classroom. *The Canadian Journal of Higher Education*, *31*(3), 175.

Parker, P. (2015). The Historical Role of Women in Higher Education. *Administrative Issues Journal: Connecting Education, Practice, and Research*, *5*(1), 3–14. doi:10.5929/2015.5.1.1

Pascarella, E. T., & Terenzini, P. T. (2005). *How College Affects Students: A Third Decade of Research* (Vol. 2). ERIC.

Pasquale, F. (2015). *The black box society*. Harvard University Press. doi:10.4159/harvard.9780674736061

Patel, P., & Cassou, D. (2015). Enabling high-level application development for the Internet of Things. *Journal of Systems and Software*, *103*, 62–84. doi:10.1016/j.jss.2015.01.027

Pauget, B., & Dammak, A. (2019). The implementation of the Internet of Things: What impact on organizations? *Technological Forecasting and Social Change*, *140*, 140–146. doi:10.1016/j.techfore.2018.03.012

Pechenkina, E. (2017). Developing a typology of mobile apps in higher education: A national case-study. *Australasian Journal of Educational Technology*, *33*(4).

Pellini, A., Hub, E. & Jordan, K. (2020). *Education during the COVID-19 crisis*. Academic Press.

Peraya, D., Piguet, A., & Joye, F. (1999) Rapport d'information sur les mondes virtuels. Rapport rédigé pour l»office fédéral de la formation professionnelle et le la technique, Berne, Suisse.

Pérez-Expósito, J. P., Fernández-Caramés, T. M., Fraga-Lamas, P., & Castedo, L. (2017). VineSens: An eco-smart decision-support viticulture system. *Sensors (Basel)*, *17*(3), 465. doi:10.339017030465 PMID:28245619

Perez, S., Massey-Allard, J., Butler, D., Ives, J., Bonn, D., Yee, N., & Roll, I. (2017). Identifying productive inquiry in virtual labs using sequence mining. *International Conference on Artificial Intelligence in Education.*

Perkin, N., & Abraham, P. (2017). *Building the Agile Business through Digital Transformation.* Kogan Page Stylus.

Petimani, M. S., & Adake, P. (2015). Blackboard versus PowerPoint presentation: Students opinion in medical education. *International Journal of Educational and Psychological Researches, 1*(4), 289. doi:10.4103/2395-2296.163935

Petrov, C. (2019). *Internet Of Things Statistics 2020.* Available: https://techjury.net/stats-about/internet-of-things-statistics/

Phelps, E. S. (1975). *Altruism, Morality, and Economic Theory.* Russell Sage Foundation. https://books.google.co.uk/books?id=fIS4BgAAQBAJ

Piattoeva, N., & Boden, R. (2020). *Escaping numbers? The ambiguities of the governance of education through data.* Taylor & Francis. doi:10.1080/09620214.2020.1725590

Pinna, A., & Ruttenberg, W. (2016). *Distributed ledger technologies in securities post-trading revolution or evolution?* ECB Occasional Paper 172.

Pisa, M., & Juden, M. (2017). Blockchain and economic development: Hype vs. reality. *Center for Global Development Policy Paper, 107*, 150.

Pittaway, S. M. (2012). Student and staff engagement: Developing an engagement framework in a faculty of education. *Australian Journal of Teacher Education, 37*(4), 3. doi:10.14221/ajte.2012v37n4.8

Pompei, L., Mattoni, B., Bisegna, F., Nardecchia, F., Fichera, A., Gagliano, A., & Pagano, A. (2018). Composite Indicators for Smart Campus: Data Analysis Method. *2018 IEEE International Conference on Environment and Electrical Engineering and 2018 IEEE Industrial and Commercial Power Systems Europe (EEEIC/I&CPS Europe).*

Poonia, P., Jain, V. K., & Kumar, A. (2018). Short Term Traffic Flow Prediction Methodologies: A Review. *Mody University International Journal of Computing and Engineering Research, 2*, 37–39.

Popenici, S. A., & Kerr, S. (2017). Exploring the impact of artificial intelligence on teaching and learning in higher education. *Research and Practice in Technology Enhanced Learning, 12*(1), 22. doi:10.1007/978-3-319-61425-0_24

Prado, J. C., & Marzal, M. Á. (2013). Incorporating data literacy into information literacy programs: Core competencies and contents. *Libri, 63*(2), 123–134.

Prandi, C., Monti, L., Ceccarini, C., & Salomoni, P. (2019). Smart campus: Fostering the community awareness through an intelligent environment. *Mobile Networks and Applications*, •••, 1–8.

Prinsloo, P. (2017). Fleeing from Frankenstein's monster and meeting Kafka on the way: Algorithmic decision-making in higher education. *E-Learning and Digital Media, 14*(3), 138–163. doi:10.1177/2042753017731355

Qin, W., Li, B., Zhang, J., Gao, S., & He, Y. (2014). *Design and Implementation of IoT Security System Towards Campus Safety.* Paper presented at the Advanced Technologies in Ad Hoc and Sensor Networks, Berlin, Germany. 10.1007/978-3-642-54174-2_27

Quaicoe, J., & & Pata, K. (2017). Basic school teachers' perspective to digital teaching and learning in Ghana. *Education and Information Technologies.* Advance online publication. doi:10.100710639-017-9660-8

Quintieri, R. (2015). *What is REALab?* https://uomrealab.wordpress.com/what-is-realab/

Rappaport, T. S., Xing, Y., Kanhere, O., Ju, S., Madanayake, A., Mandal, S., Alkhateeb, A., & Trichopoulos, G. C. (2019). Wireless communications and applications above 100 GHz: Opportunities and challenges for 6G and beyond. *IEEE Access: Practical Innovations, Open Solutions*, *7*, 78729–78757. doi:10.1109/ACCESS.2019.2921522

Redden, E. (2020). Zoombombing' Attacks Disrupt Classes. *Inside Higher Ed.* https://www.insidehighered.com/news/2020/03/26/zoombombers-disrupt-online-classes-racist-pornographic-content

Rehman, U. U., & Iqbal, A. (2020). *Nexus of knowledge-oriented leadership, knowledge management, innovation and organizational performance in higher education. Business Process Management Journal.* Ahead-of-print.

Reid, D., Bussiere, D., & Greenaway, K. (2001). Alliance formation issues for knowledge-based enterprises. *International Journal of Management Reviews*, *3*(1), 79–100. doi:10.1111/1468-2370.00055

Richman, L. J., & Parrish, A. (2017). Introduction to Themed Issue: Technology to Support and Enhance Professional Development Schools. *School-University Partnerships*, *10*(3), 1–4.

Rickey, V. F. (1987). Isaac Newton: Man, Myth, and Mathematics. *The College Mathematics Journal*, *18*(5), 362–389. doi:10.1080/07468342.1987.11973060

Rippa, P., & Secundo, G. (2019). Digital academic entrepreneurship: The potential of digital technologies on academic entrepreneurship. *Technological Forecasting and Social Change, Elsevier*, *146*(C), 900–911. doi:10.1016/j.techfore.2018.07.013

Rittinghouse, J. W., & Ransome, J. F. (2016). *Cloud computing: implementation, management, and security.* CRC Press.

Roberts-Holmes, G., & Bradbury, A. (2016). The datafication of early years education and its impact upon pedagogy. *Improving Schools*, *19*(2), 119–128. doi:10.1177/1365480216651519

Robinson, C. C., & Hullinger, H. (2008). New benchmarks in higher education: Student engagement in online learning. *Journal of Education for Business*, *84*(2), 101–109.

Robinson, C. C., & Hullinger, H. (2008). New Benchmarks in Higher Education: Student Engagement in Online Learning. *Journal of Education for Business*, *84*(2), 101–109. doi:10.3200/JOEB.84.2.101-109

Rohrer, D. (2015). Student instruction should be distributed over long time periods. *Educational Psychology Review*, *27*(4), 635–643. doi:10.100710648-015-9332-4

Rose, K., Eldridge, S., & Chapin, L. (2015). *The internet of things: An overview.* The Internet Society.

Rovai, A. P. (2003). In search of higher persistence rates in distance education online programs. *The Internet and Higher Education*, *6*(1), 1–16. doi:10.1016/S1096-7516(02)00158-6

Rushby, N., & Surry, D. (2016). *The Wiley Handbook of Learning Technology.* Wiley.

Russell, S., & Norvig, P. (2016). *Artificial intelligence: a modern approach.* Academic Press.

Russell, S., & Norvig, P. (2016). *Artificial Intelligence: A Modern Approach.* CreateSpace Independent Publishing Platform. https://books.google.co.uk/books?id=PQI7vgAACAAJ

Ryan, S. M., & Grubbs, W. T. (2017). *Curricular Collaborations: Using Emerging Technologies to Foster Innovative Partnerships. In 3D Printing: Breakthroughs in Research and Practice.* IGI Global.

Saadé, R. G., He, X., & Kira, D. (2007). Exploring dimensions to online learning. *Computers in Human Behavior*, *23*(4), 1721–1739.

Saidhbi, S. (2012). A cloud computing framework for Ethiopian Higher Education Institutions. *IOSR Journal of Computer Engineering, 6*, 1–9.

Sánchez, L. E., Santos-Olmo, A., Álvarez, E., Huerta, M., Camacho, S., & Fernández-Medina, E. (2016). Development of an Expert System for the Evaluation of Students' Curricula on the Basis of Competencies. *Future Internet, 8*(2), 22. doi:10.3390/fi8020022

Sander, T. H. (2002). Social capital and new urbanism: Leading a civic horse to water? *National Civic Review, 91*(3), 213–234. doi:10.1002/ncr.91302

Sarker, S., Sarker, S., & Sidorova, A. (2006). Understanding Business Process Change Failure: An Actor-Network Perspective. *Journal of Management Information Systems, 23*(1), 51–86. doi:10.2753/MIS0742-1222230102

Saxena, S. (2013, October 8). How Important is use of Technology in Education. *EdTech Review*. Retrieved on June 11, 2019 from http://edtechreview.in/news/2681-technology-in-education

Schiaffino, S., Garcia, P., & Amandi, A. (2008). eTeacher: Providing personalized assistance to e-learning students. *Computers & Education, 51*(4), 1744–1754. doi:10.1016/j.compedu.2008.05.008

Schleicher, A. (2015). *Schools for 21st-Century Learners: Strong Leaders, Confident Teachers, Innovative Approaches*. International Summit on the Teaching Profession. ERIC. doi:10.1787/9789264231191-en

Schneider, F., de Vries, H., Candel, M., van de Kar, A., & van Osch, L. (2013). Periodic email prompts to re-use an internet-delivered computer-tailored lifestyle program: Influence of prompt content and timing. *Journal of Medical Internet Research, 15*(1), e23. doi:10.2196/jmir.2151 PMID:23363466

Schön, D. (1988). Educating the reflective practitioner. San Francisco, C.A.: Jossey-Bass.

Secolsky, C., & Denison, D. B. (Eds.). (2012). *Handbook on measurement, assessment, and evaluation in higher education*. Routledge. doi:10.4324/9780203142189

Selwyn, N. (2016). *Is Technology Good for Education?* Wiley. https://books.google.co.uk/books?id=XLtQDAAAQBAJ

Shams, S. R., & Belyaeva, Z. (2019). Quality assurance driving factors as antecedents of knowledge management: A stakeholder-focussed perspective in higher education. *Journal of the Knowledge Economy, 10*(2), 423–436. doi:10.100713132-017-0472-2

Shea, P., Bidjerano, T., & Vickers, J. (2016). Faculty Attitudes toward Online Learning: Failures and Successes. SUNY Research Network.

Sheikh, S. (2020). *Understanding the Role of Artificial Intelligence and Its Future Social Impact*. IGI Global.

Shuler, C., Levine, Z., & Ree, J. (2012). *iLearn II An analysis of the education category of Apple's app store*. Academic Press.

Shum, S. J. B., & Luckin, R. (2019). Learning analytics and AI: Politics, pedagogy and practices. *British Journal of Educational Technology, 50*(6), 2785–2793. doi:10.1111/bjet.12880

Siemens, G., & Long, P. (2011). Penetrating the fog: Analytics in learning and education. *EDUCAUSE Review, 46*, 30.

Slade, S., & Prinsloo, P. (2013). Learning analytics: Ethical issues and dilemmas. *American Behavioral Scientist, 57*(10), 1510–1529.

Slade, S., & Prinsloo, P. (2013). Learning analytics: Ethical issues and dilemmas. *The American Behavioral Scientist, 57*(10), 1510–1529. doi:10.1177/0002764213479366

Smart, O., & Burrell, L. (2015). Genetic programming and frequent itemset mining to identify feature selection patterns of iEEG and fMRI epilepsy data. *Engineering Applications of Artificial Intelligence*, *39*, 198–214. doi:10.1016/j.engappai.2014.12.008 PMID:25580059

Sokol, A.W., & Hogan, M.D. (2013). *NIST Cloud Computing Standards Roadmap*. NIST.

Srivastava, T. (2014, May 7). Build a word cloud using text mining tools of R. *Analytics Vidhya*. Retrieved on Apri 25, 2019 from https://www.analyticsvidhya.com/blog/2014/2005/build-word-cloud-text-mining-tools/

Stanford-Bowers, D. E. (2008). Persistence in online classes: A study of perceptions among community college stakeholders. *Journal of Online Learning and Teaching*, *4*(1), 37–50.

Stein, D. (2000). *Teaching critical reflection* (Myths and realities No. 7). Columbus, OH: ERIC Clearinghouse on Adult, Career, and Vocational Education. (ED445256)

Steiner-Khamsi, G. (2003). The politics of league tables. *Journal of Social Science Education*.

Stewart, S. C., Witte, J. E., & Witte, M. M. (2019). Workforce Development and Higher Education Partnerships: Transdisciplinarity in Practice. In Handbook of Research on Transdisciplinary Knowledge Generation (pp. 369-382). IGI Global.

Stone, C. (2017). *Opportunity through online learning: Improving student access, participation and success in higher education*. National Centre for Student Equity in Higher Education.

Subhash, S., & Cudney, E. A. (2018). Gamified learning in higher education: A systematic review of the literature. *Computers in Human Behavior*, *87*, 192–206. doi:10.1016/j.chb.2018.05.028

Subrahmanyam, K., & Renukarya, B. (2015). Digital Games and Learning: Identifying Pathways of Influence. *Educational Psychologist*, *50*(4), 335–348. doi:10.1080/00461520.2015.1122532

Subramanian, S., & Seshasaayee, A. (2014). Review & Proposal for a Cloud based Framework for Indian Higher Education. *International Journal of Engineering and Computer Science*, *3*, 3689–3694.

Su, C. H., & Cheng, C. H. (2015). A mobile gamification learning system for improving the learning motivation and achievements. *Journal of Computer Assisted Learning*, *31*(3), 268–286. doi:10.1111/jcal.12088

Summers, D. (2009). David Cameron warns of ‘new age of austerity’. *The Guardian*.

Suomi, K., Kuoppakangas, P., Hytti, U., Hampden-Turner, C., & Kangaslahti, J. (2014). Focusing on dilemmas challenging reputation management in higher education. *International Journal of Educational Management*, *28*(4), 461–478. doi:10.1108/IJEM-04-2013-0046

Suppes, P. (1971). *Computer-Assisted Instruction at Stanford* (Technical Report 174). Stanford.

Swan, M. (2015). *Blockchain: Blueprint for a New Economy*. O’Reilly Media. https://books.google.co.uk/books?id=4vFiBgAAQBAJ

Sweetser, P., & Wyeth, P. (2005). GameFlow: A model for evaluating player enjoyment in games. *Computers in Entertainment*, *3*(3), 3–3. doi:10.1145/1077246.1077253

Talari, S., Shafie-Khah, M., Siano, P., Loia, V., Tommasetti, A., & Catalão, J. (2017). A review of smart cities based on the internet of things concept. *Energies*, *10*(4), 421. doi:10.3390/en10040421

Tegmark, M. (2017). *Life 3.0: Being Human in the Age of Artificial Intelligence*. Penguin Books Limited. https://books.google.co.uk/books?id=3_otDwAAQBAJ

Tekic, Z., & Koroteev, D. (2019). From disruptively digital to proudly analog: A holistic typology of digital transformation strategies. *Business Horizons*, *62*(6), 683–693. doi:10.1016/j.bushor.2019.07.002

TEQSA. (2018). *The Tertiary Education Quality & Standards Agency*. Regulatory Risk Framework, Tertiary Education Quality and Standards Agency.

Terill, B. (2008). *My Coverage of Lobby of the Social Gaming Summit*. Retrieved 7th Mar from http://www.bretterrill.com/2008/06/my-coverage-of-lobby-of-social-gaming.html

Tesoa, E., Olmedillab, M., Martínez-Torres, M. R., & Toral, S. L. (2018, April). Application of text mining techniques to the analysis of discourse in eWOM communications from a gender perspective. *Technological Forecasting and Social Change*, *129*, 131–142. doi:10.1016/j.techfore.2017.12.018

The Commonwelath of Learning. (2002). *An Introduction to Open and Distance Learning*. Available from http://www.col.org/ODLIntro/introODL.htm

The Open University. (2019). *50 Years: a movement of millions, a mission of one*. www.50.open.ac.uk

Thowfeek, M. H., & Hussin, H. (2008). Instructors' perspective on e-learning adoption in Sri Lanka: A preliminary investigation. *Communications of the IBIMA*, *6*, 124–129.

Tiahrt, T., & Porter, J. C. (2016). What do I do with this flipping classroom: Ideas for effectively using class time in a flipped course. Elm Street Press.

Tierney, W. G., & Lanford, M. (2018). Institutional culture in higher education. Encyclopedia of international higher education systems and institutions, 1-7.

Tierney, W. G., & Lanford, M. (2016). Conceptualizing innovation in higher education. In *Higher education: Handbook of theory and research* (pp. 1–40). Springer. doi:10.1007/978-3-319-26829-3_1

Times Higher Education. (2020). *World University Rankings 2020*. Times Higher Education - World University Rankings. https://www.timeshighereducation.com/world-university-rankings/2020/world-ranking#!/page/0/length/25/sort_by/rank/sort_order/asc/cols/stats

Timmis, S., & Muhuro, P. (2019). De-coding or de-colonising the technocratic university? Rural students' digital transitions to South African higher education. *Learning, Media and Technology*, *44*(3), 252–266. doi:10.1080/17439884.2019.1623250

Tisdell, E. J. (1993). Interlocking Systems of Power, Privilege, and Oppression in Adult Higher Education Classes. *Adult Education Quarterly*, *43*(4), 203–226. doi:10.1177/0741713693043004001

Tokmak, H. S., Yakin, I., & Dogusoy, B. (2019, January). Prospective English teachers' digital storytelling experiences through a flipped classroom approach. *International Journal of Distance Education Technologies*, *17*(1), 78–99. doi:10.4018/IJDET.2019010106

Touri, M., & Koteyko, N. (2015). Using corpus linguistic software in the extraction of news frames: Towards a dynamic process of frame analysis in journalistic texts. *International Journal of Research Methodology*, *18*(6), 601–616. doi:10.1080/13645579.2014.929878

Trilling, D., & Jonkman, J. G. F. (2018). Scaling up content analysis. *Communication Methods and Measures*, *12*(2-3), 158–174. doi:10.1080/19312458.2018.1447655

Trowler, V. (2010). Student engagement literature review. *The Higher Education Academy*, *11*(1), 1–15.

Tsai, Y. S., Poquet, O., Gašević, D., Dawson, S., & Pardo, A. (2019). Complexity leadership in learning analytics: Drivers, challenges and opportunities. *British Journal of Educational Technology*, *50*(6), 2839–2854. doi:10.1111/bjet.12846

Tsohou, A., Karyda, M., Kokolakis, S., & Kiountouzis, E. (2015). Managing the introduction of information security awareness programmes in organisations. *European Journal of Information Systems*, *24*(1), 38–58. doi:10.1057/ejis.2013.27

University and College Union. (2020). The automatic university - a review of datafication and automation in higher education. *UCU*, 1-55.

Univiersity of Westminster. (2020). *Using Blackboard*. Retrieved 24th June from https://www.westminster.ac.uk/current-students/studies/online-learning

Uslaner, E. M. (2003). Volunteering and social capital: how trust and religion shape civic participation in the United States. In Social capital and participation in everyday life (pp. 104-117). Routledge.

Vaibhav, A., & Gupta, P. (2014, December). Gamification of MOOCs for increasing user engagement. In *2014 IEEE International Conference on MOOC, Innovation and Technology in Education (MITE)* (pp. 290-295). IEEE. 10.1109/MITE.2014.7020290

Valentine & Doug. (2002). Distance Learning: Promises, Problems, and Possibilities. *Online Journal of Distance Learning Administration, 5*(3).

Valenti, S., Cucchiarelli, A., & Panti, M. (2001). A framework for the evaluation of test management systems. *Current Issues in Education (Tempe, Ariz.)*, *4*(6).

Valks, B., Arkesteijn, M., & Den Heijer, A. (2019). *Smart campus tools 2.0 exploring the use of real-time space use measurement at universities and organizations*. Facilities. doi:10.1108/F-11-2018-0136

Vaquero, L.M., Rodero-Merino, L., Caceres, J., & Lindner, M. (2008). *A break in the clouds: towards a cloud definition*. Academic Press.

Vasileva, R., Rodrigues, L., Hughes, N., Greenhalgh, C., Goulden, M., & Tennison, J. (2018). What Smart Campuses Can Teach Us about Smart Cities: User Experiences and Open Data. *Information*, *9*(10), 251. doi:10.3390/info9100251

Vayre, E., & Vonthron, A. M. (2019). Relational and psychological factors affecting exam participation and student achievement in online college courses. *Internet and Higher Education, 43*(May), 100671.

Vázquez-Cano, E. (2014). Mobile distance learning with smartphones and apps in higher education. *Educational Sciences: Theory and Practice*, *14*(4), 1505–1520.

Villegas-Ch, W., & Luján-Mora, S. (2017). Analysis of data mining techniques applied to LMS for personalized education. *2017 IEEE World Engineering Education Conference (EDUNINE).*

Villegas-Ch, W., Molina-Enriquez, J., Chicaiza-Tamayo, C., Ortiz-Garcés, I., & Luján-Mora, S. (2019). Application of a Big Data Framework for Data Monitoring on a Smart Campus. *Sustainability*, *11*(20), 5552. doi:10.3390/su11205552

Vlugter, P., Knott, A., McDonald, J., & Hall, C. (2009). Dialogue-based CALL: A case study on teaching pronouns. *Computer Assisted Language Learning*, *22*(2), 115–131. doi:10.1080/09588220902778260

Vohra, R., & Das, N. N. (2011). Intelligent decision support systems for admission management in higher education institutes. *International Journal of Artificial Intelligence & Applications*, *2*(4), 63–70. doi:10.5121/ijaia.2011.2406

Wang, A. Y., & Newlin, M. H. (2002). Predictors of performance in the virtual classroom: Identifying and helping at-risk cyber-students. *THE Journal*, *29*(10), 21.

Wang, J., Ma, Y., Zhang, L., Gao, R. X., & Wu, D. (2018). Deep learning for smart manufacturing: Methods and applications. *Journal of Manufacturing Systems*, *48*, 144–156. doi:10.1016/j.jmsy.2018.01.003

Wang, M., & Ng, J. W. (2012). Intelligent mobile cloud education: smart anytime-anywhere learning for the next generation campus environment. *2012 Eighth International Conference on Intelligent Environments.*

Wang, T.-H. (2007). What strategies are effective for formative assessment in an e-learning environment? *Journal of Computer Assisted Learning*, *23*(3), 171–186.

Waters, J., & Brooks, R. (2010). Accidental achievers? International higher education, class reproduction and privilege in the experiences of UK students overseas. *British Journal of Sociology of Education*, *31*(2), 217–228. doi:10.1080/01425690903539164

Wattal, S., Telang, R., Mukhopadhyay, T., & Boatwright, P. (2012). What's in a "name"? Impact of use of customer information in e-mail advertisements. *Information Systems Research, 23*(3-part-1), 679-697.

Webb, J., & Hume, D. (2018). *Campus IoT collaboration and governance using the NIST cybersecurity framework.* Academic Press.

Wei, P., & Zhou, Z. (2018). Research on security of information sharing in Internet of Things based on key algorithm. *Future Generation Computer Systems*, *88*, 599–605. doi:10.1016/j.future.2018.04.035

Welbers, K., Konijn, E. A., Burgers, C., de Vaate, A. B., Eden, A., & Brugman, B. C. (2019). Gamification as a tool for engaging student learning: A field experiment with a gamified app. *E-Learning and Digital Media*, *16*(2), 92–109. doi:10.1177/2042753018818342

Welham, D. (2008). AI in training (1980–2000): Foundation for the future or misplaced optimism? *British Journal of Educational Technology*, *39*(2), 287–296. doi:10.1111/j.1467-8535.2008.00818.x

Westfall, R. S. (1993). *The Life of Isaac Newton.* Cambridge University Press.

Whitmore, A., Agarwal, A., & Da Xu, L. (2015). The Internet of Things—A survey of topics and trends. *Information Systems Frontiers*, *17*(2), 261–274. doi:10.100710796-014-9489-2

Williamson, B. (2015). Algorithmic skin: Health-tracking technologies, personal analytics and the biopedagogies of digitized health and physical education. *Sport Education and Society*, *20*(1), 133–151. doi:10.1080/13573322.2014.962494

Williamson, B. (2017). Big data in education: The digital future of learning, policy and practice. *Sage (Atlanta, Ga.).*

Will, L. (1997). *Opportunities and constraints for the use of consultants in museum documentation.* CIDOC Jahrestagung.

Wilsdon, J. (2016). The metric tide: Independent review of the role of metrics in research assessment and management. *Sage (Atlanta, Ga.).*

Wilson, F. (1997). The truth is out there: The search for emancipatory principles in information systems design. *Information Technology & People*, *10*(2), 187–204. doi:10.1108/09593849710178207

Wladis, C., Conway, K. M., & Hachey, A. C. (2016). Assessing readiness for online education—Research models for identifying students at risk. *Online Learning*, *20*(3), 97–109.

Wolfenden, B. (2019). Gamification as a winning cyber security strategy. *Computer Fraud & Security*, *2019*(5), 9–12. doi:10.1016/S1361-3723(19)30052-1

World Health Organisation. (2020). *Coronavirus (COVID-19) events as they happen.* https://www.who.int/emergencies/diseases/novel-coronavirus-2019/events-as-they-happen

Wulff, R. L., & Palacios, G. (1991). We/They The care and feeding of museum consultants. *Museum International*, *43*(4), 188–190.

Xia, F., Yang, L. T., Wang, L., & Vinel, A. (2012). Internet of Things. *International Journal of Communication Systems*, *25*(9), 1101–1102. doi:10.1002/dac.2417

Xing, B., & Marwala, T. (2017). Implications of the fourth industrial age for higher education. *The Thinker, 73*.

Xu, Y. (2011). *Literature review on web application gamification and analytics*. Honolulu, HI: University of Hawaii. CSDL Technical Report 11–05.

Xu, X., Li, D., Sun, M., Yang, S., Yu, S., Manogaran, G., Mastorakis, G., & Mavromoustakis, C. X. (2019). Research on key technologies of smart campus teaching platform based on 5G network. *IEEE Access: Practical Innovations, Open Solutions*, *7*, 20664–20675. doi:10.1109/ACCESS.2019.2894129

Yang, K. C. C., & Kang, Y. W. (2018, October 27-29). *Global communication educators' responses to the new media landscape: A text mining approach to understand trends and future developments in communication curricula around the world.* Paper Presented at The New Paradigms in Communication Education Stream, The Asian Congress for Media and Communication (ACMC) 2018 International Conference, National Chengchi University, Taiwan.

Yang, K. C. C., & Kang, Y. W. (2020). The effectiveness of gamification on students' engagement, learning outcomes, and learning experiences. In Handbook of Research Creating Meaningful Experiences in Online Courses (pp. 286-305). Hershey, PA: IGI-Global Publisher.

Yang, C., & Huang, Q. (2013). *Spatial cloud computing: a practical approach*. CRC Press. doi:10.1201/b16106

Yang, Z. (2011). Study on an Interoperable Cloud framework for e-Education. In *2011 International Conference on E-Business and E-Government (ICEE)*. IEEE. 10.1109/ICEBEG.2011.5887174

Yan, Y., & Zhang, Z. (2019). Knowledge Transfer, Sharing, and Management System Based on Causality for Requirements Change Management. In *Proceedings of the 2019 3rd International Conference on Information System and Data Mining* (pp. 201-207). 10.1145/3325917.3325947

Yeh, H. T., & Lahman, M. (2007). Pre-Service Teachers' Perceptions of Asynchronous Online Discussion on Blackboard. *Qualitative Report*, *12*(4), 680–704.

Yin, R. K. (2013). *Case study research: Design and methods*. Sage publications.

Young, J. R. (2012). Inside the Coursera contract: How an upstart company might profit from free courses. *The Chronicle of Higher Education*, *19*(7).

Young, S. (2006). Student Views of Effective Online Teaching in Higher Education. *International Journal of Phytoremediation*, *21*(1), 65–77.

Zawacki-Richter, O., Marín, V. I., Bond, M., & Gouverneur, F. (2019). Systematic review of research on artificial intelligence applications in higher education–where are the educators? *International Journal of Educational Technology in Higher Education*, *16*(1), 39. doi:10.118641239-019-0171-0

Zhang, Y., Chen, M., & Liu, L. (2015). A review on text mining. In *2015 6th IEEE International Conference on Software Engineering and Service Science (ICSESS)* (pp. 681-685). New York, NY: IEEE. 10.1109/ICSESS.2015.7339149

Zhang, Y., Dang, Y., & Amer, B. (2016, November). A large-scale blended and flipped class: Class design and investigation of factors influencing students' intention to learn. *IEEE Transactions on Education, 59*(4), 263–273. doi:10.1109/TE.2016.2535205

Zhu, Z.-T., Yu, M.-H., & Riezebos, P. (2016). A research framework of smart education. *Smart Learning Environments, 3*(1), 4. doi:10.118640561-016-0026-2

Ziegler, G. (2019). Knowledge Management System: Designing a Virtual Community of Practice for Higher Education. In *Intelligent Computing-Proceedings of the Computing Conference* (pp. 1009-1029). Springer.

Zuber, W. J. (2016). The flipped classroom, a review of the literature. *Industrial and Commercial Training, 48*(2), 97–103. doi:10.1108/ICT-05-2015-0039

# About the Contributors

**Mohammed Banu Ali** is a PhD holder from Manchester Business School and Teaching Fellow of the Higher Education Academy who is currently an active Director of PhD supervisory at the University of Bolton's Centre for Islamic Finance and research assistant at the Alliance Manchester Business School. His research interests are digital strategy, technological innovation and organisational transformation. As a Teaching Fellow (FHEA), Mohammed as obtained a vast pool of knowledge in areas such as the Teaching Excellence Framework (TEF) and the Research Excellence Framework. He also has a growing number of publications on Cloud Computing and ERP systems adoption, as well as contributing to several co-author publications in the area of Social Media, mHealth systems, IoT and Artificial Intelligence. He has been a reviewer for several research journals where he has shared his wide pool of knowledge, experience and skills. Mohammed is also an associate editor and a member of the Editorial Advisory Board of the following journals

**Trevor Wood-Harper** holds the Emeritus Chair of Information Systems (IS) and Systemic Change at the Alliance Manchester Business School (AMBS) having been recruited in 2003 to re-vision Information Systems & Management Research and Doctor- al Education on the merger of University of Manchester Institute of Science and Technology (UMIST) with the Victoria University of Manchester (VUM). He has held visiting chairs at the following universities: Oslo; South Australia (A$500K funding); New South Wales, Sydney; Cape Town; Napier, Edinburgh; Georgia State, Atlanta and Copenhagen Business School. Currently AMBS has world ranking 37 and in the UK 6. He has acted as an external examiner for many BSc, MSc and MBA courses including LSE and Warwick. For 10 years he was a member of the British Computer Society (BCS) Validation Panel for undergraduate degrees. Also he has acted, as an advisor on university periodic research review panels with the most recent was Henley Business School, Reading.

* * *

**Mohammed Abdel-Haq** is a Professor in Banking and a Director of the Centre for Islamic Finance at the University of Bolton. He is also Executive Director of the Centre for Opposition Studies and Assistant Vice Chancellor for Postgraduate Developments at the University of Bolton. He is the Principal of Hume Institute for Postgraduate Studies, Switzerland. Mohammed has a long career in banking in major financial institutions such as Citi Bank, Deutsche Bank, ABN AMRO and HSBC. He is also the CEO of Oakstone Merchant Bank. Mohammed was the Chairman for the Advisory Task and Finish Group on Taxi and Private Hire Vehicle Licensing whose report has been recently published by the UK

Government. He was a member of the Council of the Royal Institute for International Affairs (Chatham House) from 2011-2014. In 2011 Mohammed was appointed Chairman of the UK Ministerial Advisory Group on Extremism in Universities and FE Colleges and he was a Member of the UK Government Task Force for Islamic Finance.

**Ahmed Abdulkhaleq** received his BSc in Communications Engineering with a first-class from the University of Mosul, Iraq in 2009. In 2010-2011, he worked as an engineer at the college of Electronics, University of Mosul, Iraq. In 2011-2013, he received a scholarship from the Higher Committee for Education Development in Iraq (HCED-Iraq) to complete his master's degree. In 2013, he was awarded the MSc degree in Personal Mobile and Satellite Communications with distinction from the University of Bradford, UK. In 2013-2017, he worked as a lecturer at the University of Nineveh, Iraq. Since 2018, Ahmed has been appointed as an Early-Stage Researcher (ESR). Ahmed is an author and co-author of many international journal and conference papers. His research interests include energy-efficient RF power amplifiers, Digital Signal Processing (DSP), filters, antenna array processing and reconfigurable transceivers.

**Alaa Abdulrahman S. Al-Amoudi** is a lecturer at the Human Resources Management Department at Prince Nourah University, KSA. She holds a Master degree in Human Resources Management from the Catholic University of America, USA. She is a Certified Trainer from the Technical Vocational Training Corporation. She has extensive experience in organizing conferences and leading students' unions.

**Abubakar Albakri** is a post-graduate candidate. His main field of interest is IT project management, computing security, information security and telecommunications and networking. Eng. Abubakar is currently also involved in various projects related to the latest trends in the IT field. Prior to his post-graduate studies, Eng. Abubakar has been involved in various collaborative projects with Aston University. Future plans involve publishing in high impact factor journals in his field of study.

**Omar Albakri** is an expert in telecommunications and networking. He obtained his first degree from Birmingham City University in which he obtained a first-class. Eng. Omar also has over 10 years of experience in the field of information systems, computer science and telecommunications and networks.

**Fahad Alhazmi**, MHA, PhD, Assistant Professor of Healthcare Services Administration at King Abdulaziz Universty. Dr. Alhazmi worked as Project Assistant at Tufts Medical Center in Boston, MA, USA. While his time at Tufts, Dr. Alhazmi worked on several projects including, increasing patients satisfaction, implementing calculated risk management, and improving patients' discharge time.. Dr. Alhazmi teaches undergrad and graduate level at King Abdulaziz University, his main research interests are Healthcare Organizations and Ethics, Patients Safety, and Quality Management, Healthcare Policy, Organizational Behaviour, Conflicts of Interest in Healthcare

**Chris Bamber** has been Managing Director and Dean of the Organisational Learning Centre (OLC) for 21 years. Prior to that worked as Operations Manager for a multi-national manufacturing company for 8 years and prior to this worked as Quality Manager for a leading U.K manufacturing organisation. Chris now draws upon over 38 years industry and academic experience to provide OLC with strong leadership and direction. He is Director of Studies at the University of Bolton for PhD candidates in the

Business School and research interests include analysing the roles of Entrepreneurs, Intrapreneurs and Lean Thinkers in the Modern Enterprise.

**Godwin Chukwukelu** obtained his BSc in Computer Science and MSc in Advanced Computer Science and IT Management from the University of Nigeria Nsukka and the University of Manchester respectively. He is currently working towards his PhD at the Alliance Manchester Business School, University of Manchester.

**Enis Elezi** has a degree in International Agribusiness Management and has completed a PhD by research at University of Bolton focused on Knowledge Management and Knowledge Transfer practices among British educational partnerships. Currently, Enis is Lecturer in Business and Management at Teesside University, UK. His areas of research interests include Knowledge Transfer, Organisational Learning, International Knowledge Transfer Partnership Strategies, Trust and Inter-organisational Communication Channels and Knowledge Management across Borders.

**Aniekan Essien** received the B.Eng. degree in computer engineering in 2011, and the M.Sc. degree in information systems from the University of Manchester, Manchester, U.K., where also obtained the Ph.D. degree. He is currently a Research Assistant with the Future Manufacturing Research Institute, College of Engineering, Swansea University Bay Campus, Swansea, U.K. His research interests include deep learning for time-series forecasting, artificial intelligence for smart manufacturing, and traffic predictive analytics.

**Victor Essien** received the B.Sc in Computer Science from the University of Uyo, Nigeria. He is currently working towards obtaining his M.Sc in Data Science from Teeside University, UK. Mr. Essien has vast industrial experience in software development, management information systems (MIS), and decision support for organisational improvement, having worked in a broad range of organisations in various sectors of endeavour, including finance, healthcare, insurance, and entertainment.

**Kabir Hossain** received his PhD in Accounting and Finance, specializing in comparative studies of banks' performance between conventional banks and Islamic banks from the Centre for Islamic Finance, the University of Bolton, UK. Kabir is currently supervising several PhD students at the Centre for Islamic Finance, University of Bolton, UK. Before working as a research supervisor, Kabir worked as an International Liaison officer at an export-oriented garments company Galpex Limited in Bangladesh and worked as a lecturer at colleges and coaching centres in Bangladesh. Kabir's research interests include Islamic finance and economics, financial performance measurement, non-financial performance measurement, corporate finance, corporate social responsibility, Sharia governance and regulations, and fintech.

**Yowei Kang** (Ph.D.) is Assistant Professor at Bachelor Degree Program in Oceanic Cultural Creative Design Industries, National Taiwan Ocean University, TAIWAN. His research interests focus on new media design, digital game research, visual communication, and experiential rhetoric. Some of his works have been published in International Journal of Strategic Communication, and Journal of Intercultural Communication Studies. He has received government funding to support his research in location-based advertising and consumer privacy management strategies.

**Natalia Moreira** is an interdisciplinary researcher and Project Manager with a technical focus on sustainable materials and supply chains. With a strong technical research and publication record, Natalia has been in the field of product development since 2007, advising global fashion brands and completing research on sustainable textiles for action-oriented change projects, and contributing to vital academic debates on sustainability. Natalia also has an interest in software development and has skills and client relationships in this area (in countries such as Canada, the UK, Italy, Brazil and Germany). Natalia's research emphasises direct engagement with diverse stakeholder groups involved in product supply chains, which has enabled her to successfully develop new models of sustainability futures and systems thinking in her research.

**Mark Schofield** is an experienced academic researcher of over 10 years at UK Academic Consultations. His specialist area is information systems and has a wide range of knowledge covering the multi-disciplinary area of topics ranging from cloud computing and ubiquitous technology to Artificial Intelligence and Machine Learning Systems.

**Eleanor Ward** is a poet, researcher, and educational consultant from Congleton, Cheshire. She completed a PhD at The University of Manchester, focusing on Disability and Identity in contemporary poetry. Since then, she has become a successful educational consultant, working with children and adults with complex disabilities to access education. She has been published in a variety of places, including the anthology Stairs and Whispers, the magazine Litmus, and has been short-listed for a variety of poetry prizes.

**Bob Wood** is an experienced director and entrepreneur, with a demonstrated history of working in the research industry. Research and practice covers Human Adaptiveness, Adaptive Leadership, Adaptive Culture, Ethics, Dynamic Personality, Future of Work, Lecturing, Culture Change, and Educational Technology. Strong professional with a PhD focused in Organizational Psychology from University of Washington.

**Kenneth C. C. Yang** is a Professor at the Department of Communication. His research focuses on new media and advertising, consumer behavior in East Asia, impacts of new media in Asia.

# Index

## P



## Q



## S



## T



## U



## V



## W

Lightning Source UK Ltd.
Milton Keynes UK
UKHW032019280920
370690UK00003B/45

9 781799 848462